Joan van Hove

LAUGH OR CRY

To Joan van Hove
a good friend of many
years

With love
from
Sylvia

June 10TH 2006

LAUGH OR CRY

Sylvia Hurst

Book Guild Publishing
Sussex, England

First published in Great Britain in 2006 by
The Book Guild Ltd
25 High Street
Lewes, East Sussex
BN7 2LU

Typesetting in Times by
Keyboard Services, Luton, Bedfordshire

Printed in Great Britain by
Athenaeum Press Ltd, Gateshead

A catalogue record for this book is available from
The British Library

ISBN 1 84624 064 6

*To my parents and Grandmother Hedwig
Victims of the Holocaust*

*And to the childen of Germany
Victims of Brainwashing*

Contents

Part One – Normal Times

Part Two – Change

My thanks to the following:

Maureen Fitzgibbon for typing and encouragement

Liz Finnigan for typing and encouragement

My brother Arnold for educating me in politics

Ann and Bob Elder for introducing me to a computer

The kind staff of the Stanley Library

Dr Walter Johannes Stein, my Mentor

Joan van Hove for listening

My daughter Amanda Hurst for reminding me to include the many humorous or sad episodes I had forgotten.

Hamburg Main Railway Station

Children's Transport to England on Platform 4

I was lucky, I had been included in a Children's Transport from Hamburg. Parents were not allowed on the platform; they had been told they must go home as soon as the children are assembled outside the station. Please to co-operate.

Miss Edith Rosenthal, the matron of the orphanage, had seen us off. She had arranged my place on the transport. Most of our children were boarders at the orphanage, including myself, enabling us to attend Jewish schools in Hamburg. They had been excluded from the schools of their hometown or because of some unpleasantness of sorts. I had attended the Jewish Fashion College in Hamburg.

We had arrived too early at the Railway Station.

Miss Rosenthal said, 'Children, I am sorry, I have to go. Have a good journey. Do write when you get there. God bless you, God bless you all. Here is your Helper.' She handed us over to an elderly lady, giving her the list with our names.

The lady was dressed all in grey, a sort of travelling costume, with a pink straw hat. She studied the list, then counted us.

She approached me. 'Will you look after these two.' She handed me Suzi, aged four, and Morris, aged five. 'I shall take the other ones. Stay on the pavement. Do be quiet.' She clapped her hands. I thought, I bet she is a school teacher. Once again she consulted her wrist watch. She clapped her hands again. 'It is time, come along.'

We were marched through the Station Hall. I noticed a large, white sign: CHILDREN'S TRANSPORT TO ENGLAND PLATFORM 4.

Down the steps we went, and up again, Suzi clutching my hand and Morris hanging on to the belt of my coat. I had to carry my suitcase; it was so heavy. I had always admired this suitcase, made of crocodile skin. It belonged to mother. It was the wrong choice to take. They had put a long table on the platform. It had several large cardboard boxes on it, showing the alphabet in large letters. Our helper handed over the list, one lady searched through the list whilst the other one rummaged in the boxes for our labels. She called our names; we were given a tag to hang around our neck. 'You must never, never take this off; this is important, it has your number on it!' I noticed my surname starting with an extra-large initial.

Packaged like a parcel. Yes, we were packaged like parcels, a long line of children waiting patiently for the train. There was a Helper with a baby in her arms, it could not have been more than a year old. The Helper struggled with a laundry basket; there seemed to be nappies in it – what a baby carriage! Who would send such a small child away? Perhaps it went for adoption.

The train arrived. They shooed us into the compartments, single ones for about eight people. I thought, that will make it difficult for them to supervise the children. I had not seen many helpers.

Morris, Suzi and I were joined by three more children, an older boy and a girl and boy whom I thought looked about seven or eight. The Helper picked up my label, read it, and said, 'Sylvia, you are in charge. Good luck!' and then she went, presumably to the next compartment along the corridor.

The older boy, named Helmut, helped me to put the luggage into the overhead nets, the ones used for hand luggage.

A slight squabble: who can have the window seats?

'Sit down and be quiet! Here, you can all have a sweet.' My little going-away present from the Domestic Science students at the orphanage came in useful. It worked, but for how long?

Finally the train left. I introduced the children to each other. 'This is Suzi ... this is Morris ... Helmut, how old are you?' 'Twelve last May.' 'What is your name?' 'Liselotte.' 'And yours?' 'Reuben.'

The train started to gather speed.

After a while a lady came around, offering drinks. 'Pop or milk?' 'Do we have to pay?' asked Helmut.

'No, it's free'.

I was glad it was in bottles with a straw. No messy, spilling cups. She said, 'If you have to go to the toilet, go with the older girl. We don't want you getting lost.'

For an express train it seemed to move slowly; perhaps it was not an express train.

'Let's have a sing-song,' I said. I started.

> *Ri Ra Rutch*
> *Wir Fahren In Der Kutch*
> *Wir Fahren In Der Schnecken Post*
> *Weil Sie Nur Einen Kreutzer Kost*
> *Ri Ra Rutch*
>
> *Ri Ra Roach*
> *We travel in a coach*
> *A coach as slow as a snail*
> *This is a sorry tale*
> *It only costs a penny*
> *Go and tell your granny*
> *Ri Ra Roach.*

'I am not singing that I'm not a baby,' complained Helmut.

'Of course not, you are there to help me.' That seemed to satisfy the boy. Each of the children had a turn on my lap, up and down, right and left.

'What is a kreutzer?' asked Suzi.

'In your grandmother's time, a pfennig was called a kreutzer.'

'I called her Oma,' said Suzi. (*Oma* means grandmother.)

'In your Oma's time there were not many trains, people went by coach and horses. What other songs do you know?'

(A very free translation)

> *Hoppe, Hoppe, Reiter*
> *When er Faellt*
> *Dann Schreit er*
> *Faellt er in den Graben*
> *Fressen ihn die Raben*
> *Faellt er in den Sumpf*
> *Macht der Reiter plumpf*

Peck, Peck, Peck

Hop, hop, little man
Ride as well as you can
Don't fall in the ditch
Because there lives the witch
Don't fall in the brook
Because there lives the rook
Who will eat you.
(*Let the child fall between your legs.*)

Peck, Peck, Peck

I was getting tired, giving the children turns on my knees.

'Let's count telegraph poles.' The wires were dancing along the railway lines. 'When we get to fifty, you all get a sweet.' Bribery! 'Now we have a little rest.'

The train stopped. I wondered why. I went along the corridor, to open the window on the door. After a while, I could fasten the leather strap, which regulated the aperture. I could see nothing – nothing to be alarmed about. I had heard that the SS stopped trains with refugees. Definitely no-one there. When I returned to the compartment, Helmut said, 'One is not allowed use the loo unless the train is moving.'

'I know that; it means not in a station. Ugh, disgusting! Clever, aren't we?'

Helmut produced a mouth organ and started to play Heiden Roeslein (the little red rose on the heath). I recognised the tune immediately, he played so well.

'Any of you know it?'

'What is it about?' asked the children.

'It's about a boy who wants to pick a pretty red rose which grows on the heath, a rose with thorns. The song is very famous.' I had learnt it at school. My cousin Erica told me the song was about a rape of a virgin – I kept that to myself, naturally.

Liselotte said, 'My daddy and I visited my mummy in hospital. We took red roses. That's why I have to go to another lady to look after me. When my mummy is better she will come and get me.'

'Helmut, you are very musical. You are very good!'

'I would like to be a musician, but my father said, they are badly paid, there is no money in it.'

A lady pushed back the door to our compartment. She carried a large basket with rolls. 'Egg or cheese, one or two?'

I replied, 'Six of egg and six of cheese please,' thinking, one does not know when they will give us something else to eat.

Reuben called out, 'I want ham, I don't like cheese!'

The lady was shocked.

'Reuben, listen, my lad. Children eat what they get,' said I.

By way of apology, 'Please excuse him, madam, Reuben comes from a "Reform" family,* he does not know any better.'

'Ah, so,' said the lady, still annoyed.

'We thank you, all of us. It is very kind of you.'

'Thank the Committee.' She stomped out.

We were nearing the border, I recognised the names of the towns, having looked up the various routes of the trains. I did not know the names of the port of embarkation.

'*Aufmachen*,' an SS man screamed, throwing the door open. He entered with a civilian. It was a headcount. 'Five!'

They looked at me. 'Your name, Miss,' called the SS man.

'Can't find her name on my list,' said the civilian.

When they went out, I thought I heard the door give a click. I tried the door. It was locked.

Now I was frightened.

The transport was for children under seventeen years of age; I was seventeen years and four months. Surely they would not send me back for those four months? Suddenly I realised they must have thought I was a helper. They had a list with their names, an official list, with the stamped permissions.

Of course I was not on that list: I was a child! Stupidly I had tucked my label inside my blouse because I felt too grown up. Quickly I remedied it. All right, I am a parcel, I am a child with a number.

The SS man and the civilian returned; the lock snapped back. They examined my label on my chest. They made a note, asked to see my passport, then went out without a word.

God be thanked.

I had heard that sometimes people tried to smuggle themselves out on a children's transport. Perhaps the SS were searching for escapees.

---

*Liberal Jews who don't keep the dietary laws.

God be thanked again.

Now we are over the border.

'Children, we have left Germany. Do you know where we are going?'

'England,' they said in unison.

Helmut said, 'My little brother is in a town called Leeds. The lady said they would try to find me a family there, if they can. My father said we'll go to America when our number* comes up; he'll get us then.' My father had said exactly the same. No-one else knew where they were going, including myself, all I had been told was London.

We were travelling through Holland. We were safe. They could not touch us here – not any longer.

Helmut went through his repertoire. He was good on march music; it put us in a happy mood.

'Another song, please,' begged the children. Reuben started with 'Haenschen klein'. They all knew that song.

This is the most unsuitable song – how can I stop it? Sweets – all have a sweet! My usual remedy.

Haenschen klein geht allein in die weite Welt hinein, aber Mutter weinet sehr, hat ja nun kein Haenschen mehr ... and so on.

Little Hans travels all alone into the big wide world. His mother is very upset, she cries and cries, no longer has she her little Hans...

'Listen to me, I know a story, a real true story, about a boy called Hans. He went alone, from his village in Denmark to the capital city, Copenhagen. He was a cobbler who made beautiful shoes and dancing slippers. He made red ones for a girl. They were so good she could not stop dancing once she had put the shoes on. He made golden ones for the princesses at the Royal Court, so everybody wanted his shoes.† But this is not the reason Hans became so famous, he told wonderful stories, and there were crowds of people who came to listen to his stories. He became very, very famous. His name is Hans Andersen. His stories got translated into all languages, into books; every bookshop sells his books.

'Do you know any of his stories?'

---

*Waiting number, given by US Consulates for admittance to the States.

† My invention. Apologies to Hans Andersen.

And so I told them the story of the ugly duckling.

'Can any of you speak a little English?'

Helmut exclaimed, 'I've done two years at school!'

'Wonderful. You'll be the teacher. Start with *Good morning*, *Good evening*, and *How do you do*.'

I was dead tired and left them to it.

Not having slept properly for several nights, I noticed that I was becoming irritable. This will never do. The children also were becoming bored or tired, or both. I said, 'We'll soon be there, let's have a little rest.'

It was getting dark. *Hoek of Holland*. The train stopped, children assembling on the platform.

The Pink Hat arrived. She took charge of the smaller children; Helmut was to join the older boys. 'You have been a great help. Don't give up your music, you have real talent.' I gave him a hug – which he did not like very much.

'God bless,' Pink Hat said to me. 'You are good with children.'

'Oh no, I sometimes helped out at the orphanage, weekends.' All I wanted now was sleep … no more kids, I hoped there would be no more kids.

The children were shooed up the gangway of the ship like sheep, 'Come along, come along, this way!' In a dining hall we were given a mug of soup, some bread and a bar of chocolate. The bread was white and square, which caused a lot of comment. I had seen this kind of bread before at our home; we called it English Sandwich Bread.

I was shown to my cabin. To my surprise it was an outside one, with only two bunks. 'The upper one is yours.' Father had warned me that sometimes one only gets a deck chair. The bed was made up too. I was asleep in minutes.

I awoke early. Noiselessly I climbed down the ladder. An elderly lady was snoring in the lower bunk. I had never heard her coming in. Looking out of the porthole, I could see the water splashing gently against the sides of the ship, a pink reflection of the sunrise on the sea. This is England, this is England.

Now we were waiting for our train to London. It was a long wait; they seemed to be sorting out something or other. We waited in a meadow near the railway station.

The children were divided by age – big boys are to play football, small ones to make a circle over there! Girls, hold hand, come along … I stood aside. I thought, Play your stupid games, get on with it. I was wondering what I would do in London, what sort of people had been kind enough to take me in.

Pink Hat brought to me a little girl, who was crying, sobbing.

'Look after Ilse.' She took me aside. 'She'll have them all crying; take her for a walk.'

Ilse's little face, dirty as it was, was stained with tears.

I took my hanky out. 'Spit. This will have to do, we have no water.'

Ilse was so surprised she stopped crying.

'Why were you crying?' I asked.

'I want my Mutti.' (Her mama.)

'You can't have your Mutti, she is not here.'

'That's why I am crying.'

I said, 'I'll let you into a secret. I want my Mutti, too. I never said goodbye to her when I left; she was not at home. She had gone to visit Grandpa because he was very ill. I want my Mutti too.'

'But you are a big girl; you are a lady.'

'That makes no difference.'

So we sat down and comforted each other, Ilse on my lap.

'Let me do your hair – you have lovely red hair – it's all messy … and knotty.'

'Promise not to pull it.'

'I'll try. Look, what a lot of daisies are here, we could make a daisy chain! If you'll pick them.'

I opened my suitcase to take out my little silver fish, my little treasure, my needle cushion.

'I need a fine needle to make the holes, otherwise the stem breaks. My Mutti gave me the little fish.'

We made a lovely daisy necklace.

* * *

At Liverpool Street station we were marched into a cavernous brown hall. Everything was brown – it was poorly lit. There were rows of tables with large letters of the alphabet on them.

'Find your table, according to your name, and queue next to it.'

After being marked present, we were told to stand quietly. Someone would bring a bench … presently.

Patience, patience. This was certainly not presently.

Families came to collect their children.

The hall slowly emptied. There were no children left on my bench. I reviewed my situation, seated on an uncomfortable bench in this gloomy hall.

I was here, safe in England. What would be my future?

My sister Susan, who was fifteen years old, had a place on the children's transport, which had left Stuttgart two days ago. Aunt Paula, father's sister, had arranged that. She had also managed to obtain a place for my brother Richard, then aged twelve years old. Aunt Paula had remonstrated with Father; however, Father said he was too young to go. Aunt Paula, who lived in Stuttgart, was waiting to join her son Herbert who had been born in London, which made him an English citizen.

Aunt Paula's husband Eugene had been working for a number of years in our factory in London, before World War I. Grandfather Samuel had founded this branch factory in 1871 in London Wall. He said he was horrified at the conditions people suffered in the sweat shops in London's East End, where they mostly employed, in terrible conditions, the Jewish Immigrant Labour. So his daughter Paula regularly collected, from her friends, unwanted children's clothing and other needed articles to take to Whitechapel for distribution to the poor, who had originated from Russia or Poland. The time of their Exodus had been 1880–1910, because of the pogroms there. Many of these families had got 'stuck' in London on their way to America, because of their lack of finances – the fare to America from Hamburg or Bremen was thirty-four dollars, less from London or Liverpool.

* * *

Brother Arnold, who was then twenty years old, had arrived in England by air, escorting the elderly Aunt Anna, sister of Aunt Frances. Aunt Anna, a widow, had refused to travel alone as she had never done this before, and certainly never by air.

Aunt Frances remembered, conveniently, that Arnold had written to her, asking if she would give him a guarantee; he had sent her his VC.

At the same time Father had written to her explaining that we were waiting to emigrate to the USA. He wrote that his English was almost perfect, he could work in the factory, he did not mind in what capacity. Her answer had been negative. On the phone she had been quite short with Father, saying her own family had priority on her resources. Father explained to us that she was one of sixteen children, not all of them were living. She would be in her middle seventies now.

She had come to England to work as a governess, penniless, but had married well – Uncle Adolphe, the brother of our grandmother, who ran the branch factory in London, which Grandfather Samuel had founded in London Wall. The factory was now situated in Margaret Street, near Oxford Circus. Because of the 1914 War, it had been written over to Uncle Adolphe, who was by then naturalised English. No money had changed hands. Father had left it at that; he was not interested in commerce. When Uncle Adolphe died, Aunt Frances had taken over the factory, and later on her nephew Jeffrey, her sister's son. This sister had also been a governess who had married well in England.

So strangers, not our family, had offered to take me, as well as my sister Susan. Strangers had given the guarantee needed to enable us to come to England with the Children's Transport.

I am now in England, in this depressing large hall. I am waiting for my family.

They have not turned up. Where can they be? Almost everyone has left. I'd better inquire, if I can find a Helper. So I asked.

'As far as we know, they are coming. We have not heard anything to the contrary,' answered the lady behind the desk. 'Sit down, be patient.'

I was wondering if they had changed their mind. I was scrutinising the entrance door. No, this is a delivery man. No, this is a Red Cross person. What will happen if no-one comes to collect me? There is a couple with two children. Perhaps...

She spoke with the last remaining Helper. They looked over in my direction. They came nearer, stopped. The woman gesticulated, spoke what I took for Yiddish. I could make out one word, *Schickse*, *Schickse*. This means a Christian Girl, a Servant Girl.

'Look! Blond hair.'

There were also Christian children in the Transport, from the intelligentsia, communists, writers – I believe between ten and fifteen per cent.

The Jewish Board of Guardians and the Quakers jointly had arranged the Children's Transports. There had been rumours, complaints, that orthodox Jewish children had been placed in Christian homes, and vice versa.

The lady approached and looked me over. '*Bist a Jid?*' (Are you Jewish?)

I nodded. 'Yes.'

'*Bist a Yossem?*' (Are you an orphan?)

I did not understand. 'Sorry, I don't understand. Please speak to me in English. I know English.'

'Abe,' the lady called to her husband. 'She speaks English. She is not a *Schikse*, God forbid!'

She turned to me. 'Why were you in the orphanage?'

'I was a boarder there. I went to College in Hamburg.'

'Fancy that. So sorry we were late. We came as soon as the business closed.'

The lady was really ugly, with a very large nose, wearing a peculiar hat which looked more like a beret. There was a massive Rhinestone brooch stuck in this beret. She was very, very over-weight. So this is my family. The husband was a fine looking man, tall, with a tanned face. The boy and the girl were very nice looking. The girl was really pretty, with her dark hair worn in ringlets.

I asked, 'Where do you live? In London?'

'Yes, in Whitechapel, in Jubilee Street.' She yelled, 'Abe, it's late ... let's go ... Abe, take her case!'

'Crock ... Hm ... Crocodile.'

I knew it had been the wrong thing to bring this case.

I was home ... with these good people who had signed the guaranty for me.

They had saved my life.

* * *

I could not understand why Father had refused permission to send my brother Richard. Most of the children of the Hamburg Transport were even younger. Why was Father so reluctant to leave Germany? Only after November 9th, the *Cristall Nacht*, and his time in Dachau, did he realise the seriousness of the situation.

He still carried on, as before, with his medical practice – forbidden then – in secret, amongst the local population. Twice a week he cycled to the villages, wearing plus-fours and a rucksack. It was true: he was venerated, he was the 'Healer' with paranormal powers. He felt, whilst he could help, be of use, nothing could touch him. Father was a strong personality; Mother felt compelled to follow his wishes. Twenty years ago she had married a manufacturer of corsets, he was now a doctor of naturopathy, a mystic.

I could not understand what had been happening in Germany, ordinary moral standards had given way to a kind of euphoria, sweeping over the whole country: German is best, is noble, is victorious; Hitler is now God. Who dares to say otherwise? If you do, there is always the Concentration Camp to enlighten you. So it is better not to open your mouth; it is much too dangerous. Walls have ears.

I was glad to be out of it.

White is black.

Black is white.

Who says so?

It is written so everywhere, in the newspapers. You hear it on the radio.

In the marching songs on the street.

In the rousing music.

*   *   *

In this book I am telling my story, right from the beginning, from my earliest memories. How it was that Nazism could take hold in Germany. How ordinary, good and honest people were gradually seduced into this criminal madness and the German nation made to feel great, superior, euphoric.

My book is not a Holocaust memoir.

It is the story of our Jewish Community, and particularly my family, which had played an important part in the economic development of the Town as well as the Country. It is a very personal story of Jewish and Christian children growing up together in Germany in the years 1925 to 1939.

The history dates back to 1777 when twenty families came under the protection of the local Baron, the Lord of the Village.

Unfortunately everything is true.

Sylvia Hurst
County Durham, England

PART ONE

NORMAL TIMES

Chapter 1

I Have a Ladybird

I am hiding under the bed. I don't want anyone to see me cry. The lino feels cold – it will soon warm up; or, better still, I'll crawl into the wicker laundry basket, full with our stockings and vests and linen waiting to be mended. It is dark underneath my bed. It's a big wooden grown-up bed, the same as Arnold's – he is my older brother – with a heart cut out of the bedhead, because I am three now and Susan, the baby, has my cot.

Perhaps Arnold does not like me any more. He is very cross and won't talk to me, he did not even take my cake. That's why I was crying and when I cry I crawl under my bed so no-one can see me. I am not a cry baby like Susan. I did not mean to tell tales, but he hit me so hard with his wooden wasp, it has black and yellow stripes, it's a silly toy, mine is much nicer. A ladybird, that's what I've got. Arnold and I were playing, I did not do anything and he hit me. I ran to my mummy, I wanted her to make it good. Old Miss Mary never, never makes it good, she just says: 'ZzZzz...' They talked about it and said, he is two years older, he should not hit her. If he can't behave like a big boy, he'd better have his tea at the 'Cat's Table', without a tablecloth, and no cake for him.* If we are naughty, that's where we have to eat. They gave him only brown bread and butter for afternoon tea. He would not take the cake I tried to smuggle in for him, he turned his face away.

Someone is coming into the nursery. She has black stockings on, it must be the maid, Miss Mary has beige ones. She opens the wardrobe to hang something in and goes out again. I must tell Arnold I did not mean it.

---

*The small play table in the nursery is usually in Germany called the 'Cat's Table'.

It is comfortable in my basket.

'Sylvia, Sylvia!' Miss Mary is calling me. If I don't come out she'll find me and know my corner, then I can't hide there any more.

Miss Mary says we must hurry to get ready for our walk, because it gets dark early in October, and if we are good, Arnold and I can order afterwards the dragon. Our new kite is going to be a dragon with a horrid face and a long tail. The carpenter at my daddy's factory is going to make it for us. 'Arnold, please, don't be angry with me.' And he says 'All right', but nothing else.

When we arrive at the factory we go to the carpenter's shop. Arnold tells him how he wants it made. Whilst Miss Mary is talking, not about the dragon at all, Arnold and I run out to the time clocks in the entrance hall. He puts the cards in and I turn the handle, and then it rings. I am glad he liked me again. Two ladies are coming down the stairs. They laugh and say, 'Look, Mr Julius's children.' We put more cards in. Miss Mary comes running out, pulls us away, saying we are naughty.

And where is my second glove, she is going to tie them together with a long string so I won't lose them any more. It was in my pocket all the time. The factory belongs to my father. He works in the office, I am not allowed to visit him there. My father is very tall and big and he knows everything. All people know him, they take off their hat and call him Mr Julius. His other name is Mr Fleischer, like Mummy's, Arnold's and mine, because we belong to him. Susan is only a baby, she can't talk yet. Arnold can say the whole address, but I can tie my bootlaces.

Miss Mary is very old, she has grey hair, she says because of us, so I feel very sorry. She wears a white apron which goes all the way around her. Before she came to us, she was Miss Mary to two girls, but they are big now. Miss Mary says, 'You must wear the woolly vest so that you don't catch cold.'

'No, I don't want to, it scratches. And my stockings too!' They go right up, are horrible, brown and ribbed. The ribbed ones scratch more.

Miss Mary is sure it does not scratch, she said it three times. She holds the vest to her face and says, 'Nice and soft.'

I know it is not. 'I want my mummy.'

'You can see your mummy after tea time, if you are good, you cannot disturb her now. Your brother is not making a fuss like you.'

So I wait and sit quietly on my little chair, the vest does not scratch so much when I sit still. After tea I tell mummy. She also says the wool does not scratch. I cry because she does not understand. I scream and trample the floor. They put me to bed without supper, Arnold told me it was raspberry jelly and whipped cream, my favourite.

When daddy comes to say goodnight to us he sits on my bed. 'Miss Mary tells me you were not a good girl today.'

I sob and throw my arms around his neck. 'I was, I was, I was! It's scratchy and they don't believe it. It's still red on my legs!'

He puts the light on. I am so glad it is still there.

My daddy calls Miss Mary and they both look again. 'She has the skin of a princess.'

Next day I got pure silk underwear to go underneath my woolly ones. Mrs Koester, the sewing woman, puts linings in all my woollen winter dresses. I know the difference between wool and silk and cotton. I am very interested in clothes. My mother has beautiful ones, two wardrobes full. If we are still awake when she goes out in the evening, we admire her long dress. She smells so good.

*　*　*

We had a lot of snow this winter. Once there was a long icicle on my bedroom window, but when I looked again at lunchtime, it had gone. The snowman in the garden had melted too. He was taller than my father and then every day he got a little bit smaller. His coal-eyes and carrot nose fell out and all that's left of him is a small mound of dirty snow, Daddy's old top hat, and the birch broom.

After my birthday in March the weather became warmer and we could play in the garden again. I received my presents, had a party and an iced cake with my name on it and four red candles. Arnold blew them out before I had the chance.

I like summer best, when I sit by myself in the meadow.

Carefully I look at the flowers, how they are made. Sometimes I pull all the petals out to see what happens inside. Often it's like the poppyseed on our breakfast rolls, only white instead of black. Sometimes it's all smeary.

The crickets chirp and when the sun is hot, there is so much humming. That can't all be bees? If I keep very still, perhaps this

5

cabbage white will land on my frock, there are lots of flowers printed on it. Can they tell the difference? I have been told, cabbage whites are a pest. How can a beautiful butterfly be a pest? And they said, Because their caterpillars eat the cabbage in our garden. Good riddance! I don't like cabbage, I hope they eat the lot.

I love making posies. When I wake up early the small hand on our cuckoo clock is not even at the bottom, I dress myself quietly and go to pick flowers in the garden. Only the ones I am allowed to. They say they last longer if one picks them before the sun comes up. My pet name is 'Blumen Dorle'.*

When they call me that I think I don't deserve that name, because I forget sometimes to water my flower bed. Karl, our gardener-groom-handyman, does it for me when I forget. He has never given me away. I don't know why I can only grow marigolds and pink poppies, I put in all kinds of seeds from marvellously coloured packets – all kinds of flowers – but they always turn into marigolds! My flower bed is the one under the old pear tree. It must have been the poorest ground in the garden.

Karl looks impressive in his blue uniform with gold buttons and his red, waxed moustache with points. The grown-ups always say that they cannot understand why the gentle Roesle, my grandmother's cook, married him. Karl liked his drink. I wish they wouldn't say that. Karl is wonderful.

*   *   *

When Mrs Koester, the sewing woman, makes new dresses for Susan and me I ask her for the cuttings for my dolls. I have to ask quite often, until she gives them to me.

'Don't plague me anymore, that's enough', she says, and then she gives me a really big one from a box. 'It's no use anyway.'

'Thank you.'

Miss Mary cut the dress out and I sewed it up. I have a needle with an extra large eye so I can thread it myself. When it is finished I show my doll to Arnold.

'Ha,' he says, 'it's like a potato sack. Potato sack – potato sack,' he sings, holding my doll high in the air and marching round the nursery table.

Miss Mary assures me it is a kimono dress, a polite name of

---

*Flower Dorle. My second name is Doris. Dorle is the diminutive of Doris.

6

hers for a piece of cloth sewn together under the arms, with just a hole for the head.

'I want one like my frock,' I say to Mrs Koester, pointing to my smocked dress. She shakes her head, rattling away on the machine, she has no time and she shoos me back to the nursery.

'I'll cut it out myself.' So I take a pair of scissors from the mending basket under the bed.

'What are you doing, who gave you the scissors?' Miss Mary snatches them out of my hand. 'They are much too pointed, they are dangerous.' She puts them on top of the wardrobe where I cannot reach them, not even if I stand on a chair.

I know my mummy has a pair of embroidery scissors. I'll go and ask her to give them to me.

Mother is writing letters, she does not look up and says, Go and ask Miss Mary, and she continues with her writing. I don't move and I wait, she writes some more, so I pull her sleeve.

'What is it?'

'I can't.'

She puts her pen down. 'What is it you cannot do?'

'Ask Miss Mary. She won't give them to me, she says they are dangerous.'

'Well, she is quite right, go back to the nursery.'

'But I must have them, I don't want a potato sack, I want a beautiful dress for my dolly. I want your scissors.' I start crying.

'Go back at once!'

'I want scissors, I want scissors.'

'One cannot give children everything they want.'

I cry noisily and trample the floor.

'Look at her, she is quite red with rage.'

Miss Mary comes running from the nursery. 'Be quiet at once, you bad girl. I am sorry, Madam.' She takes me by the hand and leads me out of the room.

After our supper I sit on my father's knee. He puts both fists out. 'Guess which one, right or left?'

I don't know right and left yet so I point. He shakes his head. It is usually barley sugar or caramels he has hidden in his fist. We call them 'Jump-to-bed-sweets'. I'll try again.

'Right this time.' On his outstretched palm lay a small pair of scissors with rounded blades.

'Daddy, Daddy, how did you know?'

7

'A little bird told me.'

'Which little bird?'

'The one on your window sill.'

Little birds are always telling my father what we want. I put crumbs out for them and almost never forget.

The little birds will also tell St Nicholas if we have been good children. On the 6th of December, the eve of St Nicholas, we put our slippers outside the day nursery. As soon as we are awake, we race outside to see what he has brought us. My slipper is full of sweets and chocolates, but Arnold, who wanted to be clever and put out his Wellington, finds a birch twig in it; a single sugar-ring is tied to it with a blue ribbon.

Miss Mary says, 'Evidently St Nicholas does not like greedy boys, just a warning this time.'

The legend goes that St Nicholas beats naughty boys with a birchwhip.

'I'll give you some of my sweets,' I whisper. 'Half and half.'

Chapter 2

A New Baby, a New Nurse, and I go to Kindergarten

Sometimes, on winter Sundays, Father ordered Karl to get out the sleigh, instead of the Landau or the motor car. First Father and Karl had a long discussion. Is the snow the right kind or not? It must not be drift snow, nor frozen over. That would hurt the horses. The horses were called Fanny and Prince. Because they were 'artistocrats' Karl wound yellow bandages round their slender ankles. Muffled right up to our ears, covered with coarse woolly tartan rugs, we were gliding down the streets, jingling on to the woods. The extra treat was to sit next to Karl and help hold up the reins. Sometimes the horses touched an overhanging branch and snow fell on us. I loved snowflakes, I could stare right into them for hours and it got all mixed up with my daydreams of fairies and princesses.

There was an epidemic of whooping cough. All three of us children caught it. For a cure they took us to Worishofen, a spa in the Alps – the water cure!

They called it hydrotherapy, I could not pronounce the difficult word, but I hated whatever it was. Attendants in white smocks and sandals directed the cold hose straight on to me; it terrified me. All the assurances by grown-ups – how good it was for me – made no impression. I offered to forego my 'Jump-to-bed-sweet'. I did not want to be brave or a big girl, it was too cold.

When we returned home people were asking whether we wanted a little brother or sister. Arnold firmly declared that we had enough cry-babies, meaning Susan. I was intrigued and put sugar every night on the window ledge for the stork. I did this faithfully nightly for two weeks but no baby came. Triumphantly Arnold said, 'I told you so, the stork is a cheat, he just swipes the sugar for nothing!' So I stopped putting it out.

One morning Miss Mary came in to tell us that a little brother had arrived. We thought she was teasing and refused to believe it. When finally I was convinced I put a whole basin of sugar on the window ledge and it duly disappeared. I felt I had to make up for my omission and was grateful it had been accepted by the stork.

It was evening before I was allowed to see the baby. When I asked my mother why she was in bed, she told me that the stork had bitten her in the leg. I begged her to show me the mark but she would not. That was mean. After all, a stork does not bite you every day. Mother wore a beautiful salmon-coloured nightie. It had even more lace on it than the ones she usually wore. She looked lovely. Her room was full of flowers, bought ones. She gave me some for the nursery. The baby was in a cot which had spotted muslin hangings and blue bows, almost like the baby prince in my picture book. He was horrible! I was disappointed he was such a funny looking creature. I did not dare say so, it was naughty to contradict or criticise grown-ups and they called him beautiful. I told everybody that the new baby had 'come without being ordered'. People giggled, I could not understand why.

The baby was called Richard, I became very attached to him. After a few months he looked pretty and chubby; I was allowed to help bath him. He belonged to me because he had the same white-blond hair as I had. My mother was chestnut, my father's hair was light brown. There was a photo of my father as a child in a white sailor suit, then he had long blond curls. He told me that after an illness the long hair was cut off, after that it grew dark. That was puzzling. When I went to the hairdresser after my chickenpox, I wondered if the same thing would happen to me. The grown-ups said that with the sunbathing my hair had got even lighter. They washed it with camomile and egg. The fuss they made. '*Ein blondes Judenkind!*' The maid sang to tease me, '*Wo hast du denn die blauen Augen her, bei Tietz gekaufft, 's gibt keine mehr.*' (Where did you buy your blue eyes, at Tietz [a department store like Selfridges], but they're all sold out.) This was a popular song in the 'Hit-parade'. I hated it. I started to count out all my fair relatives – there were many – 'that's where from'. After I had said on two occasions, 'This is a *common* song,' she stopped it.

At Richard's birth, old Miss Mary had left and a new nurse,

Sister Paula, arrived. I was very attached to Miss Mary, who explained to me that with the new arrival, the work would be too much for her. I pleaded with her to stay. I promised I'd make no work, I'd fold up my clothes at night and tidy my toys. It made no difference. I cried at first, but soon I forgot her.

*   *   *

It is still bitter cold outside, the wind is whistling around the house. Double windows have been attached. I open the inner one and lean on my elbows on the velvet bolster which has been placed in the gap. I want to look outside, the view is hidden by intricate patterns of frost flowers – crocuses and arum lilies, fern and the leaves of daffodils. How lovely!

It is a pity to spoil the pattern, I do so want to look out. My hot breath melts a hole, I wipe it clean and dry it with my handkerchief.

The garden is thickly covered in snow and more is falling in single flakes. The wind hits the lilac bushes, rose trees shake their heads, muffled in brown paper hats, which are tied on securely round their necks.

Some loose creepers on the house beat at the walls in intervals. Cry, cry, wind! I am warm and safe in my father's house!

A starling settles on the window ledge, looking for crumbs. Quickly I fetch some crusts from the kitchen and open the outer window. 'Here you are, little bird, it's on my hand.' He hops nearer. I keep very still and wait. 'Come on, I am not going to hurt you.' The starling does not move and looks at me with beady eyes. My hand, which is resting in the snow, starts to burn with cold. 'Silly bird, silly bird.' I fling the crust at him. The starling flies away with fright.

It is getting dark. The electric light shines so yellow in winter. The glare of the white American cloth on our big nursery table is sharp and forbidding.

I am making reins (French knitting). Sister Paula will sew it together for me to make a potholder for my mother's birthday. Mummy says she needs one very urgently, they are hard to get. My wool changes from red to green and back to yellow, pink and red. Arnold is folding stiff coloured paper to make her a box.

Father joins us. Today he is telling the story of the little fox – he is acting it with a glove puppet. He is a cheeky fellow that

11

little fox! He almost caught the baby chicken. I am the hen and I cackle, Arnold is the cock and he crows.

When I wake up in the morning, I quickly peep through the curtains to see if I'm in time for sunrise. Often on falling asleep, I tell myself: wake up in time, wake up in time, I must not miss it again. It fills me with wonder and gives me almost a sense of achievement to watch it. First comes the pink glow, it chases the mist away, then brittle white clearness with sharp needle rays. After this I cannot look any longer, the bright sunshine is blinding me and makes my eyes water. One day I hope to fulfil my ambition to look the sun straight in the eye.

* * *

My parents have arranged for Arnold and me to have lunch with them in the dining room. They say they hardly see us. Sister Paula has no time to supervise us, she is busy with Susan and Richard. We are thrilled. Eating in the grown-up's dining room, being served by the maid! Sister Paula cautions us not to let her down, not to speak with a full mouth, in fact not to speak at all until we are spoken to.

Everything goes well the first day. We're very proud. I don't think they saw the spot I made with the cherry juice, I put my plate over it. Secretly I find I liked it better in the nursery. I had to eat spinach which I hate, two spoonfuls to show goodwill and next day Mother noticed I picked the onions out of the salad which means a bad mark from Sister Paula. We have daily and weekly prizes for behaviour.

After lunch I go into the kitchen and say to Liesel, 'Don't put any onions in the salad anymore, please.'

'Who says so?'

'I do.'

'That's what I thought. When, and if, Madam tells me, I'll leave them out. Now go back to the nursery. I have a lot to do.'

'Oh, Liesel, please. I get a bad mark if I leave them on the plate, I can't put them in my napkin either, they are so sharp and make me cry.'

Liesel laughs and promises to grate them fine. 'You won't even notice.' She says that is the best she can do. For a few days she really does it, and then she forgets.

Chapter 3

The Pioneer of the Corset Industry and his Family

Grandfather Samuel Fleischer was greatly interested in stopping the horrific conditions in the Garment Industry all over Europe. He had been elected Delegate of the Garment Workers Union to represent them at the German and French Parliaments and did much to improve working conditions. In England these were equally bad, in London's East End, if not worse. He was a charitable man who practised what he preached. The new factory he had built in Germany, in 1890, was an outstanding model. In front of the building was a pleasure garden, with flowerbeds and fountain for use of the workers in their lunch break. There was a canteen which dispensed mainly drinks since workers usually brought their own lunch packets with them. Boys doing well at school could apply for a scholarship at the local grammar school. Not only did he pay the fees, he also gave grants for suitable clothing so that the lads should not feel uncomfortable amongst the more affluent pupils.

The corset factories were doing well. According to the Wuerttembergische Handelskammer, our firm was in control of the whole corset industry in America. Branch factories had been opened by him in 1871, both in London and in Milan. I don't know the date of the ones in Paris and Muehlbach, Alsace.

For his services to the country, the King of Wuerttemberg had offered him a title, but with a condition – to become a Christian. Grandfather thanked the King for the great honour, which he could not accept. He was not a religious man, but he was the doyen of the Jewish community.

He was a serious and serious-looking man. I found he looked comical on photographs taken together with Grandmother: she was six foot tall, and he only five foot four. I would have asked her to sit down! On an etching in the hall he looked impressive; perhaps it was the inscription:

200 German Industrialists
Samuel Fleischer
Pioneer of the Corset Industry

For twenty-one years he had been the head of our Jewish community. This post carried many administrative, but very few, religious duties. The congregation was very 'Liberal' (also called 'Reform'). Few people still kept a kosher kitchen. Even our Jewish butcher had many Christian customers, who claimed his sausages were the best in town.

On Grandfather's birthdays – it was almost a 'Clan Gathering' – he gave presents to all the members of the family. For instance, paintings of horses by artists he was sponsoring, bronze statues of horses, etc. Horses were his passion. He loved riding. He did not bet, only admired the 'noble' creatures. Statues and pictures of horses were everywhere, even in the servants' bedrooms.

Grandfather had died shortly before I was born. Often I was told how pleased he had been with my mother to produce a firstborn, Arnold. There had been a run of grand-daughters in the family. When the third was announced, he walked out, slamming the door, refusing to admire her.

*   *   *

Several years ago, Cousin Elisabeth, who was my senior by fifteen years, told me the following story. Grandfather Samuel had invited her and her sister Rita, with their governess Fraulein Frieda, to the Friday Night Dinner. This was always an elaborate, almost festive, affair. On this occasion, they were joined by a further guest, a 'Polacky' Jew. It was considered an honour, a privilege, to invite the Jewish Wanderers to one's home for the Sabbath. As doyen of the Jewish community, the first right of hospitality belonged to Grandfather. After the pogroms in Russia and Poland, from 1880 there was mass emigration of Jews to America. These Eastern Jews, who spoke mainly Yiddish, walked from one Jewish community to the next. On arrival at the synagogue or the rabbi's house, they were treated as welcome visitors. The rabbi's wife, and my grandmother, with the help of a notable citizen, Christian or Jewish, presided over the second-hand clothing store, as-good-as-new, asking if the visitor would like to view it. Perhaps there might be an item to their liking, perhaps boots for the children? This store was also open to the poor of our town, of any denomination.

Sabbath accommodation was provided in the loft of the house, in simple, small cubicles next to the expansive drying loft, which was for use in inclement weather. These cubicles were needed for artisans or other specialist repair workers coming to do jobs at the factory. The servants bath- and wash-room next to the boiler house was put at the disposal of the wanderers and their families.

After the Friday Night Service, the congregation dispersed; the men wearing their top hats and prayer shawls, slowly walked home. The dinner was ready, the candles had been lit on the massive dining table, which had the carved lion's heads on all of its legs, snarling at one another.

A Hebrew prayer was said by the Polacky, which he seemed to consider a great honour. Cousin Elisabeth was of the opinion that Grandfather's Hebrew was not up to it. Soup was served. The Polacky broke his bread into small pieces, dunking them into the soup. Elisabeth copied this. Fraulein Frieda was shocked, giving Elisabeth a well-earned puff. The guest was ill at ease with all these many items of silver cutlery; he knocked over his glass of red wine. Elisabeth tried to be helpful. She had heard that if you put salt on to the stain the damask tablecloth will be easier to wash in the laundry. Disaster!

The top of the salt cellar had not been properly screwed on, a whole mountain of salt was rising on the cloth. 'Miss Elisabeth, leave the table at once!' Governesses had full charge. Grandfather suppressed his laughter, Grandmother looked stern. Elisabeth spent the rest of the evening in the kitchen, normally forbidden territory, which was much more fun, tasting all the dishes, even those labelled not suitable for children.

* * *

Grandmother Emilie's visit was announced whenever we were ill. It had to be a real illness; colds did not rate a visit. She was Father's mother; Mother's parents lived far away in a small spa in the Taunus mountains.

The maid had to give the sick room an extra polish. They changed the sheets if they were only a little crumpled, even if they had no spots at all. Grandmother was feared by everybody, everybody I knew, and her visits amounted almost to an interview or audience. Always she brought with her the 'stuffed pigeon for the sick child' prepared by her housekeeper Wanda. I cannot remember any visits without pigeon. I found the pigeon tasted horrid, but it was an honour to receive it. Grandmother also brought some small gift of moral value, like containers to keep things tidy. How glad I was when the visit was over.

Grandmother's Wanda jealously 'guarded' her. Wanda – I found out later – unknown to Grandmother, would decide who was received. She would return with the caller's visiting card. 'Mrs Fleischer does not receive today but I will inform her.' Apart from this, Wanda looked after Grandmother, who often felt a little unwell, with a deep and sincere devotion. Wanda had been in the family all her life; she occupied a position of authority: 'The Fraulein Wanda'.

'Wanda, the Dragon', that's what we children called her. She always told tales about us and would complain about our shoes not being wiped, even on a fine day. We composed nasty poems about imaginary misdeeds committed by her. I remember a spy glass we said she used featured in them often (like the bad Queen in Snow White), and we had the poems delivered by hand by Mr Herd, the one-armed messenger of the factory.

The couplets were typewritten, anonymous. Mr Herd was a good sport and never gave us away.

*　*　*

Soon I would be six and going to school. I was looking forward to it. Mrs Koester made schooldresses for me, woolly tartan ones, lined – the skin of a princess – with detachable white collars, striped or checked gingham ones, 'suitable for school' as they referred to it. Then there were school aprons. It was compulsory to wear an apron in Junior School.

Grandmother was going to buy the satchel. This was another ritual in the family, she always bought the satchel for the grandchildren.

Wanda rang up to say that tomorrow morning, providing the weather was fine; Mrs Fleischer would call for me at eleven o'clock to buy the satchel.

Well before the appointed time I sat on the staircase. I kept very still, as I did not dare mess up my clothes. Finally Karl rang the bell, I opened the door and he lifted me up and kissed me. Sister Paula had said I was too big for that, besides it was unhygienic, but she was not there to see it. Karl wore his best uniform and the brass buttons were newly burnished.

'Good morning, Grandmother.'

'Good morning.' She inspected me. 'Where is Sister Paula?'

'Bathing Richard.'

'Tell her to put a slide in your hair.'

Back I went.

'I told you not to get yourself untidy. Tell Mrs Fleischer I am sorry I can't come down, I'm bathing baby.'

'I told her already.'

Grandmother indicated the seat opposite her in the Landau. 'Cover yourself with the rug.'

I was stroking the fur lining underneath.

'Don't fidget.'

Hackerle, the saddler, had been informed by Wanda that we would call.

The old Mr Hackerle stood in the doorway to greet us.

'Now, have a good look around,' said Grandmother. 'See if there is one you especially like.'

There were dozens of different kinds of satchels on display; the choice was hard. Finally I narrowed it down to two: one in a shiny patent leather and one covered with the furry side of calf's hide, processed to look like leopard.

The assistant laid both on the counter. Grandmother had been chatting with Mr Hackerle.

'Quite unsuitable,' remarked my Grandmother. 'Patent leather cracks.'

'This is good quality, Madam,' protested Mr Hackerle.

'Even so – and the other one, we're not going to a circus.'

Mr Hackerle brought one made of brown, solid cow-hide. 'This is what we usually sell for the young ladies.'

'It will do very nicely, thank you.'

'Can I wear it now?'

'Of course not. You can carry it if you like. Have you got a purse?'

'No, Grandmother.'

'Purses, Mr Hackerle.'

I was allowed to choose a lovely red one. Grandmother put one mark inside it.

'Now, you keep that till you go to school – it's school money.'

'Thank you, Grandmother.'

The young Mr Hackerle came to greet Grandmother.

'How is your wife and the new baby. It's a boy, am I right?'

Wanda kept Grandmother well informed.

Young Mr Hackerle blushed. 'Fine, fine, both of them.'

'Give her my best regards.' We moved towards the door. The two Messrs Hackerle bowed us out.

'*Gruess Gott, gruess Gott und dank schoen, gnae Frau.*' (God's greeting, thank you, Madam.)

There was an interesting story about Grandmother and her siblings. Great Grandmother had lost several babies, the reason being that she had no milk at all, and therefore could not feed them. She lost all her 'summer babies' in spite of the best cows' milk she gave them. This milk was probably far too rich. The commandant of the local prison was a friend of the family and was asked to help.

In Victorian times, when unmarried girls got pregnant, if the parent threw them out – 'Never darken my doorstep again!' – the Town 'took them in', in the local civil prison, which was housed in the castle, next to the administrative offices. Good accommodation it was, too. The young man, or the old man who would not, or could not, marry the girl, was sentenced to labour for a time. All his earnings were confiscated to pay for the expenses of mother and baby.

Often these girls were healthy peasant girls.

Great-grandmother said to the commandant, 'I am having again a "Summer baby". I need a wet nurse; all my "Summer babies" die, I don't know why. I give them the very best cows' milk. I would like to try a wet nurse. If you can get me a respectable girl, due in about May, can I have her?' Sometimes even respectable girls got into trouble. One had to promise to supply private quarters for the wet nurse and her baby, and to take full responsibility for a job or position later on, or even find her a husband.

So Grandmother and other siblings were nourished on 'Prison milk'.

Another 'milking story' concerned my mother. Arnold, her firstborn, was a tiny child. This was not surprising, mother being only four foot eleven inches. There was a surfeit of milk. The local doctor approached mother, asking if she would consider giving the surplus to a little boy who was dying because of lack of mother's milk.

So Karl, our coachman, waited with the Landau in front of the house three times a day to take the precious milk, all wrapped in nappy and hot water-bottle to the poor child, who thankfully survived.

Most evenings Father came to the nursery to play with us for an hour. He usually stayed until dinner time. Sometimes he told us stories or he read us books like the *Muenchener Bilderbogen* by Wilhelm Busch. These are comic strips of superior quality, well drawn, with very witty rhymes. We squealed with delight over the limericks. He also read us many animal stories.

I adored my father, and wanted to be his favourite. He took the 'Best Child of the Week' for the early morning walk on Sundays. How hard I tried to be the best child! We set out at six o'clock for the woods and returned in time for breakfast. Father knew the names of all flowers and animals, and could distinguish birds by their calls. One day he might tell me how Mr and Mrs Stag-beetle lived; on another he'd explain to me the medicinal properties of herbs found on the roadside. 'We must not despise our common friends. This little daisy, look at the leaves, they are good for the stomach and so is the dandelion – one could put a little in the salad with the lettuce. And here, horsetail, very good for the kidneys. Ah, Nature cures, and the doctor pockets the fee.' Father knew everything. (Actually he had one of those rare photographic memories. I never knew him to make a mistake, however obscure the subject). If the winter was hard, he would arrange for 'salt-blocks for the mammals'. He was a member of the Alb-verein; the Jura mountains were near, and he would arrange for footpaths to be cleared and marked, benches to be erected at beauty spots. He was always arranging something which would help someone.

Before returning home we did some breathing exercises. How long he could hold his breath! (He told me years later that the exercises we did then in the woods had cured me of a slight stammer.)

He had a great sense of humour and could tell little jokes (*Spaessle*) for hours. Jokes were divided into three classes: Children's; Drawing Room; and Definitely-not-the-Drawing-Room Jokes!

The latter, of course, I never heard.

Following afternoon tea we usually saw Mother for a few minutes in the drawing room. Arnold would tell her about school, then she'd ask me how Kindergarten was.

'Do you play with Helga?' Helga was the new girl; Mother knew her mummy.

'No.'

'Why not?'

'Because I don't like her.'

'Why don't you like her?'

'Because she can't play properly.'

'Why ever not? She is the same age as you.' She was born on the same day as I was, in the same hospital, next room, six minutes after me!

'She's silly.'

'Well, play with her. I know her mummy.'

'You play with her mummy.'

'Don't be cheeky.'

'I'm not cheeky.' I pulled a face.

'Yes you are, and stubborn. You are to play with Helga.'

I did not know what I had done. Mother was very cross. Why should I play with that silly girl? I was glad when it was time to go back to the nursery.

'What's the matter with you?' asked Sister Paula.

'She is sulking,' answered Mother.

'Would you like to tell me what happened?' asked Sister Paula when we had left the room.

'No ... she said I was cheeky.'

'Not "she", Mother. Were you cheeky?'

'No, I wasn't.'

Sister Paula left it at that... She never gave me bad marks for being 'cheeky' to Mother.

Chapter 4

Easter and I Wish I had the Measles

'Is the chicken for tomorrow, Liesel?'

'No, baby lamb for tomorrow, always baby lamb for Easter Sunday.'

'Can I watch, please?' Liesel was preparing a chicken; I loved to watch when she took the innards out. I counted the eggs: 'One big one, two middle size, one small one, and lots of teeny-weeny ones!'

Liesel put them in a bowl. 'They will do for the stuffing.'

'Do you think the big one would have popped out tomorrow, tell me, and would have become an Easter Egg?'

"Who knows?' said Liesel.

'Mr Easter Rabbit knows,' said I.

'Sure.'

'You've not touched anything,' said Sister Paula to Arnold at tea-time. 'Too many sweets I suppose.' Mr Easter Rabbit had been most generous.

Sister Paula was a 'too many sweets – bad for the teeth' Nanny. She would have loved to lock them all away.

Arnold sat quietly, with hunched shoulders, on his chair. He looked very white.

'It's not true. He did not eat many.' I felt I had to defend him. 'I ate much more.'

'We'd better put them away now.'

Arnold did not eat dinner either. He mumbled, 'I want to go to bed.'

'That's the first time I've heard children asking to go to bed,' said Father. He looked at him. 'He's running a temperature.'

'Straight to bed.'

During the night I woke up. People were talking. My parents and Sister Paula were standing around Arnold's bed. Then Father wrapped him in a blanket and carried him outside.

'Where are you taking him? Why?'

'Sssssst ... you go to sleep.'

'Where are you taking my Arnold?'

'Upstairs. He's not well. We can look after him much better upstairs. Go to sleep now. I'll tuck you up.'

When the maid brought my breakfast she said, 'Arnold has the measles. He's in *isolation.*'

'What's that?'

'It means nobody is allowed to see him.'

For the next week I hung around in the corridor, hoping to catch a glimpse of him. Always some grown-up shooed me away.

'Don't let me catch you again.'

After a week I was allowed to join him in the red-curtained room. I think I was rather glad I had caught it too. If only my eyes had not hurt so much! They kept the curtains drawn all the time – how I hated the red half-light. I cried, 'Red hurts me, I want green.' But they insisted that red was good for me. Nurse Vetter came to look after us. She stayed with us in the room. When we asked her for something she gave it to us right away – to our surprise. I tried this out, but after a while I could not think of anything else I wanted. So I settled down to a little sleep. When we were better Nurse Vetter played with us. She was very good at cutting out and made long paper chains for us. It was wonderful how she cut the chains in the shape of dancing boys and girls. Arnold and I drew clothes on them; he did it with pencil and I coloured them with crayons. Father bought us several large sheets with cut-outs, '*Ausschnittbogen*'. We pasted them on cardboard, standing up. There was Snow White and the Seven Dwarfs – everything was on this *Ausschnittbogen*, even the spindle on which the Good Queen had pricked her finger.

We cut out a whole zoo, with cages for the wild animals.

'Quick, quick, paste the cages on, my tiger is going to bite you,' called Arnold. Nurse Vetter was very afraid and hid under the bed.

Nurse Vetter's father had a soap factory. It was a small place. Often he stood in his yard before the wide-open factory door. He was a big fat man. The white lab. coat he wore made his red face look quite purple. Sometimes he called us over when he saw us passing and he gave us tiny pieces of highly scented soap. 'Roses for the young lady – you like pink, don't you – mimosa for the young man.' Arnold and I loved our 'stinky soap'. At home we had to use 'good soap suitable for children' which did not smell nearly as nice.

'Oh, thank you, Mr Vetter.'

Once he allowed us to look inside the factory. There was so much steam that we could hardly see the big bubbling cauldrons. We quickly came out again because it was too hot. As a sideline Mr Vetter manufactured soap novelties, like animals for children or lemons. Mr Vetter was a practical joker; he was proud of his 'Big Invention'. Together with a local patisserie he made chocolates filled with soft soap!

If we were good Nurse Vetter would bring us soap bears or squirrels and as a goodbye present we received a soap heart wrapped in cellophane with 'I love you' printed on it.

*   *   *

I had been given a box of coloured beads, for making necklaces or bracelets. Threading them was quite easy, if one took care not to drop them. Beads are hard to retrieve from underneath furniture.

On my father's desk was a pretty lamp made of multi-coloured glass, a Tiffany lamp, which had a beaded glass fringe. When the sun shone on the lamp the glass made pretty patterns on the wall and if one touched the fringe one could make coloured lights dance around. The beads were much nicer than the ones in my box, quite easy to snip off. They improved my necklace no end. The grownups praised my pretty necklace, until they discovered the source of my beads.

'Father's desk – Father's lamp – not to be touched – understand?'

Someone must have told an 'Aunt' about my necklace adventure. My birthday present was a necklace made of coral beads and silver squares. I did not like it. I told Mother I would not wear this horrid thing. She agreed it was too old for me, said it was 'Art Deco', and that was the last I saw of it. Most probably it went into Mother's secret drawer, the one for unwanted presents, always locked. When I was older. Mother explained this 'magical' drawer. The contents were fascinating, some extraordinarily ugly. 'One has to record the details of the present, here in this little book, with dates, and who gave, and what occasion. This is to make sure that one does not pass it on (recycle) to someone who knows the giver. It could upset them.'

Mother explained, 'We get a lot of these things, figurines and pictures – they are only prints – because people say we like art. One does not know what to do with them. I would be embarrassed to give them to someone, such bad taste.'

'Give them to a raffle,' I suggested.

'What a good idea. There is the Easter raffle at the Kneipp Verein, after the lecture.'

'That's settled then, as long as they don't know they're from us.' Father was the Honorary Treasurer of the Kneipp Verein.

'Arnold told me school starts tomorrow,' I said to Father. 'Please, let me get up, properly I mean, not only in this room. If I don't go they'll give my place away. Nurse Vetter says I can't go, not for a fortnight. Please tell her that I can go.'

'I'm afraid, my dear, she is right. You'll miss a few days. But it does not matter, you'll soon catch up. You're my clever girl.'

Arnold did not care if he missed lessons or not. He was first in class and considered very forward for his age – mentally only; he was still a tiny child.

Chapter 5

My First Schoolday and Religion Puzzles me

I had been looking forward to my first school day. Now it was all spoilt. Sister Paula took me to school. I had hoped Mother would take me, if only on the first day. School started at eight o'clock, Mother did not usually get up so early.

On entering the classroom the first thing I saw was the 'leopard' satchel, the one I had chosen at Mr Hackerle's. It belonged to a thin, mousy-haired child who wore a black apron and sleeve preservers (considered practical and economical, worn by children coming mainly from lower middle class homes).

The teacher walked up to me.

She limps, I thought.

She said, 'So you are Sylvia, we've been waiting for you. I've kept a seat for you. Here, in the front row.'

She's nice, I thought. I wonder how she guessed that I like sitting in front?

The teacher and Sister Paula left the classroom, talking in low voices. I wonder what she is telling her about me? I became a little worried. I've been Best Child quite often lately, I'm sure it's all right. I was relieved.

I looked around. Ah, there was my cousin Lila Guggenheim. I waved to her. In the back sat 'silly Helga'. I did not wave to her.

I became devoted to Miss Helmstaedter, my school teacher, who was a woman of early middle age with gentle ways and serene bearing. She was most kind. She never hit anyone. Cane-on-knuckles was still popular with many Junior School teachers. She wore her dark dresses which were trimmed with écru lace collars, very long, much too long for the fashion of that time. Probably she was very aware of her club foot. Her black hair was parted in the middle and she had regular features. I thought her beautiful.

She was considered 'advanced', 'enlightened', or 'crazy', according to different parents, because she taught by pictorial methods. This was unusual in 1928. Reading was fun: for every letter she drew a picture on the blackboard. So was arithmetic: we counted apples – she had brought a whole basket full. Lesson finished, she shared them out. What a contrast to the other junior class! We could hear their chant through the walls: 'Two and two makes four, four and two makes six...'

I was happy to have such a wonderful teacher. I loved her. I loved school.

A popular sport, when I grew older, was 'vexing teachers', but to vex her would have been inconceivable to me and to the whole class.

She had no favourites; she did not believe in having favourites.

In Germany it is customary that all children go to the State Junior School. There were few private schools, none in my hometown. The daughter of the miner shared the bench with the daughter of the millionaire.

There was the 'Catholic School' where nuns and priests taught, for catholic children only. The Schiller Schule was a girls' school which catered for Protestants, Jews and other minorities. All schools came under the local council. One had the same teacher right through the four years of junior school. They taught all subjects, including religion.

Miss Helmstaedter was qualified to teach in High School. She was bi-lingual as she came from Alsace Lorraine. I don't know if she was French or German. She said it was more satisfying to remain with a group of children for several years, and this was the reason why she preferred teaching in junior school. We, her pupils, felt very honoured and grateful that she taught *us* when she could have done 'better' and earned considerably more.

The Jewish children were not expected to take part in the classes on Religious Instruction, but were allowed to do their homework. I pretended to read but devoured all Miss Helmstaedter told about Gentle Jesus – also the Christian principles. Gentle Jesus, the 'Herr', the Christ Child – always kind. Why was Jehovah, who was my God, so often angry? I felt so ashamed when she said that the Jews had crucified Him. Suffering great remorse over my childish

26

faults and shortcomings, I resolved to be better and to try hard to mould my life by His teachings. Carefully, I enquired about Him at home. My Mother referred to Him as an 'Imposter', an opinion for which I did not forgive her. Arnold called Him a Prophet, a very clever man and a teacher, but said he was definitely not the Messiah. I cannot recall what my Father said. I don't think he was present at the time of discussion.

I was taught to say my prayers before going to sleep. I often forgot. I think the reason was because we did not speak them aloud. Next day I felt guilty and I would say, 'Dear God, I am sure You know I did not mean to forget. Please forgive me. I'll try not to let it happen again.'

If only I could have prayed to Jesus. I was certain He forgave Christian children when they forgot.

'Please, Jesus, tell me it is not true what she said of You. She must not say it, she must not call you an Imposter. I must not call Mother 'she'. That is rude. 'She' is the cat's mother. I am sorry. I am sure Mother is wrong, Jesus was crucified by the Jews. Arnold says that to crucify is a Roman way of killing. So the Romans must have done it. Are all Jews bad? My Father is good. You know he is. Why am I Jewish? Because God made me so, because my parents are. But Your father and mother were also Jewish. I wish I knew ... please.'

And I would close my eyes tightly and see the black and yellow shapes intermingling, stars and rays and shadows, growing bigger and bigger. And now it's all pretty colours like a kaleidoscope. And then all black again, but the yellow light darts through it, very fast. They are snakes.

I was frightened and turned over on my stomach. I pressed my palms in my eyesockets.

That was better! I like this pink colour. It has turned to blue-green now. Just like the blue lake, *Blautopf* (Blue Bowl) near *Blaubeuren*, where we went last summer on an excursion. There's a nymph there who sings under the water. Father told us the legend. Sometimes she appears to young men and they fall madly in love with her. If she likes them she marries them, and they live with her down there under the water.

Chapter 6

What are you Going to be When you Grow Up?

The keynote of our nurse, Sister Paula, was clinical kindness, efficiency and self-control. The first thing she had done on her arrival was to take off the frilly organdie hangings on Richard's coat. They were 'dustcatchers' and 'unhygienic'. I would not have been surprised to see her disinfecting the carrots which she substituted for jam at tea time. Because kissing was unhygienic, it was discouraged, especially kissing my Mother. Later we called Sister Paula 'Deda'; Baby Richard called her that. Her face was parchment coloured and she had straight fair hair, which was hidden under a nurse's cap. She was all starched apron and blue and white striped dress, and I did not think she had a figure at all. She seemed very old, while my Mother seemed to be a young woman who laughed and cried and had tempers, wore perfume and pearls and heels as high as my father would permit; it was bad for one to wear high heels – Deda wore sensible shoes. The two women were jealous of each other. Father talked to Deda for hours on medical subjects and Mother imagined things.

At this period, we saw little of Mother. Deda did not encourage it. Children's nurses insisted on 'full' charge. Our idea of Mother became associated with the inspection of clothes. Before we were allowed to leave the house we had to show ourselves. Mother looked at us critically and then would decide whether a certain beret would match a certain coat. I was told that some people considered us the best-dressed children of the town. We used this occasion to wish her 'Good morning' or 'Goodbye'. Our quarter of an hour after tea in the drawing room was abolished. We took our 'tea' in the open air, weather permitting. 'Tea' was now fruit juice and, if we had been good, raisins, figs or dates. Everything 'nice' was said to ruin the teeth. Biscuits were nice and cake very nice. We got fruit flan on Sundays and Liesel was asked to bake cakes only for birthdays and holidays.

Sometimes in the afternoon orders were sent to the nursery for us to be put into white organdie aprons, boys into sailor suits, 'not to be dirtied or crumpled', and we had to wait till Mother sent for us. Then we would be handed round the table to her lady friends and asked a lot of silly questions. How old are you? How tall are you? How much do you weigh? Do you go to school? Do you like your teacher? Are you a good girl? The ladies all smelled very nice and when I was about to be kissed, I demanded, 'On the cheek only, please.' We children discussed their scent, calling it 'stink', our little revenge for being 'paraded'. We would argue as to which lady 'stank the most'.

After tea, Mother sat in her wing chair by the window, embroidering. Occasionally, if there were no visitors, she would permit me to join her. Mother embroidered an endless succession of tablecloths. All our tea tablecloths were hand-embroidered, and we had very large tables. Sometimes she consulted me on the choice of colour, but she never took my advice. Children like many bright colours together. She would complain to me bitterly that she could not make her own clothes. She told me she would have dearly loved to have taken a course in dress-making, but her father would not hear of it. He had said, 'No daughter of mine is going to wear home-made clothes. I hate home-made clothes.' She was his only child.

I occasionally 'helped' her when she did her crosswords. She purchased the small books, saying the puzzles in the newspapers were too easy. 'What was that tributary of the river Amazon?' I found several in the great atlas in the library. 'Only four letters, please.'

I sat usually on a footstool. If the embroidery was an 'easy' one, I helped Mother, otherwise I fetched my own. It was customary for girls to do embroidery, mostly tray-cloths with daisies. I liked these afternoons; Mother was then so kind that I wished she would hug and kiss me like she used to when Miss Mary was with us. Why could I not tell her that? Why did I wait for her to make the first move? And then Deda knocked at the door and it was time to go back to the nursery. Obediently I got up, hoping that perhaps next time...

Our holidays were spent with Deda, without our parents, in Eckenweiler, a hamlet in the Black Forest. Deda's father had a small farm there. We liked the country life. We played peasants wearing patterned overalls and headscarves and carried rakes and pitchforks. Busily we were helping to make the hay, but this consisted mainly of sitting on top of the wagon and waving to the peasants on the other 'haycarts' who passed us on the dirt track. We helped to cut the corn, and this consisted of carrying the red kerchief with the cheese and bread, or even the jug of home-made cider which was drunk in this locality at mealtimes. Meal times were so different from home. The whole family sat around the bare, wooden table. They reported what had happened during the day. To the local gossip, old Mr Stuhler, Deda's father, always gave a grunt. He had no teeth and ate his soup in a disgusting manner; we children would have been severely scolded for it. We watched him with fascination. He was so daring, and nobody said 'boo'. What a hero! At home, meals were taken in silence. One had to masticate. We were allowed to speak only after permission had been given.

Deda's brother was a carpenter. His workshop adjoined the house. I loved to watch him and his apprentice, and hung around with a broom in my hand on the pretext of sweeping up woodshavings. Usually he took no notice of me, but sometimes he got angry, pretending he had just discovered me. 'You get out of here, but quick.'

Deda's youngest brother Fritz did no work; he always sat on a bench in front of the house. He was ill. He had boils which hurt him. Later he joined the Nazi Party. I was told that after he got his 'post' there the boils disappeared.

* * *

Deda was good at organising games. She persuaded my parents to buy us wonderful toys, such as a tent for playing Red Indians, a real box camera and a Doll's Nursing Home, instead of the usual Doll's House. This nursing home had been specifically made for us and was complete with running water, a first-aid room and a doll's play room for the convalescent dolls. There was even a premature baby all packed in cotton wool. We often played 'hospital', because Deda had told us stories of her training. What intrigued me most were the tales of premature babies, all packed in cotton wool. This was before oxygen tents were used.

30

On Deda's instruction Mrs Koester made nurses' uniforms for Susan and me. Arnold got a doctor's coat. Now we could play 'Hospital' properly. 'Operating for appendicitis' and 'broken arms and legs' were popular. I was told I was good at bandaging. Arnold wanted to operate on Margot, who had been Mother's doll. He said, 'Let's cut open her belly, and see what's inside – straw perhaps.' Margot's body was of flesh-coloured kid leather, she was a Jumeau doll and consequently very valuable. We did not dare, because she had been mother's favourite. She had a bisque face and hands and was beautifully dressed in the fashions of the 1890s, with handmade underwear and patent leather boots.

When next time Sister Paula took us to the hairdresser, we took Margot along. The young assistant placed the doll carefully on the high chair reserved for toddlers, spread a cloth around her neck, and gave her the fashionable twenties shingle. As Margot had a real peruke, individual hairs attached, just like a grown-up wig, he would cut her hair, which had been in a fancy coiffure. Mother was furious, of course; we had not asked her permission.

In the attic was a box full of costumes, accumulated over years from 'performances' in the family, and handed down to us from older cousins. We often acted fairytales. There were gnome suites for Snow White, fairy dresses, a Red Riding Hood outfit, and wolf's mask, a toad suit for the story of the Princess and the Frog King – my favourite; I loved 'splosh-splosh-splosh, wait for me Princess!' I designed the sets. It was very useful that Uncle David had a paper factory. He was most generous and supplied all we needed of coloured crêpe paper for the sets and costumes.

Also in the attic was a very large box containing the Marklin Railway. It had belonged to Father, and was large gauge. Unfortunately, when set up, it occupied one and a half rooms; therefore it 'came out' only at Christmas.

Miss Helmstaedter encouraged us to stage plays and she liked it when we wrote them ourselves. I sat down and wrote reams 'to order'. I kept the actions as simple as possible. I considered this a necessity because of our home-made costumes and improvised props. I was afraid the audience might not be able to follow. This was a pity, as I adored the plots of operas – Mother was an opera fan and had told me of many on embroidery afternoons – with the actors incognito, this magic word! Beggars into princes and princes into swineherds.

31

Miss Helmstaedter called me '*Kasperle*' (little clown), as I liked to entertain my audience.

My plays were always in rhyme. Sometimes the matching word was very elusive, but however far-fetched, it had to do. Our neighbour, Ette Duisberg, was far better at rhyming than I was.

I wrote lyrical ones, with Mother Earth, birds and bees and cockchafers; sloppy ones, with poor little children and guardian angels; heroic ones, with much suffering and misunderstanding, but ending in everlasting happiness. The grown-ups laughed in the right places, clapped in the right places, and were, for once, intelligent.

I was very conscious of the distinction between rich and poor and often introduced this into my play. Many of my classmates' fathers were out of work in the 1930s. Our teacher paid for special treats for the 'poor pupils' out of the school fund – her own pocket, as I found out later.

By the standards of my storybooks I assessed my family as very rich. Mother always told us, 'Be grateful – other children haven't got it.' How I wished I was poor, then I would not be told continuously to be grateful. I would have rather lived with the charcoal burners in the wood, like the heroine in the fairy tale, or, like the foundling princess, be brought up by smallholders. Everyone was so noble and they cheerfully ate dry bread.

Arnold once asked me, 'What are you going to be when you grow up?'

'Well, I don't know,' I replied. 'I've not made up my mind. What do you want to be?'

Arnold had his answer ready. 'I'm going to be Prime Minister.'

'Oh, that's lovely. I want to be Prime Minister too.'

'Girls can't be Prime Minister,' said Arnold with authority.

'Why not?'

'They just can't. But I tell you what you can do, you could marry one of Hindenburg's sons.'

Mother often said how nice it would be if I became a dress designer. After all, I was good at handicrafts and could draw quite well. When a visitor had asked me, in the presence of my parents, 'Do you know what you want to become when you grow up?' I had answered, 'I want to be an artist.'

Father said, 'Quite out of the question, my dear. That is a hunger profession.'

How right he was – I knew he always gave money to his artist friends – a lot of money!

Father said he would prefer it if I would learn something practical. But what?

So when visitors insisted that I should tell them, I felt at a loss and embarrassed and would mumble something about dress designing.

'Speak up, don't be shy. Fetch those drawings you did last week,' said Mother. 'Isn't she a clever girl?'

'May I go now?' And I left Mother to her favourite topic, clothes.

Brother Arnold was still in the Prime Minister stage, though he said now that he would not mind starting as a Cabinet Minister, the experience might be useful, even as a politician, a member of the Reichstag. Richard answered every time, 'a gardener'. He spent most of his time with the Duisberg boy, whose father was a florist, par excellence. Their greenhouses and nursery adjoined our orchard. They specialised in growing exotic plants. Richard also 'helped' Karl a great deal. Susan wanted to be a fine lady and a housewife.

Having been noisy on our afternoon rest, Susan was put to sleep in the salon, on one of the settees. She got bored, found a little loose piece on the Chinese hand painted wallpaper – it came off quite easily. Father had to ask one of his artist friends to paint in the flowers and birds. The artist, who came to stay, took over three weeks to do the work. Liesel said he made it last, because he liked her cooking. The young man had made a good job – he proudly showed it to me: one could not tell the repair.

Chapter 7

We Visit our Grandparents and Other Relatives

Deda had stayed for two years with us. She left to take another exam in midwifery. She was quickly promoted and became supervisor of an entire district in the Black Forest.

I loved Hede, the new governess, immediately I saw her. She was so pretty and she was good fun, not at all like the grown-ups. She treated us almost like equals and had 'absolutely no use for bad marks'. Hede was popular with everybody. Mother and Hede spent much time together. Mother took her often to the cinema. When Hede was invited to parties she wore very nice clothes. I loved to watch her dress and pin the flowers my parents had ordered for her onto her frock. I admired her silver shoes, which she had dyed herself, using an old toothbrush. The shoes would not lose the smell till Father gave her an ingredient he used when he made scent, a hobby of his.

Hede was so clever, so artistic. She was experienced in crafts, and taught me basket making. The long 'spaghetti' had to be soaked overnight to make them pliable, then one slotted them through the base, prepared by the carpenter of our factory. It was quite quick to do, weaving in and out. One finished off with wooden beads at the top and, hey presto, a good present for the many aunts was ready. She also taught me sewing, different types of stitches. I did not like embroidery, because it took too long; one had nothing to show for the time spent. Hede taught Arnold fret work and some carpentry. He made small boxes and varnished them.

Bedtime was the best. Hede became a tiger, a lion, a monkey. She did it awfully well. She jumped on our beds, pretending to eat us. It was great fun.

But, best of all, she was affectionate: she cuddled us, she praised us. Mother never cuddled or praised me, not even when I got ten out of ten at school, and not even when I got the very highest mark of all the girls in the district for the entrance exam to higher education – in my case, the Seminary for Young Ladies. But still nothing.

The summer holidays were spent, after Deda had left us, with our maternal grandparents. They lived in Camberg, a hydro, in the Taunus mountains. The train journey, which took almost a day, was wonderful. We had at least four changes; the last train was a slow local one which we called 'Creeper-train', or, because it frequently rang a bell, 'Bim-Bim train'. We maintained the reason was to warn the cows to get out of the way. The 'Bim-Bim' stopped very often even where there was no halt sign. Perhaps it stops at every apple tree we thought.

Mother and Hede had their hands full in every sense of the word. Each of us children had special hand luggage: toys or a jar with goldfish, things which could not possibly be sent in advance. It was a 'flying visit' for mother; she could only stay for a few days, declaring she had too many commitments at home.

We were met at the station by my grandparents and August, their chief clerk. Secretly we called him 'silly August', after a nursery rhyme. August did not deserve this, for he was most capable. He was very good natured and took our childish whims and requests seriously. August was six foot four inches tall, pale and thin; the khaki overall he wore made him appear even taller.

Camberg is a small old town, built on a slope. The medieval half-timbered houses lean towards each other across the narrow cobbled streets. The old tower on the city wall looks as if it is going to topple over, but it is quite safe – it says so in a tourist brochure! The city wall, which was crumbling and overgrown with ivy, bore notices stating, 'Sitting on City Wall is at your own risk'. The legend was that geese nesting there had saved the town from an attack by their honking, which woke the burghers. The moat formed part of the public park and gardens. The town council was modernising all the time, making everything flat and planting green grass and tulips. One had to keep off the grass. On Sunday mornings the Camberg Brass Band played there, but when it was wet, it played in the Assembly Rooms.

We children had looked at the posters in the many shop windows. The *Kur Verwaltung* (local Tourist Board), were holding their annual

35

dance. It was to be a grand affair in the Ballroom, with two bands, one from far-away Frankfurt, a tombola with good prizes, and a champagne supper, buffet style – previous booking required – all in aid of the Home for the deaf and dumb children, situated in the nearby village.*

My grandparents had received their special invitation, for they always gave generously. They said their dancing days were over, but that Hede would enjoy it.

'I have nothing to wear,' Hede moaned. As the time was short, Mother sent Hede's evening gown and her silver sandals by special courier, who came on a motorbike. It was all so exciting. Grandmother loaned her a necklace, as she said the low neckline needed something. This necklace had diamonds in it, though not very big ones, and 'dangly bits'.

Next morning Hede told us she had had a wonderful time, the best ever. Grandmother said Hede had been the prettiest girl there, the belle of the ball. We were all very proud of our Hede.

There was a knock at the door – 'A bouquet for Miss Hede'. There were two more bouquets delivered later. Who had sent them? Hede had danced every dance. She laughed; she could not remember the lads, but they had all been very nice and polite.

I liked everything better at my grandparents' house, starting from early morning. We were allowed to wash with *warm* water. Then we had *white* rolls and *white* bread, *and* it was still warm. All this was labelled 'not healthy' at home. There were usually two or three vegetables served with the lunch or dinner. I was allowed to choose, so I never had to eat spinach, sprouts or other nasty greens, 'so good for one'. I really disliked the skin on the boiled milk, freshly delivered by the farmer – but it was important to boil it for health reasons. The skin made me shudder. At home they told me off when I fished this skin out of my coffee and put it in my saucer. At breakfast with my grandparents, however, a pretty silver strainer, decorated with a garland of flowers at the rim, was put in front of my place setting. We were allowed more freedom; there were almost no rules or regulations. All that was required of us was to be punctual for meals, have clean clothes and hands, and be quiet in our bedroom after lunch for one hour and a half.

Richard never liked to sleep after lunch – Arnold and I were

---

* Home still in existence now.

allowed to read – and had to be coaxed to be good and quiet; he was put by himself in my grandparents' bedroom, in their large, old-fashioned double bed. This bedroom had French windows leading out to a balcony overlooking the street. To pass the time one day Richard climbed on to the balustrade to see if he could balance on it. He waved to Ernest, the idiot son of the neighbours who was sitting as usual in the sun in front of their house. Richard walked the whole length of the balustrade. Ernest was impressed and came nearer, gaping, just in time to catch him in his arms as he fell. Luckily it was only an eight foot drop to the ground. Ernest carried the frightened child in and handed him to Hede, who made us promise secrecy. The fact that Richard might have been killed, or so we liked to imagine, made it a particularly exciting secret to keep.

*   *   *

Grandfather was a wholesale iron merchant. His warehouses were the most wonderful places to play in, especially for hide-and-seek. Our favourite one was the storehouse for stoves and ovens; those made for hotel kitchens were large enough to crawl into.

Our favourite game was 'thundering'. We had invented this ourselves. In the warehouse large metal sheets, 2 metres by 2.5 metres approximately, were stacked against the walls. The peachy coloured ones contained copper, most others were silvery.

When one drummed with one's fist, it sounded like thunder, vibrating from quite loud to a small whisper. Tapping with a broom handle was like a military tattoo, with a metal rod it chimed, and with a nail it screeched horribly. Different coloured metal sheets gave different tones. We had our very own Metal Band; we must have made a dreadful din.

The metal sheets had other good uses: there was room to hide, when one sat on the floor behind them – a space of about half a metre.

But August had seen me. He pulled me out, slowly, gently. 'Young miss, don't ever do this again. It's dangerous.' He took my finger and ran it against the edge of the sheet. Uh, it was sharp! A drop of blood appeared, though only a tiny one. 'You could have decapitated yourself. Promise, never do that again.' I was frightened; I promised.

The large commercial cooking ranges made very good hiding

places: One crawled in and closed the oven door. They were quite roomy. When I tried to get out, the door would not open from the inside. I wriggled – no use. On the surface of the range are various graded rings, for different sizes of cooking vessels. I tried to push these upwards with my head. Finally I managed to free myself. I had bruises and my scalp hurt for days, but I told no-one about my adventure. I was not a Moaning Minnie and, besides, I was afraid they would forbid us to use the premises.

Only one warehouse, where the long iron bars leaned against the walls, was forbidden ground. Another warehouse had a room filled with all sorts of rifles, including airguns. We were allowed to borrow the latter. Target-practice was in the yard and the paper targets were pinned on a wall. Unfortunately, this wall was covered with slate and, of course, we shot it to bits and pieces. Grandfather was rather cross and withdrew our pocket money for a week to help cover the cost of re-slating. After this we used unripe elderberries for ammunition; they left a neat green splash – most satisfactory. I was a poor shot but gave the fact that I am slightly short sighted as an excuse, which Arnold and his friends accepted. The boys – Martin, Robert and Hannes – were all a couple of years older than I, and told me they only let me play with them because I could mend their torn clothes so neatly. They said their mothers did not even notice my repairs, or if they did, mistook them for their own work. Condescendingly they used to say 'not bad, considering she is a girl', or 'almost as good as a boy'. I knew I was as good as they were, but if I surpassed them in anything, they had a habit of pretending not to notice.

Occasionally, Paul, Martin's elder brother, would honour us by joining in our games. Paul was a student at Limburg University; he travelled there every day by train. He wore his peaked students cap at a rakish angle. Those caps were almost as important as the curriculum. First there was the colour of the cap, then the multi-coloured ribbon and, most important of all, the angle at which it was worn. To us he looked 'too wonderful for words'. He allowed me to cover his schoolbooks for him in the regulation blue paper, and I blushed with pleasure when he praised me: 'Quite nice.'

One day Grandmother announced that a new boy was coming to play with us. His name was Horatius, and he was staying with his grandparents for the summer holiday.

Horatius arrived in a white sailor suit, white socks and a cap, with *Bremen* (the name of a famous German liner) written on the ribbon. He was spotlessly clean.

'Hello.'

'Hello.' We stared at each other.

'My grandmother sent me.'

'We know,' Martin interrupted, 'to play with us.' We giggled. 'Perhaps next time. You see, we don't play indoor games in this weather, and we're off to the woods now.'

'Oh, but I would like to come with you, really, I would.'

And Martin said, 'What, in that get-up? With that get-up you can only sit on a chair. Perhaps August will play draughts with you. August is very good at draughts.'

I took pity on him. 'Let him come if he wants to. I'm sure his monkey-suit can be boiled.'

Horatius looked at me gratefully.

Hannes said, 'What did you say your name was?'

I was sure he had heard perfectly well and only asked to embarrass the boy.

'Horatius, Ho-ra-tius. You can call me Rats if you like,' he added apologetically.

The boys walked at a terrific pace on the road leading up to the woods on the hill top. Perhaps they intended to test Horatius. I had difficulty in keeping up with them and Horatius was certainly not used to it. After a little while we fell behind.

Arnold called, 'Hurry up, you slow coaches!'

They waited for us at the entrance to our 'secret place'. This was a small cave in which one could hardly stand up, its entrance hidden by brambles.

Robert called to Horatius, 'Ha! The way you walk I bet you haven't a decent mountain where you come from. Our Feldberg is eight hundred metres high. I've been on it four times.'

Horatius answered, 'No, we haven't got a high mountain, but my father almost climbed the Mont Blanc in Switzerland.'

Robert sneered. 'Almost does not count. How high did he get?'

'Well, quite high ... and then the weather got bad and they had to turn back. Next year he's going to try again.'

Hannes chipped in sarcastically, 'Ask him to send us a postcard if he does.'

'We've discovered this cave,' said Martin proudly, showing the new boy around, side-stepping the puddles.

39

I hoped Horatius would not notice the initials carved in the rock, presumably by lovers. One was a beauty: a heart with an arrow.

We always removed our footprints outside 'our cave', in true Red Indian tradition. Horatius helped me, brushing vigorously with his twigs.

'Hey, hey! You're making too much dust. Look at your socks,' said Arnold. 'They're black now.'

'Who cares?' answered Horatius.

'Your grandmother will,' said I.

'*She* doesn't wash them anyway; they're used to me getting dirty ... because I fight a lot.'

I thought, He's bragging now.

'I said, "I fight a lot",' Horatius repeated with emphasis.

'Why do you fight a lot?' asked Arnold.

'I like rude words.'

Hannes, who had joined us, whistled.

'I know many,' said Horatius smugly.

'Bad expressionisms', as rude words were called in our home, were strictly forbidden. How I admired the 'streetboys' who used them freely. I envied them.

'Do you know any good ones?' Even Martin, who was the eldest, showed interest.

And Horatius started, with the usual ones like 'sow' and 'shut your trap'. Then he whispered in Martin's ear.

'Not fair,' complained Hannes. 'I want to know, too. The others were nothing.'

Horatius repeated it aloud.

'What does it mean?' asked I.

'It means nothing,' said Hannes. 'He made it up.'

'Oh, no I didn't.' Horatius was annoyed. 'It's awfully rude.'

'Tell us what it means.'

He stuttered. 'I'm not quite sure, but I heard it from two streetboys. They had a smashing fight. They only stopped when one was bleeding.'

'It *is* a rude word,' said Martin with authority. 'Grown-ups use it. And I'm not explaining it to you children, and that's final.'

On our way home, when we reached the first houses of the town, we had an unpleasant experience.

Three boys, strangers, called after us, 'Dirty Jew, dirty Jew.' This was the first time it had happened to us, but other Jewish children had told me they had endured such name-calling quite often.

Somehow I felt then it was because we had used rude words ourselves, and my dress was dirty.

Horatius called, 'Let's run after them and give them a good hiding,' and he and Arnold gave chase, but could not catch them.

Horatius was the only Gentile among us. He was a good fellow. He had proved he had courage. Hadn't he taken our part?

On our return we told our grandparents what had happened. They said, 'Uneducated lot – just forget about it.'

'We have not enough suitable children for you to play with, not here in Camberg,' said Grandmother.

'Suitable children', they were always on about that one – suitable...

'Unsuitable' street children had much more fun; they were more daring. On the old City Wall sat one such, a young lad. When he saw Arnold and me he waved.

Then slowly he started to walk on his hands, along the top of the wall. We were rapt in admiration. When he came to the end of the wall, he jumped off. It was quite high. He put his tongue out, I suppose as a greeting, then ran away.

'I'm sure I've seen this lad before,' I said to Arnold. 'He is the one who peed on the front steps of the house – I told you about it.'

'There are not enough public loos here in this Spa town. When you've got to go, you've got to go.'

* * *

Arnold and I had been invited to play with Dr Plesch's children in nearby Koenigsstein – Honoria and Peter Hariold. They had a summer house there.

Honoria, what a queer name! I had never heard that name before. A honorar – that's what doctors get for services, but surely Dr Plesch would not call his daughter after that. Grandmother said the doctor was Hungarian. That might explain the odd name.

As my grandparents did not drive, we were taken in a sort of private taxi to the Taunus mountains. I somehow expected a log cabin in the woods, perhaps to play Red Indians.

Crikey, look at that! A holiday home? It was a most beautiful house, like a small château. There were Greek-style columns at the front entrance, which reminded me of the Acropolis in Arnold's book on Ancient Greek Legends. There were even more columns inside the house. The gardens were very formal – of the 'don't walk on the grass' kind.

Honoria was very kind to me. She showed me her room, which was surprisingly sparsely furnished with just a large table in the middle. Honoria explained, 'I need some workspace, I am going to be a dress designer.'

'Snap,' said I. Suddenly I was interested in her. 'Can I see some of your work?'

'Why not? I did these last week.' She brought out several sheets of paper, which I noticed was water-colour paper. I was not allowed this expensive paper.

'Oh!'

'Let's do some drawing.'

We both sat down, on opposite ends of her large table and made our preliminary sketches, what my mother used to call my 'scribble'.

'I get messy when I colour it in; that's why my table is so large.'

Honoria was sloshing about with her water-colours. I had seen this procedure before with Father's artist friends, painting landscapes.

'Your brushes are too big. Get some sable ones, fine ones,' I suggested. 'They are expensive, though.'

She let me look through her drawings. We were doing evening dresses. Mine were based on one of my mother's which I particularly admired. It had a handkerchief hemline. I had tried it on, once, when mother was out, and twirled around before the full length mirror in her bedroom. It was a creation of the Salon Wintermeyer, super extraordinaire.

Honoria's evening wear was lots of tulle – my mother would have called it predictable. It reminded me of the ballet I had seen. I had to admit she was quite right: these sorts of dresses would have been fine for girls of our age, but boring, boring.

'I'm getting one like that. I designed it myself,' said Honoria.

What could I say? Actually I did not like it all that much, but one has to be polite to one's host. 'You are lucky, such a beautiful dress!' I showed her my drawing, saying that my mother had a similar evening dress, and that I had done different versions of it. 'Her dress is in ombré chiffon by the Salon Wintermeyer in Wiesbaden. Ombré – that's shaded in different colours,' I explained.

'That's local,' said Honoria. 'My mother gets her dresses from Paris.'

They called us for tea, herb tea.

The tea trolley was most interesting; it converted to a tea-table. I had never seen one like it before. Daisy-embroidered tray-cloths were on two tiers. I wondered if Honoria had done them, but I did not ask her, not wishing to bring up this hateful subject of young girls being made to embroider tray-cloths.

The cakes were good, as good as Liesel's. There was a lovely selection. The boys too seemed to appreciate them, at least from the way they stuffed themselves.

They had played chess in the library.

'Peter Harry, did you win or Arnold?'

'My name is Peter Hariold, not Harry.' He sniffed. 'Arnold won.'

Arnold always won at chess, even when playing against the grown-ups.

(Three years later, looking at a postage stamp, I thought: I know this house, it looks like Honoria's, the one in the Taunus mountains, I am sure. I decided to ask my grandparents if they knew anything about it. Grandmother answered the telephone. 'You are quite right. It is a rest home, a recreation home for the Nazis; they have confiscated it. Dr Plesch has emigrated to England. He had inherited the house from his in-laws, a Frankfurt family. They were important people there, chemists, called Gans.' She added. 'We knew the family.')

* * *

Grandfather had just handed us children our weekly pocket money. He was very generous.

Arnold said, 'Let's go to Pinotti's'. Being a Saturday afternoon, Pinotti's Ice Cream Parlour was crowded. I adored the water ices there, especially the one called 'Sorrento' – melon with pistachio nuts, garnished with whipped cream. This, to me, was the height of luxury.

We sat on small cane chairs at a round marble-topped table. The tables were all of different types and colours of marble. I pointed this out to Arnold. 'Perhaps Mr Pinotti has brought them from his native Italy to make him feel less homesick.'

Arnold said, 'My guess is that he has bought up old wash-stands and had them cut down.'

We had an excellent view of all the other tables as we were sitting on a raised platform in a corner of the shop.

'Let's play the "guessing game",' Arnold suggested.

They were mostly visitors on holiday. A couple, taking the cure, discussed the thermal bath, saying, 'Last year in Wildbad it was better; of course, it is much cheaper here.'

'What is his profession?'

'No profession,' Arnold decided. 'Trade – no – let me think. Look how he flicks through that catalogue as if he is counting money; he's used to it.'

'They don't look rich to me,' I interrupted him.

'Don't be silly. He works in a bank.'

A thin, pale lady was sitting by herself at a table.

'A spinster, an old maid.'

'How do you know?'

'Easy that. No ring.'

'What do you think she does?'

'Now, let me see ... perhaps she works in a shop. No, look – she's round-shouldered.'

'A waitress?' I suggested hopefully. 'They're often round-shouldered.'

'No, she's too fidgety, too fussy, the wrong type ... I've got it,' Arnold exclaimed proudly. 'She's a dressmaker. Look at her forefinger: she's got a corn on it – from the scissors.'

'Arnold, you are clever.' I admired him.

It was great fun.

Two men had sat down at the table next to us and we could hear clearly every word they said. They seemed to be discussing sales figures, possibly from an electrical shop, because they repeatedly mentioned brand names.

'I am well down on last month, I don't know why. June used to be a good month with our sidelines for the holidays,' said the thin man.

'Perhaps you ought to advertise.'

'Perhaps ... it's so expensive. Since Rosenberg has that new shop front, they all go to him – it's all black glass – flashy!'

'If you would paint up yours a bit ... it could do with it.'

'What are they talking about?' I whispered.

Arnold explained to me that, since the Depression, people had cut down on luxury goods and many little shops were going bankrupt.

'He looks so worried.' I felt sorry for him. He was such a thin little man, with sparse grey hair, going bald. I listened again.

'Young Rosenberg. Of course he got in when all the decent men were at the War. The Jews are all the same, all shirkers.'

'I thought it was his mother who had the shop then,' said the other man. 'He can't be more than thirty now.'

'What difference does that make? It's Jewish money.' Arnold nudged me.

'Those Jews grab the trade, those shirkers. Sitting at home, cushy, yes, while we sacrifice ourselves at the Front Line. Yes, any decent men ... we can't make a living.'

We had long finished our ice-cream. Arnold rose. 'Let's go.'

Passing their table, he bowed politely to the men, 'Gentlemen, perhaps you've never head of the RJF [*Reichsbund Juedischer Front Soldaten*], the Association of Jewish Front Line Soldiers? They have more than sixty-five thousand men,* frontline Jewish soldiers, and only soldiers who have actually fought at the Front Line are eligible. Good day.'

We stalked out. They stared at us open-mouthed.

Father was a member of this Association as he had spent over three years at the Front Line. He had been the Regimental Runner. He spoke French like a native, this came in useful when he took messages through enemy lines. He told us that a very rude French curse had once saved his life when he was challenged. He was promoted to Kaiserlicher Gefreiter, a great honour, as he had refused a commission. He had been decorated with the Iron Cross and the *Wurttembergische Verdienstsmedaillie*.

Father told me that to the best of his knowledge, he had never killed anyone. He did not believe in legalised murder. And he was the best shot of his Regiment, so it is unlikely that he would have killed anyone accidentally. Even now he won prizes at rifle competitions.

* * *

The food at my grandparents was much more interesting than the food at home. We particularly liked the things which Father had labelled 'not good for children'. We got a small bar of chocolate every day; at home they said it was constipating. There was a cream cake for each of us at tea time, and every day it was a different one. 'It's real cream, butter and eggs,' said Grandmother.

---

*84,352 Jewish soldiers fought in World War I, 1914–18. 10,089 died. 65,418 were frontline soldiers.

'It can't hurt them.' For our visit, as part of the 'fattening-up', she had bought a hundred extra eggs, and halfway through the holiday she bought another hundred. (In my mind I could hear Father say, 'excess of albumen'.)

Every week Grandmother weighed us and noted our progress in a little book.

'It might not be Food Reform', she said to Mother, 'but they certainly thrive on it. And the good air, of course.' Camberg was not an industrial town.

We sunbathed naked every day. One morning, Richard, who was then three and a half years old, bit me on the thigh. I was astonished how much it bled, and he was equally surprised.

Grandfather took him by the hand and quietly explained to him that he-who-bites is a dog, and if a dog bites, one has to chain him up, for in Germany it was customary to chain the larger type of dog to their dog-house, during the day, particularly Alsatians. He chained Richard to the veranda railings. First Richard screamed, then he cried; after a little silence he said he did not want to bite any more.

*   *   *

I was looking forward to Friday night dinners, which were special and festive.

With freshly washed hair, fingernails inspected, a 'best' dress on, I was allowed to wear my gold locket, the one my late great-grandfather Leopold had given to me at my birth. It was heart-shaped, opened up and had quite a large diamond on it. Susan had received a similar one, with a ruby. They called it 'starting the girls off with a little jewellery'.

As a treat Grandmother Hedwig sometimes allowed me to help with the preparations. I found the dining room very old-fashioned. Cousin Elisabeth said all that carving, those scrolls, that Art Nouveau was 'out'. She called it '*Firlefanx*' and '*Schnoerkel*' and 'Dust-catchers'. Clean, simple lines were good design. I had told her that I rather liked old-fashioned things, in clothes and in furniture. Victorian ladies looked so romantic. The huge sideboard with its massive top glass cupboard, carved with floral scrolls, was definitely Art Nouveau. On the wall below the windows hung a long Gobelin carpet: putti, naked ones, were dancing on the olive green background, horrible with their fat legs. I mentioned how I disliked these twee creatures. Grandfather said the Gobelin kept the draft out; it had thick padding on the back. The long dining table stood before a very high, over-stuffed sofa. That's where my grandparents sat; no-one else was allowed to sit there. Extra bun feet had been added, to get the greater height needed for dining. Grandfather liked his comfort. On either side of the table, six chairs had been arranged for us; if one put the wooden leaves in, the table could take twelve.

The white cloth had been spread. Grandmother had fetched an additional green runner to go beneath her lace cloth of the same size, to show up the beautiful pattern.

'Oh, this is Point de Venice.' I was proud to air my knowledge, which Father had taught me; he had an antique lace collection. 'Yes, a good copy. Chinese, all handmade, from your father. He gave it to me for my fiftieth birthday.' Very carefully she took from the glass cabinet the Baccarat 'Roemer' glasses, all different colours, with fine etching. 'I always wash these myself.'

I put the candelabra in the middle of the table. 'You have to leave room for the centre piece, we are having *bouquet de légume.*' The centre piece was very important, usually composed of flowers or fruits from the garden. Cook had allowed me to help. I cut out the fancy daisy shapes for carrots and beetroots, cooked *al dente*, using new cutters ordered from one of the catalogues which came with the hotel cooking ranges. All the vegetables you could think of would be arranged on an extra long dish, like a floral bouquet. Cook was very proud of her art work. There were cauliflowers, tomato roses, stalks made from strips of leeks or chives, every vegetable of the season was represented, but I liked my 'daisies' best. All this was done for the second course, a last minute job.

When all were assembled, Grandmother lit the candles. Grandfather said the prayers, always the same, in German, praising God. He finished with a short Hebrew prayer. Then, speaking Kiddush, he blessed the wine and the bread, which was special and had a plait on top. He took a sip. We all got a little of this blessed wine in our beautiful glasses. And then, best of all, he blessed everyone, including Hede. A full glass of the wine was put on the window sill, for the prophet Elijah, and the front door was left ajar, should he decide to honour us with a visit.

I felt very loved, very secure. I wished my father would celebrate Friday night, the Sabbath. Hede said it was like the Christmas Meal at her home. We were lucky, to have it every week. I believe Mother would have liked to celebrate Friday nights.

When I tried to discuss this with Father he explained that the Christian Mass celebrated Bread and Wine, and was, after all, based on the Jewish tradition. He did not want to celebrate the Sabbath.

The meal was very fine: usually roast chicken, with stuffing. Chicken was special at this time and very expensive. Hede said that it was a pity to eat the *bouquet de légume*, one should photograph it. Several kinds of puddings followed, all wonderful. Then kisses for the children ... and so to bed.

* * *

A delicious smell was wafting from the kitchen. I put my head in. 'Oh, you're making biscuits.' I noticed a small ball of left-over pastry. 'What are you going to do with that?'

Cook was in a good mood. 'What would you like? Perhaps a *Hampelman*?' (A gingerbread man, without the ginger.)

'No, I would like a tiger.'

'Right, come after lunch.'

Grandmother had told us about 'centre pieces', made for the Sabbath Table. Mrs Rothschild, who lived in Frankfurt, had a chef who made very fancy ones, usually baked from bread dough or like a cake. When children were present he made castles or a Noah's Ark or a Zoo. However, the children were not allowed to eat the centre pieces; they were given away to children's charities.

'Is he still working for the Rothschilds?'

'No, that was some time ago. I was told he went to Paris, to their cousins, the Baron Rothschild's place.'

'Why did he leave?'

Grandfather chipped in, 'Paris is very interesting to single young men. He was an excellent chef. When the Prince of Wales, the son of Queen Victoria of England, had lunch with them, he was so impressed with the food he took the chef to England with him.'

'To pinch his chef, that must have made the Baron mad!' Arnold exclaimed.

In the kitchen my tiger was cooling down, resting on a plate. Cook had decorated him with stripes of chocolate and icing sugar. Unfortunately the pastry had spread, so he looked more like a cow. Cook saw I was disappointed. 'It will taste just as good,' she comforted me.

'Of course. Thank you.' I carried my plate outside. Arnold inspected it. 'Not bad. Can I have a bit of your zebra?'

It was a wonderful holiday.

*   *   *

One of the best treats was to be invited to Strasbourg to visit cousin Frederike, who was the same age as me. She also liked sketching and we used to go to interesting sites together.

The journey alone was exciting. Father had escorted me to Stuttgart to catch the D-Train, the one which had all the fancy inlaid marquetry panelling. One had to pay quite a bit extra to ride on this super fast train. My parents had chosen this train because it stopped only once, in Karlsruhe. I was a big girl now, I could travel by myself. After the Karlsruhe stop the attendant brought me a jug of hot chocolate, so I was not quite without supervision.

Strasbourg is fantastic, with lots to do and see. There were river trips, museums, the old houses overhanging the street in the upper stories, having gargoyle waterspouts and other grotesque carvings. My favourite was the Judgment of Solomon on the outer wall of the Cathedral. Frederike and I tried our best to sketch it. My pencil drawing was no good at all, but I took a good picture with my box camera. The Cathedral was fine if one did not go near it at bell ringing time, when it boomed so loudly that it made one's ears go gribbely.

The older cousins took us fishing on the River Rhine and the Ill. We would go out early in the morning, fishing for trout and pike. Pike is an ugly fish with a long, pointed snout and many sharp teeth, and is a local speciality. Because I am squeamish, cook removed the head before serving it, saying that I was silly. But she served the *Truite bleu* (blue trout) in the correct manner: tails tied to the head to form a circle on each plate. They must be alive immediately before they are cooked to retain the blue colour. This was the reason for the large metal-lined baskets the boys took with them to carry the fish home in. The fish went into a tank in one's garden, to await the table.

But the Alsace pastries and cakes were the best, even finer than our Liesel's.

*   *   *

There were also frequent return visits from our Alsace family. Lilo Guggenheim's and Eva Fleischer's mothers were both born in Strasbourg, cousins naturally.

The nicest way to travel and also the cheapest was by Post Bus, which left Strasbourg via Kehl, crossed the Rhine Bridge and proceeded all the way through the Black Forest. It stopped at every village, and at a wayside inn for refreshments, but even so was faster than the railway, which had to go the long way around. This scenic route was absolutely wonderful. I imagined what it must have been like in olden times. Coach and horses, the horn blowing, tra-ra tra-ra.

Mr Kuhn, our chauffeur, collected (and delivered) the party of children with their nanny at the terminus in Tuebingen, which was not far from our town.

*　*　*

Jointly our French family were owners of a large house in Baden Baden, which was used as a guest house by the whole family. It was permanently staffed by a housekeeper and her handyman/gardener husband. There was always open house. These holidays were much in demand, as Baden Baden was considered the finest spa in Europe and was only 25 km from Strasbourg and 75 km from our town.

Visits to Baden Baden usually only lasted a few days. We enjoyed swimming in the tepid thermal waters, which were in great contrast to the Kneipp Bad Woerishofen (specialising in cold-water cures), which was Father's favourite. There the mountain water was icy-cold. The only consolation of visiting Woerishofen was the hotel fare. We children were allowed to choose anything from the Table d'Hôte menu, which was silver service. Arnold counted with satisfaction the many little dishes served; I too was impressed. Hede soon put a stop to it. I think she was sorry for the waiter who had to carry this heavy load, or did her disapproval belong to the 'spoiled children' category?

*　*　*

Our town had been a famous Spa since the 16th century.

The reigning Duke of Wuerttemberg, on a visit to Paris, had been poisoned, whether by malice or accident has not been established.

By the Grace of God and the curative waters his Highness the Duke Christof recovered. He showed his gratitude by bringing his retinue, building sumptuous buildings and spreading the fame of our town.

In the 19th century the Spa became an insitution for the mentally handicapped. A Dr Landerer, a very enlightened man, ran it very ably, employing many of his patients, this was very therapeutic as well as an economic boon to the establishment.

Once, on an errand for Father, we passed the entrance to the spring.

'Let's go inside and have a look,' said Arnold.

'Ugh, this water is yellowy.'

'Must be sulphur. Sulphur and brimstone,' said Arnold.

'Looks like witches' brew, no wonder it cured the Duke,' said I. 'It tastes absolutely revolting. Why is it that always "healthy tastes nasty"?'

'Perhaps it's better for bathing.'

We were not impressed with Christof's Spa.

*   *   *

It was sad when Hede left us. She was friendly – too friendly – my father said, with a law student.

'This is no match for Hede,' said Mother. 'Anyway, he can't marry her for years. When, and if, he finishes his studies, he'll have to repay his grant and keep his mother.'

I found the situation extremely romantic and Mother's 'practical attitude' disconcerting. He was a cobbler's son; his father worked and died in poverty. Liesel said he was a rotten cobbler, that's why he was so poor. I hated Liesel when she said that – who has ever heard of a rich cobbler? But my parents felt they had to act responsibly.

We children sensed that on her day off something forbidden and exciting happened. We asked her if she was meeting her young man, seeing that she dressed so carefully. Hede replied, 'No, no, no. I am visiting a sick aunt.'

When she returned we made her tell us all about the sick aunt. We asked what the doctor had said and if she had progressed, almost putting the answers in Hede's mouth.

She enjoyed the game as much as we did. After she left us, she stayed at home, with her parents who lived in a village in the mountains, an hour's bus ride away. She often came to visit us and once I spent a week's holiday there.

Chapter 8

'The Queen Mother'

On our return journey, Father met us in Stuttgart when we changed trains. It was almost a fight as to who would be allowed to sit next to him.

The following day we called on Grandmother to pay our respects. Wanda came to the door and told us that Grandmother was unwell and could not possibly receive us all. Only one child – Sylvia.

Grandmother was propped up in bed. I could hardly see her in the half-light, as the shutters were closed, allowing the air to come through the open windows, but not the light.

This bed was enormous – actually made of two three-quarter beds put together with one headboard. It occupied the greater part of the room.

'Bring a chair,' said Grandmother. 'No, not an upholstered one. Children don't sit on upholstered chairs.'

'Are you better, Grandmother?'

'Yes, thank you. Now, tell me all about the holiday. Four weeks, that's a long time.'

'We've had good weather – look, I'm quite brown. Oh, it's too dark to see. But it rained for three days, just when we had planned to make the steamer trip on the Rhine. We had to postpone it, and we went the next week. It took three hours. It was smashing.'

'It was *what* did you say?'

'It was very interesting, Grandmother.'

'Very nice.'

'And one Sunday we went to Wiesbaden, with the car. There we saw two Scotsmen, "in skirts". Exactly like the one I have got, the same pattern, except mine has pleats all the way round.'

'The correct name is kilt – it is their National Dress. I believe it is worn there even in towns. When I was your age, National Costume was still worn in almost all villages around here. It is a pity. Now they wear it on holidays, or as a tourist attraction.'

'Perhaps they don't like ironing all those many petticoats.' Liesel had told me that. Grandmother ignored this remark. I continued, 'Then we went to the Kur Saal for tea. We had to leave the car outside the park; one is not allowed to drive a car in the park, only a carriage. They put two tables together for us in the restaurant. There was a big band – I counted twelve men – they played for one if one sent a little note. They played "Blue Danube" for me, but not all the way through. People danced. Some of the ladies were terribly painted.* They must have been from Berlin.† Or perhaps they were foreigners. At the table next to us sat a negro. He was not black at all, only brown.'

'A mulatto,' corrected Grandmother.

'Arnold says not all negroes are black, it depends where they come from.'

'What language did he speak?'

'I don't know, he was by himself. We couldn't hear what he said when he gave his order to the waiter because of the band. Grandfather said we mustn't stare, as it's bad manners, and he told us he knows a negro gentleman who is Professor. Have you ever seen a negro?'

'Yes, many times.'

'But they never come to our town.'

'After the war there were negro troops with the French Occupation Army in the Ruhr Gebiet.'

'He had a gold tooth, it looked funny.'

'Who?'

'The negro gentleman.'

'Many white people have gold teeth; you shouldn't take notice of it.'

'But I do. Farmer Wettgenstein has three. Big ones, in the front. Mother says one should not put them in front.'

'What else did you do?'

'Lots of things. We visited Uncle Emile in Bad Nauheim. He was supposed to be free all afternoon. He was called away right

---

*Heavy make-up, even visible make-up, was considered not 'lady-like' in our family.
† In South Germany, Berlin was considered a 'Babel'.

in the middle of tea. They phoned for him from a Hotel, for an American. Uncle Emile was a heart specialist. When Uncle Emile came back he was cross because it was not his patient; his colleague had just been there. He said it was not etiquette, and that the porter should have known better even if the patient was a millionaire. Uncle Emile says that it's mostly not heart at all, it's wind or overeating.'

'Is that a watch you are wearing?'

'Yes. Grandfather bought all of us watches. It's real gold.' I took it off so that Grandmother could see it better. She wore thick glasses because her eyes were very weak. She took her magnifying glass from the bedside table and examined my watch carefully.

'I thought so,' she said. 'It's *not* gold, it's only *rolled* gold.'

'It's from Switzerland, and it is a good watch, and it's got jewels inside.'

[I wore this watch for twenty years, and only once did I have it overhauled.]

'I cannot understand your Grandparents. Children of your age [I was then eight], do not need watches, gold or otherwise. I do not consider it right; it is not done. Gold watches – children's – tut-tut. I suppose Susan received a watch as well?'

'Yes, Mother is keeping it for her.'

'You can ask your mother to keep yours till you're older. Did Richard get one too?' Her tone was sarcastic.

'No, he got a balloon.'

Wanda came in with a tray. Grandmother took meat broth for her elevenses. She said, 'We must not tire Mrs Fleischer. I think it is time for you to go.'

Quickly I got up. Taking my watch from the bedside table I slipped it into my pocket.

'The chair, please,' said Wanda.

'Sorry.' I put it back. 'Goodbye, Grandmother. Goodbye, Wanda.'

I put my watch back on my wrist. Twenty-five minutes I had stayed there.

Why is she so horrible? Whenever we get a present from Camberg she runs it down. She runs Mother down too. She *thinks* she is nice to me; I wish she would be nice to someone else instead. I am supposed to be her favourite – because I look like her, many people say. 'Quite the old Mrs Fleischer', or 'Such a resemblance'. The worst of this is that Mother says it too, often. I think Mother

54

and Grandmother hate each other. Whatever Mother does *they* find fault with it, Grandmother and all of Father's family. I think they are jealous because people say that Mother is an attractive woman; they say that mother looks like a young girl. I'm glad I did not tell Grandmother about the fashion show. I can imagine what she would have said. She always says things like, 'I should have thought your mother had sufficient clothes', or 'Your mother is clothes mad', or 'Those crazy clothes they make at the Salon W. are quite unsuitable for your mother; she is a married woman now with four children'. I think Grandmother talks like that because she is past clothes. She only wears black silk now, and her dresses go right down to the floor. And the Aunts! They are plain dowdy. That is what Hede calls them. Hede thinks Mother's clothes are very chic and anything from Salon W. 'Just fabulous'. Fabulous. I like this word ... fabulous, just fabulous!

'I don't want to look like Grandmother. She is old and fat and much too tall. I don't want to be like her,' I told Mother.

Mother said, 'Why ever not? She is a very clever woman; she's well read, well-educated. When she was young, she was beautiful. You should be honoured' – Mother actually used this word – 'that she has chosen you to be her favourite and that she asks for your presence so often.'

To be truthful, I did enjoy it when she invited me last spring to help her prune the roses. She explained it awfully well; I think I could do it now on my own. I'm not sure, though, if I could cut across in the right angle. She never let me try. Perhaps it needs practice.

She likes me to accompany her on her walks, if one can call them that. I trot along next to her and we walk slowly round the block. Sometimes we call at Eberton's, the market gardener. The vegetables look beautiful in their willow baskets, good enough to paint. But for Grandmother that's not good enough, not fresh enough. So they go into their greenhouse and pick some more. I wouldn't do it. It's an honour to serve Grandmother. They don't seem to mind but I am embarrassed. Fortunately, we don't go there often because Karl grows most vegetables in the garden.

Grandmother's nickname in the town is 'The Queen Mother'.

Grandmother is very knowledgeable and always right. My Grandmother in Camberg is also knowledgeable, but with her other people are also right. Susan is her favourite – fair is fair. I wish I could be hers and not 'The Queen Mother's'.

One of the highlights of the holiday had been a visit to Mother's dressmaker, the Salon Wintermeyer in Wiesbaden.

They always showed a new collection in August. One morning we received the invitation cards, printed in 'script' with a gold border. I was already impressed.

Grandfather said, 'If Sylvia is going to become a dress designer, we had better take her along.'

This was to be my first Fashion Show.

I was afraid we would be late; Mother was always late. She would insist at the very last minute on having a skirt pressed. I told her to wear another suit. Mother laughed and said that it was courtesy to wear something bought at the Salon. I thought, why did she not see to it the day before? Things like this made Father furious; there were often rows about 'being kept waiting'.

They were showing ski clothes when we entered. 'We've hardly missed anything,' said Mother. 'They always start with sportswear.'

We sat down on small golden chairs. It was crowded.

'Why ski clothes in Summer?'

Mother said, 'Ssssh, I'll explain later.'

The mannequins looked very pretty, like dolls, with heart-shaped mouths and very arched eyebrows. They were even more painted than the ladies we had seen at the Kur Saal. Mother whispered, 'Make-up is permissible on the stage' – and there was some sort of stage.

My Grandparents made little comments like, 'Now this would suit Irma [my mother]', or 'What unusual colours! It would be just right with your hair.'

When the show was over we were given tiny open sandwiches with sharp things on them, like smoked salmon or anchovy. There was champagne. As they had nothing else I got some too, diluted with *Seltzer Wasser*.

Mother had liked several outfits. She had clapped often, but had said just as often, 'not for me', or, 'if I were tall' – Mother was barely five feet and a petite figure – or 'very impractical'. And when they showed evening dresses she said laughingly, 'This is the perfect dress for our town.' I can remember that they were very low cut, front and back.

The sister of the owner came along and greeted us. She was exactly the same size as Mother, so Mother was saved preliminary fittings. We made an appointment for the afternoon when it would be less crowded.

Then we had lunch at a big hotel. We had cold salmon from the Rhine and *Zeller Schwarze Katz*, a Rhine wine. I was allowed to choose it; I knew it had a pretty label.

Grandfather tried to persuade Grandmother to order some clothes for herself but she wouldn't hear of it, saying, 'Fashion is for our Irma.' Older ladies wore black or very dark colours.

Mother said, 'Papa, I don't need anything, not a thing.' But after a short walk in the park we went to keep our appointment.

Finally they chose a lilac georgette dress, the skirt of which had bands of hemstitching. It was called a 'small evening dress'. For day time they ordered a two-piece in cocoa-coloured wool with a plaited skirt, made of stripes two inches wide. I remember the clothes well; I can recall many of the clothes I've worn after the age of four, well enough to draw them, more particularly because I was shocked when I heard the price. Mother whispered, 'It's a Salon.' We were dealing with *haute couture*.

At home Mother was considered extravagant with clothes. The fact that Grandfather usually settled her bill at the Salon W. made it even worse. The ladies of Father's family bought their clothes to last – the cloth was certainly the best quality – while Mother had new clothes every season. The simple ones were made for her in our home town. Mother often said 'they were ruined' by the dressmaker because of her provincial taste. 'She can sew,' said Mother, 'but she has no feeling for clothes. They are all peasants.' And mother would shrug her shoulders and pass them on to the maids, who were delighted.

But I was flabbergasted. To spend so much money on clothes! Perhaps Father's family was right after all.

One of my paternal grandmother's sayings was, 'Better one give it (the money), to Charity, than to hang it on one's back.'

Mother's response was, 'It's also important to keep people in work.' There was a great deal of unemployment in 1930.

When the new clothes arrived, packed in striped boxes with layers and layers of tissue paper, I could hardly wait till Mother tried them on.

'Fabulous. Just fabulous.'

Chapter 9

More About Religion

Our cook, Liesel, was a jolly round peasant girl. She had big pink arms and looked very solid in the black-and-white check cotton dress and voluminous white aprons which were starched stiff like a board. When I heard her singing – she often used to sing for hours – I would put my head through the kitchen door. 'Do you need any help, Liesel? Can I come in?'

'Hmm ... all right then.'

She would find a little job for me, perhaps setting a bowl of apples in front of me. 'Do you think you can peel these without cutting yourself?'

'Of course I can. look – in one piece,' and I would proudly hold up my long, long snake.

Liesel had a beautiful voice. I begged her to sing for me one of the folksongs of the countryside, and when I knew the song I hummed the tune. My favourite was, '*In einem kuechlen Grunde da geht ein Mühlenrad*', which is a sad folk song about love and broken faith. This song made me thoughtful and I knew that I would never break my promise to my beloved.

'Yes,' agreed Liesel. 'It is very wicked. Now, cut the apples, in slices. Mind that they are even. And here is the lemon water.'

'What for, Liesel?'

'You sprinkle it on the apples, then they don't go brown.'

'Oh.'

Since Deda's departure we baked cakes again. Every Saturday Liesel baked, usually three or four cakes or tarts – when we had guests, more.

Karl had brought in a large basket of apples, windfalls, so we made apple flans that Saturday. Mother did not mind if I helped with the baking, but she strongly objected if we children went into the kitchen at meal times. 'You must not disturb them,' she used to say, or 'I don't like it if the children listen to their gossip', as if they would ever say anything in front of us!

'Here, you can scallop the edge of the flan, like this.' She critically watched me. 'Yes, that's quite nice.'

Whilst they were in the oven, I helped Liesel with the washing up. I sniffed. 'I think they are ready.'

Liesel consulted the large kitchen alarm clock. 'Soon.'

I helped to lift out the flans, but too energetically and one broke. 'Oh, I'm sorry.'

'Look what you've done! One does not dig like that!'

'I said I was sorry.'

'We'll have to keep this one for the kitchen.'

'If we eat it right away nobody will know it was broken,' I said hopefully.

'Cake is for Sunday,' remarked Liesel in a severe voice, but her eyes were smiling. She cut me a large piece.

'Thank you. Where is yours?'

Liesel shook her head. 'I'm getting too fat – and then I'll get the sack!'

'Don't be silly, nobody gets the sack for getting fat!'

'Look, this dress hardly fits me now.' She showed me where it was tight. 'Your mother has only two sizes, large and small. I couldn't expect her to have some more made ... ha, ha, ha. So no cake – well, only on Sunday.'

I had two pieces.

Liesel was a devout Catholic. Her free time was spent in the Catholic Society for Young Women, a very strict club run by the nuns.

'If you behave yourself and don't let me down, I'll take you with me tomorrow. We are having a special performance. The Herr Pfarrer [the parson] is going to attend.'

It was a hot, sticky afternoon, so I wore my coolest dress which was sleeveless.

'Oh, my goodness! You can't wear this, it's wicked!'

'Why, Liesel?'

'You must not bare your arms. The Herr Pfarrer will be shocked.'

Everything was wicked, according to Liesel. She once had told me that she bathed with her vest on as it was wicked not to. When I asked her, for I was rather worried, if it was wicked if I bathed without a vest on, she replied soothingly, 'No, no, dear. It's different for children of the *Herrschafts Volk*.' [Children of the gentry.]

Grumbling, I changed into a long-sleeved dress. I could see that Liesel would not otherwise take me.

The doors of the church hall opened, the nuns filed in. We waited and waited. Finally, the Herr Pfarrer arrived, his housekeeper a respectful distance of three steps behind him. After exchanging a few words with the Mother Superior, he sank smiling into the one and only armchair. He folded his podgy hands over his chest and nodded for the play to begin.

It was a boring play, apart from the dance of the devils.

Wicked servant girl, Karolina, steals gold from her employers to buy a red dress for the dance. She means to return the gold on quarter day after she receives her pay.

Good girl Johanna is helpful to all, assisting the old and frail.

Fire breaks out behind the cellophane windows of a house. Karolina redeems herself by rescuing the baby from the house. She is burned so badly she is dying.

The devils are waiting to snatch her soul. They are getting a cardboard fire ready...

This was by far the best part of the play. The devils were schoolchildren of all ages, who had been rehearsed by the local ballet mistress. Frolicking and leaping about, they swung their long tails most effectively. One tail was over-long so the girl kept slinging it over her shoulder. Their costumes were super, considering they were made of the black lock-knit gym bodices with black stockings on arms and legs – not forgetting the red horns.

...Then the priest enters. He holds the crucifix and, with thunder and lightning, all the devils disappear.

Peace and order is established; the stage is flooded with pink light.

Angels are singing *Kyrie eleison*, joined by the schoolchildren behind the stage. The angels are taking Karolina up to heaven.

When the lights went on I noticed that Liesel was crying. 'A beautiful play, it was,' she sighed. 'Karolina, she is Mrs Weidiner's Mary. I know her. She is really a good girl.'

'I am sure she is,' I replied. 'I recognised Hilde Schmidt. She was the second largest devil.'

The play seemed so short. 'What comes next?'

'It is finished. We'd better go home, now.'

'So soon?'

'What time is it?'

Proudly I looked at my watch. I had never told Mother that Grandmother disapproved children having watches – old-fashioned and mean, that's what she is. 'Seventeen minutes past four.'

Liesel pondered, wrinkling her forehead, then said, 'Perhaps we have just enough time to listen to Herr Pfarrer's address. You know, this is not my free Sunday.'

We sat down again.

The Herr Pfarrer had mounted the stage. He was flushed from the heat which hung like a damp cloud in the hall. He coughed to restore silence. He congratulated the Ladies Society on their fine performance and thanked them for the play. He hoped the attendance at the service next Sunday would be as good – ha, ha, ha – and he wagged his finger at us. The restoration of the bell-tower would start shortly, the target having almost been reached, and he announced that a collection would now be taken.

I was not prepared for his. I had only one Mark in silver, my pocket money for the week. I did not dare take change from the plate, but when Liesel praised my generosity I was consoled. If I got into difficulties during the week, Arnold would lend me some money.

I did not like the Pfarrer's speech. He seemed to be a different person, not at all like the priest who celebrated Mass in the morning; then he was quite awe inspiring, and gave me a religious feeling. Or was it the dark coolness of the church, the first light falling through the stained glass windows? I was puzzled.

Although I had obtained permission to watch the play, my parents did not know that I occasionally went with Liesel to early Mass.

In Summer I awoke at sunrise, often before our cuckoo clock in the nursery had called five times. Picking up my neatly folded clothes, opening the door carefully lest I woke Susan with whom I now shared a room, I stole into the lavatory to dress there. I tied my shoes together by the laces and hung them round my neck, and tiptoed in stocking feet downstairs. I sat on the bottom step and waited for Liesel.

Once I met my father coming downstairs. He rose early to work in his laboratory. He looked at me, surprised, saying after a small silence, 'Oh, you are up early.'

I was afraid he would ask me why, and I breathed more easily when he passed on without questions.

Often, when sitting on the stairs, I wondered if he would catch me again. What would I say? Would I lie, saying I was picking flowers in the garden? I often did this before going to school. Tell him the truth? Would he tell Mother? I was certain Mother would be angry – very angry.

Liesel and I never discussed this, our secret; we had an unspoken understanding. We chose the least frequented path to church, leading through the cemetery. Here we passed a large angel, almost lifesize, who was guarding an overgrown, neglected grave.

'A beautiful angel, an expensive angel,' said Liesel reverently. 'One ought to clean him; it is a shame.'

True enough, the Angel, who was made of some copper alloy, was mouldy green.

'Yes, let's do that!' said I. It took us several times before we had scraped off the worst and Liesel shone him almost bright with metal polish. After that I felt almost proprietorial towards this angel.

I much preferred going to church than going to synagogue, in spite of the fact that Liesel made me stay in the last row and wait for her there. Sometimes she allowed me to dip my hands in holy water or light her candle. I felt praying was much easier when one knelt down; I wished we could have done this in synagogue. The synagogue looked austere in comparison with the church. I missed the paintings, the gilded saints, the stained glass windows with the stories they told. I had been informed that 'pictorial representation is not customary in synagogues.' On High Festivals Mother took me to synagogue. Father went only on Yom Kippur, and on the remembrance day of his father's death, to give a donation, after he had been 'called up' to read a piece of the Thora scroll.

This synagogue was a medley of Victorian and Oriental style and there was red coconut matting on the mosaic floor. The ladies wore their best clothes and discussed their hats, and the men wore morning coats and toppers. I am sure there must have been some genuine religious Jews amongst the so-called 'liberal' ones, but I cannot remember any among our acquaintances. The Rabbi was a brilliant man; everyone said he would have made a good lawyer or historian. He had written several books. He was short and slight, but had a dynamic personality.

Some half-hearted attempt had been made to teach Hebrew to the Jewish children. I'm afraid I hardly managed to read a line; it was lucky for me that the prayer books had a German translation on the opposite side to the Hebrew. The translation could not have been very good: the spelling was phonetic, and the language neither beautiful nor moving. The Jewish religion did not attract me. There was one line which upset me greatly. 'An eye for an eye and a tooth for a tooth.' I thought of Gentle Jesus offering the other cheek.

My Mother said sarcastically whenever Christianity came up in the conversation, 'Look at them with their 'Love thy Neighbour' – and look at their hatred and brutality.'

I thought, the Christians I know are kind.

Father had said there are many religions, rather like languages – Buddhism, Hindu, Moslem … they all instruct people how to live a better life. The form of worship does not matter much, but that's where the trouble is. The varied churches think and preach they are the only way to heaven. 'Daddy, why don't you go to the synagogue?'

'In the woods, in nature, I feel nearer to God.'

Our library contained many books on different religions. I looked at them, put them back; I did not understand them at all.

Chapter 10

The Water Tower and I Enjoy Reading 'Der Stuermer'

Our local newspaper had not accepted an advert about a Nazi meeting. At that time the press had not been taken over by the Nazi Party. To remedy this, handbills for this public meeting were delivered to many houses of the town.

There was to be a guest speaker, all the way from Munich.
The theme was to be:

The Pestilence of the Jews
The Jews were the traitors of the Reich, it was their fault we lost
  the war
They are profiteers, usurers, swindlers
Honest Aryans should no longer be exploited
Deutschland Erwache [Wake up]
Entrance Free

Liesel gave this handbill to me. She said, 'I wanted to put it in the dustbin, but now I think your parents should see it. This is absolutely terrible. They must be mad, those Nazis.'

Mother said, 'Don't be upset, it's not worth it. Rabble, hooligans. The Jews have always been the scapegoats.'

That night there was fighting in the street between the Nazis and Communists.

Arnold fetched the flyer out of the waste-paper basket. He explained to me what 'usurer' meant, I had not heard that word before. 'All those lies, lies,' he said. It was the first time we children experienced antisemitism in our town. We had always felt the Jews were respected – in our town...

Our parents would never discuss anything serious or important with us children. Father said, 'Religion, money, politics, do not make polite dinner table conversation.' Yes, they believed in the 'ostrich policy'. Brother Arnold read the daily papers, he liked to have an audience to air his knowledge. He was considered very clever by everyone, whilst they said that I was naïve, dreamy and gullible, though not without intelligence. I showed him the hand bill. 'Why do those Nazis hate us so much?'

'Bemmerle, I am going to wise you up a bit. It is convenient to blame someone, when one is poor or unemployed. The world situation is very bad, all over, not only in Germany. First we had the Inflation, remember, when people lit their cigars with banknotes and then came that Wall Street Crash.'

'That was terrible. Father told you off for showing me the newspaper with the men leaping out of the windows. That really frightened me. Collapse of High Finance, whatever that is. What has that to do with us?'

'I'll tell you. America had been lending lots of money to Germany, and then they wanted it all back, took it back. So there was not enough dosh left here. Our Reichs Chancellor Bruening, he's not much good – they call him the Hunger Chancellor – you know what he did? He reduced the unemployment benefits, the state ones too. Perhaps they did not have the money to pay out. And he told employers to cut people's wages to the amount they paid in 1927. The people working in Government positions also had their wages cut. Well, if you are unemployed, you have nothing to lose. The Nazis promise them full employment and God knows what else.'

'But what has that to do with the Jews?'

'Absolutely nothing. The Nazis tell them the Jews want to dominate the world, to exploit the masses, that Jews are the reason for the unemployment. Believe me, in the last Reichstag elections, Württemberg had the fewest Nazi Delegates of the whole of Germany, and also the lowest unemployment as well. Even so, business is bad. Places going bankrupt, lots of them.'

Father had to put his workers on short time. He thought it was better than reducing their hourly wage, or sacking them. Someone told me he sold goods at a loss, waiting for better trade conditions. The top end, the lovely satin pyjamas with the lace incrustations, sold well, and also the very cheapest stuff, the Liberty bodices and the fleecy knickers – we called them the 'Monster Fleeces'; they were supposed to keep you warm. The middle of the market was 'dead', so they said.

These 'Monster Fleeces' went right down to the knees, with elastic, and were huge, made of heavy brushed material. When we undressed on sports afternoon, I had seen the poorer pupils of the class wearing them, those who did not have warm clothing or coats. Some children wore plimsolls; some had toes sticking out. There was a poster in school asking for grown-out clothing and boots. I asked mother if I could take some, but mother usually sent all the cast off children's clothes to the clothing store in the Rabbi's house, which was open to all denominations. Father told us that his mother had been in charge of the Ladies Association for twenty-five years and would be annoyed if our clothes went to other charities. One girl came to school in a stunning bright red outfit, a sort of suit. She told everybody it had been made from her granny's red flannel petticoat which they had found in the loft. Many children wore knitted pullovers, some with patches on the elbows. Some had alternating stripes. I thought the colours were badly matched; then I found out the reason: old pullovers were unravelled, one made hanks of wool over the chair back, washed the hanks and then rolled them up in a ball for re-knitting. Because of the patches, or holes at the elbows, one could not use the arms, so one had to introduce different wools from other garments.

I was afraid to think that some of my class mates were starving; they did not have a sandwich at break time. Maria Gais, with whom I shared the bench never seemed to have one. What could I do? I asked Liesel to give me two, saying I was starving, which surprised her. I had previously got into trouble for bringing half of my sandwich back: wasting food in our house was a crime; everything on the plate had to be eaten up, clean ... other children would be glad of it, etc. My half sandwich would be served to me instead of the pudding. One was not allowed to put food into the waste paper basket in school as this would attract mice or rats. I told Maria about missing out on my pudding – could she help me out, please? 'They are so strict at my house about finishing one's food.' Problem solved.

When, in 1930, the elections came I took little interest in politics, being then only eight years old. I asked my classmates what their father's had voted: Democrat, Nazi, Communism, or Centre. I was not interested in the small obscure parties. My parents had, I believe, voted for Party No. 8, but I cannot remember what party this was.

Arnold had told me that many people were no longer satisfied with the Weimar Republic – they wanted a change. They liked neither Nazi nor Communist, because of their street fights, so they turned to the smaller parties. This produced a large increase at the Reichstag, from twelve in 1928 to one hundred and seven in 1930. Dr Joseph Goebbels was in charge of the propaganda, a job he did very well. Many of the speeches he wrote could only be described as Jew-baiting.

I noted that most of the parents of the poorer pupils voted Communist. Someone had told me that Communism means sharing everything and this had made a great impression on me. I tried to convert my father, who in turn explained to me that the poor man will not usually share once he has acquired wealth, and so only a rich man can really be a Communist. This ended my brief, if fervent, association with the Communist ideals.

One of my father's friends, Dr Friedrich Wolff, belonged to the Communist Party. He was a well-known doctor and writer, whose plays were performed in the big theatres. This was in contrast to Uncle Arthur, who thought he was a writer, a view the family did not share. Later on, however, his books were published in France. A prophet is without honour in his own country.

Uncle Bernard, my father's older brother, was a lawyer. He used to speak to his daughter Beate in improvised verse only, at least always in our presence, and Beate would answer in the same way. They would keep it up for quite some time. We 'ordinary' people were very envious of that gift. Beyond this we considered fat Uncle Bernard with his tight Roman curls and tiny feet, which made him wobble, a perfect horror! He loved teasing us, especially by inquiring innocently about our mainly vegetarian diet. Did we eat anything besides grass? What did it taste like? I interrupted him: 'Perhaps I can wangle an invitation to dinner for you from Mother' – he pretended he had not heard me and continued. He couldn't see why more people did not try it, it was very healthy for cows ... and so on. Luckily he seldom visited us. Had he done so more often he would have known that there was always meat for guests.

Aunt Paula, Father's sister was always kind to us children, but she did not like Mother.

Uncle David Fleischer, a second cousin of father, was very

popular with us; he brought us lovely presents. He was a handsome man, very tall and athletic, an expert skier. Hede had a crush on him, saying he looked most distinguished with his white hair and sun-tanned face. We children could always rely on him to supply us with fancy paper novelties.

We also liked Uncle Georg Adelsheimer, a friend of Father's. He took us to the local patisserie for cream cakes. 'No more than one', Father had said. Uncle Georg ordered 'a very large portion' for us. He was an entomologist, a Herr Professor. To look at his collection of beetles and spiders gave one the creeps. He was writing a book on scarabs. He laughingly explained to us that this included cockchafers and dung beetles.

Collecting cockchafers was a local sport. Thousands appeared in the woods in May. One had only to shake the trees and they fell down like crab-apples. They reminded me of musicians playing in a band because their wings looked like the tails of a brown morning coat and they wore black and white waistcoats. We bored holes in cigar boxes and lined them with beech leaves. If there was a 'good' year the Town Council paid ten pfennig per hundred for them – they were considered a pest. I was not allowed to sell mine, as it was 'unfair to compete with the poor children'. Cockchafers take four years to complete their cycle of reproduction, and the older children would tell me in confidence when to expect a good year.

*   *   *

Since Deda's departure, 'bad marks' had been abolished, but I missed the Sunday morning walks, the treat for 'the best child of the week'. Father was usually in his laboratory by the time I got up and sometimes I could persuade him to take me then, as well as on some weekday afternoons.

Father seemed to know so much. He explained to me how there is a balance in nature, that if one completely removes a 'pest' one might at the same time destroy the main part of the diet of a useful animal.

From far off we could hear a drill going.

'They are sinking a new well for a water tower,' said Father, 'now the town is growing.'

I watched the men drilling. To my regret the hole itself was hidden by a fence.

Father stood next to me, thoughtful. After a while he walked over to the foreman, whom he knew, and spoke to him. The foreman gave a sign and the labourers sat down and started their vesper or break, at which the working class usually ate sausage and bread and drank a bottle of beer.

Father was talking to the foreman who kept on shaking his head when even Father pointed to a certain place.

After a while, he and I continued our walk. I noticed that the foreman had gone off in the opposite direction.

'Daddy, what were you talking about?'

'I've told him not to waste the town's money. They'll never find water on that spot, even if they go down a mile. I showed him where to sink the well. Mind you, the water, it's not far off. He's gone to phone the Town Hall. I've told him to say that Mr Fleischer said so.'

I knew Father was reputed to be able to divine water. At that time I was not surprised at anything my father could do – to children grown-ups are omniscient and omnipotent – but I knew other people did it with a hazel twig. 'You did not use a twig, Father. How did you know where the water was?'

He stretched out his hands. 'In my hands. I don't need anything, just in my hands'.

On our way back we saw the men drilling, still in the same place.

The foreman came over to us and said apologetically that his instructions were to continue. The Departmental Chief at the Town Hall had been very rude about it all.

'I'm not surprised,' said Father to me. 'Besides, the man is a Nazi.' Father indicated the place where he believed water would be found. 'They won't have to go very deep there,' he said.

After a week they started drilling in that very place and that's where the water tower stands today.

*   *   *

It is difficult to say when Nazism became significant in our life. At first, the grown-ups made good-humoured jokes about the Nazis, then they spoke about them more and more frequently. If on the streets we should see a 'Brown Shirt', which happened rarely as it was illegal, we thought it was almost as good as seeing men from Mars or the chimpanzee from the zoo. On our way to school we passed the Litfas Columns. The usual advertisements were there, programmes of theatres and cinemas, meetings and public lectures. Sometimes overnight the Nazis pasted their newspaper *Der Stuermer* (*The Storm Trooper*) on it. This paper was semi-legal, and appeared to be designed to breed hatred, greed and envy. It ran wonderful comics, mostly about Jews. Jews were invariably horrible lecherous men who had long noses almost meeting their chins; they were portrayed either as fat men with thick golden chains over their paunches and sausage fingers studded with large rings, or as wizened old men with black skull caps. The Star of David was embroidered on their sleeves or pockets. The things those Jews did! They lured innocent little Christian boys to the synagogue with promises of sweets. They had need of little Christian boys at their awful ceremonies. Sometimes the little boys escaped, but more often they were slaughtered and boiled. There was a strip cartoon about a Jewish money lender. The poor widow borrows money on her house so that her son can finish his studies. The interest she has to pay to the Jew is so exorbitant that she falls into arrears and soon loses her home. She has to go out scrubbing floors. But the nice man from the Nazi Party avenges the poor widow. He kills the nasty Jew and also allows her son to join the Glorious Party, and they all say '*Heil Hitler*' and live happily ever after.

There was also a story about International Jews, whose object was to dominate the whole world with their money and bribes. I asked Arnold.

International Jews? He answered, 'In a way *we* are – our family have factories in different countries. But that is good; it brings employment to the population, if one pays the people properly. I think they mean people like the Rothschilds; they were bankers to Royalty. They made their money by Pigeon Post.' This was a fascinating story. 'At the Battle of Waterloo, where the outcome had been doubtful, Mr Rothschild in London had been informed by Pigeon Post before all other people, and so he could make "a killing", that means, a lot of money.'

'Arnold, you know such a lot.'

'I'm interested in finance.' This was proved in later life, when he became an accountant and business advisor.

Some of the people said, '*Der Fuhrer sorgt fuer uns*' [The Fuhrer looks after us], in just the same way other people might say, 'The Lord protects us'. Hitler, in his speeches, had promised them so much. He even once promised a husband for every German girl.

It never occurred to me to think that the Jews in these cartoons could possibly mean us. Once a little boy called after me, 'Jew, Jew, Jew, pork is good for you'. He was a little boy and stupid; anyway, we ate pork, though not very often because, Father called it hard to digest.

A friend of Father caught me reading *Der Stuermer*. After this it was strictly forbidden to 'waste time reading this rubbish'. Comics were not allowed in our house; only good literature should be read, even by children.

Arnold and I had a new game: 'Hitlers'. He was much better at it than I, being more inventive. He drew 'Hitlers' whose armlets and badges and buttons all had swastikas on them. There were swastikas on their ties, and he monogrammed their handkerchiefs. And all these 'Hitlers' were either waving flags or raising their arm in salute.

When we got tired of this we painted people in fancy dress, or I sketched gnomes, elves and princesses. Arnold was contemptuous of this; he called it soppy and 'girl's stuff'.

But it did not sound comical at all when my parents spoke about the Nazis. They would discuss the latest outrage, how the 'hooligans' had smashed several plate glass windows of a large Jewish store in Berlin, or how at a street corner meeting they had beaten up a perfectly innocent onlooker because he had a crooked nose. A dirty Jew! The man was in fact a Turk, a carpet dealer, and he had complained to his consulate. There had been quite a fuss. It was rumoured that a substantial order had been put in his way.

Of course, all this could not happen in our town; it could happen only in a large city like Berlin or Munich where the people did not know each other.

'It is easy to be incited to hatred,' said my father. 'If you don't know the other fellow, you will believe all sorts of lies, especially if you hear the same lie often enough.'

'Who are the Nazis?' I asked Father.

'The undesirable element.' He explained further. 'Work-shy people, dissatisfied and misguided people, people with a grudge.'

'Then they make the Jews scapegoats,' my mother added.

Father continued. 'Some are opportunists and some of the youngsters just love uniforms and waving flags. Unfortunately, there are also quite a few of the old Wehrmacht officers; they've been promised big positions in return for their support.'

The persecution of the Jews had started and therefore I had to cling to Judaism. I thought, only rats leave a sinking ship.

No longer did I attend church; Liesel never said anything to me. I felt I had been a traitor.

I believed the persecution was the result of the Jew straying from God. Once I reproached Father for not going to the synagogue. He had said he felt much nearer to God when he was in the woods, with Nature but this answer did not satisfy me completely and left me disquieted. I did not dare press him to explain further; he seemed reluctant to talk about it. If ever he went to synagogue it was to please Mother. On his bedside table was the New Testament.

'Daddy, why do you read this?'

'It is a most interesting book, my dear.'

Chapter 11

About Servants and Nature Cure

In our locality the staff for the 'Good Houses' usually came from the surrounding villages. These positions were then much sought after. Often the servant girls married a local tradesman or assistant *Geselle* (Journeyman) to the butcher or baker, or perhaps someone they had met at the May Dance. When this happened they would approach the lady of the house and say, 'I've got a cousin [or a friend] who would like to go into service in a good house', in order to pass on the position to someone of their acquaintance.

In a 'Good House' a thrifty girl managed to save all her wages because she was provided with uniform, shoelaces, soap and all toilet accessories, even with cinema money every fortnight.

It was customary for visitors and guests at dinner parties to leave a tip on the kitchen dresser for Cook to share out amongst the staff. As most entertaining was done at home, the amounts left as tips were often considerable. The staff looked forward to the extra work – the larger the party, the better.

At Christmas, friends and relatives gave the servants Christmas boxes, mostly linen or cutlery.

After a few years in service, a girl had collected her dowry. At that time the majority of young men expected a girl to have a dowry, linen, household goods, and a little money. 'You can't get married on nothing,' they said.

Grandmother's former cook, Roesle, had married Karl. They had one child, Hannes. He was married and lived far away, in Leipzig. He never came home to visit.

Hannes was brought up in our family, and had spent his childhood in Grandfather's house, often running little errands for his mother, such as fetching herbs from the garden. He was one of our children.

73

Uncle David's boys, Herman and Walter, were the same age; they went riding together and rifle shooting with air guns for target practice. Hannes was the best at archery, and won junior competitions. The grown-ups were surprised by his interest in art, I did not think it was surprising when there were so many fine paintings hanging on our walls.

A good looking boy, red haired like his father, and with the regular features of his mother, well spoken, polite, he was popular. Grandfather had paid for him to attend the grammar school. Then he got an apprenticeship in Uncle David's paper factory, where there had been an up-coming demand for tissue paper, crêpe paper, paper serviettes, etc., and much was exported. This was surely more interesting than corsets. Hannes had served his apprenticeship and passed the examination of the Chamber of Commerce, so he was sent for 'experience' to a rival paper factory in Leipzig, a large concern. He had become an exceptionally good-looking young man. The owner's daughter fell in love with him – she was an only child.

Trained in the paper trade, industrious, cultured, he was considered a suitable husband. They married. I was told it was one of the largest paper mills in Germany.

Karl and Roesle had extracted from Hannes a promise that he would never divulge his parentage; they explained that it would destroy his chances. I pondered about this: it seemed so sad, so wrong. I thought, if my grandfather had adopted him, he could have come home to see his blood parents – but Grandfather had died in 1920.

It was very upsetting. Why did the family condone this? Karl and Roesle's wishes? Victorian snobbery?

Father handed over Hannes' very infrequent letters, some of which included snapshots of his children, to a very grateful Karl and Roesle.

I could not understand why grown men doffed their hats to me when they passed in the street when I did not know them. It had happened several times; I was embarrassed. I discussed it with Arnold. He said, 'I just touch my cap in return.' The Grammar school boys wore their student caps with pride, every year a different colour per form. He had orange this year.

Liesel must know, I thought, she is a local girl.

'Well, I tell you. It's because you are like a checkered dog –

everyone knows a checkered dog. They do that to honour your father. Well, half the population works for him, or some of your family.'

This was a gross exaggeration, though it might have been true in my grandfather's time.

Liesel claimed that she knew her place. She had her hierarchy:

The Pope
The former King of Wuerttemberg
The Count of Rechberg, a direct descendant of the Hohenstauffen Kaiser Barbarossa (Friedrich II), the Holy Roman Emperor, who drowned in the river in Palestine during the Holy Crusades. Local people were still singing songs about him and his ravens.
The *Herrschaftsvolk* (Gentry – that included us)
Ordinary decent people
Not-so decent people
Louts
Absolute rubbish

Mother also had her hierarchy. I thought mother stuck-up, at least by the standards of my fairytales, in which poor people like charcoal burners were always so noble. Mother was a strong believer in people knowing their place. Her hierarchy was:

God
Families of Good Standing
The General Population
Common Folks – they did not know better
Criminals

I worked my problem out myself. To the lifting of the hat, I would curtsey back: a full curtsey, just as we would make to elderly aunts, dignitaries and famous people.

From the age of fourteen many girls started to sew for their bottom drawer. 'Putting by for getting married', was spoken of with the same reverence as going to church. There was a great surplus of women in Germany after the last war.

Servants felt they belonged to the family, and therefore thought it only right to ask their '*Herrschaft*' for advice if they had a regular boyfriend and intended to get married. Enquiries were made about the character of the lad by the family and, if necessary, a better job was found for the young man. Those weddings in the villages were jolly affairs – and the christenings too, before the year was out.

It was Susan, then aged eight years old, who told me about women carrying babies in their tummies. She would say to me, 'Look at this lady – I would say about seven months.'

'How do you know?'

'Well, I just know.' And she would adopt a knowing air.

'Oh, there is another one,' said I. 'How many months do you think?'

'Don't be silly. She's just fat.'

I felt stupid. Arnold then joined in the conversation and said, like a wise old man, 'I advise you girls to get an encyclopaedia and look it up under "ovum".'

Even after I reached puberty I did not associate the bearing of children with love. Illegitimate children seemed to be a social thing; I thought only servants and factory girls had them. I had never heard of people in our circle having illegitimate children, and if I heard that so-and-so was a naughty girl and had had to be sent to Switzerland, it meant nothing to me; I thought they were sent there to a rather strict Finishing School.

Father played an active part in the local *Kneipp Verein* (a Nature Cure Association), of which he was the Hon. Treasurer. As the Chairman was a bachelor my parents entertained most of the lecturers. These visitors often stayed for days, even weeks. A retired Captain, Olav von Muende, who travelled in Health Food and gave lectures on 'Breathing', called our house the Hotel Fleischer. When he was in the district the Hotel Fleischer was his headquarters. I thought the show my mother sometimes put on was as good as in any hotel. The table would be elaborately laid with much silver, cut glass and floral decoration. Five to seven courses were the usual, unless the visitor was what Arnold and I called a '*Fanatischer Kracher*' (a fanatical old codger). The wine was carefully selected to match the food. Father was considered a connoisseur and our cellar was well stocked. Some wine growers would send Father a case to sample, if they thought it was especially good. Many people, including the largest grocer of our town, would ask Father's advice as to which wine to buy.

Mother always managed to serve the 'right' menu, even if it had to be nut cutlets. She took great trouble to find out what they liked to eat. Some of these 'lecturers' were famous, others just eccentric.

Arnold and I were allowed to stay up and eat with the visitors, providing we promised to be extra good, to behave ourselves, not to speak unless we were spoken to, etc., etc. One evening when the maids forgot to serve him – they had started on opposite ends with the pudding, which was something special too – Arnold did not say a word. A promise is a promise.

I listened attentively to the conversation. They mostly talked 'shop', so I was soon reasonably well-versed in Nature Cure and Diet. I was very interested in my Father's work and admired him greatly.

By this time Father had qualified as a Doctor of Nature Cure. His patients were mostly poor people who came to him from the surrounding villages. They religiously followed his advice. It did seem that he possessed the power of healing and people also said he was clairvoyant. He could foretell the illnesses people might be going to suffer, and as they rarely took his advice about preventive medicine there was ample opportunity to prove his 'prophecies'. Some of my parents' friends looked on his gifts as hocus-pocus, more suitable for party entertainment. He was teased in a good-humoured way but he only got annoyed when people suggested he should be making money out of his gifts. We children were strictly forbidden to discuss this.

Twice a week he held surgery in the villages. He visited the sick. The rest of his time was spent in his laboratory (he rarely went to the factory now), where he made or mixed most of his remedies himself.

His laboratory had an alchemical quality about it – only the skull was missing. There were thousands of little bottles, pestles and mortars of various sizes, oils and tinctures, things to measure, things to weigh. On the window sill stood a large bottle of calendula to be exposed to the rays of the sun, which would improve its goodness and potency.

Herb-women called frequently; he had his own herb-women who gathered for him at the right phase of the moon. Such was his reputation that they would get up when it was still night to climb a mountain to pick something for him at sunrise. Father would have said 'sunrise', 'full moon', or 'in the mid-day sun', and so it was done. Some of the women would take no payment, saying they were glad to help, as Father had looked after someone near or dear to them.

At home patients called by appointment only. Occasionally they came long distances – as a last resort – but this was not encouraged. Quite often friends or acquaintances asked for his opinion when they did not 'like' their own doctor's diagnosis or treatment – a situation which needed much tact and humour. Father had a great deal of the latter, but of tact, very little. He referred to certain surgeons as butchers. He maintained that there was far too much surgery when less dramatic remedies might have helped equally well, if not more effectively. Many complaints treated almost exclusively by surgery in the thirties are treated nowadays by other means. It was not that he disliked surgeons; he was great friends with the Chief of our Municipal Hospital. This doctor also belonged to '*Naturfreunde*'; in fact he introduced again to our woods certain species of birds which were extinct in our neighbourhood.

One afternoon the elder of the Misses Sanftmuth, the grey haired Miss Hermina, called. She urgently wanted to see Father, but he was not at home. I asked Miss Hermina if she would like to wait and showed her into the drawing room. We knew her and her sister Bella well; they kept the local Health Food Stores. Miss Hermina was very upset, I could see she had been crying. Mother rang for tea, peppermint tea – Miss Hermina would have no other. Haki, her lap dog, wrapped in a sheet and blanket, lay cradled in her arm. She kept on talking to him, repeating, 'No, I won't let the nasty man put you to sleep, I won't. You'll see, Haki, Mr Fleischer will help you. I know he will.' She told me that the veterinary surgeon had advised her 'to put the poor creature out of his misery' when Haki did not respond to treatment.

I said, 'Miss Sanftmuth, Father is no vet, you know.'

'He'll do it for us,' she pleaded. 'The Herr Vater is most kind.' Herr Vater or Frau Mutter, an archaism, was used by people sometimes as mark of respect.

'What next!' said Father, when I told him Miss Hermina was waiting. 'Doctor X [the vet], won't be very pleased, but now she's here, I'll have a look at it.'

Afterwards I asked Father what was wrong with the dog. He replied: 'Haki is not as ill as all that. It's eczema. He's a nervous little doggie – it can't be much fun to live with the old ladies.'

'It is *not* a Dog's Life,' said I, very pleased with my witticism.

A week later Arnold and I were sent to deliver some ointment and tincture for Haki.

The Health Food Stores were situated in the old part of the town. The house had been a private residence before, and the windows of the former parlour had been only slightly enlarged to hold the display. Against a background of crêpe paper were stacked, by size, a variety of tins and boxes of Health Food. There was a little note in each window, in copperplate: 'Customers please note, that in the interest of hygiene, only dummies are on display.'

It was always dark inside the shop, as not much light penetrated the crêpe paper. Two lamps with celluloid shields swung from the ceiling. When one got used to the half-light, one could see that they sold everything from walnuts in sacks to Health Hair oil and Health periodicals. The shop was crammed full with goods, displayed on shelves covered with white American cloth with a scalloped edge, and the Misses Santfmuth prided themselves on being 'up to date' and well stocked.

Miss Hermina insisted that we came into the sitting room, in order to show us Haki's progress.

'We're so grateful to your Herr Vater, aren't we, Bella?'

'Yes, very grateful.'

'You really must see – all new skin. Show it, Haki.'

Obediently the dog got up from its basket next to the tiled stove. Wearing a knitted coat, Haki stood there, trembling, and looked at us with gentle eyes.

'Please Miss Sanftmuth, don't disturb Haki,' said I, when she started to take his coat off. 'Don't.'

'But Haki wants to show you,' she insisted. 'Look at the pink skin. Isn't it wonderful?'

I am not squeamish, and I like animals; nevertheless, I felt nauseated. Thinking about it now, I believe it was the whole situation, rather than Haki's sores, which were quite clean. Arnold saw my discomfort and, coming to my rescue, said, 'We really must go now. We're late.'

'Just a minute,' said Miss Bella. She went into the shop and returned with two biscuits. 'Here you are.'

Seeing that we hesitated to accept them she declared, 'They are oat cakes, very healthy. Die Frau Mutter won't object.'

79

'It's not that,' said I. 'It is so near our dinner time.' The biscuits were grey in colour and looked revolting.

Miss Bella appeared hurt by our refusal, so Arnold suggested: 'Perhaps we could have them as "Jump-to-bed" sweets.'

Miss Bella beamed, 'There you are. What well brought up children.'

'Thank you, thank you and goodbye.'

Outside the shop we examined the biscuits. 'They smell funny,' said Arnold. He handed them to me.

'Goodness,' I exclaimed. 'They are hard, like stone. I bet they've had them for ages. Let's give them to the birds.' I tried to crumble them up without success. I had to stamp on them.

Several pigeons swooped down immediately.

In fairness, I must state that these oat cakes were probably quite fresh. We were not aware that it takes several days before the moisture of the air softens them.

A month later a large cake arrived, home-baked. It was tied with a ribbon and there was a card: 'From Haki, with gratitude.' The writing was spidery, as if someone had guided a child's hand. The things they made that poor dog do!

It was a good cake, made after an old-fashioned recipe, not a Health Reform one.

In one of the lectures sponsored by the Kneipp Verein, the lecturer had spoken about the benefits of '*Wassertreten*', walking barefoot in a brook. Father had taken us to do this very thing sometimes, on a hot summer day. Children, of course, love plunging in water; that it was 'beneficial for the health' was coincidental. During conversation Father had mentioned the fact that he sometimes took his children to a small stream in the Beecherwood, whereupon Miss Munsell, an ardent student of Nature Cure, asked if she might join us the next time we went. Father consented and promised to inform her in good time. A meeting point on the outskirts of the town was arranged.

'Oh, there is Miss Munsell,' said Father. 'The lady with the light blue dress.'

'Which one?' asked Susan, 'Two of them are wearing blue dresses.'

'The lady in the *light* blue dress, the tall one,' answered Father.

Miss Munsell came over to greet us. 'Hello, Mr Fleischer. I've taken the liberty of bringing some friends along. I do hope you don't mind, but we're all so interested in *Wassertreten*. Is it all right? Thank you so much.'

'I think I've seen you at the meetings,' said Father.

The ladies fussed over us and exclaimed, 'Aren't they delightful!'; 'Such a darling, his hair is really corn colour!' (meaning Richard, then aged four). 'You must be very proud – four lovely children, Mr Fleischer.'

'Yes, they are all right – when they are asleep,' answered Father. 'We had better go ... I had no idea that *Wassertreten* was so popular.'

Arnold nudged me and whispered in my ear, 'It's Father who is popular. They've got a crush on Father. They're all old maids. They're terribly old – at least forty, and Miss Munsell is fifty, I'm sure. Just look how they hang around him, asking him this and that!'

'But they're only talking about diet,' said I. 'They're interested in Nature Cure – and another thing. Mother said they can't help being old maids when all the men who could have married them were killed in the War.'

The two ladies in blue wore linen dresses, the other two were dressed in folksy looking handwoven skirts. Most of the Nature Cure ladies were dressed like this; they thought it was the correct attire for an outing. They also liked mauve wool and middle partings, or plaits coiled round their head. The colours were usually pleasant, but the styles so hopelessly home-made and ill-fitting. Often the ladies adorned themselves with large silver or copper brooches and bangles. They also wore their Kneipp sandals.

We wore our Kneipp sandals too. These are open Grecian type sandals with a moulded inner sole, said to be healthy as it supported the instep. Father wore plus-fours, which he usually donned for cycling and other sport. Arnold and Richard were in leather trousers; most boys wore these in summer.

There was one particular spot in the Beecherwood which was much favoured by us and we headed towards this place. The stream was shallow there with large flat stones, 'strewn' in its middle. One could jump from one to the next if one was careful.

The ladies went into the wood to remove their stockings. When they finally, very gingerly, stepped into the water, they kept on telling each other how cold it was, how healthy it was, and what fun it was. They waded slowly, with gathered skirts, one behind the other.

Richard was skipping from stone to stone. For a child of his age he was surprisingly agile.

'Look out!' I called. Too late. With a big splash he had fallen in, right next to the ladies. Richard scampered out while the ladies were inspecting their wet skirts.

'Ricky, you'd better apologise,' I said to him.

'I couldn't help it.' He was grinning all over. 'Honest.'

'Ye ... honest, you rascal.'

The ladies were sitting in the sun drying their clothes. Again they discussed the merits of Wassertreten. Father joined them. They told him that they knew other ladies and gentlemen who were interested.

'Miss Munsell,' said Father, 'as it seems so popular, we have to organise it, and I am wondering if you would consider taking charge of the whole matter. I'm rather busy, as you know. So what about it?'

Miss Munsell gave Father a radiant smile. 'If you think I'm capable of it, I'd love to. I'd absolutely love to. But, Mr Fleischer, does that mean you won't be coming?'

'Of course not,' Father reassured her. 'I'll meet you here when I can, time permitting.'

Miss Munsell was delighted. She said she would have cards printed, and do it properly. Perhaps Miss Sanftmuth would give her her mailing list of the Nature Food customers. Father suggested it would be much better if she relied on personal recommendation, as you know the people then.

'You're so right, Mr Fleischer. We don't want *everybody*.'

After supper we told Mother all about our successful outing.

Mother said, 'It's ridiculous, Julius. I wish you wouldn't do it.'

'Mummy, Miss Munsell is going to organise it, not Daddy,' said I.

'That's a blessing,' observed Mother and she sighed. I knew what that sigh meant. Father was no longer the man he had been when they got married.

Father had changed a great deal.

Chapter 12

Albert Einstein

The only really famous visitor was Albert Einstein: he was a distant cousin. Originally they were called Loeb (that is Jewish for Levi), then changed their name to Doerzbacher, the village they came from. Later they changed their name to Koch, because one was a baker. The Kochs married the Einsteins.

His maternal family also originated from the village, as well as some of his paternal relatives. Four Doerzbacher boys had married four Rosenthaler girls, what my mother called 'the *Vetterles Wirtschaft*'. As a child, he and his sister Maja spent many of their school holidays with our family, as our children were of the same age. My Father and he became lifelong friends. They had much in common, but their secret esoteric side is not well known, as both discouraged any talk of it. They both had a horror of hocus-pocus, and claimed that at least 90% of the so-called Spiritualists were of the fraudulent cross-my-palm-with-silver type. Father said that mediums were sometimes deluding themselves; even if some were genuine, he did not believe spiritualism was a good thing. Father very seriously believed his extraordinary gift of medical clairvoyance was God given; his one-ness with nature was a part of it. The latter he shared with Albert, both claiming they could feel the forces of the Universe and the Cosmos. It was instinctive. Albert said, 'I know it, but have to work it out yet.' Their serious discussions about such things as magnetic rays and forces took place in the library (the *Herren Zimmer*). One was not allowed to disturb them. Albert said he found our home '*gemuetlich*', which means comforting and relaxing.

Albert and father called each other Herr Vetter (Mr Cousin), a jocular address, and used the familiar 'thou'. They were both fond of making '*Spaessle*' (jokes) of the South German or specifically Swabian brand, sometimes very broad indeed – never malicious or filthy, always witty, but definitely not of the drawing room kind. Albert entertained us at our lunch table. People said, '*Des Albertle and des Juliusle, die habe was zusamme.*' (Albert(le) and Julius(le), they have something in common.)

It was strictly forbidden for us children to discuss Albert with anyone outside the house. Father said, 'It's no concern of the people. We do not wish him to be gawked at.' Albert called the dinner invitations he received 'feeding time at the zoo'.

He liked Swabian food, especially *Spaetzle*, a dish made with eggs and flour hand-scraped from a small wooden board into salted boiling water. (Nowadays they have a machine to do it, and it does not taste as good.) This was his favourite. 'How come, Irma, that your *Spaetzle* are better than Elsa's?'

'It must be the Saur water [natural spring water from our local source]; it's very gassy,' answered Mother.

Elsa tried it, using Seltzer water and various other types, but she could not obtain ours in Berlin. 'It does not have the same taste,' reported Albert, on his next visit. Father suggested the mineral content of the water must be different. He would see if he could find the analytical content of the various spring waters.

Einstein frequently related a story about an experience on a Stuttgart tram. The tram crawled upwards, from the centre of the town to the steep surrounding hills. He was deeply occupied with a difficult mathematical problem. As he had not solved the problem by the time he reached the terminus, he took another ticket, back to town. He was calculating aloud and had not noticed that the conductor – who did not know him – had been standing next to him listening. That official tapped him on the shoulder, then tapped his forehead, saying with pity in his voice, '*Eh, Kopfrechnen, Schwach.*' (Mental arithmetic, feeble.)

Another favourite concerned his wife (he referred to her as his 'old lady'), who was always scolding him for leaving his belongings behind in hotel rooms. 'She complains that when I am travelling alone I throw into my suitcase only what I can find. Well, I am not particularly worried. So what! So, one time, before going on a journey, she made me promise to be careful. I gave her the promise: Yes, yes, I will be careful, I will leave nothing behind. I'll pack the case properly. When I returned, she was amazed –

the case was in perfect order. She wondered who had packed it for me. I did not let on. When I took my shirt off, however, she suddenly knew why – I had never opened the blasted case!'

Trouble with suitcases – this was nothing new. It started when Albert was a boy. He and his sister Maja had been invited by their Aunt Gella, who lived in our town, for the holidays. She had been very annoyed with him because he had left his suitcase on the train. If Maja had been with him, it would never have happened. Finally, the suitcase was located, though not before Aunt Gella had bought a change of clothing for him. Then the good Aunt Gella exclaimed, 'That boy will never come to anything, mark my words!' She said it more than once, to all and sundry.

Albert always forgot to tip the maids, so father would put some money on the kitchen dresser, pretending it was from Albert. It did not occur to me that he might be hard-up for money. We thought he wore horrible clothes, they did not suit him, black, funereal, they looked like hand-me-downs, badly fitting. This he wore when he visited the Bernheimers. Elsa stayed with them, they were also cousins. With us he sometimes wore a pullover. He said, *'Ich muss jetzt gehn und muss mei Maentele schuettle, ich komm gleich zuruek'*. (Literal translation from Swabish, 'I must go and shake my overcoat there, quickly on-and-off, I shall be back in five minutes'.) It was what he called an *'Anstandsbesuch'*, an obligatory visit.

∗   ∗   ∗

Once, when Father was complaining yet again about the inefficiency of allopathic doctors – their poison medicines, their operations which were not needed – Albert said, 'Surely there are *some* good doctors. One of my best friends in Berlin, Plesch, is very good; he looked after me. Talented medico, quite exceptionally so. Julius, I think even you would approve. Sometimes he works together with your homeopaths. An interesting character, very artistic. A sort of Society chap – claims he is on intimate terms with some of the crowned heads of Europe and the Corps Diplomatique.'

At the mention of Dr Plesch, I had pricked up my ears. I entered the conversation. 'Daddy, on our last holiday, in Camberg, I met a girl called Honoria Plesch. Arnold and I were invited to their place in Koenigsstein, in the Taunus mountains. *Her* father is a doctor, but we did not meet him. They have a fantastic place, like a château.' What had impressed me most was the architecture. I did not think ordinary people had places like that.

Albert replied, 'Honoria? Yes, Plesch has a girl called Honoria, about the same age as you, Sylvia. Yes, he has a summer house there, I believe.'

'The same one then, this Plesch,' said Father. 'Not my kind of person.'

They said Albert was famous for the Relativity Theory, but I did not understand what they were talking about, so I asked him. He answered, 'If two lovers sit on a bench for one minute, that is a short time. However, if you sit on a hot stove for a minute, that is a long time.' Then he looked at me, and said slowly, 'You look like Elsa. You are the spitting image of her at just about the same age. I have a photo – I'll bring it next time.' He never did.

Once at a lunch I mentioned that the teacher had suggested, that a girl called Straub should have extra coaching, otherwise she would have to repeat the class. Straub exclaimed that she had no time, not with her extra duties at the BDM (*Bund Deutcher Maedels* – the Nazi organisation for girls). 'She comes to class in her brown uniform,' said I.

'Repeating class is not such a bad thing,' said Albert. 'I had to repeat a class.' And my Father, to our great surprise, said he also had had to repeat a class. He, with his photographic memory! He had handed in a blank paper at the main examination, at the end of the year!

'It was so boring,' he said. 'The teachers were stupid louts!'

Albert agreed, and they blasted the teachers as 'stupid asses'. 'No wonder one fell asleep – so boring, repetitious, and all this rote, rote, rote. They would be better on a parade ground with the military,' declared Albert.

Mother seemed surprised. 'Elsa tells people you were top of the class,' she exclaimed.

'Well,' said Albert, with a smile, 'I cannot remember. I leave this to Elsa. She tells nice stories [*nette Geschichtle*].'

He was not very popular with us children; he forgot to bring us presents. Then he would give mother some money to buy us chocolate, which we were not allowed as it was 'bad for the teeth'. So the money was put in our saving boxes. What good is that?

Albert and Father met quite often in Stuttgart, when he was changing trains, for his lecture tours took him all over the world.

One lunchtime, I remember Father reading to us a letter he had just received from Albert who was travelling on a large cruise liner. The Einsteins were not wealthy, and had therefore purchased passage in an inside cabin on the lower deck. When the Captain realised he had such illustrious passengers, he upgraded them to the No. 1 State Cabin, the very best on board. They were given a place on the Captain's table which, however, only caused Albert annoyance and embarrassment, because people, under various pretexts, wanted to talk to him. 'Feeding time at the zoo, no peace, again.' Subsequent, meals were taken in their cabin.

A little about Albert's background, for those not familiar with him:

Albert Einstein was born in Ulm, in Bahnhofstrasse on 14 March 1879, two years older than my father. His parents were cousins, in the usual family tradition.

Their small electrical shop was not a success – this venture was too advanced for the time and locality. In 1880 they moved to Munich, where they had relatives. The electrical business they started there was prosperous at first, then strong competition made it fail. The family 'helped out'. When Albert was fifteen his parents moved to Milan and he was left behind to finish his studies. He hated school and was bored. He was only good at mathematics and music. He wanted to be a musician but his father said that was a 'hunger profession' – the same attitude that was held in my family.

Our family had a well established corset factory in Milan since 1871, one had connections. Albert's father got a large contract to supply the electricity for a small town near Milan. This was a wonderful opportunity to get established. However, his costing for the work had not been right, it turned out not to be profitable, what a shame. The family 'helped out'. Albert was alone in Munich, he hated his oppressive school, he was not comfortable in his digs, he complained about these in no uncertain terms to my Father when he came on holiday to us. He was upset and lonely. To leave the school was not easy, but a doctor helped him, gave him a certificate to say he needed southern sunshine and warmth. Most probably it had been very cold in his digs, people did not heat bedrooms, usually. The sitting room was crowded – he could not do his homework.

Albert's Italian was not good enough to enter a school in Italy to study for Matura, therefore his mother took him to German speaking Switzerland. He did not pass the entrance exam for the Polytechnic in Zurich – no wonder, he was too young.

He was accepted in the Technical Department of the Grammar School in Aarau, and boarded with a Professor Winteler. This was a lucky choice and he was happy there. They had children of the same age. The Professor gave him one-to-one tuition, at no extra charge. Albert responded and caught up with his studies. He called Mrs Winteler his second Mama. He passed his Matura and now could enter the Polytechnic in Zurich.

I know very little about his first marriage. Our family made many nasty remarks about Mileva, his first wife. They called her a Xanthippe.* When Albert got seriously interested in her, they were dead against it, especially his mother. She was the only female student in his class: this was very unusual, universities did not normally accept females. It was said that they fell in love. His mother said she did not like this Hungarian girl, this Mileva Maric. Mileva wrote up Albert's thesis, and she was his 'sounding board'. Albert needed to talk out loud, to become clear about his thoughts. He did that with my father as well. She apparently failed her own examination twice. When I was told that, I wondered if the examiners marked her down, to teach her a lesson? At that time I was going through my feminist stage. Did she actively help him? I don't know. Albert got his degree, but only after his second attempt. His paper was considered too short. Only after Albert's father had died did Albert and Mileva marry. They went on to have two sons. There were always financial difficulties. In his student days an aunt had 'helped' out. He had only a very junior position at the patent office in Berne. Again the family 'helped' out. When he became famous with his 'Relativity', people started to take notice of him. He wrote other important works at that time. The Nobel Prize he received was not for the Relativity Theory. By that time, around 1921, his marriage had broken up and he had become involved with Elsa, his cousin, who 'understood' him. The Nobel Prize, a great deal of money, he gave in its entirety to Mileva, who had demanded it as compensation for the divorce. Mother had said she was 'skinning the bear',† before he received the Nobel Prize. The family said he was mad, but he replied it was to shut her up, it was worth it. (*Das Maul Halten!'* – Albert's words, very rude.)

---

* Xanthippe – the wife of Socrates, proverbial as a scolding and quarrelsome woman.
† 'Skinning the Bear' – deciding what to do with the proceeds of the valuable bear skin, before they even had shot the bear.

In our family they referred to Mileva as '*das Ungarische Luder*' (a Luder is a girl who sleeps around). If my Father knew anything, he was not letting on. I had never heard of Lierserl (the daughter born before they married, whom they gave away), and Albert did not talk about his boys, who were living with the mother. I had never met them. I have to mention, my father had a very tolerant attitude towards illegitimacy, he used to say – 'the way of manufacture is exactly the same', or 'a fully grown premature birth', or, 'a little too much friendliness'. Generally speaking, if anything like that came up, it was 'not in front of the children'. Mileva was an emancipated woman, who had studied at the university with the men. To me, she sounded fabulous. Elsa, his second wife, was a hausfrau, a derogatory term which Mother used sometimes. Actually Elsa was artistic, interested in drama and poetry, and one of her daughters was a sculptress. I had never visited them, as they lived in Berlin.

Albert Einstein had dual nationality. He had 'got rid' of his German one, as a schoolboy of fifteen, and he became a Swiss citizen at the age of twenty one. He had been stateless for four years. This had been discussed at great length at our dinner table, his dual nationality.

When he became Professor, in 1914, at the Kaiser Wilhelm Institute in Berlin, he refused to accept German nationality. After much pressure he relented in 1918. Non-German nationals who held important positions were presented with the doubtful gift of German nationality, often after considerable persuasion. They were called the '*Muss Preussen*' (Prussians by compulsion).

The Swabians never liked the Prussians, they generally referred to them as *Sau Preussen* (Prussian pigs). Even educated people like Father and Albert called them names. In the Napoleonic War, the Swabians had fought on the side of Napoleon against the Prussians, and the Arch Duchy of Wuerttemberg had been elevated to a Kingdom. This was in the beginning of the 19th century.

Albert would have been safe from persecution had he been solely of Swiss nationality. The Nazis put a price on his head, a very high one – 50,000 RM. This astonished him, 'Am I worth that much?' Friends persuaded him to leave Berlin at once, where he had been resident for years. He seemed to be unaware of the very real danger he was in. This was in October 1933. He and Elsa went at first to Belgium. I had been told he knew the Queen of the Belgians, they had made music together. Father read out a letter to us at lunchtime. The Queen had given him a bodyguard, but he wrote that they looked so much like policemen, that it made him look more conspicuous. The University of Princeton offered him a post, which he accepted. He lived and worked there until he died in 1955. Elsa had died in 1936.

His first wife, Mileva, lived in Switzerland until she died in 1948. I was told she was very vindictive, she told people she had been left destitute by Albert. She went on public relief. This was not true at all. His older son, Hans Albert, became a specialist in water and hydraulics. He became quite famous in this field in the USA. He used to pretend he was not related to his famous father. He had two sons and one adopted daughter whom we believe to the daughter of Albert Einstein (by that time Elsa had died). Albert's younger son spent much time in a Swiss sanatorium. I thought he had TB, this is the reason people go to a sanatorium. Later I found out it was a mental institution.

My family has not been in touch with any of the Einsteins since the war. Aunt Paula used to hear news of them sometimes.

Chapter 13

For Better or for Worse

Before the First World War, my Father was a confirmed bachelor. I was told that only once Father had thought of marriage. He was very young then and fell in love with Aunt Emmy, a second cousin and 'poor relation' who had been given a job in the factory. She was gay and cheerful, but much older than Father. The disparity in their ages was given as one of the reasons for the family's opposing the marriage. The other reason, which they claimed was the main one, was the already great amount of intermarriage in the family! My great-grandparents, my grandparents, and several uncles had all married cousins.

I was told by a friend of the family that, in her opinion, Father fell for Aunt Emmy because she was sweet-natured and such a contrast to his rather overbearing mother. She did not think he had been really in love with her.

Aunt Emmy was sent away. A corset shop was opened for her in a town in the Rhineland. She never married.

Mother used to say, 'The men in Father's family marry relations because no-one else is good enough. Aunt Emmy was an exception and probably the reason for that was that she had no money.'

Father's family was very clannish; Mother suffered because she was treated like an outsider. Even Mother's considerable dowry, 150,000.00 goldmark, did not 'buy' her a place in the family.

When the First World War ended, Father longed for a normal life. He wanted marriage, a home of his own, and children. He said, 'Three years at the Front is enough for anyone'. He had always loved children, and had been a 'favourite uncle' for years.

He met Mother by chance at Uncle Emile's. It was love at first sight. I wondered then what Father had been doing at the house of a heart specialist; he had never had heart trouble. I later found out that he had had influenza, and the porter in the hotel recommended Uncle Emile. Father asked to be introduced to the charming young lady.

Mother was then an attractive girl of twenty-four, with chestnut hair and the pink and white complexion of a redhead. Father was thirty-six and considered very handsome.

During their courtship and engagement, he arranged for flowers to be sent every day. Twice a week the patisserie in his home town posted delicacies, elaborately packed with ribbons and bows. Why Mother imagined he had packed these parcels himself, I don't know – men don't usually do things like that; it was a disappointment to her when, later in her marriage, she was introduced to the young lady in the patisserie who had done the packing.

When Mother was in a good mood, she would tell me about her former admirers. I marvelled that she had had seven marriage proposals before she met Father, but she said, laughingly, that at least three of them were on account of the dowry the young men hoped for. She would tell me about the balls and fêtes she had attended, and of the whims her father allowed her to indulge.

'You never let us do anything like that, Mummy.'

'My dear, there are four of you. Imagine each of you wanting something different.'

Sometimes Mother would tell me of the year she had spent in Finishing School. Young ladies wore white; they were not permitted to wear anything but white, even in winter. Most nationalities were represented, but only three languages were spoken: French, English and German, for a week each at a time. If one were 'caught' speaking in the wrong language, one had to pay a small sum into the kitty. There was usually enough in the kitty every month for an outing for all the girls to the theatre or concert hall. Occasionally certain 'approved' students were invited to share the dancing lessons with young men present. These young men had been carefully selected. It was all very honourable and strictly chaperoned.

It was on embroidery afternoons that Mother told me such stories. If there was an opera on the wireless we listened to it, but Mother did not allow us to listen indiscriminately. She called popular music 'fairground music'. She used to mark the Radio Zeitung with red pencil for the whole of the week. It was music Mother loved, and opera in paricular; she was not interested in the other Arts.

She played the piano, having taken lessons for many years, though she did not play nearly as well as her father who could not read a note. When the music came to an end she sometimes told me the story of the opera. I marvelled how she could remember all the plots. She laughed and told me that she had heard them probably a dozen times. Every fortnight she visited the Stuttgart Opera House, for she had an annual season ticket.

'Mummy, don't you get bored with it? The repertoire can't be as large as all that.'

'No, I never get tired of it. Besides, I can change my seat at the Opera House for one at the Hof Theatre, if I let them know in good time.'

'Don't you mind going alone?'

'Well, I know some of the regulars.' She shrugged her shoulders. 'You know your Father is not keen on it, unless they perform *Carmen*.'

Father's favourite was *Carmen*. He had seen or heard various versions of the story forty-seven times, seven of these by a group of dancers in mime, during a visit to Spain.

Mother loved dancing, Father hated it. Mother loved parties, a social life, gossip. Father loved nature and solitude. At first he still accompanied Mother to social events, or the theatre, but in later years Mother would go alone, unless it was a function or dinner where his absence would be noticed and commented upon. However, she accompanied him to most of his Nature Cure meetings.

Mother usually sat in her wing chair forever embroidering. I would fetch a small stool for myself and put it next to her. Sometimes I did a little on the corner of her work. She would be delighted and say I was a great help, remarking on how the work had progressed. I couldn't help her often because I had so many tray-cloths to do. Embroidered tray-cloths, the standard birthday present from us for aunts, must have been invented to plague little girls. Aunts have birthdays all the time. Besides my natural aunts, great aunts, cousins and friends of my mother called 'aunts', these were the wives of Father's friends. My calendar in the day nursery was full of red marks – the dates when each present had to be finished. The two grandmothers, however, rated a more substantial present.

I selected the tray-cloths myself in town, carefully choosing the ones involving the least work. I could not trust Mother to buy them for me; she was bound to get a 'pretty one' – meaning of course one *covered* with embroidery. If I found a rather sparsely decorated one, I would buy several at once and put them by. The one consolation for all this labour was the birthday presents those aunts gave me – some even asked me what I wanted.

Those embroidery afternoons were good days, they became rarer and rarer.

Now there was much tension in the house. Father and Mother had 'discussions' at meal times. They would begin when Mother aired her grievances.

'Why is it,' she said, 'that I can never have Kuhn when I want him?' There were three cars, one belonging to the factory, but only one chauffeur for the use of the 'whole' family.

'He was on an errand for Arthur.'

'Why don't they send Herd?' (The factory messenger.)

Neither Father nor Mother could drive.

On another occasion Grandmother had got Wanda to phone to say that Sylvia's and Susan's dresses were much too short.

'You tell me, what concern is it of hers?' Mother challenged Father. 'Why don't you tell your mother to mind her own business.'

At his point, Aunt Paula rang to tell Mother that the sewing woman was with her till the end of the week.

'Why don't you send those short dresses over? She could do them for you right now,' Aunt Paula offered. 'They only need letting down a couple of inches.'

'Thank you, Paula,' Mother replied. 'You're very kind, but I have *my* sewing done in *my* house.'

I knew that my skirts were shorter than those of my schoolmates – Mother had said they were dressed like peasants – but children like to conform.

'Mummy,' I said, 'I could lengthen them myself.'

'No-one has asked you.'

'Really, I can sew quite straight.'

'Will you be quiet? Go to your Aunt Paula ... or to your grandmother. That's where you belong. You look like her. You've got the same taste as her. Why don't you go?'

Father said, 'Irma, the child was only trying to be helpful.'

Mother was so angry, she went on and on about it and the local taste, or lack of it. She said, 'I would not let my girls walk about the way she dresses hers in dresses handed down from generations,

94

unpicked and made over – "the material is still good". Ha! I dare say it'll last another twenty years!' Aunt Paula felt virtuous about her economy – I don't think she realised that the clothes were hideous and outdated, whilst we were considered the best dressed children of the town. Mother continued, 'By the way, Julius, don't forget there is the concert tonight. We'll have to eat earlier.'

'What concert? I did not know I was going to a concert.'

'Of course you know – in aid of the Mothers' Fund. You promised.'

'I've got to go to Lorch. I don't know if I'll be home in time. Sorry dear. They only rang before lunch and it's urgent. Now look, I won't be very late. I'll meet you at the concert.'

'You've got time for everyone else except me. You never have time for me. Everybody comes before me.'

And then Mother started to cry. She cried more and more. We children looked at each other. Father rose and fetched Mother's drops.

'She doesn't understand him,' I thought. 'Can't she see that his patients are more important than a silly concert? Everybody needs my Father. I would be glad to be married to such a wonderful man. She always worries him with silly things ... and it all started with my silly skirts, and it's altogether silly, and I wish she would stop crying. I wonder why her neck gets so red when she cries – mine doesn't. I wouldn't cry about a thing like that. And Aunt Paula's taste – puh! – Mother is quite right. Why can't she tell them to go to hell? That's what I would do.'

Oh, no, you wouldn't, said another voice in me. Who says I wouldn't? I would just love to be rude to Grandmother. Just once, really rude ... And then they can send me to Reform School ... I don't care.

'Can we get up now?' asked Arnold.

'Of course, of course.'

Mother retired to the bathroom to wash her face.

I went to my room and got my homework out. My pencils needed sharpening – where was the sharpener? I did not feel like sums. Then I remembered another of those birthdays. Collecting my traycloth and silks together, I counted the days, subtracting two for transit. 'I'll make it if I send if off tomorrow. And the letter.' I hated writing birthday letters; they showed them round and criticised them for style.

Mother was sitting in her armchair. I could see by the way she was stitching that she was still angry.

I fetched my stool.

She looked up. 'Have you no homework?'

'Not much. I'll do it later.'

'You'd better do it now, and do it properly,' said Mother. She was still cross with me.

Back in my room I continued with my sums. I found myself doodling and outlining the shapes of my doodles, drawing faces with stern expressions and unsmiling mouths.

I wondered how long Mother would be cross with me.

There you go again, I said to myself. You will open your big trap. When will you learn to keep quiet? Miss Sylvia, you have a genius for saying the wrong thing. Why don't you learn from your brother, Arnold? He's diplomatic. Susan, darling Susan, can do no wrong. And if anything does go wrong, Mother excuses her: 'Too much is expected of that child', or 'It was an accident'. Yes, if darling Susan breaks something, she knows what to do. She comes running to Mother and cries, so Mother has to comfort her. But if I break something, that's a different story. At best, I'm called clumsy – usually it's carelessness – or why don't you look what you are doing? And I break less than she does.

My Ricky is a sweet, sweet rascal. No-one can be angry with him.

The sums won't come out, blast!

Concentrate!

Perhaps they *don't* come out. Some don't.

Three times I have checked it now. If it's wrong, it can stay wrong. I wonder where my pencil sharpener is?

Susan comes into the room.

'Have you seen my pencil sharpener?'

'No, I haven't. You needn't shout at me.'

'You usually have it when I am looking for it.'

'Not this time. Here you can borrow my new one, if you put it back.'

'No, thank you. I'll use a knife.'

'Don't make a mess. Last time you made a beastly mess.'

'Yes, Miss Tidy.'

Later in the afternoon I went into the garden to cut flowers. Several rooms had to be done. This was my chore, but I liked it.

I hated laying the table, which I did alternately with Susan. Susan was not 'old enough' to do flowers. Mother said I did it very artistically. I took great trouble over the arrangement for mother's dressing table. This would please her. Mauve was her favourite colour and the Michaelmas daisies looked good with red berries and copper beech.

I distributed the other vases, leaving Mother's till the last. I washed my hands, combed my hair and then put on a clean apron. Mother approved of aprons. I knocked at the bedroom door. 'Oh that's nice. What a lovely combination!' I was relieved.

It was all right again. I liked to help mother dress when she was going out. She let me put her scent on her hankie.

'Can I put it on this lace one?'

'If you like, but please give me a plain one as well, the border is scratchy.'

I had not thought of that, only how nice the guipure lace trimming looked.

'Which gloves, Sylvia. What do you think?'

'This pair matches exactly.' I held them to the light.

'So it does, but they're too long.'

'I'll bring the drawer.'

What a selection! Neutral shades predominated. Pastel coloured ones were wrapped in tissue paper.

Mother's drawers were so neat and tidy, her underwear folded neatly, the linen tied with mauve ribbons which had adjustable clasps on the sides. The maids were not allowed to touch the drawers in case anything got disturbed.

When first married, Mother was not able to dress herself alone, so I was told. 'Spoilt, spoilt, spoilt' – that's what Father's family called it, and how they loved to exaggerate. 'Not a good Hausfrau' (which was quite unjustified), they said. Mother laughed at that. 'If your Father had wanted to marry a "good Hausfrau", he would have chosen one of the local "peasants".' I suppose her 'helpless' ways enchanted Father.

The story goes that, returning from the honeymoon, Mother was found sitting on the bed crying. No lady's maid had been engaged for her. 'How can I dress myself?' Garments had many tiny buttons on the back. 'Who will do my hair?' Her long chestnut hair. which had been put at night into plaits, was elaborately coiffed in the day time.

97

'I do hope your Father will not be late,' Mother said. 'I don't like to go by myself. Everybody will be there: you know how it is – "where is Julius, is he not coming?" – I hate it when I have to make excuses all the time.'

'But doctors are called away to patients.'

'Your Father is no doctor – a doctor of Nature Cure, that's different. Well, I suppose he does some good work, some wonderful work. Those Cures! It's embarrassing. Do you know, last week on Market Day I had just bought two kilos of grapes and was going to pay for them. The seller – I had never seen her before, not a regular – imagine what she said to me: "I can't take money from you, Mrs Fleischer".'

She absolutely refused to take the money. Then she said, in front of all those people. 'She walks ... she walks ... Mr Fleischer did it. God bless him.' I laid the money on the stall, but she picked it up and slipped it in my shopping bag. Please, Mrs Fleischer. We're so grateful. My Lore, she had not walked for years. We had a specialist in once too, a fine gentleman, from Stuttgart.'

'She wanted to tell me all about it in front of all those women! So I said quickly, "I am glad for you", and I went. She called after me, "Any time, I'll be honoured" ... I had not even finished my shopping; I had to go again in the afternoon.'

'Your father was not a bit like that when we got married. I had no idea. I thought I was marrying a corset manufacturer, or the son of one. Before the war your father worked in the factory; he travelled abroad then, and in the first years of our marriage as well. He hardly goes to the factory now. That's very bad for business. Too many people are allowed to sign on his behalf. One of his secretaries is building a villa. I'm wondering where the money is coming from; he can sign anything. They should have allowed your father to study medicine. He always wanted to study medicine. Who will take the German factory over? Your good-natured Father. But is he running the factory? No.'

Father, like any other Victorian or Edwardian *pater familias* did not discuss financial affairs with Mother. To talk about money was vulgar, certainly not ladylike. Mother said that the Fleischers were brought up as though they had a bottomless sack of money, and she suspected that when the supply ran out Father sold properties. She added that it would have been better if her own father had administered the factories. Once upon a time there were over 1,000 employees in the German factory alone, not counting the workers in the factories abroad.

I have a photo of my father as a young man, holding a corset. In the background one can see the medals won – Gold Medals – at world exhibitions in Paris, London etc., from 1867 to 1915. There is also a picture in a book, dated 1890, showing 'Fleischer's Electrique Corset', a patented and registered trade mark. The mind boggles! What were its uses or benefits? But Father seemed no longer to be interested in the factories, except as a source of orthopaedic corsets to help people, and artificial busts for ladies who had lost their breasts through cancer. I had once looked at a folder on Father's desk – naughty, naughty … not allowed. I had quite a shock. These photographs were terrible … these poor people with their distorted bodies! I was glad the subjects wore black masks. I was so sorry for them and glad if Father could to something to help.

Since corsets were no longer fashionable in the twenties, the factory had changed its production. Only the older generation still wore the traditional article – we children called them armour plating. The new line was corselets, made of shiny lock-knit jersey, without bones. They also produced fleecy knickers, with elastic around the knees, and Liberty bodices, for ladies and children, which had four dangling elastics with either woven-in buttonholes for buttons which had been sewn on the top of the stockings, or suspenders – clip-on things with teeth. There was a new very successful line in ladies' pyjamas in pastel-coloured lock-knit with contrasting trim, a design called 'Sappho' (*marque deposé*).

Mother explained, 'The name your father has chosen is not very suitable, but I doubt if people would know. Sappho was the chief priestess in "Lesbos", that's an island near Asia Minor … near Turkey.'

'Did they wear pyjamas there?'

'Certainly not.' Mother showed me a book with Greek ladies. 'Look, all draperies. Those are square pieces of cloth, just pinned at the shoulder.'

Needless to say, I had never heard of lesbians.

*   *   *

One year the snow had come down in big flakes and now the sun was shining, the children of the town came to enjoy it with home-made sleighs and contraptions made of thick wooden board, which worked surprisingly well. We had been told the best hill for tobogganing was the one situated right next to our factory. Arnold and I asked Sister Paula if she would take us, as we were not allowed out by ourselves. Arnold pulled the sleigh, a neat polished job made out of slats, which had a bell attached.

We climbed the hill where there were a lot of children waiting their turn to glide down the slopes. We knew none of them. Why were they hostile to us? They called out, 'We don't want these posh kids.' They must have seen Sister Paula in her nurse's uniform waiting at the bottom.

'Hoity-toity, la-di-dah, this is our hill. Get lost! Buzz off!'

Arnold said politely, 'We'll wait our turn.'

'Oh, no, you won't,' called a big boy. He gave our sleigh such a push, that it careered down the hill all by itself. There was nothing else to do, but go home.

Sister Paula asked Karl to recommend another 'good hill' – as a local man he would know – telling him the 'street children', as she called them, would not let us use the hill adjoining the factory.

The next day it was raining, and over night it froze hard. This made the snow sharp like needles, and one could hurt oneself – it was no use going sledging. Mother called us into the drawing room, saying, 'I know you are disappointed. I have a special treat for you. They are performing *Hansel and Gretel* in the Stuttgart Opera House. You can have my seats. Sister Paula is to come with you. Kuhn [our chauffeur] will take you and bring you back.' We knew the melodies from *Hansel and Gretel*, because Mother had sung them to us, accompanying herself on the piano. I put on my best dress, the pale blue silk one. Arnold wore his brown velvet suit, with the frilly pink shirt which he hated. He was told 'any more fuss and you can stay at home.' It was magical – we had not been to the grown-up theatre before. We came home very, very late. There was only semolina pudding with cherry jam for supper. They said a meal would be indigestible at such a late time. We had missed dinner, we were very hungry.

Next day there was a 'good snow' again. We set off to a different location. When we passed the 'best hill' we noticed the gate had been nailed closed, and a large notice read: '*Privat Eintritt Verboten*'. Sister Paula explained that Karl had been furious – 'The cheek of it, stopping our children,' he had said. 'This is Fleischer property.

I am going to tell madam, and ask for permission to put a notice up.'

Arnold said, 'It serves them right.' However, I was sorry, we had spoiled the children's fun.

Opposite our factory, on the other side of the street, was a large piece of ground, a meadow, which some years earlier, Father had decided would make a suitable vegetable garden. He engaged two gardeners to dig it over and plant it for the use of the poor of our town. The general destitution, the aftermath of World War I, had hit the people heavily. Locals were allowed on two days a week to collect their vegetables, all for free. The gardeners insisted they would hand out the produce, as they did not want their work trampled.

Our grandfather had planted his orchards largely with apples, as they were doing well in our locality. There were also *Zwetschgen* trees, with their delicious deep blue plums, pointed at each end. Black-currant and red-currant bushes lined the pathways.

I helped to wrap up the apples in waxed paper, to be placed on wooden trays and stored in the loft, where they would keep till Christmas.

After the family had collected all they wanted from the orchards, there was always a great surplus, so the poor of the town were invited to help themselves; they came with baskets; some even brought ladders. It would have been a shame to let the fruit go to waste.

PART TWO

CHANGE

Chapter 14

The Seminary for Young Ladies – Politics are not Included in the Curriculum

Shortly after my tenth birthday, I entered the Seminary for Young Ladies, having duly passed the entrance examination with the very highest marks.

In summer school started at seven o'clock, during the winter months at eight. The lessons were arranged in 'short' hours: we had five lessons and were finished by lunchtime, except on sport afternoons. This enabled the pupils, including those who lived in the surrounding villages, to get home for lunch since there was no arrangement for school dinners.

When the deafening bell announced the mid-morning break, the girls raced down the wide stone staircase, yelling to their friends to hurry up. Everybody tried to be the first at the entrance in order to have the best choice of the rolls. Two baker's women stood behind large washing baskets, filled with all kinds of rolls; Laugen Bretseln were greatly favoured, and there were never enough to go round so there was pushing and shoving. The milkman stood at the opposite side; it was more peaceful there. School milk was a fraction cheaper than that sold in the shops.

When I was very late in the morning I would run through Mr Vetter's yard, thus cutting a whole corner off the distance. If he saw me he called: 'Some time, when you're not in such a hurry, we must have a little chat.' I would curtsey and run on.

Next to the seminary were the Public Gardens and the 'old cemetery'. On winter mornings when it was still dark, boys would hide behind the graves, their heads covered with sheets, and play 'ghosts', in order to frighten 'the stupid girls'; many of the girls would rather walk the much longer way all around the cemetery.

How could one be quite certain what one saw was not a ghost?

Where the cemetery adjoined the Public Gardens was a Garden of Remembrance, and the newly erected War Memorial. There had been a great deal of discussion amongst the City Fathers and councillors over what form this should take. Finally, they had decided on a Pieta* in grey stone by an artist called Nussbaum, a local talent. It was to be a great memorial – the town was rich and could afford it – six metres high and carved on the site.

I often walked past, hoping to see something, but Mr Nussbaum worked behind scaffolding. Once I caught a glimpse of the artist himself. What a disappointment! He did not look at all as I had imagined. A sculptor? He looked like Mr Pinotti, the ice-cream man, and he also wore a white overall.

Walking past the memorial every day, I had time to get used to it. It was a 'modern' Pieta. Standing closely in front of it I became acutely aware of the foot of the dead man, bent upwards with a hollow instep. It was a funny foot – I felt I wanted to count the toes.

At the seminary I missed the friendly atmosphere of Miss Helmstaedter's class, the personal interest she had taken in us. Now it was us against them.

Most of the classes were taken by men, whose approach to teaching was varied. But the standard of teaching was fairly high, most of them having obtained a doctorate or the equivalent of an MA. The school believed in discipline and passing exams; the rest was left to the teachers' discretion.

Dr Kocher took French, German and Literature. His French was good. He often referred to his student days, spent partly at the University of Toulouse. To get the right accent, that little extra, you have to learn it in the country, he used to say. He had endless patience when it meant getting the pronunciation right; he would make us hold our noses and practise. Otherwise he had the proverbial quick temper of the redhead. He even occasionally threw a book in desperation. The girls said that if he was wearing brown shoes he was in a good temper – black for bad temper. This 'knowledge' had been handed on to us by former pupils. However, he nearly always wore black and I was not superstitious.

Father knew him well and once asked him how I got on. 'Bone-

---

*It has since been replaced by a more warlike creation.

lazy', was the verdict. Dr Kocher promised to cure me of it. I had a good memory and therefore considered it superfluous to prepare lessons as it was mainly repetition. So when Dr Kocher asked a question and no-one put up their hand, it was always my turn to answer. I would bluff and say the first thing that entered my head which, to my surprise, was often right. If the answer was wrong, however, I was given lines to do. He would say, 'If Fleischer does not know it, it's sheer laziness; she did not do her homework.'

The constant repetition made me feel drowsy; I was bored, so I read romantic and historic novels, or travel books under my desk. He spotted my lack of attention. The girls said that his bi-focal glasses were for the purpose of 'catching out' pupils sitting in front and at the back, at the same time. Slowly he would creep nearer until he stood in front of my desk. By that time someone would have given me a warning – perhaps a shove with their foot – so I would have managed to put the book away.

'Now tell me, what do you think of it? What would you say?' With luck I might have caught his last word or a friend might have whispered to me. In that case I would answer the question correctly, but sometimes I would expound an elaborate theory on the wrong subject. By the silence of the class, or its suppressed giggles, I would know I was on the wrong track, whereupon I would become nervous and talk more and more.

Dr Kocher would smile at me – always a bad sign. 'You may sit down. That was very interesting, though not quite what we were talking about. Perhaps you will *write* about this equally well – at home. We haven't the time now. Not less than two pages.'

I felt this was persecution on Father's orders and therefore did not bear Dr Kocher any grudge. After all, he was quite right – I had not prepared the lesson.

Miss Holder was the biology mistress. She was a dainty white-haired lady who considered herself very refined. She wore tussore dresses in pastel shades, mostly pale green. They were old fashioned, more so because of their boned stand-up collars. These were the subject of much speculation and we eventually decided that she must be hiding a scar.

Her entrance into the class room was always the same.

'Good morning, my dear children,' she would say in her falsetto voice. 'Margaret, open the window. Not a breath of fresh air in here.' She would walk over to the window and inhale deeply.

Whilst she stood there, she would continue with her commands. 'Lisa, take a duster and wipe my desk and chair so that I can sit down.' Then she would carefully spread her skirts.

'Now, here we have the corrected homework. Charming little mistakes, really quite charming.' She would quote something, then say to the girl in question, 'Perhaps you would enlighten us, my dear. We would like to know what you meant, wouldn't we, children?'

The class would giggle, though sympathetic to the pupil.

Miss Holder was unpopular.

In the game 'Imitating Teachers' I'm afraid she fared badly. She was easy to take off and we made her say absurd things. Irony was resented more than bullying. She seemed to delight in stripping us of our dignity.

Mr Gilling, the Maths master, had great ability; he was a born teacher. There was not a pupil who could not follow his explanation – even 'silly Helga' could. She was still with me in the same class, scraping through the exams with difficulty. Her parents, an intelligent couple, coached her.

Mr Gilling was tall, handsome and very friendly; he never showed annoyance and was adored by the whole school. At the beginning of term pupils of different forms would ask each other: 'How many hours with Gilling?' 'Six – you are lucky. Fancy, six whole hours with Gilling.'

The girls who had a 'bad crush' on him brought elaborate bouquets to school, stripping their garden of the best. He never took flowers home, so as not to show favouritism.

The crush was extended to his family – his pretty wife and his four small children. When the fifth one arrived he received dozens of matinee coats and booties, knitted by schoolgirls.

Some of the teachers were actively disliked. To play tricks on them – especially if one got away with it – gained one prestige.

The history master was a fat gentleman with a red face and a shiny bald head. He was the only bully amongst the teachers. We nicknamed him 'Teach', as he was a plain *Reallehrer* (secondary school teacher), which is a very low rank in the teaching hierarchy. He had never been promoted.

I considered him stupid; he seemed to know only what was written in our current school books. I loved to confuse him by asking him difficult questions, in the hope that I might trip him up. It flattered me to think that he might be a little afraid of me.

'Teach' was in his element when a pupil could not answer his question. It gave him an opportunity to show his power. In a booming voice he would repeat the question, whilst he advanced on the victim. His face changed colour with anger, his small eyes glinted. Some girls were so frightened they burst into tears. Then he would shout, 'So, we have a Kindergarten now. God, the stupidity, I have to suffer. It's got to be heard and seen to be believed. Whatever possessed me to leave the Boys' College – I must have been out of my mind.'

With his pointer he would beat repeatedly the girl's desk. 'Stupidity ... Laziness! Oh God! What a Kindergarten.' But he did not hit us – it was not allowed in the Seminary.

If he attacked a girl belonging to my 'camp', I tried, if I could not prevent it by a well-timed interruption, at least to avenge it.

My knowledge in history was good. I devoured anything I could get hold of, either from our library at home or from the newly opened Lending Library, where they stocked some historical novels. Fraulein Frieda Heller, the lady in charge there, helped me with my selection. Once or twice she'd even bought in a special copy for me, second hand; she said the general demand was for love stories. Fraulein Frieda was nice to talk to and she was interested in history. I was not surprised that Uncle Georg Adelsheimer was often in her shop.

Armed with my newly-gained knowledge, I would ask 'Teach' tricky questions.

He would hum and haw, then say, 'We cannot go into that now. I'll come back to this later on.'

The girls would grin, knowing what would come next.

'Teach' would slip out of the classroom at the first opportunity, go to the School Library, staying there anything up to a quarter of an hour, till he had found the answer to my question. On his return he would say, 'By the way, coming back to your question...'

After a while, he connected his shouting fits with my 'punishment' of him, and they happened less frequently.

He then often checked himself before it got to the 'yelling' stage. He would glance over to my desk. There I sat, chin in hand, with my best 'I-dare-you' face. So instead of growling, he would say, sneeringly, to the girls, 'Never mind, learn it at home. I can't plague myself with you girls. God ... whatever made me leave the Boys' College?'

At the end of term he announced that in the next lesson we would take the examination papers. As the yearly report was based on the outcome of this examination, the girls swotted feverishly. Even I read the primer through, as well as looking up a few books on the subject which I had found in our library.

'Teach' had handed out the papers. We were ready to start. I felt him staring at me. He was. I smoothed my hair. I wondered if I had an inkspot on my cheek.

He screamed, 'Fleischer.'

I rose, 'Yes, Sir?'

'You pick up that piece of paper. A crib! I caught you. Hoping to get away with it. Yes, weren't you Fleischer?'

Puzzled, I bent down and picked up from the floor a small piece of paper. I said, 'Excuse me, Sir, may I explain?'

'Explain', he gaped at me. 'No explanation is needed. Put it in the waste paper basket. At once!'

It was not a crib, but I put it in the waste paper basket, as told, and returned to my seat.

'Fleischer,' he screamed, 'you sit here in front.' He pointed to an empty row of desks. No-one sat on these; they were a smaller size. 'That will stop Lendt passing you any information.'

I shared a desk with Lisa Lendt, a Jewish girl.

'Teach' went over to my desk and examined it for open history books and other incriminating evidence. He found nothing. He seemed satisfied he had caught me out at last.

At our next history lesson, he came back with the marked sheets. He glared at me. As usual, he sat down at his desk and discussed the work, giving some explanations. Then he called me out.

'Can you tell me,' he shouted, 'where you kept your information? In your sleeve, perhaps? How did you know what I was going to ask? I'd prepared a brand new paper.'

'I didn't, Sir.'

'Ninety-three per cent ... Ninety-three per cent. Way ahead of all the others. The next is Reiher with seventy-six per cent. Fleischer, where did you get the information?'

'From books. I like history, Sir. I'm fond of the Greeks, Sir. I read a lot,' I answered smugly.

'That does not excuse you using a crib. And what do you have to say to that?'

'I tried to explain before, Sir. It was a shopping list for my mother.'

The class hooted with laughter. This should have pleased me. Yes, for a minute, and I looked at 'Teach'. My God, he looked miserable! I could not enjoy my triumph. He was slumped over his desk. He did not stop the laughter in the classroom. Finally, it died down.

I was still standing next to his desk; he had forgotten to dismiss me. I retreated gradually, backwards, step by step. There was silence.

After a while he indicated with a gesture that he wanted a girl to distribute the examination papers.

Silence again.

It served him right, I thought. He had it coming to him. Why do *I* feel so uneasy, *I* have not done anything. Haven't you? Which side are you on? He's a bully and it serves him right. That big, fat blob!

I couldn't see his face, only his bald scalp. He stirred a little, then looked up. His face was white. He looked at me. His mouth opened as if he were going to speak, but he closed it again. I would have liked to say to him: 'Don't look at me like that – I can't stand that pleading look – say something. You ought to admit you were wrong, the girls would respect that.'

He slowly got up and, shuffling towards the door, he mumbled, 'Page two hundred and ninety-five. Reading. One paragraph each. You there, you start.'

We read to the end of the chapter. Then we read it again ... and a third time. The reflections of the sun from the window opposite danced on the blackboard – nobody told us to draw a curtain. The sunbeam danced all over us. 'Teach' returned in time to dismiss the class. He gave no homework that day.

And I felt sorry for him and somehow ashamed. Fool that I am.

Trudi Fahner came over to me and said, 'How do I know it was not a crib?'

'My dear Fahner, you missed your chance. You should have looked in the waste paper basket. I couldn't care less what you think.'

'Hmmm.' She walked away.

Our class was divided into two camps. There were two leaders – 'big mouths' might be a more correct description – Trudi Fahner and myself.

She had great physical courage, and would do anything for a dare; I mean *anything*.

Every fortnight we went to the local swimming baths. The bathing cabins and benches were situated in the upper gallery. There were notices everywhere that it was dangerous to jump down from there – *Lebensgefahr* – mortal danger. Several times Trudi had jumped from the upper gallery; she was the only one in our class who dared. Once a boy had almost killed himself; he had badly hurt his spine.

She approached me. 'What about it, Fleischer? Do you fancy doing a double from the gallery with me?'

'No, thank you, Fahner.'

'Scaredy-cat.'

'If it pleases you, call me that. My Mother does not allow it.' I *was* scared.

'I did not ask mine.'

Several girls were standing round. Trudi's supporters started to chant: 'Scaredy-cat, scaredy-cat.'

'He's back,' called a girl. She was referring to the Bath Attendant.

Thank goodness, I thought. It's not worth it – it's silly. I *am* scared, I'm even scared when I jump the six-metre board. Still, I jumped every time we went, for appearance sake.

There was clapping. Trudi Fahner had made a beautiful double turn dive from the six-metre board. I could not do even a single turn from that height.

The Seminary had a well equipped gymnasium but I disliked the equipment because, however much I tried, I was bad with bars and climbing and ropes.

Trudi could do the most number of pulls on the bars – I managed no more than two. To make up for the weakness in my arms I trained myself in acrobatics. Handstand, spagat, bridge, swan, were all postures which depended upon skill rather than strength; I excelled in these. Hoping to improve my strength, I used to wrestle with Arnold, but lately I had given that up – my breasts were developing and hurt at the slightest pressure.

Since Hitler had been made Chancellor at the end of January, 1933, several of the girls did not dare associate with the Jewish pupils; their parents had forbidden it. There were four Jewesses in my class: my cousin Lila Guggenheim, Lisa Lendt, 'Silly Helga', and myself. There was no open anti-semitism, just a little tension at times. Little things occurred, perhaps accidents; perhaps one was touchy.

During our mid-morning break I sat down next to Lila, wanting

112

to talk to her about my grandmother's forthcoming birthday party. Lila had been invited as well.

Trudi Fahner joined us. As she shared a bench with Lila and they were friends, I could say nothing, though I would have liked to say, 'Buzz off, we're talking about private matters.' She offered a sandwich to Lila and me. Lila took it and exchanged one of hers. I said, 'No, thank you.'

'They're good,' Trudi said. 'They are ham.'

'I don't want to deprive you of your sandwiches.'

'Perhaps you don't eat ham – your religion. Sorry, I forgot.' She said sanctimoniously.

'Not every day and not *your* ham – I had some yesterday.' Our family had not kept a "kosher" kitchen for several generations. Father said it was an outmoded law, no longer needed. Moses invented these health laws for two reasons: firstly, in a hot country food deteriorates quickly, with no ice cabinets or cold store rooms; secondly, animals, especially pigs, had trichinas or other diseases – that's why the Rabbis had to inspect the meat. They called pigs dirty.'

Arnold said, 'Pigs *are* dirty, I have seen them wallowing in mud.'

'Perhaps they do that to keep cool, like elephants.'

Arnold laughed. 'Pigs are not elephants.'

Trudi Fahner was the first in our class to wear her Nazi uniform. She wore it every day to school. Lila still shared the bench with her. The Nazi uniform did not seem to disturb Lila. No politics in the Ladies' Seminary: that's what Dr Kocher had said.

After the excitement about Hitler becoming Chancellor had died down, Dr Kocher had given a little lecture. He said, 'Our Germany will be strong again some day.' And he spoke of the Treaty of Versailles, the humiliation, crippling Germany – '... our wonderful, beloved Germany.'

He loved Germany. To him it was the best country in the world.

He concluded on an unusual note: 'By the way, I would like to remind you, all of you, that politics have no place in school. I do not wish to hear of any persecution of the Jewish pupils. This is a Seminary for Young Ladies – politics are not included in the curriculum.'

Politics, I addressed him silently, why, you're talking politics yourself. I suppose you don't like what Hitler says about the Jews. You know better.

113

I told Father about it.

Father said, 'Kocher is no Nazi, he's a good fellow. But you mention the Treaty of Versailles to him and he's off. He is a good German. I hope we all are.'

The sentiments Father expressed were shared by many German Jews. The *Central-Verein-Zeitung* (a Jewish newspaper) wrote on the 25 March 1933: 'Nobody can rob us of our German Fatherland... In that we fight this battle we carry out a German, not a selfish-Jewish fight.'

In June of the same year, the *Juedische Rundschau* (another Jewish paper), said: 'The Jews are not enemies of the State. The German Jews desire and wish for the rise of Germany, for which they have always invested, to the best of their knowledge, all their resources, and that is what they wish to continue to do.'

Our Jewish community was well established. The Jews were respected. They were good employers, but the fact that most of them were employers and not employees was exploited by the local Nazis. The workers, however, were getting a fair deal, their fathers and grandfathers had been getting a fair deal; it was common knowledge that the Jewish employers paid better.

The people of the town said, 'We don't understand all this about "bad Jews". We don't know any. It must be some foreign Jews they talk about in the papers.' And to make up for it, the greengrocer picked for us the choicest fruit.

Some of the local shopkeepers put up signs saying: 'No Jews wanted' on their shopfronts, but these shops were not those normally patronised by the Jewish community.

Arnold used to read the newspapers carefully – and I don't mean only the sports pages. He was keenly interested in politics. As a little boy he had wanted to be Prime Minister.

He knew I would never read that part of the paper by myself so he lectured me on politics. He said my ignorance was 'appalling' and that he felt I had to be instructed. It was very important.

In 1932, we had three national elections within the span of five months, and although the number of Nazi delegates in the Reichstag had slightly increased, they did not have the majority. But the Nazis became more and more powerful. By the summer they had managed to get lifted the ban which prohibited them from wearing their uniforms in public. They marched in the streets.

The Communists, too, marched in the streets.

We children had strict instructions to return home immediately if we saw either of them. It was not safe. There were many clashes between the Nazis and the Communists; every day there was something in the paper. People got killed. People got wounded. It was dangerous to be an onlooker. Several hundred people were killed that summer in the streets, and over a thousand wounded. Martial Law was declared in Berlin.

Arnold told me that the 'Ruhr Barons' and other industrialists were financing the Nazis because they feared the Communists.

The workers were earning pitifully small wages; I was sure this was the reason why they were Communists. Why did those Ruhr Barons not give them a rise? They should look after their workers – my father looked after his. Then the workers would no longer be Communists, and the Ruhr Barons would have no need to finance the Nazis to keep their workers in check: everybody would be happy.

Arnold called me a *Kindskopf* (baby fool). 'They don't want peace, they want power. They're arms manufacturers, or have you forgotten?'

Dr Schacht, the financial wizard, recalled that at Nuremberg on 20th February 1933, he collected from some of the leading magnates, 3,000,000 marks in 'voluntary' donations to the Party, at one single meeting. These industrialists were happy to use the Nazis as their strong arm men.

I could not understand why President Hindenburg allowed all these 'goings-on'. He was a General Field-Marshal, Supreme Commander of the German Army; surely he could put a stop to it. Arnold said that at eighty-five he was too old. One should pension him off, he added disrespectfully.

And then, to crown it all, Hindenburg himself had given the Chancellorship to Adolf Hitler, on 30th January 1933. This proved to me that Hindenburg was senile. Everywhere they showed pictures of the old President walking together with Adolf Hitler, and shaking hands with him – one could not get away from it. Nazi flags and banners were everywhere.

It was rumoured that some of the Communist leaders had gone to Russia and others had gone underground. Hitler had banned all Communist meetings, and the rallies of the Social Democrats were broken up by Nazi thugs. Newspapers fell in with the new régime, or were closed.

Reichs President Hindenburg had appointed a personal friend, Franz von Papen, to be his Vice-Chancellor. He in turn appointed his friends, aristocrats, who were inexperienced, to the Cabinet. Was it a sinecure, or did he want 'Yes-men'? People referred to them as the Barons Cabinet (*Junkers Kabinett*). It was not a popular move. The comic papers portrayed them as elderly gentlemen, in frock coats and top hats, whilst the Nazis and Communists were vigorous strong lads with lots of muscle.

To make speeches in different towns, Hitler hired an aeroplane. Air travel was most unusual at the time; the population was impressed.

Von Papen seemed to favour the Fascists, the Nazis. He elevated them to auxiliary police, hoping thus to control them. However, the street battles continued as before.

I asked Arnold why von Papen favoured the Nazis.

'He does not favour them, he needs them. Together with his Centre Party they are strong enough to oppose the Social Democrats, who are the biggest party in the Reichstag, and so prevent them from having the majority vote.'

I did not understand politics. If I was honest, I did not want to understand it!

One often heard that people had been taken into protective custody – a euphemism? Protective! They were tortured, or even murdered. In June 1933, the Wuerttemberg State President, Eugen Bolz, one of the Centre Party's leading men, was arrested and severely beaten. This outrage was only whispered about, as it was now dangerous to talk openly. Everyone, of all the parties except the Nazis, found this absolutely dreadful – a State President!

Then followed the persecution of the Catholic Church Delegates – they were to resign or join the Nazis.

The Nazis were well organised. Their propaganda Minister, Dr Goebbels, was very efficient. Hitler's speeches were relayed in public places: unemployment would soon be a thing of the past. Flags were everywhere...

Again the magnates were happy to use the Nazis as their strong arm men.

Then: 'The Reichstag is burning – the Communists have set the Reichstag on fire.'

Everyone talked about it, speculating how it could have happened. The Reichstag fire, which occurred on 27th February, was topic number one in all Germany. It even made the elections, which had been scheduled for the next week, seem less important.

According to the newspapers, a Dutchman, Marinus van der Lubbe, a Communist, was the arsonist. He had been caught red-handed at the scene of the crime. He behaved like a lunatic; he seemed half dazed when he was interrogated and he certainly gave all the wrong answers, incriminating himself in a most stupid manner. Some people said he had been hypnotised. Others went even further and maintained the Nazis themselves had put him up to it. It was said he had been a fire raiser before. It was a great mystery. I could not understand how one man could get such a big fire going in just a few minutes, and in a stone building too. He was found guilty and decapitated on 10th January 1934 in prison in Leipzig.

Hitler used this Reichstag fire incident to wheedle additional powers – a decree 'for the protection of the German people and the German State' – out of the old President. This decree suspended the parts of the constitution which guaranteed individual and civil liberties, including freedom of the press.

There were mass arrests of Communists, 10,000 at least it was rumoured. Goering, all important man at the Reichstag, advocated shooting them all. Such action might possibly have caused a civil war. Goering maintained this was the start of a communist civil war, for a Soviet Germany. People were frightened.

The general election on 5th March 1933 was the last in Hitler's Germany. The Nazis gradually got rid of all the other parties.

When President Hindenburg died on 2nd August 1934, the Nazi Cabinet had passed a decree the day before to the effect that the offices of Reichs President and Reichs Kanzellor be united. Hitler was now supreme ruler in Germany.

But Hitler was in Berlin – and Berlin was far away.

Chapter 15

'It's Piffle to Wear White Aprons'

On the morning of Grandmother's birthday Wanda rang up to say that white aprons should be worn, it was Grandmother's wish.

'Mummy, must I? I'm too old to wear an apron at the table, I am not a baby.'

'It's her birthday. It won't hurt you, just once. Wear the organdie one, the frilly one. It suits you.'

'Must I? All right then.'

I tied an artistic bow around my present. Thank goodness I managed to finish it in time – I was glad to see the end of it.

Shortly after Christmas, I had asked Grandmother what she wanted for her birthday.

'A stole, to wear in bed.'

In spite of the thick needles I used, the progress was slow. I was annoyed with myself for having been so stupid as to ask her. I might have got away with something like a tea-cosy or a set of covered coat hangers.

So I was knitting, knitting forever ... for three months. And now it was finished. The stole was on the short side for someone of Grandmother's proportions, but it was wide enough. I had crocheted a lilac border with scallops around it.

As it was her seventy-fifth birthday, an elaborate programme had been worked out by the children of the family. For weeks we had been rehearsing our play and the dances.

Susan, dressed as a huntsman, spoke the prologue.

Cousin Erica, Aunt Paula's daughter, danced a fiery Cossack dance. She was a clumsy girl, but one did not notice this overmuch because she stamped to her heart's content and swung her over-long arms about like flails. She danced with determination. Her

118

costume was very good indeed; it had been carefully made by a 'real dressmaker', not the sewing woman.

Applause.

Then it was my turn. I danced a lyrical dance to the sentimental strains of 'La Paloma'. I had chosen this piece, which I considered great music. I wore a three-quarter-length tulle skirt, three layers, made by myself. The dance was a kind of *Les Sylphides* interspersed with leaps and backbends.

Applause.

Lila, dressed in the National costume of Alsace Lorraine, recited a folksy poem. Lila's mother came from these parts, and she had borrowed a genuine costume for her.

Applause.

Arnold and I carried a small table in. Then we arranged two rows of glasses of all kinds, shapes and sizes, on it. It had taken us several weeks to collect these. We had made the rounds to friends and relatives until we had 'tuned a set'. They called us a nuisance, but it had been worth it. Arnold played, with two pencils, the 'K & K' (Koenig and Kaiserlicher March).

After the second round I fell in, and we had a really grand finale.

Applause.

Interval.

We went to admire the presents whilst we were waiting to join something like a reception line to wish Grandmother happy birthday. Everybody, but everybody, was there – even cousins of the third degree. 'And who are you?' they asked. 'How nice to see girls in white aprons, one does not see if often enough nowadays.' 'More flowers.' 'Another telegram, put it over there with the others.' 'Ouch!' – an elderly gentleman had pinched me on the cheek.

Now it was my turn. 'Many happy returns, Grandmother.'

'Not too many, I hope.' She raised her eyebrows. 'Thank you.'

Oh dear, I had said the wrong thing again, as usual.

But Grandmother smiled. 'Wait, don't go away – I have not thanked you yet for the shawl. I have always wanted one just like that, not too heavy.'

She seemed so genuinely pleased that I felt guilty about my mean thoughts. And she was right. It was a shawl – too short to be called a stole.

'I'm so glad you like it, Grandmother.'

She was sitting on a small settee which had been produced especially for the occasion.

She looked different. What was it? Her hair looked whiter. She wore an elegant floor-length lace dress, black over grey; she wore her diamonds, a sort of choker like old ladies wear – no, it was not that. It was her face. She was smiling. I had seen her amused before, but smiling? Not actually smiling.

Uncle Daniel's sons, Herman and Walter, had promised to help me. They shooed the guests out of the salon, which took some doing. Then they arranged the chairs for us, in rows, in front of the double doors of the salon; these folding doors did duty as a 'curtain'. Inside we had stretched sheets on string to make a small stage.

The play was called *The Suitcase Exchange in Error*. It had been a joint effort and had been 'written' by the whole cast. It was a story of opposites.

An actress and her manservant travel to the mountains to escape civilisation, 'before they go mad', they say. In the same compartment travels a farmer, who is returning from a conference about fertilisers. They pick up by mistake the wrong suitcase, because the two are identical. The mistake is not discovered until they start to unpack – the farmer at home and the actress at the Hotel Alpenwiese.

The contents of the cases vary greatly.

The farmer's wife is shocked when she finds the frilly underwear. She reads aloud a love letter which has been composed in most romantic terms. The farmer protests his innocence.

The actress and her effeminate servant unpack the farmer's suitcase. They are also convinced that the case is their own. It is too late. They are paying the penalty of civilisation, of the unnatural life of the city. They realise they must have gone crazy, because wherever they look is fertiliser or manure. The case is filled with samples of fertiliser or manure. There are pamphlets and books about manure; everything has turned into manure. They also find a single woolly hand-knitted sock.

We were all on the stage at the same time, unpacking the cases and commenting alternately.

As we were short of boys in the family and we didn't want outsiders, Arnold took four parts. For instance, when, as the ticket collector, he reported the respective losses to the policeman, he wore the collector's cap. Then he took it off and put on the helmet, and answered as the policeman. This had been my idea. The argument between the doctor and the lawyer drew a lot of laughs.

There was polite, embarrassed laughter from the front row, where Grandmother and the ladies from her Ladies Circle sat. The second row, the parents, were apprehensive, but the back rows, the younger members of the family, the third cousins and the servants, found our play hilariously funny.

It all ended well with the help of the policeman, the ticket collector, the doctor of the lunatic asylum and the lawyer. Arnold called them his 'character studies'.

The general verdict was: 'How strange children are nowadays,' though to our faces they called us budding playwrights.

Mother commented that the play was hardly suitable for the occasion. Father said he had enjoyed it, and that there was more to it than met the eye. Herman and Walter were laughing quite loudly. They were heard to say, 'It's hilarious, this play about "shit".' And, 'Fancy that, the children wrote it all by themselves.' Some of Grandmother's lady circle friends seemed embarrassed.

After having been thanked and congratulated, we went to the dining room for our well-earned tea. It was a good spread, worthy of the occasion. 'Good children start with bread and butter.' They had not forgotten this one. Several small plates with bread and butter stood on the table.

The centrepiece was the, by now traditional, meringue and whipped cream gateau, the speciality of the Patisserie Bliederhauser, decorated with two small doves. They also did storks, horseshoes, and sugar roses. Grandmother always ordered doves.

Hannah, as the eldest (she was fourteen) was in charge. Nannies had not been invited as the children had come with their parents.

'I'm not going to eat bread and butter,' said Eva, Hannah's younger sister who sat next to me. 'I can eat that at home. Not unless I get sausage with it. I am going to ask for sausage.'

'You wouldn't dare.' I was astonished. My mother belonged to the 'Children-take-what-they-get' school. 'It's not polite.'

'Shut up. You are a young green vegetable (*légume verte*). I wouldn't dare? I'll show you.' She rang the bell.

'Sausage, please,' she said to the maid. This maid had been loaned for the occasion by Lila's mother. It was customary to borrow extra help from relatives for parties. 'If there is no sausage, ham will do.'

The maid returned with a large plate of assorted sausage. 'If you want anything, just ring. Don't come out in the kitchen, for goodness' sake. It's like a railway station out there.'

Eva smirked. 'See.'

I retorted, 'If it had been our Liesel all you would have got is a telling off.'

When we had eaten our way through the éclairs, cakes, fruit flans and jellies, Hannah started to cut the meringue gateau. She handed to Eva the piece with the doves on it.

I tried to snatch it. 'Not fair,' I snorted. 'Arthur's children (as the children of Uncle Arthur were generally referred to), had the doves last year. Now it is the turn of Julius's children.'

'What about guests?' asked Ette Duisberg. 'My mother says "guests come first".'

'This is a family matter. Don't you mix in.'

Eva quickly got up to collect the doves from Hannah, but in her hurry, she knocked over her glass of raspberry juice. It made a huge stain on her dress.

'That serves you right,' I said with glee. 'You should have worn a white apron. Why didn't you wear a white apron? I'm sure Wanda rung you as well.'

'My mother said "white aprons are piffle – what's the good of white aprons? They show every spot. It's different for you – you're a young green vegetable, you need it."'

'Need it yourself,' I picked up her skirt. 'Look, who needs an apron now?'

'Don't touch me.' She pushed me away. I pushed back. In no time at all we had a good fight going, all the children participating except Lila and Richard.

Richard had been waiting for an opportunity to try out the possibilities of the slippery parquet floor. Judging by his delighted shrieks of 'Whee!', it was satisfactory. He was the youngest, then six years old. Indeed, he could have fought with Erwin, Eva's younger brother, who was nine. He was about to charge him when Susan pushed him away shouting, 'Erwin is mine.' Richard often challenged older boys. He was very strong and a cut knee or open lip meant nothing to him.

Susan had a love-hate relationship with Erwin. Ever since they had been toddlers they had played together; they had hit each other, cried, kissed and made up. They were going to marry each other – in our true family tradition of cousin marrying cousin.

Cousin Lila was a well-brought up child, a little 'goody goody'. I was not surprised to see her sitting in the far corner of the room on a rug chest. She was absorbed in the study of the decoration, a battle of the Huns, ivory inlaid in dark wood.

Lila's maid came running in. 'The noise, please, the noise,' she moaned. She stood at the door, wringing her hands.

No-one took the slightest notice of her. So she went out, returning with Fraulein Wanda.

'Children, will you be quiet, at once?' called Wanda and clapped her hands energetically.

We looked up and then continued fighting. The opportunity was too rare – what a joy: Arthur's children versus Julius's. Ette sided with Arthur's – Hannah was her bosom pal – and Erica, who was wearing a white apron, with us.

Meanwhile Wanda had returned with reinforcements, the grown-up sons of Uncle David. They had been away to university studying and Herman was now a 'Herr Doctor'.

'Herr Doctor,' said Wanda, addressing him with his brand new title, 'see what you can do with them – they won't listen to me.' She disappeared.

Walter closed the door. 'Children,' he boomed, 'go on, kill yourselves, I'd like to see some broken heads.'

Herman started to laugh. Then both of them laughed and laughed. When they had finished laughing they separated us.

I could never tell them apart, they looked so much alike. Was it Herman or Walter who wore the glasses? I couldn't remember. They were both six feet two inches tall and very heavily built.

'Look at you,' Walter said to me. 'Shame on you. Your pretty apron is all torn.' He tried to look stern.

I glared at him. 'I don't care.'

He patted me on the shoulder in a patronising manner and said, 'You girls are all alike – Rita was just the same when she was told to wear an apron.'

'How is Rita?' I asked politely. After all it was not Walter's fault I had to wear an apron. 'Why did she not come home on holiday?'

'She spent the Easter holidays with Ellen's family in Karlsruhe. They only had ten days – she's gone back to Montreux for another year. To perfect her French. The second year is a secretarial course.'

Rita had been away in finishing school in Switzerland. Ellen was her room mate. I had met Ellen once. She wore orange-coloured lipstick and rather more than was permissible in our town. She was very attractive, so everybody said. I projected onto her an air of sad mystery. Rita was an orphan. Both her parents had died in an aeroplane crash in the twenties, a time when almost nobody travelled by air. It was in all the papers. It was a pity it had not been a Zeppelin crash – that would have been even more interesting. She would have been famous then. Ever since the accident she had lived at Uncle David's; he was her guardian.

Herman let out a whistle, loud and long – it was a beauty. When all was quiet he made an announcement. 'Arthur's children go to the cloakroom now to tidy up. And when they've finished, Julius's go. After that we play ball in the garden. March!'

Meanwhile Herman and Walter had picked up the plate with the doves and put it high up on the ledge alongside the pewter.

They supervised our game for a while, just to make sure we would not start fighting again.

It was exceptionally warm for May. They served our ice-cream in the garden.

Then it was time to go home.

'No-one got the doves, after all,' I said to Arnold, whilst we were putting our coats on.

'We'll see about that,' he whispered. 'You watch.'

We tip-toed, hand in hand, back to the dining room. And there the doves were, still sitting on the ledge, too high to reach.

'I'll fix you, ye doves of peace.' Arnold took his sling out of his pocket. A perfect shot. He got both of them. It made a lovely mess.

Chapter 16

An Unusual Piece of Soap

Mother usually asked us after we had finished our lunch, 'And how was school today?'

I always said, 'All right, thank you.' I felt a polite question deserved a polite answer. If I had let on that I was given lines to do, mostly for inattention, Mother would have given me some more on top of them. Mother had been educated in a Convent School, where she had received prizes for good behaviour – Grandmother had shown them to me on our last visit to Camberg – I would never get any of those. Yes, it was better to keep quiet about certain things.

'Nothing ever happens in your class?' Mother asked.

'Nothing which would interest you. In French today when Dr Kocher asked Ella Straub to tell the story in her own words – you know, a summary – she couldn't do it. She'd learned the paragraph by heart and rattled it off. "No, no, in your own words, you are not a parrot. Can you tell the story in German at least?" he asked her. She hadn't a clue. I think she ought to repeat the class, the time we waste on Straub.'

'You don't like her much, do you?' Mother asked.

'No, I don't. One can't like everybody.' I didn't want to tell Mother that Straub was another one to turn up in Nazi uniform; we had several now in our class. It annoyed me, that's all, but Mother took things like that seriously. Dr Kocher had suggested that Straub should be coached, but Ella had answered aggressively that she had no time, with three times a week duty in the *Jung Maedels*. Better keep quiet, I said to myself. What about Mr Vetter? You must tell about that; it might happen to Susan as well. So I decided to tell the Vetter episode.

125

'I was a bit late this morning – not in school, I just made it before the bell. You know, it's quicker if I cut through Mr Vetter's yard. He was standing in front of his door; he called me over. I waved and I was going to run on. He shouted, "Come over here, you." So I stopped. He shouted, "Can't you read?" I had no idea what he was getting at. "Of course, Mr Vetter, I can read." "Then read that!" He pointed to the board in his yard: KEEP OUT. PRIVATE. BY ORDER. "Keep out. Yes, Mr Vetter, I'll keep out." He was really nasty.'

Arnold chuckled. He seemed highly amused.

'It's not funny.' I was furious. It was no laughing matter.

'I'm not laughing about you,' he said. 'Don't you know he manufactures Swastika soap now?'

'No. Swastika soap, what's that?'

'Soap with the Swastika on it. Ha, ha, ha. It's inlaid – Swastika to the last piece. Perhaps it's for washing after you have committed crimes in the name of the party.'

'Daddy, did you know that too?'

'Yes.'

'You never told me. I would not have gone near his damn place.'

'No need for swearing.'

'You should have told me. You should have told all of us.'

'My dear child,' said Father, 'we have so many Nazis now, where should I start? They'll get over it – they'll come to their senses. It's just a phase.'

Arnold said, 'I've looked in the chemist's window to see if they displayed a piece of the soap. Nobody seems to. Perhaps they are afraid the Communists will bash the window in.'

I changed my mind about keeping quiet now we were talking about it. 'Several girls in our class come in everyday in the brown uniform; it's hateful. Fahner started it, and Fahner is the worst.'

'Fahner?' Father inquired. 'Fahner. There are not many Fahners here – only one as far as I know. What does her father do?'

'He's an Inspector – on the Council.'

'Same one, then. Well, well. He is married to a Levi from Esslingen. Glove manufacturers, the Levis.'

'Had a good dowry that Levi girl,' said Mother, 'so I'm told.'

'You mean her mother is Jewish?'

'Yes.'

'Does she know? Surely she can't. But why do they let her go to the *Jung Maedels*?' I was stumped. Big mouth Trudi Fahner, an *Mischling* [of mixed blood] – that's what the Nazis called it.

'Why don't you ask her?' suggested Mother. 'Next time she opens her mouth about the Jews.'

I knew that I never would. I would not tell her that she was an Mischling, if she didn't know. Let someone else tell her.

I did tell Lila what I had found out. She was still sharing the bench with Trudi Fahner and I challenged her about this. She told me she would rather wait till next term than make a fuss now. To change one's seat a teacher's permission was required. One had to give an explanation – it would draw attention to oneself.

I liked to keep in the background now. No longer did I have a 'camp', no longer did I 'protect' the girls from Teach's wrath – it was not necessary because he seldom lost his temper now.

He's getting mild in his old age, was the opinion of some girls. 'He's scared,' said others.

*   *   *

I declined the honour to be the Fox at the paperchase. Paperchase was most popular on sports afternoon. The girls voted me Fox because I knew every hiding place in the woods. I did not offer to arrange the plays for speech days. So it was arranged through the Party. Instead of Beethoven or Schubert, we sang Die Fahne Hoch and the Horst Wessel Lied (two Nazi songs). I learned to keep my mouth shut; that was very important now. Nobody dared to say what they thought – so much appeared to be wrong and upside down. Gone were the aesthetic values of the Weimar Republic – the Third Reich was much grander. The ruffians who died in the Munich putch were declared 'national heroes'. The new Bible, *Mein Kampf*, had grammatical errors – I had seen an early edition; the later ones were tidied up. I could not imagine that intelligent people would fall for that. Arnold said to me, 'You've answered it; you said *intelligent* people.'

I was glad, I told myself, of the extra time I had now. The time could be put to better use than arranging silly things, silly childish things. I knew I was no longer a child. But did the others know it too? I believe some did. I was given adult books to read. I read every available minute. It was an escape. It was a drug. I needed it.

I was very unhappy at that time – everything went wrong. I was twelve and my eyes were opened.

127

My father was no longer a God, his judgement no longer infallible; I could now see Mother's point of view as well.

She was justified in many of her complaints and she was right when she called Father an ostrich. What Father did not wish to hear, he did not hear. I had seen, on more than one occasion, that Father put letters in the drawer of his desk – unopened. Mother said he should have sold the factory a long time ago. The factory was an institution – many people depended on it for their daily bread – so it ran at a loss. Father, most reluctantly, cut down on staff. Fewer shops stocked Jewish goods; shops who had been supplied by us since about 1870 cancelled orders.

Property was sold from time to time.

It was not only property which was sold. One day we discovered that the stable was empty. Karl explained that Fanny and Prince had recently been sold. No, he did not know who had bought them. One morning on my way to school I met Prince. He had become a coal-horse. Prince, the aristocrat, no longer with yellow socks around his ankles, a coal-horse! Admittedly the cart was small. It belonged to a not very prosperous coal-merchant, who was sitting on the box seat. I talked to Prince quietly, so that the man should not hear us.

'Giddy-up, giddy-up.' Prince shook his head. The coal-merchant became impatient. He cracked his whip. 'Giddy-up.'

After this meeting I carried lumps of sugar in my pocket, always hoping to meet Prince. I never did.

Bills were not settled punctually. Ssh, not in front of the children. One does not talk about money. To talk about money is vulgar.

Mother stressed at every opportunity the need to economise. She set a good example. She stopped her daily long-distance telephone calls to her parents, waiting until they phoned her, which after a while they did every day. She studied her housekeeping accounts, comparing the price of certain foods at different times of the year. At parties I was allowed to help with the preparation and with the drying of the dishes, whereas previously we had had extra staff for the occasion. We had less regular staff. We children were required to run the errands and to go for the 'Sauerwasser' [mineral water]. There were three natural springs near the town, an important source of local revenue, as the water was bottled and sold for its medicinal properties. It was free for local inhabitants. Schoolboys took on the job as 'Sauerwasser boys' in order to earn their weekly pocket money. It was a bore to push the small cart, specially constructed with compartments to hold the quart bottles with spring clips. We did not dare complain; in fact, we felt we earned our pocket money now. I helped with the monthly laundry, mostly ironing and folding, as we now had only one washerwoman, and one ironing woman, instead of two of each.

Mother believed that much money was saved in this way.

I was worried by all this talk of economy and tried to find out what was happening. My parents made me feel that my questions were quite improper and out of place.

I learned to keep my mouth shut. Father had been angry when I had asked him some questions about the factory and when I heard that the land was up for sale. He told me that was no concern of children.

I wished Mother would see that I sympathised with her often. I was sorry for the annoyance I had caused her on so many previous occasions. She had always said I was 'contrary' or that I 'never listened'. Life was not easy for her. And when I had formerly blamed her for all the quarrels my parents had, I came to realise that their incompatibility was caused mainly by their different views on life, and it was Father who had changed.

Mother had never been accepted properly by Father's family. They made derogatory remarks about her – quite openly – and then Mother, rightly or wrongly, held Father responsible. She flew into a rage and quarrelled and Father left the room, slamming the door.

My wonderful Father, whom I still admired as much as before, had feet of clay.

I grieved because I could talk to him no more – he was distant, removed. Sometimes he accepted my help with the chores of the laboratory, like sterilising bottles or running errands, but more often he declined, saying he preferred to be alone, that he had special work to do.

I tried to keep out of Mother's way, for she seemed to dislike me on sight: nothing I did pleased her, and I tried hard to please her. I'd steal away then and cry with self-pity.

When she was irritated with me over some trifle, she would remark frequently how much I was getting like my grandmother. 'You hold your head like her.' 'You look like her.' I learned to keep my mouth shut. I conquered my desire to answer back – one

129

of my faults – but my stony silence and the martyred air I put on when I thought I had been wronged infuriated her more than any of my cheeky answers had done. She slapped my face. There I stood, a good bit taller than she was; I said nothing, I did not move. The silence put her ill at ease and sometimes she became slightly hysterical.

Consoling myself with daydreaming and reading, I looked forward to the time when I would be old enough to leave home.

I developed a mania for books. Usually I read until three in the morning, although the rule was lights out at 10.30. I read with a torch under my bedclothes, until my parents retired. My complexion grew pale, almost green; I lost my appetite. The medical comments about my condition – puberty, growing pains – were very interesting. 'If only you knew,' I thought, 'you wouldn't be so kind.' I felt awful, a fraud, especially when Mother went out of her way to tempt me with special foods. However, it did not stop my reading. I was hungry for words, devouring any book, but preferably good ones.

Lion Feuchtwanger's *Success* made a great impression on me; he had caught the atmosphere of a community similar to ours. I knew people almost like the characters he portrayed. I was impressed by the girl, Joanna – by her courage, which enabled her to take from life what she wanted.

It made me smile when I remembered that my mother had told me, 'Never let a man touch you nearer than the elbow.' I did not condemn her as old-fashioned, just thought there were different kinds of women. In the good books, when the heroine loved, she loved, whilst in women's magazines only the wicked girls tempted upright young men and made them stray from the straight and narrow path. Of course, in the end, the young men settled down with someone whom one did not touch nearer than the elbow, and lived happily ever after.

Jacob Wassermans' *Joseph Kerkhofen*, which described a transference of power, also made a great impression on me. I read H.G. Wells' *A Short History of the Universe*, and I thought he must be the cleverest man alive to know so much. I read Tolstoi's fairytales and I loved him for writing the one about the shoemaker-angel. And then I hated him for disappointing me with books like *Anna Karenina* and *The Kreutzer Sonata*. He was pure in the fairytales.

My judgement was ruthless, negative and fanatical; in adolescence one does not know compromise. Galsworthy, I considered superficial, Warwick Deeping's *Sorrel and Son* – which was a bestseller at that time in Germany – sentimental.

I liked Gottfried Keller and Hoelderlin. Hoelderlin's Tower, where he was kept during his madness had been pointed out to us on excursions. To live in a tower right by the river Neckar, to see the reflection of the bridge and the willow trees in the clear, clear mountain water, and not to see it because one is mad? The handsome young Hoelderlin was a romantic figure. We assumed he went mad because of his unrequited love for Suzette, his Jewish employer's wife. Schiller, who was revered as a local deity, bored me: we had to recite in school '*Die Glocke*' (The Bell), till the bim-bam-bums grew out of our ears. Even Goethe meant nothing to me. Father had an early edition which he treasured, and if Father liked it, it must be good. I felt perhaps I was too young for Goethe. I also did not understand Shakespeare and thought *Hamlet* consisted of an awful lot of murders and ghosts, like any other grisly paperback.

I never lost my love for Wilhelm Busch. What can I call him? A cartoonist? Though, when I was older, I no longer appreciated him. Grimm's *Fairy Tales* were a treasure and Hans Andersen's *Little Mermaid* moved me to tears every time.

Robinson Crusoe had been a favourite of mine since I was a small child. I often pondered over what I would do if stranded on an island. What are the essentials for survival? In the encyclopaedia I looked up the poisonous tropical plants because I was amazed that Robinson Crusoe never had the slightest stomach ache from the plants and fruits he ate. I tried rubbing pieces of dry wood to make a fire but it never worked and I decided that this method must be a myth; it occurred to me that a magnifying glass would be more useful. It was doubtful if I would be able to salvage so many helpful things – for instance, he had enough gunpowder to last him for twenty-eight years!

One had to read Karl Marx. Everybody apparently had read *Das Kapital*. It cropped up so often in conversation. Dutifully I went to our library and took away this rather large book. I could not get on with it at all and, after a brief struggle, I put it back again. The print was too small: it tired me and the dry way in which the people were represented, emerging as numbers, hordes, multitudes, called 'The Exploited Proletariat', took the personal angle away. Should I feel sorry, or guilty?

It was almost a kind of Jewish 'patriotism' which made me borrow the works of Jewish authors – we did not have many of the modern ones, apart from those belonging to Arnold. I enjoyed them: Stephen and Arnold Zweig, Franz Werfel and Max Brod, Thomas Mann and his brother Heinrich. I tried Martin Buber, but could not understand him. I found him obscure and was relieved that Arnold shared my point of view. At school we had 'done' Heinrich Heine – and anything we had 'done' was done to death. This was before the Nazis banned his books. We had to stick paper over his poems in the school anthology. In the later edition, *Lorelei* was described 'traditional'. Still, my favourite book was Lion Feuchtwanger's *Success*.

The Nazis not only banned the books, they deprived the Jewish writers of their German nationality, making them stateless. This meant they could not travel, as some countries refused entry to 'stateless' persons.

In an effort to understand my Father, I started to read medical books. I picked the illustrated ones; still it was difficult. But it improved my knowledge of biology, if nothing else. There were books on mysticism, on spiritual healing, herbs, and on Mazdaznan on the shelves; unknown to Father, I tried to read them. It made me feel good to read them, but though I had understood the words, I rarely grasped the meaning. Reading passages through again and again helped sometimes. I could not ask Father; I did not dare. I was afraid he might be annoyed with me for reading his books without his permission, or he might say 'not for children'.

There was much I did not understand – Radiestesia for instance. I was sceptical. How strong was the conscious or the subconscious influence? I knew Father to be scrupulously honest, and I trusted him. His control over the life force – was that the 'prana' mentioned in the book? Someone had told me that Father gave Absent Healing. Was this connected with the Magnetic Healing he practised? He had treated me on several occasions. Some of his strokes – he did not touch me – were warm, some cold. I could feel how it affected the blood circulation and I felt better for it. I did not *imagine* that I felt better; there was a sense of well being, a glow. I doubted if it had been suggestion. Was it love? Perhaps it was a kind of love.

Father never touched people. His hands always remained about five centimetres above the skin, the air varying from hot or cold. One could feel one's blood pulsing. He was never wrong in his diagnosis: he could see the organs, even before the illness had manifested itself physically.

But he never knew that I read half the night, or if he did, he never let on. He was aware that I was unhappy and that I suffered from the misunderstandings I had with Mother. He arranged for me, after a bad row, to live for a while at Aunt Paula's. I was invited to keep her daughter, Erica, company – Mother accepted and I stayed with them for several weeks. It widened the gulf between Mother and me. And, as I shared a room with Erica, I had to stop reading at twelve o'clock; that's when Erica stopped. I did not share her taste in books; she was fond of stories for young girls, an unexpected contrast to her looks and personality, for she looked and walked like a boy. The rest did me good, as well as the absence of tension. When I returned home, there was peace for some time between Mother and me.

*　　*　　*

One afternoon I met Olaf von Muende, the retired Captain, in the street. We children used to call him Uncle Olaf. I had not seen him for a long time, so I called across the road. He did not hear me, which was not surprising as he was quite deaf in one ear, an injury from the war. I caught up with him and he rather absentmindedly greeted me. I asked him if he was giving some lectures on 'breathing'. If so, I'd like to go. Was he coming to see us? I was sure Mother would be pleased to have him for dinner.

He told me he was on a flying visit, and he was pushed for time. I was surprised when he mentioned that he had booked into the Hotel Turkei, a commercial hotel, for the night.

I could see he wanted to be on his way. Father told me that he admired Uncle Olaf for the work he had organised after his dismissal from the Wehrmacht. The Wehrmacht had practically been dissolved; professional soldiers were not needed any longer, and work was now hard to get.

He had started a self-help programme for the men formerly under his command, under his supervision. He had been a qualified engineer before joining the army. They built their own houses – not only that, but the roads, sewers, and the electrical work needed.

133

There were even allotments for later on, to grow your own vegetables. Von Muende was very keen on vegetables properly grown without 'poisonous additions'. He used his lecture tours to encourage people to donate funds for this very worthwhile undertaking.

In former years, he had stayed in the 'Hotel Fleischer', sometimes for as long as two weeks. He got on particularly well with Father, but he also had great charm, and Mother liked him – most ladies liked him, but he insisted that I was his sweetheart. I was his sweetheart until I was too old to sit on his lap, and then I was his dearest friend.

'Why is he staying in the Turkei, Mummy? There are other hotels?'

'It's reasonable and very central,' answered Mother.

'He has not given any lectures for a long time. Do you know why?'

'Your Father has not arranged any for him, I suppose that's the reason... His sales must have dropped since the Misses Sanftmuth don't stock his lines any more.'

'I was wondering why you sent to the Reformhaus [the other Health Food stores in the town], for the Grunella.'

'No, I don't think he'll ever sell another grain of Grunella to the Sanftmuths.' Mother smiled.

Then I remembered something. 'Is it because he did not see Miss Bella home after the lecture?' Miss Bella had been offended because the Captain had accompanied a young lady, a pretty redhead, who lived in Charles Street.

I had thought it very wrong of Uncle Olaf – after all, old age comes first. He should have seen the old lady home first, and after that the young lady – and the first opportunity I had, I told him that. He had been most amused and bought me a bar of raisin and nut chocolate made with pure cane sugar – he was particular about food. Charles Street ... I remember Mrs Koester telling me, 'Respectable people don't live there.' I did not mention that to Uncle Olaf; his friend was surely most respectable.

'Well, it's something like it,' answered Mother.

'Mummy, do tell me. I want to know. Why don't they buy from him any more?'

'All right then. It's no secret – probably the whole town knows, she's told enough people. You know him – *kuess die Hand, gnaedige Frau*, and so on. It does not mean anything; it's his way of being

134

polite. When your Father resigned from the Kneipp Verein – after that Nazi from Berlin had given his lecture, the one who talked the nonsense about pure race, and Jews ... ironically it was your Father who had arranged the lecture... Coming back to what I was saying, von Muende thought it would be better if he did not accept our hospitality, quite rightly, so he stayed with the Misses Sanftmuth for a couple of days. I'm absolutely certain he did no more than kiss her hand. Well, it was enough for Miss Bella. She considered herself engaged.'

'What! She must be crazy!' I could understand her falling for him. He was a handsome man: tall with a touch of the military, without the heel kicking.

Mother continued. 'Without the lectures, it's most probably not worth his while to stay long. Hotels are expensive.'

'Not the Hotel Fleischer.'

'He was very welcome – a nice man, a friend of your Father's.'

However, the nice man, the friend of my Father, did not even telephone; he was in a hurry.

Chapter 17

Lebensraum

'Mummy, do you think I could take the lace, the one from the lace drawer, to school?'

'Whatever for?'

'I told Miss Hertzler [our handicraft mistress], that you had a whole drawer full of handmade lace. She was interested and asked me to bring it along to school – of course, only if you'll permit it. Do let me take it, please, Mummy.'

I could see Mother was not very pleased with the idea. 'Ask your Father,' she said. 'It's his lace, anyway.'

I had as good as promised in school that I would bring it. It would be awful if I had to own up in front of the whole class that my Mother had refused permission. When we had finished supper, I addressed my father: 'Mother says I have to ask you if I can take your lace to school, to show the class. Please.'

'Why do you want to take it?'

'Miss Hertzler was telling us about the lace they make in the Sudetenland, the *Kloeppel Spitze* [Bobbin lace]. She showed us some photos in a book, but one could hardly see anything, so I said we had lots of lace at home. She asked me to bring it along. Please let me, Daddy.'

'I don't think it will do any harm – I am sure Sylvia will take good care of it. What do you think, Irma?'

'It's your lace, don't ask me.'

Father was taking pieces of blue paper out of the drawer. The lace was tacked onto it. There were collars, jabots, lappets and cuffs, small mats, cloths and runners. There was also a box of motifs and lace wound on cards, mostly Valenciennes. He pointed to a coarse lace, made in a thread which looked like linen. 'This is a Torchon, though not from the Sudetenland, and this one here, same family, comes from Malta. This one here, from Belgium, is more complicated but still a cousin of the bobbin lace. Why are you so interested in bobbin lace? Do you want to learn to make it?'

'Oh, no, I would not have the patience. They have been telling us in school about the poor people in the Sudetenland, and that the women make that lace so that they should not starve.'

'So! Is that what they are telling you in school? They have been making lace for a long time, perhaps hundreds of years. It's their native industry. A cheap lace, used mostly on pillowcases and around tableclothes, look, similar to this one.' Father showed me a narrow trimming. 'We used this one on corsets in your great-grandfather's day, also these motifs. Corsets were then made to last; they were much more expensive in those days. Remind me to show you our collection in the factory. The old corsets were part of the dress; a lady could receive in her boudoir dressed in a corset and skirt.'

I picked out a beautiful piece, a collar.

'*Point de Venice*, a precious lace. This collar is very old – possibly eighteenth century. It was said that the lacemakers were paid with the amount of silver pieces which could be laid on the work and in the case of an extra fine piece with gold ducats. Lace was frequently made in convents and by the aristocracy. It was so costly in olden days that it was often smuggled from one country to the next.'

There were several examples half finished. One could see how it was made. It was tacked on coloured linen, with the design drawn in white ink. I found this most interesting.

Father advised me to look at some books in the library. I took the books to school as well.

Miss Hertzler displayed only the simple pieces. I was disappointed. She said the Maltese was Sudetenland lace. I did not dare correct her. She mentioned again the poverty of the Germans in the Sudetenland and how essential it was for these brave women to supplement the meagre income of their husbands. 'Yes,' she said, 'the Germans outside Germany have a raw deal.'

*   *   *

Our teachers often talked about the colonies Germany had lost after World War I. Everybody had colonies: the English, the French, the Belgians. Not only did Germany have no colonies, but our German brothers had to live oppressed in places like the Sudetenland and Siebenbuergen in Hungary. Did we know that the people there were German, spoke German, in fact knew no other language? '*Lebensraum*', as they called it, was discussed in geography and in history extensively.

One day, during our French lesson, there was a knock at the door. A pupil from Dr Tiefelbein's class, which was next door to ours, brought a large, rolled-up map.

Dr Kocher hung it up over the blackboard. He continued with the lesson.

I looked at the map. It was an old one of Czechoslovakia, called Bohemia on the map. All the towns had German names. I speculated as to what the connection between Bohemia and our French lesson might be. The only thing which came to my mind was the Carolingian Empire.

Then there was another knock. Dr Tiefelbein entered, together with a short, thick-set man. He introduced him as Herr Schultze, our friend from the Sudetenland. 'He has something to tell you, girls.'

Herr Schultze explained to us, pointing to the map, that Bohemia (or the Sudetenland) had always been German. How hard it was for the people there under the tyranny of their Czech masters! He told us of a man, a family father of seven – and all his children still of school-age – who had lost his job because he spoke only German, a job which he had held for years, a job his father had held before him. *Arbeitslos* (unemployed), that dreaded word – unemployed for months and his children starving! This was one case out of many.

In the schools, too, it was forbidden to speak German. Forbidden! 'And German is the mother-tongue of those poor children. Girls like you!'

Herr Schultze wrote something on the blackboard. 'This is Czech – listen carefully.'

It sounded very strange.

'Now you read it,' he called on a girl sitting in the front row. 'No good.'

Herr Schultze called on the next girl and the next one.

'You must try harder,' he shouted. 'You are not trying.'

'I am trying, I'm sorry, Herr Schultze, I... '

'Do you know what would happen to you if were a Sudetendeutches kind?' A whip swished through the air, again and again. 'This is what would happen to you. You're lucky you are here in Germany in the Fatherland, safe in the Fatherland.'

It was truly terrifying. I was sure I could not learn this difficult language.

'And now,' Herr Schultze continued, 'I want to show something of the work of our people, our brave people, who continue to struggle so heroically.'

He went to the door and helped an elderly man to carry a table in. 'Girls, come out here and watch carefully.'

The man was a glass-blower. He demonstrated his art whilst Herr Schultze explained. First he drew a big, coloured bubble, then a long-stemmed glass, several animals, then another glass which looked as if it was filled with red wine.

'A joke,' laughed Herr Schultze. 'Ha, ha, ha!'

He nodded encouragement. We all laughed. He made a sign. The glassblower went outside. Dr Koecher took the map down and sent it to the class next door. Herr Schultze arranged the glass novelties lovingly on teacher's desk.

'Girls,' he said, 'this man has been unemployed for a long time. His only crime is that he is German, Sudeten German. I am sure you'll want to help all you can. We must help people like him and, of course, the children. Which of you will collect for the poor, starving children?'

I eagerly put my hand up.

Herr Schultze surveyed us. 'In the back there, you don't want to help?' He looked hurt.

When all the hands were up, he gave the collection forms out. 'And whoever collects the most can have one of these as a memento. Six wonderful prizes for helping our friends. Heil Hitler!'

Already on my way home I collected several subscriptions. When I asked Mother for a contribution, she said, 'Certainly not. They are all Nazis.'

In vain I tried to explain to her that it was for the starving children and the glass-blower. In the end I subscribed to it myself, half my weekly pocket money.

In school they counted the number of subscriptions not the amount of money. I received fourth prize, the glass with the red wine attached, not the crocodile I had hoped for.

Chapter 18

Why I Stole

A few weeks later, Herr Schultze returned. This time the Headmaster accompanied him on his round of the classes. He read us a letter of thanks which he said he had just received from a child living in the Sudetenland. It brought tears to the eyes of several girls.

'You have been magnificent,' exclaimed Herr Schultze. 'Your whole town has been magnificent.'

We clapped.

'With your Headmaster's kind permission we are planning to put a play on, to be staged at the Liederhalle. The proceeds are to go to our noble cause. We are getting a producer from the Hof Theater to rehearse you; also a mistress of the Ballet School, specially from Stuttgart.'

There was much guessing as to who would be chosen to act in the play.

The solution was simple; because the Liederhalle was hired out in the evenings, rehearsals had to be during school hours. Our Head announced he would allow only girls with good marks to miss lessons.

I was overjoyed. To act on a real stage – I had always longed for that!

We lined up in the big, empty hall. It looked miserable, all bare wooden boards. When I had been inside this hall before, it had been bright with lights, tables covered with white cloths and decorated with masses of flowers.

The boys lined up opposite us.

Herr Schultze and the producer walked up and down looking us over. They stopped at a tall girl, spoke to her and patted her on the shoulder. She curtsied.

Then they stopped in front of me.

'What is your name?'

'Sylvia Fleischer.'

'Now, Sylvia, listen to me. Imagine it is winter. Snow outside, thick, thick snow. You have a step-brother. You don't like him. You order him to go out into that snow to pick strawberries for you. You tell him he cannot come back until he has filled a basket full. You're hoping that he's freezing to death. Sylvia, could you play a girl like this?'

'No, Sir, I couldn't. I'm not like that!'

'Never mind.' The producer shrugged his shoulders. 'You can play a fairy instead.'

I was so sorry for the step-brother that I quite forgot to curtsey. Little did I know then that I had turned down one of the leading parts in this fairytale, which turned out to be an 'improved' version of Grimm.

The Ballet Mistress took us in hand. It was all very simple.

Arnold said Schultze had picked on me because I was blond and blue eyed. This was quite rare in our schools, where the population was mainly Celtic.

Hop and down, and jump and down, glide around and once again. 'Graceful, girls. Remember that you are fairies, not kangaroos.'

I was the seventh fairy.

Each actor was expected to sell tickets. They were not numbered but there were three kinds. The red tickets, which were for the back of the hall were the cheapest, the blue ones were for the middle, and the white tickets for the red plush armchairs in front. These cost two marks for adults, half price for children, a fortune, I thought. I doubted if I would sell a white ticket.

However, selling tickets was surprisingly easy – the red ones went like hot cakes, my school mates being the best customers. The family bought blue ones. When I was given another batch of red tickets I was reminded that the white ones had to be sold as well.

I must sell some white tickets. I rehearsed what to say on my way home from school.

'Would you like to sit on a red plush armchair, Madam?'

'No? I don't believe you, Madam. The view is far better in front.'

'You're saying you are far-sighted.'

'I'd never have guessed it. I would suggest you wear your reading glasses, Madam.'

'What are you jabbering about, Sylvia?' A girl came up to me. I had not seen her for a long time.

'Hello, Gustel. Was I talking aloud? I'm worried about selling these wretched white tickets; they are so dear – two marks!'

'I saw on the Litfas Column that you're in the play.' There was admiration in her eyes. Gustel had been a classmate in the primary school. We had often walked home together.

Augusta was her proper name. If I was honest with myself, I never really liked Gustel, and I first walked home with her because I did not want to be a snob. Her parents were poor. If they had been rich I could have ignored her.

I was sorry for her because I thought she looked so ugly. She had straight, brown hair, which always got in the way of her nickel-rimmed glasses. These glasses did not fit very well and she was forever taking them off to rub her nose. I was sorry for her because she was so stupid – she could not do the simplest sums.

One day she had told me tearfully that the teacher had written to her parents and suggested that Gustel would benefit from a special school. Her father was furious and had given her a good hiding, saying he was not going to have a daughter who went to the 'idiot's school' – it was sheer laziness.

On the way home I tried to coach her a bit. She was not nervous with me at all. After a while I did not find her so ugly any more.

Her father maintained that the hiding had done her good, as no more letters were received.

Once Gustel's mother invited me for a '*vesper*' (high tea – a meal eaten by the working classes). It had all been very embarrassing. She said I was a good girl helping her Gustel the way I did. She was ever so grateful. There was '*Leberkaes*' (a local sausage speciality – eaten hot). I did not want to be greedy. Besides, I thought, they are very poor and I have no right to eat so much – they might be short. There was dinner waiting for me at home.

When Gustel's mother offered me beer I refused. We were not allowed beer; they said it was bad for children and made them stupid. Gustel drank a whole glass. I wondered if it was the beer which had made Gustel stupid. Gustel's mother appeared hurt by my refusal. She mumbled something about my being used to finer things and went in a huff to the kitchen.

After vesper I suggested we should play for a bit. Gustel's toys were not interesting and she had no games. I did not want to play with her doll; it had lost an eye and this disturbed me. We ended up doing Gustel's homework. I was glad when it was time to go.

Mother remarked that the choice of my friends was surprising when there were so many 'nice' girls in my class.

I could not explain to Mother; she might have thought that I was showing off.

Since I had been going to the Ladies Seminary, I had not spoken to Gustel, though once or twice we had waved to each other across the street.

'Two marks is a lot of money,' she said. 'Why don't you sell them to your rich friends? You know all the rich people. That's what I would do. I wish it was me. Sylvia, can I come with you? I'd love to help you sell tickets, please.'

I was hesitant.

'Come on,' she said, 'be a sport.'

'All right then.' We agreed to meet later. Gustel had to go home to tell her mother where she was going.

I waited for her as arranged, outside my house.

'You're late,' I scowled.

'I had to get washed and changed.'

Gustel's hair had been scraped back tidily and was held in place with a diamante-studded hairslide. She wore a party frock. It was frilly and there were lots of bows on it.

'Why are you wearing a dress like this? Is it your May Day dress?'

'Was. It's old now. I'm getting another one.'

'Couldn't you go home and change?' I was wearing a simple linen dress.

'Whatever for? My mother told me to wear this dress.'

I had drawn up a long list of houses, mostly of people who had children.

At the first house we called, the lady was out.

At the second, they had tickets already.

'Third time lucky,' said Gustel.

Alas, at the third, the maid called over the garden wall that the children had chickenpox and were in quarantine.

At the fourth house we were successful. Two white tickets for child and Nanny, and a red one for the maid.

The spell was broken. We sold and sold. We even rang the bell on houses where I did not know the people at all.

We ran out of blue tickets; a lady let me use her phone to reserve another batch. I was told by headquarters that red was sold out – in fact, everything was nearly sold out.

When I mentioned this in the next house, the lady took the tickets immediately, all white ones.

'Aren't people funny?' I was puzzled. When there was plenty and they had a choice, they wouldn't buy.

Gustel was thoroughly enjoying it. She kept saying with reverence, 'Isn't it marvellous? Those houses, all those carpets, they must all be millionaires.'

'Two more calls, that's all.' I looked at my watch. 'I'll be late otherwise. We must go to old Mrs Bollinger – she's got heaps of grandchildren, seven or eight. She is a sweet old lady. I bet she'll have white.'

'But that's all the way up the hill,' protested Gustel.

'If you're tired, sit down over there on that wall and wait for me.'

'All right then, I'll come along.'

I opened the Bollingers' garden gate – there was a trick to it – to save the maid the long walk down the drive.

Wolf, the Alsatian, ran towards us, barking.

'Wolfy – good boy, don't you remember me?'

The dog barked furiously.

'He's very old,' I explained to Gustel. 'Wolfy, good boy,' I said, advancing.

The dog growled.

Then I noticed that it was not Wolfy at all; it was another dog.

'Don't move,' I whispered to Gustel. The dog padded towards us menacingly, growling, barking. Gustel was frightened and retreated.

'Didn't you hear me? I told you not to move,' I shouted after Gustel as she ran down the drive. The dog went after her.

'Wilhelm, Wilhelm,' I called as loud as I could. I tried to whistle to the dog but I could only produce a feeble noise.

'Wilhelm, Wilhelm!'

Finally, Wilhem the gardener appeared. He called the dog off.

'He's a sharp'un, police trained. Didn't you see the notice on the gate, Miss Sylvia?'

In other circumstances I would have been thrilled if Wilhelm had addressed me as 'Miss'! He must think I am a young lady now, I thought.

We went to fetch Gustel. Wilhelm held the dog by its collar.

'No, Wilhelm, I did not see the notice. Frankly, I wasn't looking. Tell me, what has happened to Wolfy?'

'Was getting old – was sick. Poor dog. Madam had to have him put to sleep.'

'Is Mrs Bollinger at home?'

'Yes. Madam is in the greenhouse, with the cactuses – cacti.'

'He jumped on me, he bit me,' cried Gustel.

'Where? Show me.'

Gustel examined her leg. She couldn't find any mark. 'My dress, my good dress!' she wailed.

We discovered two tiny holes, hardly noticeable.

'Thank goodness for that.'

'They are trained to hold, not to bite,' explained Wilhelm. He patted the dog. 'Good boy, good boy. Friends ... friends.'

'Yes, yes. But do take him away, he makes her nervous. I know the way.'

'Very good, Miss.'

'Who is it, Wilhelm?' called Mrs Bollinger from the greenhouse. She popped her head out. 'Wait on the verandah, girls.'

Mrs Bollinger was wearing a leather apron which must have belonged to the late Mr Bollinger. It almost reached the ground, hampering her walk as she hurried towards us.

'I'm so sorry about the dog. I'm so sorry he scared you.'

'It's my fault, Mrs Bollinger. I shouldn't have opened the gate. I should have rung the bell.'

'Just a minute, girls.'

Mrs Bollinger went inside and returned minus the apron, carrying a large plate of home-made biscuits. 'Help yourself.'

I told Mrs Bollinger about the play and that there were only a few tickets left.

'I certainly will take some, if my daughters have not bought them already. I'll phone them right away.'

Mrs Bollinger took a long time. Gustel was stuffing. I felt uneasy. The plate was almost empty.

'I'll have four tickets please. In front, if you have any left in front. Veronica has bought already.'

I knew she would take white.

We rose.

'Would you like some lemonade?'

'No, thank you,' I answered. 'We must go, we're late.'

'Thank you for calling on me.'

'Thank you.'

Walking down the drive, Gustel said, 'Mrs Bollinger wore an awful dress. It had holes, and it was faded!'

'What did you expect her to wear for gardening, a silk dress?'

'But the Bollingers are stinking rich. How many servants has she?'

'As far as I know, only Maria and Wilhelm.'

'It's a huge house – only two?'

'Most of the rooms are closed.' I knew that. Last year we had been invited to a party for her grandchildren. We had played hide-and-seek because it rained. It had been a good game, much of the furniture being covered with dust sheets.

The enamel plate on the gate said: BEWARE OF DOG. There was a chalk mark next to it.

'See that sign, Gustel?'

'You should have looked before.'

'Not that one, the chalk mark. It's beggar's language. It means, 'Bites'.' I proudly aired my new knowledge.

'My Father has a book on it; all the beggar's signs are in it. They chalk it, or scratch it on the walls to warn the other beggars. I can't remember them all. For dogs they have two, "bites" and "lapdog". Some are funny, like "miser" and "soft touch". My Father said the beggars are only afraid of one, and that's "labour force". Would you believe it, some people ring the police, and the beggars, the young ones only, get conscripted into the Labour Force – they make them go, against their will!'

In the Depression of the thirties and afterwards, the beggar was an accepted sight in Germany.

There were different kinds of beggars, including many men who in normal times would not have dreamed of begging. Jobs were hard to get and harder to hold. Every advertised vacancy had its queue of applicants waiting patiently, often long before the appointed time.

The beggars made the rounds in the more prosperous districts of the towns. Country districts were favoured only by those who preferred a day of casual labour to begging.

Already as a small child I knew what to expect when they rang the bell.

The young ones would say, 'I am a journeyman (*Wandernder Geselle*), travelling in search of work.' They usually wore a rucksack or had a bundle knotted on a stick.

Then there were the tidy, neatly dressed, though shabby ones. Their shoes were always well-polished, down-at-heel, black. 'I am a commercial traveller, but I have been unemployed for so many months, or years. Will the lady be kind enough to buy these matches, or combs, or mending wool, etc.' One gave them a small sum, though one did not want the proffered matches.

There were also 'real' tramps and vagabonds. They often smelled strongly of drink.

The cooks were allowed, at their discretion, to offer the beggars a meal. If they were clean and tidy, they would be invited to sit in the kitchen with the staff. Some beggars offered to help with the chores, like sweeping the yard or beating some mats.

If it was not mealtime, they were usually given a few pennies. Our Liesel was strongly against this.

'Wicked, wicked!' she exclaimed. 'They'll only drink it. Down at the "*Schwartzen Mann*" ["Black Man"], you can see them there. That's where they meet their cronies.'

It was true. Much of the begged money was spent on drink. To counteract this, householders would buy tokens which could be exchanged in grocery stores for anything except alcohol. Restaurants accepted tokens, and so did some clothing stores.

There were women beggars, too. They mostly begged for clothes and shoes. I believed every word of their hard-luck-tales, till I saw Mother's old winter coat displayed in a second hand dress shop. It had been I who had persuaded Mother to part with it.

Mother was against giving clothes to beggars. She said cast-offs were the 'perks' of the staff, and she knew enough poor, deserving people.

'I'm thirsty,' said Gustel.

'We'll soon be home.'

'I am thirsty now. Why did you tell Mrs Bollinger that we did not want any lemonade? I did.'

'Why didn't you say so then?'

'Because you said we had no time.'

'Maria would have had to make it first. That takes ages.'

Bottled lemonade was sold in restaurants, but most people squeezed lemons as required.

Gustel repeated, 'I'm thirsty now.'

Suddenly I knew what she meant. There was an ice-cream wagon standing at the corner. They sold fizzy lemonade.

'Would you buy me some, please, because I am so thirsty from all this running about?'

'One lemonade, please.'

'Aren't you having any?'

'No. I can wait till I get home,' I said nastily.

Gustel took her time. She made the bottle last as long as she could. I was getting fidgety. To be late for meals at home – that was terrible.

'I'm sorry, I have to go. Thanks for your help.' I raced home.

The next day when I came out of school, Gustel waited for me. The Ladies Seminary finished a little later than the Elementary School (*Volks Schule*).

'I have been waiting for you.'

'So I can see. What do you want?'

'You forgot to give me my ticket.'

'What price do you want?'

'That's up to you.'

'I don't care where you sit.'

'I mean, it's up to you – it depends on your ge-ne-ro-si-ty.'

'If you think I am going to buy you a ticket, you're very much mistaken. Why should I?'

'I like that! When I've worked all afternoon so hard for you.'

'For me? For the *Auslandsdeutschen* you mean. And they are your *Auslandsdeutsche* as much as mine.'

'I could have earned some money doing errands.'

'I was not aware that you had a job as an errand girl. Have you?'

'No, but I could have done.'

'And – it was not my idea you should come along.'

'Without me you would not have sold nearly as much.'

'I can't remember that you did much of the talking. I don't think you opened your mouth once!'

'It was good that I came along with you – you being Jewish and all that, the people might have thought it was for a Jewish play. That's what my mother said.'

148

I was speechless for a minute. 'Tell your mother,' I hissed at her, 'Herr Schultze – that's the organiser – said that we must be proud to make our sacrifices.'

I stalked off.

The following day, Gustel waited outside the school again. I saw her before she saw me. I was afraid she might make a scene, so I turned round and went out the back way.

The day after that she was there again. It was no good – I had to have it out with her.

I walked up to her. 'Gustel, listen to me. You're wasting your time. I am not going to buy you a ticket, so don't bother me. Go home.'

She was following two steps behind me.

'Go home!'

'Not before I have my ticket.'

'Buy one yourself.'

She ran and stood in my way. 'I think there is something you should know. My mother is going to write to Mrs Bollinger and ask her to pay for my torn dress – my very best dress, too.'

'Don't make me laugh. One could hardly see the holes, they were so small.'

'There was a big tear, I did not see it before.'

I knew she was lying.

'My mother is very annoyed that I worked so hard all afternoon and now you won't even give me a ticket. And another thing, dogs who bite are not allowed to run around without a muzzle. My mother is going to report that to the police.'

'In your own garden? Go to the police?' I was just going to say, Do what you like, I don't care, when I had second thoughts. It was not true, I cared very much. Mrs Bollinger had always been so kind to us. She was no Antisemite. On the contrary, since all that Hitler business started she had made a point of inviting Jewish people to her house. I did not want to upset her. What was a lousy ticket against that?

'All right, Gustel. On condition you forget about these teeny-weeny holes and no reporting to the police.'

'Let's have it.' She greedily held her hand out.

'I've not got one on me. We had to give them back. I'll let you have one tomorrow – I'll have to get it from the Box Office.'

'Mind you do. I'll be waiting.'

They announced during the afternoon session that the response to our efforts in selling tickets had been so good that twice as many tickets than the Hall would hold, had been sold. Therefore 'dress rehearsal' counted as a performance. Red tickets were now for the 'dress rehearsal' performance. This would be published in all the local papers, but they expected us to tell the people as well.

What a job! It meant at least twenty calls for me.

I tried to purchase a red ticket, hoping someone had returned one. No such luck. A blue ticket, please. Sorry, only white. Two marks! I did not have two marks. Children under twelve paid half, but Gustel was over. Two marks. Where was I going to get it from? A blue ticket would have cleaned me out completely, including my milk money for the week. I'd have to borrow it. I was not successful. Arnold was broke – so was Susan. Father was not home; I could have asked him for an advance on my pocket money. Mother did not believe in giving advances; she said there is no sense in giving weekly pocket money if it is not weekly.

I spent the rest of the afternoon running around telling people about the change of time. At suppertime there were still some calls to be made. 'Mother, could I phone, please? I must let them know.'

I spent a long time on the telephone.

Mother was cross and asked me if the *Auslandsdeutsche* were going to pay for all these calls. 'I've had enough, quite enough,' said Mother. 'We've heard nothing but "The Play" for the last two weeks. Perhaps you would run an errand for me, Sylvia, if you can spare the time. A litre of milk – I don't want to be short in the morning. Take some money from my purse, it's in the kitchen.'

I took the milk money from the purse. The purse was full of change. I took an extra two marks. I stole the two marks I needed so badly.

Stole. Stole. Stole.

I'm going to put it back. Next week. Some of it. It will take at least three weeks if I don't have the school milk. Thief. She'll never notice. Most probably not, but *you* know it yourself. Meaning to put it back! Just like Karolina in the play. Well, I'm not going to die. I had to have it – that Gustel might have made a rumpus at Mrs Bollinger's. I couldn't be sure. She had no case, no case at all, but Uncle Bernard, Father's lawyer brother, had told me that people often sue for nothing, hoping the other party will settle out of court.

After supper the telephone rang.

'It's for you, Sylvia.'

'Who is it?'

'I don't know, they must be friends of yours.'

I took the receiver. I replied, 'No, I'm sorry.'

'No, I've got no spare ones – we had to give them back.'

'At the box office.'

'Try tomorrow morning.'

'I couldn't tell you.'

'No, I cannot reserve them for you.'

'Try tomorrow morning.'

'No, for the last time, and will you please leave me alonc.' I screamed and slammed the receiver down.

'Whatever is the matter?' asked Mother. 'Who was it?'

'Oh, some friends of people I sold tickets to. I don't know them. I'm fed up – I'm fed up! I hate those stupid tickets, and I hate Herr Schultze most of all. Sacrifices, sacrifices! That's what he said we must make.'

Suddenly I started crying. 'I just hate those tickets.'

And then I was sick, very sick.

Mother brought me some peppermint tea – we always got peppermint tea when we had been sick.

She sat down on my bed. 'You're over-tired. That's what it is. Do you want a hot water bottle?'

'No, thank you.'

'Do you want to tell me about it?'

I shook my head. How could I?

She smiled. 'You never tried to sell me a ticket.'

'But you said you would not support them, that they're all Nazis. Besides, you wouldn't like it. You're used to proper theatre. It's a silly mish-mush of a play. A bit of Grimm, a bit of dancing, a bit of old German Gods. Imagine – Herr Schultze is playing the God Donar! He looks revolting anyway. You're not missing anything.'

'You'll feel better in the morning.' Mother put the light out.

She was so nice to me – I wished she would always be nice to me like that.

'You don't deserve it. Thief.'

I was sobbing into my pillow. I was crying for my lost integrity. Never again could I say, 'I'm honest and trustworthy'. And the other voice said, 'What's two marks? You are going to put it back – why are you making such a fuss? It was the lesser evil.'

I justified myself until I fell asleep.

* * *

It was not only children who were 'almost conscripted' into the various branches of the Hitler Youth, almost everyone was joining the Party. It was the done thing.

A general upsurge of patriotism was manipulated, encouraged, praised. It made one feel good to belong.

Germany was going to be great again.

One had the chance, the opportunity to be part of it, to help. What better use could be made of one's spare time than to help the *Vater Land*? The social side was a bonus – one had not expected this; it was great.

The patriotic lectures, the rousing speeches, the songs, gave one a feeling of euphoria.

THE FUEHRER LOOKS AFTER US.

He reduces unemployment.

He started massive road works – the Autobahn.

He developed small private airports into large military ones.

He 'cocked a snook' at the Treaty of Versailles, that shameful treaty which had crippled Germany for so long.

He mobilised an army.

He created the *Arbeits Dienst* (labour force) – young men working as navvies for pocket money, living in spartan lodgings and gaining the gratitude of the German Reich. The youngsters marched, singing patriotic songs, shouldering their spades, on their way to work. No longer did they stand at street corners – they had better things to do.

The women and girls gave their spare time willingly, for free, they were honoured to look after the lads of the *Arbeits Dienst*: to cook, to clean, to do the washing. It was for the Reich, so different from doing the chores at home.

The socialising was great. One belonged. The Depression was over.

Adolf Hitler had succeeded in reversing the Depression.

What a man! What a Fuehrer!

Deutschland, Deutschland ueber alles, ueber alles in der Welt.

An economy drive had been recommended by the Reich: it was

the much publicised *Ein-Topf*-Sunday (One-Pot-Sunday), to happen every four weeks. For Sunday lunch one was to cook one single dish, in a single saucepan. A good example was meat stew, with root vegetables and potatoes or barley. The money saved was to be donated for the needy of the town. Many people had been hit hard by inflation. Since 1931 the town had a charity called *Winter Hilfe* (Help in Winter). Ladies, Christian and Jewish (Arnold called them the do-gooders), collected clothing, blankets and other goods. The Rabbi took a very active part. There were coffee afternoons, where the collected articles were brought. In particular demand were children's clothing, and boots and shoes. Mother considered it a very worthwhile charity. Father said it was unhealthy to wear second hand shoes, as people walk differently. Mother answered that it was far more unhealthy for the poor children, in all weathers, to go bare-foot and wear only plimsoles in winter. I agreed with Mother. We were growing out of our shoes so fast, sometimes in months, and they were not to be passed to siblings. It was a very good thing great-aunt Johanna in Limburg had three shoe shops; she kept us well supplied and, I believe, never sent us a bill.

The Nazis took over the *Winter Hilfe*, incorporating the *Ein-Topf*-Sunday. They claimed it was all their own idea. The Fuehrer looks after us. They came to collect, house to house, rattling tins, and dressed in Nazi uniforms. Mother asked them politely to remove our name from the subscription list. She told us her donations would go to the Jewish Charity shop in Stuttgart.

We liked these one-pot dishes; they tasted very good. Richard was particularly fond of them when he came home from boarding school some weekends. In the afternoons he would meet his friends, to walk to the Jewish sports meadow, situated outside the town.

One day he was stopped in the street by two men. They said they were researching for an article what people had eaten for *Ein-Topf*-Sunday. 'We had Irish Stew,' replied Richard. 'It was great.'

'Please, would you stand over here, for the photograph,' said a third man, with a camera. Richard had not seen him before.

'You don't want my photograph,' replied Richard.

'It's just what we're looking for. We'll write up your "great lunch".'

'It was a great Jewish lunch,' said Richard, and he quickly ran off.

153

Richard was very good looking – blond with grey-green eyes – a fine Nordic specimen.

*   *   *

In the past, Father had taken us on many 'educational' excursions. The family was very art orientated. He had pointed out and explained works of art and architecture, of archaeology and geology. He always seemed to know a 'story', which went with whatever he was showing us. There were many Romans remains in the neighbourhood – I found these a bit boring. They seemed to consist mostly of holes in the earth, a few stones and a tablet to say what had been there and in which museum it was now. Father told us the story of a local innkeeper he knew, a keen archaeologist, whose dearest wish was to make a find. All his spare time he spent digging. Lo and behold, luck was with him. He found a dagger. It had an inscription on it too. And this was on his birthday! His companions were very envious. However, they had the good grace to congratulate him. Unfortunately none of them knew Latin, so he took his treasure to the priest who translated: 'To my friend the Innkeeper of Lorch, with the best wishes on his birthday from his friend, Julius Caesar.'

Several times we went to the Minster in Ulm, which was imposing and very grand, it had the highest steeple in the world. Father told us the story of the Tailor of Ulm, who claimed he had invented a flying machine. The townsfolk turned out to see the spectacle. His wings attached securely to his arms, the tailor climbed the tall steeple.

The Tailor of Ulm – he tried to fly – the wind and the devil – they took him high – and then in the Danube, he fell.

He showed us the Ulmer Spatz, a memorial to a starling, made of gold, a starling with a straw in his beak. The masons, when building the Minster in the early Middle Ages, had had a problem – how to get an extra long beam through the door. Work had come to a standstill, but the starling, carrying his straw horizontally, had shown them.

We looked at the carvings and at the stained glass windows. There is now, over the main entrance, a beautiful stained glass window, commemorating the martyrs of the Holocaust.

We went for excursions to the Schwaebische Alb, and the valley of the upper Fils River, the Wendt Tal, where we climbed the rocks – though without telling mother!

We heard tales of the Robber Knights. A wild lot they were, swooping down from their mountain stronghold, plundering the merchants and their retinue of their goods, or abducting virgins, their poor wives donating chapels and churches for the good of their husbands' souls.

These small white-washed country churches were situated halfway, or even on top of the mountain. One reached them on a dirt road, strewn with stones. On the way up, at intervals, were crosses, roofed over, depicting scenes of The Passion. One was supposed to kneel and say a prayer at every cross, for penance. I, too, felt very much in need of penance, but I don't like to think what Mother would have said had I knelt down.

These churches looked plain from the outside. Entering, however, the interiors took your breath away with their carved and gilded baroque splendour. The paint looked as fresh as if it had been applied yesterday. At the altar, life-size figures of saints smiled at you out of their radiant rural faces.

Father took Arnold, Erica and me on a walking tour. (Actually we used the railway quite often.) First he showed us his *Alma Mater*, in Tuebingen/Reutlingen. I liked the old town, with the many black and white buildings, particularly the Rathaus, its painted front and interesting clockface.

We stayed overnight in Hechingen, in the Baruchs' House, which belonged to Albert Einstein's in-laws. I remember how impressed I was with the bedroom they offered us. It was high up in the house and had four single beds. I had never before seen a bedroom with *four* beds in it. We speculated about this marvel. I suggested, perhaps many grandchildren. Arnold thought it was more likely for servants, or employees. Formerly, in Victorian times, these had had to 'live in'. The Baruchs were textile merchants, Rudolf Einstein having taken over the firm and married the daughter, Fanny Koch.

Next day the most extraordinary thing happened: Father took us to a shop and bought new socks and knickers for all of us. The young lady who had served us made a parcel of what we had taken off, to send our dirty laundry home for washing. Father explained that the little rucksacks each of us was carrying for water, sandwiches, fruit (also our swimsuit, towels and toothbrush), were heavy enough!

Next on the itinerary was Hohenzollern Castle, the Stamm Schloss (family seat), of the Kaiser. We were tired, having climbed the steep mountain it was built on. We had to wait quite a long time to be let in. I did not like this place, because one had to walk on druggets (protective cotton covers on the floor). There were also ropes on both sides. One could not see anything which looked interesting, not properly.

Afterwards we went swimming in the Danube.

'Are you sure you can swim?'

'Oh,' I bragged, 'I am a good swimmer.'

The Danube was like a torrent, fast flowing, it swept me away, downstream.

How glad I was to grab an overhanging branch and find I could pull myself to shore. This was my secret, my adventure. I told no-one. Better be careful next time you are bragging, I said to myself. I could have drowned. No-one had seen me.

The next episode happened several years ago. It had been raining all weekend, so our outing was by car. Mother too came with us; she was not fond of walking excursions.

We had been invited by Mrs Einstein for afternoon coffee. She lived at that time in Laupheim, in Swabia. It was here we had a great shock. Richard, aged three years, had sneaked out of the house; he climbed into the car and somehow got it started. Very slowly the car rolled down the drive. Mr Kuhn, who was taking coffee with the maid in the kitchen, heard a noise, ran out and caught the car as it banged into the gates – he was just in time. Only some lights were broken. Richard was quite unhurt, not a scratch on him!

Chapter 19

Of Razors and Rabbits

It had been a long hot summer.

One closed the shutters early in the mornings to keep the sun out. After lunch one dared not go outside without a large-brimmed hat. Some people used parasols they had raked up from their attics.

Most of the children spent the afternoons at the lake, or, parents permitting, at the river.

The river was far from clean or healthy as the factories discharged all kinds of waste into it. At the Calico Works one day the river was red, one day blue. Children tried to dip their hankies on sticks into the water, hoping for a 'dye'.

The river was out of bounds to us. It was dirty – unhygienic; in fact, not 'nice'.

Most Sundays we went for an excursion. In former years it had been much fun to plan them. Father had brought maps and timetables and we had all sat around the large nursery table. We might even have looked up our route on his large relief-map of the Alb, which was more detailed than the one we had in school.

But the planning was now an almost tense affair. It was not, 'Where shall we go?' It was, 'Where *can* one go?'

I was longing for a swim, a real swim. Lisa Lendt's pool was so small and there were always crowds.

'Daddy, let's go to Lake Ebnis. Let's go boating. You promised to teach me that special trick with the rudder.'

'I'm afraid that's out. They put the sign up last month. Julius Guggenheim told me.' 'The sign' was: JEWS NOT WANTED.

'What about Boll Spa?'

'There were signs on the lemonade and ice-cream stands. Of course they have nothing to do with the management, but ... better not.'

Everyone put in suggestions.

I said, 'I wish we could go somewhere for a swim.'

'Schurrenhof,' said Father.

'Schurrenhof?' we all repeated in unison.

The Schurrenhof settlement had a regular stand on market days for their produce: early tomatoes, strawberries, melons. People came to stare – they stopped and bought because the quality sold was up to standard.

There was always a couple serving, though every week it seemed to be a different one. The men looked biblical, with long wavy hair down their backs. I imagined Samson must have looked like that. They wore skin clothes like trappers and, in cold weather, a fur-skin thrown over their shoulders. Men and women wore home-made sandals. The women's dresses were homespun, usually of blue linen, and they had shawls instead of coats.

People said that the Schurrenhoefler were nudists.

The Schurrenhof was a settlement of artists – free thinkers, a back-to-nature movement. They tried to be completely self-supporting. They grew their own food, built their own houses. They spun their yarn and wove their cloth, they dressed skins and made sandals and boots. They taught their children – and I was told that they taught them well.

They stood gravely behind their stands, looking very handsome and strange. They spoke little, but sometimes they had a chat with Father.

Now Father told us that they had invited us several times, saying they would be pleased to show us round. 'The children will like the swimming pool,' they had said. And another time they had said, 'If the children would like to bring their friends, they're welcome.' Yes, they had heard about the signs. It was sad.

So Schurrenhof it was.

We had decided to walk part of the way, then take a bus. No longer did we have a car.

We set off early in the morning in the direction of the Beecherwood. We took the road that led past Mr Schneider's new house. From far off, we could hear his peacock cry; it is a terribly penetrating sound. Mr Schneider had 'collected' all kinds of strange animals – we children said this was the reason why he built his new house so far out of town: he had to. In his yard, in front of the house, were the wire-netted enclosures of his 'pets'.

'Can we stop and look at them?' asked Richard.

'We have no time.'

'Just for a minute,' begged Richard.

'No. Come along.'

I knew why my parents would not let us look; it was better this way. Mr Schneider might have been embarrassed. I liked Mr Schneider, he was so cheerful. I wondered if he was still cheerful.

Ever since I can remember, Father had gone to Mr Schneider's barber shop to be shaved. On weekdays Father went to the shop and on Sundays one of the young men called at our house.

A week ago, Father had a cut on his face. He had shaved himself, with an old fashioned razor.

He had gone, as usual, to Schneider's, but found the shop closed. There was a typewritten note at the door: 'Closed until further notice'.

As Father knew Mr Schneider well, he phoned him at home. Mr Schneider seemed very distressed and told him what had happened. One of his assistants, Kipfl, had been sharpening a razor. He had made a characteristic gesture while discussing politics with a customer – politics in general and Adolf Hitler in particular. The following morning a horde of SS men in their black uniforms and jackboots had invaded the shop. They had dragged Kipfl away with them, calling, '*Raus, raus, alles raus,*' hardly giving people time to wipe the foam from their faces.

They sealed the shop up.

Mr Schneider went to the police station, but the officials shrugged their shoulders.

Mr Schneider called on the City Councillors; he visited the Mayor, protesting that he was not even in the shop at the time. It was useless. They said, 'We feel for you; we're very sorry, old chap, but we're helpless. Besides, that fellow Kipfl has been associated with the Communists. Now, if you were a member of the party, that would be a different story...'

So even Mr Schneider, the formerly very active Secretary of the local Social Democrats, joined the Nazi Party.

The sun was standing high. We picnicked in an opening in the woods on a mossy, gentle slope. Then we buried our litter, orange peel and egg shells. Father lit a small fire on a stone to dispose of the paper – we had collected quite a bit on our sticks on the way. Richard loved spearing it up. Father could get quite annoyed about the 'litter louts'.

We waited for the country bus, together with the peasants and their wives. One could see that they had been to church. They wore their Sunday best, all black. The men's suits were usually a bit tight, and their necks overflowed their stiffly starched collars, old-fashioned high collars. Some wore gold coins on their watch chains. Once one was married, it was customary to wear black to church; only the young girls wore ordinary summer dresses.

I had imagined the Schurrenhof a Garden of Eden. Now I found everything was utterly utilitarian. Life was hard. Primitive life is. Our guide was a gentle giant, wearing a loincloth.

We were shown a field where flax was growing. We saw the looms. We saw wool – coarse, uneven hanks dyed in various colours, which had been hung up to dry.

The schoolroom was brown. The living quarters were all brown, brown like the rich soil around us.

The fields and gardens were beautifully tended. In a meadow, some naked children played. Then we swam in the pool. It was not a very good pool. The water was brown. None of us remarked on it, however – it would have been too ungrateful.

We purchased some special vegetables. I cannot remember what it was, except that Mother was very pleased with it.

We went home by a different route. First we walked for a few kilometres, then picked up a local 'Bim-bim' train, a very slow train serving the villages and hamlets. The oldest wagons were used for these trains; ancient fourth-class compartments, with narrow benches along the walls. Father told us that a lot of floorspace was needed by the peasants for their baskets and small livestock. Not all of them were rich enough to own a horse and cart, or oxen and cart, to take their produce to town on market day.

The long compartment was almost empty. At the next stop, a troop of Hitler Youth joined us. They planted their Wimpel (a small three-cornered flag), in front of us, and saluted smartly: '*Heil Hitler.*'

We saluted back, '*Drei Liter.*' (Three pints.)

It had been decreed that the greeting used by all good Germans should be '*Heil Hitler*'; even in school this form of greeting was compulsory. Gone was the old-fashioned, 'Good morning, Mr Teacher.'

First people joked about it but they soon got used to it. Now, even if one went into a shop to buy something, one was expected to use the salutation, '*Heil Hitler*. I want two pounds of cabbage, please.'

Willy Reichert, our beloved Swabian comedian, who reigned at the Stuttgarter Friedrichsbau (a Variety Theatre), had been very puzzled by it all at first. When someone had greeted him in this manner, he pretended he had misheard and instead had been offered three pints. He put his hand up. '*Dank schoen – Drei Liter.*'

And when they saluted out of the window, he did likewise. Again he pretended had misheard: '*Ja, ja's regnet wirklich net.*' (It's not raining) – and he examined his hand.

I wish I could have been there and heard it. Of course, such joking was soon banned, but Reichert was so popular that the Nazis did not dare touch him.

So we cheerfully said every time: '*Drei Liter.*'

The Youth Group sat down. They hardly talked; they were too tired to talk – in fact they looked exhausted. Judging by the size of their rucksacks they must have spent the weekend away.

I thought I would not like to carry one of those in this heat. I knew where they had been – the Schwaebische Alb. They had silverthistles tied to their rucksacks. Masses of them! What a cheek! Did they not know that silverthistles were almost extinct and were protected?

Father said, 'Soon there won't be any left.' After a while he added, 'Those children are over-tired. Someone should tell their leader that it is wrong to force-march them in this weather.'

'They do a lot of this lately,' said Arnold. 'Especially since that "rabbit affair".'

The 'rabbit affair' had to do with Friedrich Gaessle, a small timid boy, the smallest of his class. He was a year or two younger than Arnold and went to the same school, the Gymnasium.

Friedrich had reluctantly joined the Hitler Youth. He only went because all the other boys belonged to a group. By the end of 1936 the Hitler Youth numbered over seven million; the rest of the children were conscripted in March 1939. He would much rather have spent his spare time with his rabbits. They were white Angora rabbits and he loved the beautiful, docile creatures. He had received a couple for a birthday present; now he had nine, not counting the two he had given away.

Friedrich was very proud of his rabbits. On the way home from school he sometimes picked dandelion leaves for them, as his Group was doing 'duty' several times a week; they called it that, it sounded more important, although most of the time was spent with games. They had a certain amount of lectures – Party indoctrination – and a great deal of physical training. Summer weekends were often spent camping. Sometimes they went on marathon marches. Then the boys returned home limping, with blisters, exhausted; they dared not complain. To make strong, hardy bodies, to create a manhood fit for the new Germany – this was the aim of the Hitler Youth. There was no room for weakness, softness and other alien attributes.

The Youth Group Leader had accepted Friedrich's invitation to the Group to look at his rabbits.

Mrs Gaessle had baked several large *Zwetschgen Kuchen* (large, flat yeastcakes covered with fresh prunes, a local seasonal dish), and laid them out on wooden trestle-tables in their garden. There was new, sweet cider, home-brewed – a whole barrel full.

Friedrich was very happy playing the host. He urged the boys to eat and drink – quite unnecessarily, as they had come prepared to stuff themselves.

It was his big day. Usually he felt at a disadvantage because he was so small. Today he felt ten feet tall.

After the meal, a slightly tiddly crowd went into the yard to admire the rabbits. All was spick and span. Friedrich had spent several hours cleaning the hutches, and he had white-washed the front.

With pride, he took out Sebastian, his favourite. He stroked him and gave him a lettuce leaf, which the animal nibbled from his hand.

While he was talking to him affectionately, the Leader was watching him with mounting disgust. 'You can hold him, if you like.' Friedrich offered him to one of the boys.

Two boys tried to grab Sebastian simultaneously. They were pushing each other, almost fighting over the rabbit.

'I want to stroke him.'

'No, I had him first!'

'It's a real disgrace. My men [he always referred to them as "my men"], drooling over a rabbit. This emotional behaviour has no place in the party. I cannot allow it. I am responsible. Now there must be a punishment. You two!' He beckoned to the lads who had been fighting over the animal. 'You take the front legs, you take the hind. Now, tear it apart, to prove to me that you are men... That's an order!'

162

'But it's my Sebastian,' cried Friedrich.

The other boys had to hold him back forcibly. He screamed and became hysterical when the blood spattered everywhere.

'Dismissed,' called the Leader. 'March!'

The Group, now very subdued, went home.

Friedrich stayed away from school for several days. His mother sent a note excusing him, on account of tonsillitis.

When the 'rabbit affair' was discussed, it was in whispers. Some parents said they condemned cruelty to animals, others declared that they did not want their sons to behave like whimpering old women.

When Friedrich returned to school none of the boys dared to talk to him. The Biology Master gave a special lecture on rabbits. By means of diagrams on the blackboard he showed that if the rabbits' rate of multiplication was not checked the world would be overrun with them. They would become a pest, as they were in Australia.

The Group Leader forbade the boys to discuss it. He said it was his holy duty to toughen them up and guide them to become worthy of the Fuehrer. He reminded them of the oath they had taken when they had graduated to the Young Volk.

'Repeat after me: In the presence of this blood banner, which represents our Fuehrer, I swear to devote all my energies and my strength to the saviour of our country, Adolf Hitler. I am willing and ready to give up my life for him, so help me God.'

The Group went on long route marches, singing mainly Nazi songs.

Heil Hitler!

Chapter 20

The Glory of the Party

At home our circumstances had altered considerably. Although we could by no means pretend to poverty, we lived much more simply. I believe this was mainly due to the Nuremberg Laws which forbade Jews to employ female domestic servants who were less than forty-five years old. The reason given for the introduction of these laws was that the young girls had to be protected from their 'lecherous masters'. By the time a servant had reached forty-five, she hoped to be either a housekeeper or a head-cook; there was no shortage of these, but cook-generals or housemaids at that age were much harder to come by.

Now Mother did the cooking. It was a novelty for her. She had taught Liesel many fancy dishes, foreign dishes and exciting salads. However, Mother was not used to handling gas and so food was sometimes burned. Once she was past the 'food burning' stage, however, our meals were better than ever. There was always something different, a little surprise. She baked wonderful cakes too and even made home-made confectionery.

Mother had run the house most efficiently, but she had not done the actual work. She said that in practice the work was far more tiring than in theory. Mother was healthy but she did not have the strength of the peasant girls. She did the housework with courage and determination and the air of a martyr, never skimping anything. She often told us how she 'sacrificed' herself by cooking, counting laundry and dusting. At that time, all the staff had left, but Mother employed a daily woman who arrived at seven o'clock in the morning and stayed till after lunchtime.

I think it was from a feeling of guilt that I helped her – as much as I could. Because I disliked being told what to do, I sometimes rose as early as five o'clock in the morning and did as many of the chores as I could manage before school. I did not expect praise – and I never got any. 'It is the least you can do,' said Mother. Perhaps I should have got up earlier; perhaps I was slow – I was certainly tired.

Those Nuremberg Laws were just some of many puzzling laws and decrees affecting Jews. They made no sense to me.

It was against the law for a Jew to marry a Christian. The Nazi Party encouraged people to dissolve their mixed marriages. There was a great deal of talk about 'Aryans'. If you were more than one-eighth Jewish, you were considered racially impure. If a Jewish man had a Christian girlfriend, it was automatically assumed that the 'dirty Jew' had seduced her. This was called 'Racial Disgrace'.

Public swimming baths were forbidden to the Jews so that they should not foul the water. This did not affect us very much. Several of our Jewish friends had swimming pools of their own. I went to Lisa Lendt's most of the time.

Even park benches carried a notice: NOT FOR JEWS – though not those which had been donated by Jews in our town in the good old days.

When the local papers became more partial to Nazism, Father cancelled first one, then the next one, then the third. After all, he knew most of the people who worked on these papers and he took it personally. As one had to keep a daily paper, we ordered the '*Stuttgarter Tageblatt*. Stuttgart was twenty-five kilometres away and the editors of the *Stuttgarter Tageblatt* were a million.

Goebbels, the Propaganda Minister, had said in a speech: 'We shall treat the Jews like flowers, but we won't water them.' I thought, so far, God has done the watering, I don't think he has waited for Mr Goebbels. However, no-one talked about the other things Goebbels had said, or written: 'The Jew is responsible for the misery in Germany, he lives on it'; 'He is the real cause of us having lost the Great World War'; 'The Jew is the plastic Demon of the Decline of Mankind'; 'The Jew is uncreative. He produces nothing, he only handles products'; 'The Jew is our greatest misfortune'; 'He who thinks German must despise the Jews, the one thing makes the other necessary'; 'We are the enemies of the Jews, because we belong to the German people'.

Those things had been said and published as far back as 1930. Then the people in our circle thought no-one of culture and education was likely to take Dr Goebbels, the 'fanatical dwarf', or Adolf Hitler, the 'trumpeter', seriously. These speeches were just rabble-rousing.

Most of the men in the street wore one uniform or another. There were the Black Shirts, called the SS (The Hierarchy), Brown Shirts, called the SA (Storm Troopers – ordinary Nazis), the Labour Force, (enthusiastic youngsters who worked like slaves for the love of the Third Reich and pocket money), and this took care of the most able-bodied civilians. Our small local aerodrome had been enlarged and taken over by the Luftwaffe, so there were plenty of grey-blue uniforms about. Many men would go to work in their Nazi uniform, and change then into overalls, as they were often on 'duty' straight after work.

When applying for a job at the Labour Exchange, it had become routine, after one had given name and address, to state one's Party Number. If one did not have a Party Number, they regretted they had no jobs. It was dangerous for an employer to give a job to a man who could not produce his Party Membership Card – one had to show allegiance to the Third Reich.

Membership would begin at an early age. There was the Hitler Youth, which in outward appearance was like the Boy Scouts and Cubs. For girls there was a similar organisation called *Jung Maedels*, *Bund Deutscher Maedchen*, or B.D.M. for short. On any festival or excursion, the children turned up in their brown uniforms. All the children had uniforms, except of course, the Jewish children.

Our local May Day Celebration was considered the great event of the year. The best party dress of the girls was referred to as the May Day Dress. Everybody got a new dress to wear for the procession – a fluffy, frilly one. There was always a fun fair, merry-go-rounds, stalls and tents, and other attractions. All schoolchildren received free ice-cream, a bottle of milk and a roll containing a large hot sausage and mustard, with the compliments of the town.

In the morning was the procession of schoolchildren. Everyone came to watch, and the shops were closed for a couple of hours. Decoration, flags and flowers were everywhere along the route. 'Look, here is my Heini.' Proud mothers waved to their offspring.

Every class tried to get a float together if possible, or had decorated carts drawn by horses wearing plumes. Figures of fairytales were very popular. In the last year of Primary School we had done Snow White and the Seven Dwarves.

What should we do this year?

We were busily discussing it and not agreeing over anything when Dr Kocher announced that the Town Council had decided, in appreciation of our Fuehrer, this May Day to take the theme, 'The Glory of the Party'. Any suggestions?

Finally it was decided that we would carry a large photo of our Fuehrer, framed in flowers.

Good, that was settled.

The next day, Dr Kocher told us that our wonderful idea had been shared by many other classes. In fact there were five classes each of whom wanted to do the portrait of the Fuehrer, so the teachers drew lots for it. We were offered a choice between Leo Schlageter and Rosenberg. The girls chose Rosenberg – he was better looking. A local photographer let us have the enlargement at cost.

'Girls,' said Dr Kocher one morning. 'Imagine! Our May Day is going to be included in the weekly newsreel – to be shown all over Germany!'

So the Town Council decided on an athletic display – by all schools – as an extra. Then orders came that girls of each class must wear the similar-coloured wreath in their hair.

Our class was given yellow – a difficult colour. Arnold suggested dandelions as a solution.

In former years the mothers had chosen the wreaths to match the dresses and complement the complexions of their daughters.

The last Sunday before May Day we had a dress rehearsal for the display; uniforms were ordered for the march through town.

Straub, who was a leader in the *Jung Maedels* had been chosen to carry our Fuehrer's portrait. She carried an empty frame for now.

We assembled. The Jewish pupils stood apart at the end of the column. We wore navy skirts and white blouses. All the others wore their uniforms – brown skirt and white blouse.

Trudi Fahner joined us, conspicuously dressed in a dirndl.

Well, I thought, it has caught up with you. But I said nothing.

Lisa Lendt asked her innocently, 'Fahner, is your uniform at the cleaners?'

I nudged her. 'Leave off.'

'What do you mean, Sylvia?'

Trudi Fahner came closer. She whispered, 'I no longer belong to the Jung Maedels. That's what she means. Who told you, Fleischer?'

If looks could kill.

'My father told me – a long time ago – he knows your grandparents, glove manufacturers. Esslingen, that's where they live.'

I stopped, because suddenly I felt sorry for her.

'Forget about it, Trudi. I certainly won't talk. I promise.'

'That's mighty kind of you,' she said snootily.

Trudi Fahner was popular; after all, she was a dare-devil. The girls of my class were surprisingly good about this delicate situation. Trudi spread the story that one of her great grandmothers had been Jewish – bad luck, this.

Fancy, denying her own mother! I was shocked. But a promise is a promise.

The May Day celebration was said to be a great success.

I never saw the newsreel. I was told there was a close-up of me.

Arnold grinned. 'The camera man was from Berlin, he couldn't have known you were Jewish. How many fair girls are in your class?'

'Only four, including me.'

'All Alpines – *Rundschaedels* [Celtic]. Ha, ha, ha.'

Most of my classmates were dark, and did not possess the desired long Nordic cranium. Once a man had come round the school measuring our heads. The longest cranium in the whole school belonged to a cousin of mine, a Jewish girl, Hilde Fleischer.

This, however, was the last year Jewish pupils were allowed to partake in the May Day festivities.

PART THREE

HISTORY AND POLITICS

Chapter 21

*Protection Money (*Der Schutzbrief*) and the Code Napoleon*

The Jewish population in my town was divided into two groups: the ones who believed in emigration as an immediate and urgent measure, and the other group, to which my parents belonged – or I should say my father – who maintained that Nazism was a crazy and unreal dream, and that the bad times must pass. After all, the people behaved in such a foolish and ridiculous fashion, one could not possibly take them seriously.

However, just to be on the safe side, Father went to the American Consulate in Stuttgart to obtain a Waiting Number. These had reached by that time an almost 'astronomical' figure. Every year, the USA took a certain number of European immigrants, fixing different quotas for the various countries. For English speaking countries, the quota was large and never fully taken up. On the other hand, the number of citizens from Middle Eastern or Asiatic countries allowed into the USA was very small.

The two groups were subdivided again: the people who believed in Zionism, and those who were against it.

My father's friends said they were 'Germans of Jewish faith' (and not very Jewish at that). They were Individualists; they did not like any fanatical group of people, whether religious or political. But slowly, particularly because of our multi-national background and almost against his convictions, Father considered the possibility of migration.

People who had felt the danger and realised at an early stage that they had to emigrate were able to take most of their possessions and money with them. They had elaborate crates, called lifts, built in which to ship their furniture and their belongings.

171

In our circle one believed in academic education. That was all changed now. The world seemed to have no use for intellectuals and professional people. Only artisans, skilled craftsmen, peasants and domestic workers were wanted.

The Zionist Movement trained young persons in Agriculture, both theoretically and by practical work. Training farms were set up. Teenage boys and girls prepared themselves for the life and work that would await them on a Kibbutz. Mother said she was surprised how the Jewish people took to this heavy physical labour. Farming had not been a Jewish occupation; she'd never heard of a Jewish farmer or peasant and she was wondering why? Father told her the reason was simple. Jews were not allowed to own farmland before the beginning of the nineteenth century – at least not in our locality. At that time there was a general decline in farming; people were looking for other ways to make a living.

'Restrictions and persecutions are nothing new,' Father continued. 'Here in our very own town, the whole community was wiped out in the year of the Black Death. It was claimed that the Jews had poisoned the wells. That the Jews drank from the same wells, and that they succumbed to the plague like their Christian brothers, did not make any difference. All the Jewry in our town were murdered, as were those in all neighbouring towns and villages.

It was exactly five hundred years later, in 1849, that Jews returned to the town.

In 1777, the Barons, who owned the village, granted their protection, free of charge, to twenty Jewish families.

The legend relates that the Barons, as usual, were hard up. A friend had suggested to one at a card game, 'Why don't you get yourself some Jews. You will soon be all right.'

The Baron was an enlightened man with rather fewer prejudices than normal at that time. It is clear by the Letter of Protection that he took in the Jews from humanitarian, as well as economic grounds. The *Schutzbrief* (protection document) was called an 'agreement', instead of the more usual 'grace'. After the number of twenty families was reached, the admission charge was fifty gulden for men, twenty-five for women. It was a favourable 'agreement'.

The protection was irrevocable for as long as Jews were 'suffered' to live in the Holy Roman Empire.

The *Schutzgeld* (Protection Tax) was twelve gulden per family,

172

per annum, plus another gulden in lieu of the usual free labour his subject performed – road repairs, forestry, harvest work, etc.

The Baron was willing to forgo his usual due of poultry, but not the tongue of all animals. He must have been very partial to tongue, because in a *Schutzbrief* of a later date, it is stated that only ox tongue was to be delivered to the castle, not lamb's or goat's. Free trade was allowed in all commodities except salt, which prerogative belonged to the Baron. The import of beer and spirits was forbidden, as was bread. 'His' Jews were to come under the same jurisdiction – the same as 'His' Christians in matters of law and trade, etc.

In return, the Jews were to enjoy all rights and free religious worship. The Rabbi and his family paid no yearly *Schutzgeld*. The Baron would punish anyone who interfered in any way with the Jewish cemetery, just as he would were it consecrated Christian ground.

Building ground was supplied free by the Baron at a given site, and Jews were not, by punishment of explusion and a fine, allowed to buy houses, ground or arable land from Christians.

The Jewish women were to enjoy the same female freedom as the women in Burgau. (I presume this refers to immunity from '*Le Droit de Seigneur*', which custom was abolished only under Napoleon.)

There is no mention of the Jews having to wear special garb or a badge.

The Jews were to pay all the usual local taxes and dues to the Baron, just as the Christians did.

In the case of a Jew wanting to leave the Schutz, he had to pay ten per cent of his money and goods, as did a Christian – this to be declared honestly, instead of the usual swearing on the Bible.

These are the main points of the rather lengthy *Schutzbrief*.

The Jewish community was at first poor, having been rather 'stripped for their worldly goods' by their former 'protectors', they referred to it as a 'bad *Schutz*' (protection). Later the community of the village prospered, Christians and Jews alike.

There had been a state of semi-serfdom in villages all over the country, in most of the small principalities, the immediate jurisdiction belonging to the Lord and Master. It was Napoleon who abolished all that (the Code Napoleon). He elevated the Kurfuerstentum Wuerttemberg to a Kingdom under Koenig Friedrich II.

The Wuerttemberger soldiers had fought together with the French against the Prussians, which were referred to then as the '*Saupreussen*' (Prussian Pigs), exactly the same as in my childhood days, before Hitler came to power. Temperamentally and ethnically, the Wuerttembergers were closer to the French than the Prussians, and at the Court of Wuerttemberg, French was spoken.

In 1806 all the inhabitants of the village, including the Jews, swore allegiance to King Friedrich II. The Barons were deposed, their power broken. However, the Jews received the complete and full rights of citizenship only after a special law had been passed on 25 April 1825; the King, who had always been friendly to the Jews, had papers drawn up years before, but had not managed to get them passed in his parliament. (Wuerttemberg was more advanced than the rest of Germany. Their Parliamentary system was similar to the English one).

Amongst the new rights and duties were Military Service, also the supply of men for the Royal hunts.

Jews could now travel more freely. The ghettoes or near-ghettoes, were abolished.

It was expedient for Jews to take on surnames. In 1816, an application was made to the county administration for sanction. Most families took the name of their town of origin, for example, Adelsheimer, Bernheimer, Doerzbacher. Some Jews chose the German version of their Christian name, like Gutman (good man) for the Hebrew name Tobias. Others took their profession or trade as a surname, Fleischer (butcher), Koch (cook). The last restriction to be abolished was the one governing mixed marriages, in 1869 (re-instated by Hitler in 1935).

After 1806, Jews were admitted to the trades guilds, which had been closed to them before. This was a great step forward. Jewish boys served their apprenticeships with Christian masters. Conditions were not good, there was friction, and even the considerably higher *Lehrgeld* (fees paid by the apprentices for tuition), would not make up for their refusal to work Saturdays. The dietary laws were almost impossible to keep, in fact these were the first to go in this process of assimilation.

Weaving seems to have been a popular choice of the young Jews as well as anything in the catering line. There were four inns in the village, one since 1821, and the innkeepers were either master butchers, or master bakers.

From the first quarter of the nineteenth century, it had been a

174

tradition for the sons of our family to enter a weaving apprenticeship, according to the regulations of the guilds. In my father's time, the sons were no longer apprenticed; they were sent to study at Tuebingen University or at the Technical High School in Reutlingen to become textile technicians or master weavers, which certificate my father duly obtained. My ancestor, Daniel Rosenthaler, born in 1824, made, in partnership with Steinhardt and Gutman in 1851, linen and cotton fabrics; each of the partners starting on his own in 1856.

Daniel Rosenthaler had been experimenting with the making of menswear for export to North America. This seemed to upset the local Tailors' Guild, whilst the cloth weavers, on the other hand, felt it would vastly benefit them.

So the family called a meeting. 'We don't want to upset anyone. Let's produce something which no-one else does.'

Corsets were the answer. In 1849 they had made some, woven ones, more like bodices.

The corset industry in Stuttgart was founded by my family in 1849. Prior to that a retired French, one-armed officer had tried to set up the industry in Stuttgart, with financial help from the Wuerttemberg state. But he was unsuccessful and his 'factory' closed after a few months.

In 1855, great-great Uncle Daniel started a large new factory; he was joined two years later by my great-grandfather Bernhard Rosenhal(er), and my great-grandfather Aaron Fleischer from Muehlbach. The quality of the goods produced was high. Gold Medals were won, all over the world. According to a report from the Chamber of Commerce, the firm employed more than 1,000 workers on 600 looms in 1867. Work from the home industry was taken in at thirty branch offices. This was beneficial for the mainly agricultural population, who could thus supplement their meagre income. Handmade lace and embroidery was used for better corsets.

In 1871 a branch factory was opened by my grandfather, Samuel Fleischer, then only twenty years old, in London, and another, in Milan. Export to North America flourished until the introduction of the Mackinley Bill. Great-grand Uncle has been described as the founder of the corset industry, grandfather Samuel Fleischer as the pioneer.

The corset industry was not the only one in which young Jewish weavers from the village excelled. Several important cotton mills were set up, first using hand looms, later mechanical looms. Hand

175

looms were not displaced for years. Julius Kaufman was the first to install four mechanical looms in the town, harnessing water power from a local brook to drive them; however, he still employed 900–1,000 workers on hand looms. The brothers Ottenheimer employed 500 hand weavers. One cotton and linen mill, owned by Moritz Fleischer changed over after thirty years of production to the making of paper, becoming one of the most important mills of paper in Germany.

The Jews were fruitful and multiplied. From the fifty-one souls who had received the protection of the Baron in 1777, the Jewish population in the village had increased to 500 in 1837.

The new factories were a great economic help to the country, for the mountainous hinterland with its relatively infertile soil – the Schwaebische Alb – was beautiful, but the people were poor, and a bad harvest could spell disaster for all.

Christians and Jews worked together more and more. They got to know each other; they became friends. Judaism became a religion, not a way of life. And, like most religions, it was neglected.

In 1868 eleven Christian and Jewish lads together founded the 'Merkuria', a mercantile club. Its function was purely social and its early membership equally divided between Christians and Jews. The Merkuria was the first inter-denominational club of this kind in the Kingdom of Wuerttemberg.

The club held dances and musical evenings. Grandfather Samuel, a founder member, then aged nineteen, administered the funds, until he went to the Franco-Prussian War in 1870, on the French side.

Father often took us to the Merkuria Club House, which was situated at the outskirts of the town near the Beecherwood. It was a popular outing for us children as there was a small zoo there. One could always count on meeting a good crowd of children there: those of Father's *Kegel Brueder* (skittles partner), or of the 'Brothers' of the Rifle Association, who practised in the Merkuria. Lila Guggenheim's father was champion at skittles; my father was champion shot. Playing skittles was popular and there were several skittle alleys in the town.

While the gentlemen played and the ladies drank their coffee and gossiped, we would be going through our ritual of trying to annoy old Trotty-Pooty. Trotty-Pooty was an ancient, dignified turkey, who strutted slowly around. We tried to anger him by waving something red. Someone had told us that it worked if one

176

did it properly. We chanted, 'couter-couter-couter, we're redder than thou', hoping this would result in his comb swelling up in rage. The turkey looked at us disdainfully, made a little noise – we claimed he had sneezed at us – and walked away.

We couldn't get these animals to co-operate. The peacock wouldn't spread his tail for us; it was a beauty and only a teeny-weeny bit moth-eaten at the end. The snakes were lazy and the lizards were asleep. Father explained it was too cold for them in the open air.

We were most successful in the monkey house. Sometimes, on summer Sundays, they put on a chimpanzees' tea-party. One did not have to induce the monkeys to throw banana skins at one; they did that without waiting to be asked.

It was a long time since we had been to the Merkuria Club house. No longer did Father play skittles, nor did he take part in rifle competitions.

On fine Sundays, Arnold and I went on excursions to the nearby mountains with our Youth Group. This was run jointly by the *Central Verein* (CV), and the Zionist group in our town. Normally those two did not see eye to eye at all, but in the case of the youth they had 'buried the hatchet'.

One could describe the situation – in an over-simplified way – by saying that the members of the Zionist movement believed in Palestine and the members of the *Central Verein Deutscher Staatsbuerger Juedischen Glaubens* (Central Association of German citizens of Judaic Faith), to give it its full name, believed in Germany Jewry. Father and his circle belonged to the CV.

This association had been founded in 1908 for the express purpose to combat attacks on German Jews and Jewry. In the past, the association had had little reason for activity in our town, so its function had been more one of instructing the public. Approximately twice a year lectures were given by famous Jewish speakers, and these lectures were well attended by both Christians and Jews alike.

The German Jews were patriotic.

The Zionists held there was no real home land except Palestine; everything else was in a stage of transition. The local Zionist group was now gaining ground; it had always been supported by our so-called 'Polish Jews'. The younger generation was mostly German born, the older people for the most part stateless. Many had settled in the town, around the turn of the century, often 'on

177

their way to America'. Conditions in the town were good; there were plenty of jobs, jobs in positions of trust – and so they had stayed on.

But they never quite belonged. The reason for that was not that they were Polish or Russian Jews, but that they had not come from the village.

Almost all the Jewish families from the village were inter-married, heavily so. They were clannish. We children sometimes used to work out in how many ways and how many times we were related to each other. Perhaps once from the maternal side and twice or even three times from the paternal side.

It was the custom that one's son married the daughter of one's business partner, or vice versa. The practice ensured that the firm, often a factory, was not drained of its capital. Some marriages facilitated a much desired merger. And, of course, if one married a cousin, the money stayed in the family as well.

One made a suitable marriage. Love marriages were in books, for *Goyim* (Christians), and rebels, like my Father.

My Mother, too, did not 'belong'. She was treated like an outsider. True, she came from a much respected family of German Jews. True, she had brought an enormous dowry – 150,000.00 gold marks – but she was not related, only an 'in-law' (*nur angeheiratet*), nor had she come from an approved Swabian village. Father's family held that Mother, therefore, 'did not understand'.

Mother suffered, though not in silence. She would angrily exclaim, '*Solch eine Vetterle's Wirtchaft!*' (Hodgepodge of cousins.)

Whilst the local 'old families' appeared to have rarely mixed with the 'Polish' Jews, the difficulties experienced in Germany by all Jews brought them together. It was the 'Russian' and the 'Polish' Jews who came to the fore in the matters of Youth Movement. They organised the sports activities, the excursions, the social evenings, whether they were educational or cultural.

Our group had chosen as our Group Song one called, '*Die Gedanken sind frei...*' (Thought is free). It was a German song we had learned it in Primary School.

> Thoughts are quite free
> Who can guess them right
> Quickly they flee
> Like shadows at night.

178

Huntsmen with bow
Can't shoot them, we know
Thoughts are quite free
And always will be.
(Translated by E. Ries)

We were a kind of 'Jewish *Wandervogel*'.

If on some excursion we met a group of Hitler Youth, and they called after us '*Saujude*', or sang the song which had the refrain '*Jude verrecke*' (Jew perish), we answered with our '*Die Gedanken sind frei*', and marched on as if nothing had happened.

Some of our local Jews, those who were still relatively rich, had donated a playing field. It was situated right next to the town's mineral spring. Every week we children took our turns in 'mineral-water-duty'. The water was fetched in specially designed clip-top bottles; it was naturally very 'gassy' and needed these extra-strong fastenings lest it explode. When we went to our sports field, we 'killed two birds with one stone'.

Susan and I went every week to the Keep Fit classes which were held there in summer. The instructress was a tall young woman.

She was very good, considering she was no professional.

Stop-watch in hand, she would say, 'Go!' We ran.

We jumped. Easy.

'You must learn to fall properly. One-two-one-two-one-two. Relax now.'

She was really quite nice; she had taught me to do somersaults. Some of the girls had a crush on her. She said she was delighted with our progress, how we took to discipline. We were a credit to her. We were to call her Aunt Felicia.

Aunt Felicia was married. She had two children, but they were too small yet to come to the playing field. Her husband was a partner in a textile mill. So was her father, though not in the same mill.

The boys had their drill on the other end of the field. In games we joined up. Those could be fun.

One or other of the boys would usually offer to strap my mineral water bottle box to his bike. It was terribly heavy. I was very grateful, for it unbalanced my bike and when on the road, which was one of the main traffic routes in South Germany, the big lorries

179

ploughed past us, making me nervous – they appeared to 'suck one' under.

I hated sport. Everybody else seemed to love it. Father approved for it was healthy. All my friends went.

I would much rather have stayed with my books at home, 'unhealthily' shut up in my 'stuffy' room, 'getting bad eyes' and a 'round back'. Yes, indeed.

Chapter 22

Art and Sex in the Third Reich

I used to like art at school, especially at primary school. For the last two months, however, art was another of the classes where I read secretly.

It was because of 'her'.

Now, our art mistress, Miss Trauthagen was always picking on me. At first I had not taken much notice, when she did it to the others. We did not know what had come over her. She certainly was changed, everybody said so.

She used to be easy, and apart from telling us what she wanted us to draw, she had left us in peace. She never corrected the drawings, nor did she show one how to correct it oneself. They did not believe in it at that time.

Since she had been to the *Tagung fuer Lehrer in Deutscher Kunst* (Seminary for Teachers in German Art) which had been arranged by the Party, she was certainly different.

First we had a discussion on the theme. Then she gave 'suggested lines of treatment'. 'Make a plan, girls,' she had said. 'Work systematically towards your goal. Clear thinking is essential. You must have a system. I am expecting neat work from you from now on. Have discipline in your work.' And she reminded us that every sheet would count towards the final mark.

We always used a pencil. Sometimes we coloured our work afterwards with water colours. They did not allow pastels or oils – and we no longer used crayons as in junior school. If one wanted to, one was allowed to ink it in.

The first time she had 'picked' on me, the subject had been 'The Wood in Summertime'. I was using the side of my B6 pencil, to put in the shade, when I became aware of someone standing behind me.

181

'What on earth are you doing?'

I turned around. What did she want? Anybody could see what I was doing, tree trunks. 'Excuse me, Miss Trauthagen, I don't understand.'

'That black smear, what is that supposed to be?'

'The shade on the tree trunk.' She must be blind.

'And that?'

'Leaves.'

'Good that you told me, I would never have known.'

She was being funny now. 'Beecherwood,' I said, 'near the Slate Valley.'

'Fleischer,' she exclaimed, with a shudder, 'your paper is all black on top.'

'Well,' I answered, 'the leaves are black when one has been in the bright sunlight.'

'Leaves, I can't see any leaves there.'

I defended myself and tried to explain, thinking how dense grown ups are. 'One can only feel them, one cannot see them, not at first when one comes into the wood. You know, Miss, at the Slate Valley, the light is different all the time, because of the open spaces.'

'I would advise a change of location then, my dear,' she said sarcastically. 'I'd like you to start again.'

By now everyone was looking and listening. She made me tear my paper up.

She addressed the whole class. 'We're not starting here with things like that.' She mimicked me. 'One cannot see them, one can only feel them! Personally, I like to be able to see what I am looking at. What next? *Entartete Kunst* [degenerate art]. We are not going to have that here. Not here.' She shook her head.

'Leaves are delicate things,' she explained. 'They have veins, they breathe. Girls, first the trunk, then the large branches, then the medium sized branches, then the smaller branches, the twigs and the stalks. Every leaf grows on a stalk.'

The way she recited it made me think of '...big fleas have little fleas and so ... infinitum'. I suppressed a grin. She saw it. The way she looked at me... Ha, I bet she was sorry they were not allowed to hit us.

She stood over me until I had done it in the prescribed manner.

It looked like a botanical drawing. 'Now it looks quite reasonable,' she said, and passed on, to make someone else 'happy'.

Once the bell had gone, the girls raced to the rubbish basket to retrieve my 'masterpiece'. A few went so far as to agree with me that it looked just like that at the Slate Valley, but most of them seemed to be rather glad that I had made a fool of myself.

Next week we had a lesson on '*Entartete Kunst*'. We were told it was Art which was foreign to the German Spirit. This was the greatest condemnation of anything. Miss Trauthagen showed examples. The girls found it hilariously funny, especially the portrait of a woman who had two faces all in one, front view and profile. Miss Trauthagen said that she presumed the painter had been short of canvas. And she smiled, as she always did, not opening her mouth, with the corners turned downwards instead of upwards.

Once I had done a caricature of her. It had made the rounds during class and was much admired, but when it was returned to me it was so grubby and crumpled that I had to throw it away.

When I told Father about our lesson on *Entartete Kunst*, he had said, '*Solch ein dummes Geschwaetz!*' (What silly talk!) 'Did she say whose work it was?'

'No.'

'It sounds like Picasso.'

It was not like Father to pass derogatory comments about teachers. 'The way we work now is very academic,' I said. Father smiled.

It had been quite some time since anyone had used this term in our house in this context.

'Why don't they come any more, Daddy?' I meant the artists.

'They are too busy with German Art. German Art seems to be quite profitable these days.'

'They' were Father's artist friends. I could remember them well. I had been very impressed. They never brought us presents like the other visitors, but then they were different and one could not expect it. They did not even leave the customary tip on the kitchen dresser for the maids.

As a young man, Father had spent a lot of time in Munich with the artistic set. He did not speak much about it but what he said sounded absolutely wonderful. Bohemian life – a magic phrase! They must have been a very happy lot. And they only worked when they felt like it! And if they did work, they wouldn't talk to you, and were rude; that was because they were happy. However, more often they did not work.

Father and Mother had spent most of their honeymoon in Munich, though they had intended to spend only two days there. They stayed longer because Mother said she was enchanted. Father was popular in Munich, especially after he had won the first prize with his 'poem'. The *Munich Illustrierte* had offered a prize for the best poem, written in the spirit of the Muenchener Carnival.

Father's poem had consisted of only two lines. The papers carried the news, the national ones too: First prize to Herrn Julius Fleischer, *Fabrikant* (manufacturer), for his poem, which we regret is not printable.

Sometimes the artists came and stayed with us; some stayed for weeks. The maids were not over fond of these visits. They complained to mother: they never got up, the bedrooms couldn't be done at a reasonable time, they used perfectly good towels as paint rags, they had even torn them up, they were not punctual at meal times (they were not going to say anything about that – obviously they weren't used to a decent life), they rang the bell for coffee in the middle of the night, and then they did not even drink it.

Mother promised to speak to them about the coffee – and also that Liesel did not like to have her behind pinched.

My parents gave many invitations, and sometimes, as a result, the artists made a sale.

I loved those occasions. Arnold and I were allowed to stay up, although often they went on quite late. I took great trouble with the floral decorations, wiring them to make them 'artistic' and did not mind when no-one seemed to notice. These people were different. One of them was always drawing on the tablecloth. I suggested to Father he should frame it. It went to the wash just the same.

They were witty and used rude words and told jokes, but they kept the 'good' ones for later when the men took their cigars. They talked about art, but mostly about money. How much so-and-so got for an absolute piece of rubbish, and how so-and-so, just for a joke, put the highest price on his worst painting and it had sold first. Most of the other artists were 'no use'; sometimes they were 'all right'. 'Academic' was a dirty word. 'Academic' was even worse than 'petty bourgeois'. An academician was a doddering old fool. I thought I could detect an undertone of admiration, or was it envy?

The painter Krauss had been one of Father's protégés.

Father had financed a trip for him to the Middle East, making only one condition: he wanted the first choice of paintings. It was too bad that the King of Wuerttemberg wanted the same paintings; Krauss honoured his promise.

But I found Krauss's Arab scene, the one all that fuss had been made over, garish.

I much preferred his 'Cabbage Field', which hung over the sideboard. Apparently someone had said this painting was just 'so much smear', and this remark had been carried to Father. It irked him. He and his friends would stand before that picture and discuss why it was not a smear. People who could say such a thing were obviously Barbarians and Philistines. Of course, by academic standards it might be a smear.

I studied that picture carefully. It was a glory of purples and mauves, pale blue and lime green, and white. Close up one could see nothing except thick spoonfuls of paint, but if one stood far enough away one saw a cabbage field, all neatly planted, the sort any German farmer could be proud of.

My favourite picture hung in our salon. This painting was of a corner of a room: bright sunlight fell on a grand piano and on the parquet floor. On the wall behind the grand piano hung many pictures – more than we had. It was the light in that picture which fascinated me. The artist, a Professor Wolff from Munich, had painted it all broken up in the colours of the spectrum. It had no name. Someone told me it was a room in a castle in the Tyrol. I decided that must be right; who else but the owner of a castle could possess so many paintings? If we were living in a castle, I would live in the tower, like a princess.

Father collected etchings, which he kept in folders, and miniatures, which hung in the corner about Mother's sewing chair.

I admired the beauty of the ladies on those miniatures. They showed a great deal of bosom, very delicate and pale blue. The Empress Josephine's dress was pretty, with tiny panel puff sleeves. The King of Rome looked very sad and romantic. The Rococo ladies had porcelain faces, black ribbons around their necks and small double chins. The double chins suited them; they did not suit the ladies of our acquaintance.

Most of these miniatures were in ivory frames, a few were in ebony and only a single one was in a fruitwood frame; I believe it was pear wood. This miniature was of a beautiful lady with almond eyes, with much bust showing, in fact, all of it. She was wrapped in a garnet-red wool shawl. The picture was unfinished at the hands and draperies.

I asked Father why it was not finished, and who she was.

He did not want to tell me, and I had to plague him quite a bit before I got something out of him.

He told me the lady ran away before the painter could finish it. The lady's father had managed to buy it, lest it fell into the wrong hands. Exactly who she was, he would not tell me. The lady was a relative – I must be satisfied with that. 'You must not ask me more,' he said with emphasis.

She had run off with her aristocrat lover who was not even young, but had been an old profligate. No, he did not marry her, he set her up. It was all a long time ago. Anyway, customs were different in the eighteenth century.

'There were many beautiful women in your family,' said Father, 'and they did not all run away either.' I was not to talk about it. 'Your mother wouldn't like it.' It was a long time ago, *Le Droit de Seigneur*.

I knew Napoleon had done away with that. People had considered it an honour. Arnold said, 'I bet the young Lord was more experienced than the bridegroom. You know, that's important for the first time.'

I said, 'If it was an old Lord, how about that?' I was grateful to Napoleon.

'Virgins,' said Arnold. 'They are more trouble than they're worth. Give me an experienced woman any time.'

'Arnold, you have not had any!'

He did not answer. He looked superciliously at me.

'When? Oh, do tell me.'

'A gentleman does not talk of his affairs.'

'I don't believe it, not unless you can prove it.'

'I don't have to prove anything to you.'

'At least tell me how old you were when your first...'

'Ha. All right. Fourteen.'

He could see that I was trying to remember who had been his girlfriend at that time. He was not having that.

'Hey,' he interrupted my thoughts, 'nobody you know. One does that with cheap girls.'

Mother always warned Susan and me not to make ourselves cheap. I looked at him questioningly.

'No. Real cheap girls. Not whores exactly, cheap girls.'

'Were you in love with them?'

'I quite liked them. It's different. One wants them, and they want you to be good at it. Afterwards they expect a present, a money present. Remember, two years ago, when Rolf and Kurt and I cycled all the way to Camberg? We stayed at a small inn in Heilbronn for the first night.'

'Oh, yes, I remember.' I had been impressed with this marathon run. Arnold and his friends had undertaken a real endurance test. 'Go on.'

'After I had gone to bed, the waitress came into my room. She was my first one.'

'Had you asked her to come to your room?'

'Of course not. But those cheap girls, they know.'

'How?'

'She said, the way I had looked at her. Well, I couldn't help it. Anybody would. Her breasts stuck out like two turrets.'

'You had not said anything to her?'

'No, one has to be careful. All the way. And some of them try to rob you afterwards. They go through your things if they can.'

'Did she rob you?'

'I hardly had anything on me. None of us did.'

'I bet that made her mad.'

'Shut up! She got enough. She cleaned me out. I had to borrow in the morning from Rolf, for the hotel bill.'

I remembered that trip well. They had tried to prove on how little they could travel.

'Robbing – that's disgusting,' I said.

Arnold shrugged his shoulders.

One thing was certain: I was never going to be cheap.

'What about your conquests?' asked Arnold.

I found that kissing business was very over-rated. Not a bit romantic, like it is in the books. When the boys escorted me home they planted a peck on my cheek. That was customary. Half the time they only kissed the air.

'Oh, nothing,' I said.

At the last New Years Party, which was held at the Jewish-owned Station Hotel – all functions were held there since Jews were no longer admitted to hotels, theatres, or cinemas – some man had tried to kiss me.

187

'Come on, Bemmerle [a slightly sarcastic diminutive of "baby"],' Arnold said, 'let's have it. One good story deserves another.'

So I decided to tell Arnold what had happened at the party.

I had worn my new dress. It was quite long, almost mid-calf. Mother held that a short dress was no longer suitable.

It really had been a good party; everybody was there. They had a cabaret. The chansonette was wonderful, that Madame Lipinskaja. It had never occurred to me how amusing the story of the Princess and the pea really was, with the prince hiding under the bed. After all, it was a fairy tale by Grimm, one you told to little children. There was also a new song called 'Our Herman'. It was very popular in Berlin, she said. Herman Goering, the important Nazi, was a good-looking tall, fat man. He had been an important flyer in World War I. Medals proliferated on his big chest and stomach.

'Medals to the right, medals to the left...' His sleeves got caught up in them when he heil-hitlered. I assumed he was rather pleased with the publicity; no-one had as many medals as Herman.

In the interval a young man started a conversation with me. I know it's silly, but I was flattered. He was a grown-up, and not bad looking either.

'Who was he?'

'I don't know. He said his name was Emmanuel and that he was staying with relatives over the holidays.'

'How old do you think he was?'

'Oh, pretty ancient. At least twenty-five. He offered to introduce me to Madame Lipinskaja. He said he knew her.'

'Did he?'

'What, know her? How do I know. I never found out. He took me behind stage, behind the curtain where they keep the props, to wait for her whilst she was changing. No sooner had we got there than he said, "What about a little kiss?" I said, "No thank you."'

The cheek of it. He just grabbed me – he was holding my face in both his hands.

I hissed, 'Let me go. I'll tell my Father.'

He laughed. 'I'm not doing anything.'

'You let me go, or I'll scream.' I wouldn't have screamed, how could I? With all those people there. And he knew that too.

'I'm only thirteen,' I said, hoping that would do it.

He didn't believe me. 'We have all been thirteen once.' And he was looking me up and down, calculating how much bust I had.

'You are getting quite nice,' Arnold interrupted.

'You're just as bad!' Arnold took that to be a compliment.

Should I continue with my story – he was not even taking it seriously.

'He was a perfect beast!'

'Don't shout like that. All right, what did he do?'

'He was squeezing me hard. He did not even let go when I stepped on his foot. A pity I had my silver slippers on; they have no heels. He was kissing me all over my neck. I was struggling and trying to kick him. I could have spat at him. He called me a wild cat. Luckily someone came then. I felt so ashamed. Euch!'

Arnold said, 'Struggling gets them more mad. You must not lose your head; you must use it, Bemmerle. You should have asked him for a glass of water, or lemonade, or something. Then you can give him the slip. Of course you must ask very nicely, otherwise they get suspicious. Let them walk about with the glass for a little while, looking for you. That'll cool them down.'

'Oh, that's clever. I do hope I can think of it. He was horrible. And I'm not your Bemmerle! How did you know about the glass of water? I suppose it was your own experience.'

'Not yet, not yet. I shall try to work my charm on them.' Arnold was so entertaining; he was popular.

'Perhaps,' I said to myself, 'I should be glad that they look at me.' I scrutinised myself in the mirror. It was a laugh – I was the Germanic type. I would have much preferred to look exotic. It would have been more mysterious.

I was not going to let just anyone kiss me. Not unless I loved them, or at least, liked them very much. What about the other thing? I could wait till I got married. One could not always get married. Suppose the Great Love came along. Great Love. In books. In films. No, really, if the Great Love came, what did one do? If one could not get married, one waited. Decent girls wait. Yes, one waited until one became an old maid. One was respectable, but nobody looked at one except one's cat – if one had a cat. I knew several old maids, nice ladies; they had waited until their young men could afford to marry them. When the time came, the young men married someone else.

When one listened to the mothers talk – those who had grown up daughters – it made one sick. They were spreading out a big

189

net to catch a good fish. The trouble was there were not enough men to go round, since the Great War.

Catching husbands. Perhaps it was better after all, to have lovers. Yes, lovers and illegitimate babies. Those Aunt Millies of the magazine – the ones who did the heart-to-heart columns, with their advice on how to catch, hold and ditch a man – I bet they were all written by men who were having one on. The marriage advertisements – the newspapers were full of them – too, were very interesting: Brunette, *vollschlank* (full-slims, a polite word for moderately fat), aged thirty-nine. 'Serious offers' meant that they were respectable. 'Holidays, share expenses', meant they were easy.

I wondered if people really answered those adverts. Did they use the Marriage Agencies who offered different services for friendship and marriage at moderate fees? Was this the last resort?

Times were changing. The younger generation went to holiday camps, arranged by the Party. The outdoor life was very healthy. Plenty of exercise. They exercised in the nude, without as much as a g-string on. A healthy body, a healthy mind: a German. Parents were uneasy, though they hardly dared voice their fears.

The older people went on *Kraft durch Freude* (strength through joy) trips, which were also arranged by the Party. One could pay for them on the instalment plan. There were sing-songs, folk dancing, camp fires, marching, motor excursions, even cruises by luxury steamers and plenty of good, clean Nazi fun. One was no longer lonely. One had never had it so good. If one did not wish to keep the resulting baby, one could always make a present of it to the Party. They had great need of pure-race German babies, and they were only too glad the birth rate was going up.

Mother said, 'They need cannon fodder.'

The older girls in the BDM had lectures on German motherhood. Motherhood ennobles, with or without wedding rings. The stigma of unwed motherhood was outdated.

Before one could get married, one had to get a certificate of marriage-worthiness (*Ehetauglichkeitzeugnis*) and one had to prove one's pure-race Aryan descent. This was sometimes difficult. From 1933 they had licensed *Sippenforscher* (family researchers), whose help could be enlisted, to find the needed documents.

They were also useful in cases where one found a Jewish grandparent or great-grandparent. They could help prove that the Jewish grandparent in question had been cuckolded by the Christian

190

lover of the Christian grandparent, with true Nordic cunning (a term much used then), and one could therefore apply for a Befreiung (liberation from the stain of Jewish blood).

In the case of an officer of the SS, a family tree going as far back as 1750, to prove non-Jewish descent, was required.

So great was the desire for race-pure German babies, that special luxury resthouses were established for the use of SS officers. There, preferably blond, but more often dark, German maidens did their holy German duty and presented the Fuehrer with race-pure babies. Arnold said, 'Perhaps instead of saying "I love you", they say "*Heil Hitler*".' These babies were then reared in children's homes under the auspices of the Party, homes which were suitable for the children of the élite.

Mother maintained that decent girls are virgins on their wedding night. I had read statistics in a *Stuermer Kasten* (glass covered display of the newspaper) which proved that decent girls were a dying race. I really did not know what to think.

My favourite heroine, Joanna, from Leon Feuchtwanger's book *Success*, had slept with everybody – well almost everybody. At first she had done it to get a reprieve for Martin who was in prison. Everybody respected Joanna. She was no 'cheap' girl. But she was a Munich girl, and I remembered Father had told us they were very gay and bohemian in Munich. Perhaps, because she was an emancipated woman, she could get away with it. She was well-educated.

My family believed in education – education suitable for young ladies. The times were changing. No longer were girls expected to sit around at home after Finishing School in Switzerland, filling in with welfare work, Kindergarten and other jobs, which were preparation for getting married. No longer did the parents arrange balls and invitations to, as Arnold would put it, 'advertise the merchandise'.

I was going to be a well-educated girl, so that people would be pleased to give me a job, a proper job.

'Miss Sylvia,' asked the little voice in me, 'how exactly will you achieve this? Where, may I ask you, and who is going to pay for it?'

That was the question. Jews were no longer allowed to attend universities, colleges, art schools. Everything in Germany seemed to be closed to them.

191

Luckily for me, we could still attend the Ladies' Seminary. I would stay there for another two years, pass my exams, and then perhaps I could go abroad to a college. Switzerland, England, Paris ... I think Paris. It was good for dress design. Besides, I had relatives there.

Who was going to pay for it? Apart from the money, the foreign currency presented problems. Well, who ... ? Father couldn't. 'When the time comes, I'll get round someone.,' I said to myself. 'One of our relatives. Mother's family – they liked me, they had no girls themselves.'

We were now very patriotic at the Ladies' Seminary.

History, German Literature, Geography: all these lessons were taken up exclusively to show how wonderful the Fatherland was – or would have been if we had not lost the war, which was due to having been stabbed in the back. There had been traitors, international traitors: the Communists, the Social Democrats, the Jews. In Geography we were shown the border lines of Germany, the ones which were by right ours. We inked them in in our old atlases. Soon we would get our New German atlas.

Germany's National Anthem was: '*Deutschland, Deutschland, ueber alles, ueber alles in der Welt*' (Germany, Germany, over all, above everything in the world). It was not new and had been sung long before Hitler came to power. Nor was *Lebensraum* a new idea. It had been advocated by Kaiser Wilhelm and his Chancellor Bismarck. The people living to the East of Germany, the Slavonic races (Poles, Czechoslovakians, Russians, and the peoples of the Baltic States) were considered inferior (*minderwertig*), and should service Germany, particularly with agricultural products and labour – slave labour.

We were initiated into the glorious German heritage of cultures. We did the *Niebelungen Lied* in the ancient German language. We did nothing else for the whole of the year in our German Literature lessons. Much was made of the quarrel between the two queens, Kriemhilde and Brunhilde, the quarrel on the cathedral steps where they called each other names like *Kebsweib* (an archaism for concubine or whore.) The teacher did not say which was the better translation. We also designed a family tree of the German gods. The mighty Wotan was on top, then the fiery Donar, and all the rest of them; and who begot who, legitimately and illegitimately. Half gods and quarter gods, we had to learn them all off by heart.

The origin and abode of the gods and notables was rather hazy. Was it Walhalla, Thule, Atlantis, Iceland or even the Teutoburger Forest? In Munich, many people knew about it. Their members were all Aryans. They preached the superiority of the Aryan Race. They belonged to the Thule Association. They were all anti-Semitic, because the Jews stood for everything evil and corrupt. Adolf Hitler was very active there; he was their best speaker.

Rosenberg was the expert on German Mythology. He was not bad looking. Baldur von Schirach, the Youth Leader, was better looking, according to my class mates, because he looked more Germanic. They all were members of the Thule Society.

To link up, in our art lessons, we were allowed to draw the two queens and colour them with watercolour. I used the thirteenth-century Countess Uta von Naumburg as a model. Her statue is outside Naumburg cathedral. She was beautiful, the most beautiful, of all the medieval ladies. I got full marks for my Kriemhilde. I did not like Brunhilde; I gave her a helmet, a double chin, and an enormous bosom. Still, I got full marks for her too.

By that time I had quite a good collection of art books. Most of them had been birthday presents. It was a motley collection.

The Italian Renaissance was well represented. My paternal grandmother had given me a set, bound in red linen with gold tooling, one volume almost every year. Relatives gave books only on classic painters or sculptors – safe presents. My first book, Raphael, I had received when I was six years old. When I had an upset over something or other, I would go to my room and look at my books and let them console me. I would sit and look and dream.

I loved my little books the best. Most of them I had bought out of my own pocket money. They were well produced, on good paper, with fine coloured reproductions of the *Jnsel Verlag*. I never tired of looking at the Bordersholmer Altar by Master Brueggeman, carved out of some coarse-grained wood, the swirling pattern of the grain accentuating the movement, or the Codex Manesse, the knights so gallant with garlands in their wavy hair and the ladies so innocent and utterly lovely with their children's faces.

When I was given money instead of a present, I sometimes indulged myself and bought a large art book. I had a Daumier. I was almost frightened when I looked at it; the injustice of life was so real there, it felt true, it was menacing. I had also bought a book on Archipenko. I was fascinated and wanted to understand. I thought, now I shall know how men think of women, what they think of them, and about them. These women had mountains of thighs. The first time I looked at it I was dumbfounded. How dare he? One had only to listen to the boys and men talk and one could easily see that he put down on paper only what they felt. If one wanted representational work, one could get a camera. On the other hand, if their girlfriends really had thighs like that; they wouldn't look at them twice, the girls would surely waddle. I went to the various encyclopaedias and looked up what 'abstract art' and all the other terms meant.

Abstract: That which comprises in itself the essential qualities of a larger thing or of several things. What the thing meant, not what it looked like, a kind of shorthand for the initiated. Most people did not know that shorthand and the artists, who were no artists, traded on it. The books written on the subject were hard to read, I couldn't get on with them at all. With all that talk about Degenerate Art in the papers and everywhere, one had to know what they were talking about. Finally I came to the conclusion that they (the Nazis), must be crazy. If they had called the women like those done by Archipenko '*Entartete Kunst*' (degenerate art), though I would not agree with that judgment, I could understand it. An old aunt of mine, seeing the book lying on my table, had been so shocked, that she had remonstrated with Father. Father had smiled that special smile of his, and said he agreed it was rather an unusual choice for a young girl.

It was amazing what the Nazis called *Entartete Kunst*. Works by the French Impressionists! Surely those were 'tame' enough?

That's just what they were not – tame. They said what they wanted. And the works of Cezanne, Gaugin and Van Gogh were put in the cellars of the museums to join Picasso, Matisse and all the rest. Museum attendants often talked to me when I was on my own. Once, one had said to me nostalgically, 'You should see what we have downstairs in our cellars, Miss. It's a shame! And we paid a lot for them too.' 6,500 modern paintings were removed from public view.

Now we got German art. Clean and wholesome. All in classical nudity. Only once had I gone to an exhibition of this. One particular piece troubled me. Where had I seen that girl before? I knew her, that girl with the two coils over her ears, with that large permanently

194

fixed grin. On the way home it came to me: it was the girl from the margarine advertisement, the one which said, 'Ella [brand name of margarine], tastes so good.' It was on hoardings everywhere. The young men looked too like posters, like those with the invitation to join the *Arbeits Dienst*. One could almost see those statues coming to attention and saying *'Heil Hitler'*.

With the books it was the same. The best of German literature had been burned publicly. That had been Goebbel's doing; he was in charge of the Reichs Chamber of Culture. As early as 1933 they had their book bonfires. Of course most of the books burned were by Jewish authors: the works of Mann, Zweig, Wassermann, Feuchtwanger, Schnitzler and Freud. They also burned foreign authors like Gide, Proust and Havelock Ellis. They did not fit in with the policy of 'German Culture', which from now on had to serve the progress of the Third Reich.

Every manuscript or play had to be submitted to the Ministry of Propaganda before publication.

Nearly all writers emigrated.

They even burnt The Code Napoleon. No, I could not believe it. The Code Napoleon had liberated the whole of Europe from serfdom. Did they not know that?

Nazi students started book burning fires in most university towns. They had sacked the Jewish professors, all the Jewish staff, even the Nobel Prize winners, and replaced them with Party members.

The Nobel Prize professors emigrated.

Books with a setting in the mountainous districts of Bavaria or the Allgau seemed very popular now. They bored me; if one had read one, one had read all of them.

The theme was always the same: about cows and *fensterln* (entry though the bedroom window by the hero). *Ja, ja, dann kam das kind* (yes, yes, then came the baby). After the christening, the hard father would relent. He had to bless the marriage between that 'penniless beggar', a foreigner from Prussia, and his daughter, his only child and heir. The preacher had openly hinted at things in his sermon – about hellfire, camels and eyes of needles. He had looked straight at him, Alois, all the time. So his dream of merging his farm with the *Gestadtner Hof* had come to nothing. Damn it all! They grew the best and largest turnips there; they were special, those turnips. And he, Alois, had hoped to feed his cattle on them. How else could he get a prize at the annual cattle show?

No, not all was lost. The 'penniless beggar', his son-in-law, had studied animal husbandry. How could he have known that? They never told him anything. His daughter – after all, she was his girl – could really pick them. They got the second prize. Who knows? Perhaps next year they might even get the first prize.

This formula seemed successful. It sold. Many books written for local consumption were in a similar vein. The people living in the mountainous districts identified with them.

Fensterln became even more popular. 'Foreigners' tried it. The rate of illegitimate birth went up.

It was not my concern what those 'yokels' did. I was not even shocked. I disliked the way they wrote about it because the characters were not sympathetic.

The book *Kleiner Mann, was nun?* (*Little man, what now?*), by Hans Fallada, had made a deep impression on me. The heroine there was pregnant too. But it was different. The young man had sold cattle fodder. Still it was different. They loved each other, there was tenderness, they were family. It was a beautifully written book, all about the Depression in Germany. That was outdated now. The Depression was over, thanks to Hitler.

Hitler took a personal interest in the cultural life of Germany. After all, he was an artist too. He had made a living out of art in his Vienna days. The Fuehrer could do everything; that's why he was the Fuehrer.

* * *

They were building the House for German Art in Munich. Hitler had helped to design it. It was going to be ready next year. Hitler personally supervised the selection of the paintings. Of the fifteen thousand submitted, nine hundred were hung. He did not entirely approve the choice his committee had made, and he kicked holes with his jackboots in some of the paintings.

The story circulated that Adolf Hitler's favourite bedtime book was *The Treasure of the Silver Lake* by Karl May. Arnold owned that book. I had read it years ago; I read it again. But Red Indians and treasure hunts were no longer my taste.

Chapter 23

About Education

By now most people I met addressed me as Miss – I was almost fourteen – only my friends still called me 'du'. I felt quite grown up, terribly old. My schoolmates seemed to me like children, I had little in common with them.

They giggled all the time. It irritated me. They stood in corners and swooned over film stars. It irritated me. They passed to each other, under the benches, little slips of paper on which were written the titles of 'interesting' books, complete with the number of the page where the 'bit' was. It irritated me. If these notes reached my desk, I 'lost' them.

The pace in school was too slow for me, the endless repetition unbearable. The knowledge was handed out in minute doses, and then it was chewed over and over again.

On the whole the teachers here were all right They never persecuted one, as they did in other towns. Not yet, not yet, said the little voice in me. No, they wouldn't be like that here. A girl in the class above me, named Ilse, had had to leave her school in Gunzenhausen because it was awful there for her. She now lived here with her aunt.

I wondered why they let us remain in the school. Was it that they did not believe what the Nazis said about us Jews? That must be it. They knew better. They never said anything nasty to me, or to any of the other Jewish girls in my class. Perhaps they had not forgotten that my family established in 1869 a scholarship fund which made it possible every year for three talented pupils from poor families to transfer from elementary school and get a higher education in the grammar school of our town, quite apart from the scholarships awarded to bright sons of our staff in the factory.

Scholarships in our town were not awarded purely on the basis of talent; there was a means test, and only poor students were eligible. I found our school fees high, even if Susan, as the third child, paid less. Everything had to be paid for. School books were a big item, especially that year.

'What again?' asked Mother. 'Can't you get the old one from your cousin Erica?'

'No, it's no good, they use different ones now.'

On many days the atmosphere in the class room was tense. The trouble was one was just sitting waiting for something to happen, particularly on days when there had been a nasty bit of propaganda in the newspapers. The girls discussed it in whispers during their break, I could not hear what they were saying, but one could tell, by the way they stole glances at us, when they thought we were not looking, that they were speculating as to whether, for example, that nasty Jew Lendt in Berlin could possibly be a relation of Lisa Lendt's.

I realised that I had become touchy. If anything went wrong in school it was because I was Jewish. I told myself I must not imagine things; things had gone wrong before as well, in the old days.

I rarely got lines now, and I read just as much under my desk. Did I become more skilled in my surreptitious reading or was it that they did not care if I paid attention or not?

The teachers were all right, even if they turned up most days in their Nazi uniforms. I had learned not to see the uniform any more.

The new teacher, Dr Beck, always came in uniform. He had replaced Gilling. Nobody liked him, but it was not his fault that Gilling had left. When Gilling came to say goodbye to us, he told us that it was only because of promotion, and he needed it with another baby on the way. That was his sixth. Some girls had cried. I was sorry he left; he was a wonderful teacher.

Dr Beck was very young looking, no older than a student. His duelling scars were hardly healed. He taught botany and zoology. He was very scientific and used many long words. He knew many more than I did – he dazzled the girls with them. However, he did write them on the blackboard, so that was all right.

He took us through Mendel's Theory. He had prepared a pretty card, with white and red carnations, and of course pink ones –

they were easier to draw than sweetpeas. He demonstrated the effect one red carnation could have amongst white ones: pink ones, red ones, the pure white strain was never the same again. The pink carnations were apparently the trouble; one did not know where they belonged, to the whites or to the reds? These hybrids were not recognised as belonging to either parent species. The girls looked at Trudi Fahner – she was a pretty girl.

Arnold claimed that Eurasian women were the most beautiful of all – not that he knew any. Admittedly, they looked gorgeous on the pictures I had seen.

I liked pink carnations. I was also fascinated by the 'fancies' and picotees. Father had a book with lovely colour plates of the old-fashioned 'flakes' and 'bizarres'. Carnations were my Father's favourite flower.

'Sir,' I said, 'Dianthus, this carnation, won a prize at the flower show in Stuttgart. It's a pink one.' Actually it had got only a mention, but I wasn't going to tell Beck that. I had taken note of it because Father was so fond of carnations. 'It is the wider implications we are interested in,' said Dr Beck. 'You must consider the mixing of a good with an inferior strain.'

I dearly would have loved to say to Dr Beck, 'Why don't you tell the bees and the butterflies?' I didn't dare. I was a coward.

We cut templates for the simple five-petalled wild carnation. Our homework was to colour them in. I took great trouble over my pink and red ones.

One couldn't argue with Beck. Anyway, the carnations were bi-sexual and the class would think I had brought it up for that reason.

I made an additional sheet, copying fancies, bizarres and picotees from the book, all the red/white mixtures I could find.

Dr Beck pretended not to notice my extra sheet when he inspected our homework; my classmates certainly did.

All this irritated me.

The Jews were not inferior, no matter what the Nazis said. History proved that. I'd never realised there were so many famous Jews, or half-Jews, the 'pink' ones. Arnold and I made a list. Arnold said the baptised Jews were to be represented as red with white hats on.

There had not been many Jews in the Reichstag of the Weimar Republic. The German Foreign Minister, Walther Rathenau, had been shot by a lunatic.

I was very interested in the story of Jew Suess, who had been Wuerttemberg's Finance Director and unofficial Prime Minister under Herzog Karl Alexander in the eighteenth century. He ended up being hanged publicly, in a cage, though he was innocent of the crime of which he was accused. A special grandstand had been erected for the members of the Court. The ladies, who had been his amours, fainted. Everyone had turned out to watch the spectacle. It was a public holiday. Jew Suess died, reciting a Jewish prayer.

Was he really the illegitimate son of the Field Marshall Baron Georg Eberhard von Heydersdorf? His mother had been the beautiful Michaela Suess, an actress and a member of a troupe who performed at the various courts of the principalities in Germany.

We decided that the Jews had done best for themselves in England. There had been a Prime Minister, and a Viceroy – the Bernheimer girls bragged about this. There were also many members of Parliament.

Perhaps Jews were accepted at the English Court because of Prince Albert of Saxe-Coburg-Gotha. And perhaps Albert, because he was 'unofficially' half Jewish was accepted by the English Parliament. There was haemophilia in Saxe-Coburg-Gotha. The Jewish banker in Paris had thick red blood.

Father was of the opinion that mixtures often had interesting results, different qualities complimenting each other. Once he had said to me, 'Take a little Robber Knight, a little of Jewish merchant, a beautiful devout woman, shake well and, hey presto, what do you get? A god-fearing pioneer of Industry.'

In school almost every week there was some parade or other. We had to assemble in the playground, in our gym hall or were taken to some part of the town to line the streets and cheer if some important Nazi was on his way through.

If it had been Hitler, that would have been worthwhile, but it was usually only a Gauleiter, or someone we had never heard of. To remedy that, we were given a lecture on our return to our class room, to inform us who the important man had been, and what precisely he did for us in our glorious Third Reich. Many lessons were cancelled because of these parades.

It irritated me.

Some girls could quote long passages from *Mein Kampf* by heart. They had learned it at Hitler Youth, where they chanted selected passages in unison. I found *Mein Kampf* hard reading and aggressive – malicious gibberish, in fact.

It irritated me.

Mein Kampf became a bestseller. In Germany it replaced the Bible. Many schools gave copies to pupils on graduation day, though not ours. Brides were presented with it on their wedding day. I had not heard that it was given for a christening present, not so far. Hitler's royalties were fifteen per cent and he paid no income tax. By 1940, six million copies had been sold.

Mein Kampf contained the outline of the future German stage, the Nazi conception of life (*Weltanschaung*) and directives on how Germany could become the Lord of the Earth.

It was almost as though people prayed to Hitler instead of God. The priests who did not fall in with the new creed were sent to concentration camps. Some priests, however, were more amenable to the new doctrine. Preaching against the Jews made popular sermons. In one church in Berlin, after a particularly vicious sermon against the Jews, there was a hush. Then everyone saw it, everyone heard it, even though they could hardly believe it: our Lord Jesus Christ climbed down from the cross, went over to Mary and said, 'Mummy, let's get out of here. They've got no room for us Jews.' That was the story, anyway, and it spread quickly. I wish it had been true.

Lila's father, Uncle Julius Guggenheim, had two sisters living in Zurich. They had sent him a newspaper cutting of a court case. He showed the newspaper cutting to my father and Arnold. The subject was 'The Protocols of the Elders of Zion'. This was based on a completely fabricated and forged document, which had originated in Czarist Russia, and had also been reprinted later in Paris. The subject of the book was 'Jew-baiting' and it had been banned. Arnold told me that if a book gets banned it gets publicity, people rush to buy it, sales increase and it gets reprinted secretly. Books on the Vatican's forbidden list have a large turn-over. The 'Elders of Zion' was full of lies about the Jews wanting to dominate the world, about wrecking the economy, about enslaving the gentiles, but people believed this garbage. Arnold said he thought Adolf Hitler's book *Mein Kampf* was based on it. The funding for the court case had come straight from Berlin. Arnold was not surprised. 'It figures,' he said.

Whenever there was any unpleasantness at school, however indirect, it brought our problem uppermost. Would they let us stay on in the Ladies' Seminary, or would they throw us out?

There was no local *Judenschule*. Richard was a boarder in Esslingen, in the Jewish orphanage for boys. He liked it there; they had beautiful grounds and a wonderful view, for the building was on top of a hill.

There was nothing like this for girls in the district.

For the past two weeks, my mind had not been on school matters. Mother was not feeling well, and might have to go into hospital for a minor operation. She, however, insisted she was only going for a check up and seemed more concerned with what would happen to us children. Grandfather was then in poor health, so Grandmother could not come to look after us.

I told Mother not to worry; I would look after everything. I was a big girl. 'You won't be there long. I'll come and report every day,' I said. I made out a specimen menu and a list of the daily and weekly chores. To my surprise this seemed to satisfy Mother. I knew I would be able to do it, given the chance, but I had not expected that Mother would share the good opinion I had of myself and entrust the running of the household to me. Mrs Woehr, our charlady, was very reliable and had promised to come a little earlier in the mornings. She regretted she could not stay longer as she had to see to her husband's lunch, and in the afternoons she had another job. In winter she usually had come at eight o'clock. I gave my instructions and the shopping list to her before I left for school at 7.45.

Everything went according to plan. I usually got up at half past five. After making coffee for Father, I did the library, which served as Father's study, and his laboratory. I was well aware it was an honour to be allowed inside, let alone touch his things.

However, he was not very pleased with me when one morning I 'tidied' the many rows of bottles. I had felt very energetic and those bottles looked so untidy, so I had arranged them by size and shape, mixing up tinctures and extracts, oils and so on.

After the laboratory, I dusted our 'works of art'; Mrs Woehr said she was afraid to touch them. Mother usually did this herself. How the time was flying! I chased Susan out of bed – it was her turn to make breakfast. She was 'sooo ti-red'. I scolded her, saying it was more work getting her out of bed than preparing the breakfast. No further prompting was required after that.

My grandmother, Emilie Rosenthaler, aged 6, with her mother. Photo taken about 1860.

Grandfather Samuel Fleischer.   Grandfather Moritz May.

My two brothers

Arnold, born 1920 (approx 24 years old here).   Richard, born 1927.

My parents in about 1919.
Julius, born 1882, and Irma, born 1894.

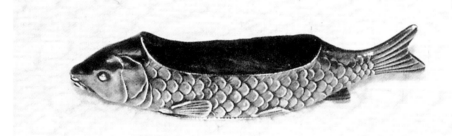

My little fish - this is a silver mid-Victorian pincushion, a precious gift from my mother.

A letterhead from about 1890.

Villa Fleischer, it was built in about 1890 and later was the residence of the
Oberbürgermeister (Mayor).

Photo courtesy of Amanda Hurst

Father in about 1910.

Arnold, Great-Grandfather Leopold, Sylvia, Mother, baby Susan and Grandmother Hedwig, in about 1923.

Arnold, Sylvia and Susan in about 1923 with our fully-trained children's nurse.

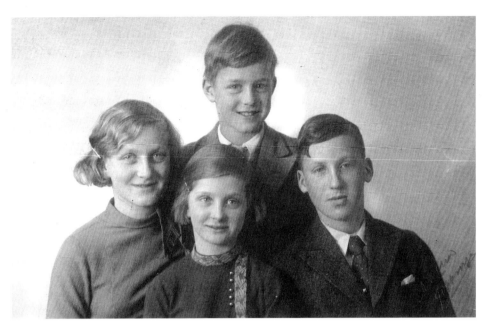

Sylvia, Susan, Richard and Arnold, 1933.

Richard at 4 years old with Hede and Sylvia (aged 9).

My cousin Eva Fleischer, about 20 years old.

Arnold, Susan, Erika, Sylvia and Richard on holiday in Eckenweiler.

Susan aged about 21 years old on her engagement to Philip Nassau.

There was no need to rush home in order to prepare the lunch, Mrs Woehr had cleaned the vegetables, and I always chose a dish which needed little cooking time. How proud I was when the family asked for second helpings! By then I could cook most dishes, besides there were cookery books to help out; it was an adventure. I studied the calorific and vitamin content of my menu in order to produce a balanced diet. I even got around to baking cakes and pastries and took the best ones to hospital for Mother.

Mother was well cared for. The Chief Surgeon, who was one of Father's friends, looked after her personally.

I visited her almost every day, though I hardly got a chance to talk to her as she always had visitors.

I would leave the previous day's menu on her side table, together with clean nightdresses and anything else she had asked for.

I took great trouble with the ironing of these nightdresses selecting only her best ones, which were of pure silk with heavy lace encrustations. They were a bother! If the lace was right for ironing, the silk was too wet. If the silk was right, then the lace was crinkly. But I was not to be beaten. Finally I managed it with the help of a damp handkerchief. Mother could not fault it; there was not a single crease.

Feeling very smug and self-satisfied, I thought the grown-ups made a big fuss about 'running a house'. I did not find it difficult at all.

Arnold said, 'When the machinery is set up, any fool can "run" it.'

'You do it then,' I retorted.

'All right,' he answered. 'I'll cook dinner this week.'

Now it was I who asked for second helpings and, somewhat grudgingly, had to admit that he was the better cook.

For Mother's homecoming we baked a large *torte*, a joint effort. I decorated it and wrote on it with butter cream 'Welcome Home'. It was not very legible, but according to Richard, who was home for the occasion, it looked different from 'Happy Birthday'. 'Any donkey could see that,' he said.

Mother was pleased with the *torte*. She said everything was nice and clean, except the lace curtains. These were absolutely shocking. What was she to do? She could not take them down now, with all the visitors. Every day ladies came to visit and enquire after her health. The weather had been bad, and the curtains were rather soiled as Father liked the windows wide open, no matter what the time of year. She was very cross with me about the curtains.

It hurt me that she seemed to see only what I had forgotten. I stalked off in a temper, but when I reached my room I cried and cried.

Amongst the callers was Aunt Felicia. Whilst Mother was getting dressed – after her afternoon rest – I showed Aunt Felicia into the sitting room and kept company whilst I was waiting for the water to boil for coffee.

She said she had missed me at the Keep Fit classes. I had sent word that I had no time to attend; she was very particular about notes of absence.

I fetched a dish of '*Gutsel*' (small assorted pastries, like petit fours), telling her proudly that I had baked them myself.

She seemed astonished, so astonished that she asked Mother if this was really so. Mother told her that not only had I baked, I had run the house as well in her absence. I could see Aunt Felicia looking around the room for hidden dust, but I was not worried. I had dusted very carefully that morning, knowing what the '*hausfraus*' were like.

A week later Father suggested that he and I should go for a walk. It was my birthday. This was a treat indeed. It had been quite some time since we had been together in Beecherwood. The first buds were showing and there were a few primroses.

Father enquired about school. I told him about all the parades and how I was fed up with them. One did not learn anything, there was no time. They had increased the hours of sports and 'recreation'. 'If one is good at sports, one can get away with anything – even flunk tests and exams! You can be as dim as you like.'

'Would you like to leave school?' asked Father.

'I don't know ... I might as well stay on until they throw us out.' I was thinking, if I stay at home, Mother will soon be tired of having me under her feet. 'What with the propaganda, it's pretty unpleasant. One has got to sit and listen to it.'

'All the teachers?' asked Father.

'In one way or another. I don't think they actually *mean* to be nasty to us. I wish I could go with Lila to Switzerland.'

'Yes, my dear. If only I could afford to send you.'

Father looked at me with pain in his eyes.

'Anyway,' I said, 'we've no foreign currency,' hoping this would console him. I was sorry I had mentioned it. 'I don't want to be a secretary. Lila says you can become a bi-lingual secretary in that school in Neuf Chatel. It would bore me, and I don't want to sit on my boss's lap either.'

I thought, If I had the choice, I'd rather go to university. I did not want to be a 'young lady'. You're letting your fantasy run away – be realistic, girl! Once and for all, this foolish thinking must stop. Those dreams are sheer self-indulgence. Don't waste your time with things you know can never be. And from then on I really did put these thoughts out of my mind and started to cultivate a more realistic attitude. 'If it were not for the social side, I doubt if many girls would go to Switzerland. They mostly only do languages, secretarial stuff, or domestic science,' said I.

'Domestic science is very useful nowadays, especially if you have a certificate.'

German Jewish women and girls emigrated, on Labour Permits, to foreign countries, particularly England. People became tired of hiring German cooks and chambermaids through agencies, and finding then, after they had sent the permit, the new 'staff' were not qualified for the work. The refugees were said to sit in the kitchen and cry, complaining that they had never done work like that before, that they had always had a maid at home. This may have been an exaggeration, but most people insisted on seeing a reference of at least a year's service.

'I thought my cooking was all right,' said I.

'Yes, you did very well when your Mother was ill,' agreed Father, 'though it would not help very much if you tried to get a job abroad. They would ask for a certificate or a reference.'

'We don't do domestic science in the Ladies' Seminary, they do it at the *Volks Schule*.'

'Tell me,' said Father, 'do you like Aunt Felicia?'

'Why do you ask? I've not been to her classes lately. She is terrific – in sports. I don't really know her, apart from the classes.'

'I had a long talk with her yesterday. She told me that she had heard from the girls at the Keep Fit classes how unpleasant it was for you at school. Did you know that she has a Diploma in Cookery? She trained under a first class chef in Stuttgart.

'Yes, she showed it to us when she had us to coffee in her house. She got honours.'

'She has offered to take you as apprentice, for a "household year".'

(This household year, together with the 'land year' had really been a Nazi invention. 'Labour is holy' said the Nazis. They made it official in order to take away the stigma, of being a domestic servant, or a peasant. Country girls spent a year in a city household, for keep and pocket money, and City girls a year on a farm or in a farm camp, for keep, fresh air, and pocket money.)

In the evening I discussed it with Arnold. I said if I was going to do a Household Year, why could it not be with some of our relatives in France? (There was a French branch of the family, a numerous tribe.) French cooking was famous – more famous than Aunt Felicia's chef, surely. And I would learn the language properly. Dr Koehler always insisted that a language could only be 'perfected' in the country. When I had 'practised' with our French cousins, I realised how right he was. We had relatives in England too.

Arnold said, 'You're forgetting, you're just fourteen. I don't think our relatives would have you – "a child". They would say, "Too much responsibility". I know, and you know, that you're not too young, but they don't know that.'

'She's got a Diploma in Cookery.'

'What kind?' Arnold was interested in cookery.

'Only from some hotel, I think. I can't remember. She's got two people in the house, a cook and a cleaner.'

'What are you supposed to do?'

'I am to be her apprentice. She's worked out quite a programme; it's very impressive. She said she'd show me everything. Apart from the usual, she wants me to go two afternoons a week to sewing classes, to the nuns. She's offered to give me ten marks pocket money a month.'

'Ten marks a month! That won't hurt her, ha! What about free time?'

'Every other Sunday afternoon and evening, and one evening a week after dinner. She said she can't give me more afternoons because of the sewing classes.'

'That's not much free time,' said Arnold.

'She said I can sit in the garden in the afternoon with the children, so that someone is there to keep an eye on them.'

'Well, I suppose it's all right. There is really not much point in staying on at school.'

Most Jewish children left school prematurely for some reason or another. My classmate Helga was emigrating; her parents were

206

shortly going to the USA. That would leave only Lisa Lendt.

Arnold was transferring from the Gymnasium to the School of Commerce. He was to attend there part time, the remainder of the week as apprentice in Uncle Daniel's paper mill. This was a wonderful opportunity for him; the mill exported to countries all over the world. There was an office staff of eighty there. He was sure he would learn a lot.

He did. He was the youngest man ever to take the exam for Diploma Kauffman at the Wuerttembergische Chamber of Commerce. He received his mercantile diploma at eighteen.

To be an apprentice anywhere was no bed of roses. The older 'colleagues' took advantage of the youngsters; one had to expect that.

To attend the Ladies' Seminary was also no bed of roses.

I asked Mother for advice. She answered, 'Do as your father tells you. He never asked me. You can do as you like.'

She seemed somehow annoyed. I did not know why. Perhaps she was glad to be rid of me. I had been very sulky after the 'curtains affair'.

I decided to accept Aunt Felicia's offer.

I was almost fourteen years and one month old when I left home.

Chapter 24

'You Will be a Servant all Your Life'

Father 'delivered' me to Aunt Felicia's; it felt just like that.

He said, rather absentmindedly, 'Behave yourself', and 'God Bless you', and then he went.

The children came in from the garden. The boy grinned at me nervously, the little girl curtsied. Her mother said, 'This is not necessary, this is Sylvia.'

Aunt Felicia showed me to my room; it was a proper room, not a servant's attic.

Then I was introduced to Emmy. The cook, Emmy, looked me over, eyeing me with suspicion. I was told to obey her. 'If she says, come, you come; if she says go, you go.'

Somehow it gave Emmy satisfaction to pile the nastier jobs – such as scrubbing the front door steps and emptying the rubbish – on her former employer's grand-daughter.

Emmy was very fond of her old father, a bent, white-haired old man with the proverbial stick and slightly neglected clothes. Whenever I was sent to town to do the shopping, she took me aside and asked me to get her one or two bottles of white wine for her father. After I had been there a month, Emmy became ill. She cried. She told me she was sick. I helped her upstairs to her attic. The dinner that night was a cold one, which I could manage easily by myself. I asked Aunt Felicia what I might take up to Emmy. She replied contemptuously that Emmy did not need anything, only sleep. She was drunk! Aunt Felicia questioned me – no wines or spirits were missing – had I bought anything for Emmy? I replied, 'Oh, no, only for her father.' I could not understand this; I thought drunks were noisy men who sang in the streets late at night after the beerhalls were closed. I had never seen a lady drunk.

208

Emmy left the following week. During that week she did not honour me with a single word, but sent smouldering glances in my direction.

Shortly after Emmy's departure, the daily woman stayed away. When she came to collect her wages, she told us how sorry she was – she liked the job, but her husband had difficulties because she worked in a Jewish house.

She was not, or could not be, replaced.

There was now no time for me to go to my sewing classes, so to make up for it Aunt Felicia gave me all the mending to do. This included her personal things.

She maintained it was the same whether I learning sewing with the nuns, or with her at home.

She inspected the work most carefully before she passed it but she never showed me a single thing. I think I could have taught her, judging by 'old mends'.

Having no staff she did her own bedroom and bathroom. I had to do the rest of that very large house: stairs, passages, hall, the lot! She cooked lunch and dinner; I helped by preparing the vegetables.

The washing up and drying was my job; pans were inspected to see if they were shining brightly, which needed elbow grease – these were pre-Brillo days!

Aunt Felicia was an excellent cook, and made elaborate dishes. I felt she was quite justified in being proud of her achievements in pastries, patés and sauces, especially her sauce mousseline. She swore by her 'Escoffier'.

There were invitations to dinner every week, for it was then customary to entertain at home.

I would have loved to watch her do her 'special' dishes. After all, her cookery training was one of the reasons, if not the main reason, why my parents wanted me to be her 'apprentice'. But there was no time.

However much I rushed when I knew she was making one of her dishes, I just could not manage to be in the kitchen in time to watch her. The important part was over.

Occasionally I was allowed to stir something.

I was always in good time, though, to wash the saucepans, and she used stacks of them. Then Aunt Felicia would go upstairs, have a short rest, dress herself and come down beautifully groomed

– the perfect hostess. You would never believe that she had seen the inside of a kitchen.

'Big laundry day', once a month, was a nightmare every time. I used to get up at five to do my ordinary housework in order to be finished by seven, when Aunt Felicia would be ready to start. All the laundry, including bed linen and men's shirts, was washed at home. In the basement of the house was a laundry and an ironing room. Aunt Felicia operated the washing machine, a boiler/agitator type, non-electric, and supervised me. Because there was no wringer attachment, nor arrangement for rinsing, it was my job to do this by hand. How I hated those large Turkish towel bathsheets, when they were wet they weighed a ton! The master often used two clean shirts a day; commendable as this was, on laundry days I detested him – forty-five to fifty-five shirts were the average. It was customary for gentlemen to have dozens of shirts. In the old days, at home, we had two washerwomen and two ironing women, one to do shirts and collars only. Aunt Felicia had the reputation of being a most efficient woman, and laundry work was part of the curriculum. Luckily for me, or for him, Aunt Felicia agreed to send his white starched collars away. I learned to operate the steam-mangle, a small household model, well enough to do even aprons and plain pieces of underwear. I liked this steam-pressing very much. It was very restful; the hum of the machine lulled me. I could then daydream. I had always been good at ironing and had started to press my own hankies at the age of seven. When everything was finished, I would survey with satisfaction the gleaming stacks of linen. But I had no time to gloat over it – hurry, hurry – I had to repair some of it before it could be put away.

The laundry was hung up in Granny's garden, our lawn being too small to take the load. Granny Rothenberg, Aunt Felicia's mother, lived next door. She was a great friend of my Father's, an old flame – he had called her adoringly his 'moss rose'. She was still lovely, with her classical features, white hair, and smooth skin. After watching me from her window, struggling with the sheets, she often came out to help me hang them up. She mumbled that I was being exploited, and that one ought to tell my Father, '...by my own daughter, too...'

If only she had. My parents were of the opinion that 'the children are spoilt'..., 'wait till you are with strangers, then you'll appreciate your home'..., 'one does not complain, it is not done'..., 'discipline is good for one'..., 'learn to keep your mouth shut'..., 'only servants gossip about their masters...' etc.

Every Friday night the family, which included me, were invited to Granny's for dinner. The atmosphere there was so festive, so cheerful, that I resolved to work harder and to forget my misery. When I was small, I had read romantic Victorian books about girls of noble birth who had to serve a wicked woman or a witch. They did it cheerfully, without complaint, and I reproached myself for my inefficiency. Thinking things over in bed at night, I despised myself for being so resentful and truculent, but sometimes I cried from self-pity and sheer exhaustion. Aunt Felicia complained that I was slow, quite often calling me a 'slow coach'. On afternoons it was one of my duties to cycle into town to do the shopping. I wished she would get the shops to deliver or order the groceries over the phone. Then her husband could have picked them up when he passed the shops; I did not think his chauffeur would have minded. Sacks of potatoes are heavy.

'Where have you been? Visiting your parents, or talking to your friends?' She looked at her watch. 'I needed the sultanas, for my cake.'

'I came back straightaway,' I said, trying to defend myself.

She would not listen. 'Don't lie to me.' She was furious.

'I'm not.' I stood there, open-mouthed, not knowing what to say. There had been lots of shopping this time. The basket attached to the back of the bike had not been large enough to contain everything on my extensive shopping list. The rest had to go into a net; I hated this! Nets swinging over front handles were always banging against one's thighs! Everything was so heavy. I had to push the bike uphill. The gradient was at least one in seven in some places; with the best will, I could not pedal.

'My cake... Don't lie to me again. I am late.' She slammed the door.

Sometimes her malicious behaviour left me speechless. I had been told that one does not answer back to grown-ups. Surely...

Looking back now, I realise that I must have worked very hard and quickly, but the work was too much for one person, no matter what their age, even in a working day of fourteen hours minimum. Was I in the right? I was never quite certain of this and lost confidence. If only I could have run away. But where could I go? I did not care for the idea of returning home in disgrace, by

211

breaking the agreement; and disgrace it would be – Aunt Felicia would see to that. When she talked about me to her friends she had referred to me as 'that idiot child', or 'this imbecile'. I had heard it myself. Yes, I thought, she is right. I must be an idiot to stay with her. Sometimes her malicious behaviour left me speechless – I gaped at her, open-mouthed, unable to utter a word in my defence. I couldn't tell my Father; the wonderful relationship we had had as a small child was no more. He was a stranger now.

He called occasionally at Aunt Felicia's house. The first time he came, I thought he had come to see me. But he hardly talked to me. He only said 'You look well', and 'I'll see you on Sunday', and then he went straight into the drawing room. I did not see him leaving; Aunt Felicia must have shown him out. I was upstairs doing bedrooms. Several times he had come, and it had always been the same. I wondered why he came; I did not dare ask him. Perhaps he was treating Aunt Felicia – she had a rash. But she went to that 'specialist' in Stuttgart. The one did not exclude the other. But I had not seen any of his ointments standing about, though I had looked in their bathroom cabinet.

I had a terrible suspicion, which I hardly admitted to myself. I only hoped I was wrong. I knew that things at the factory were going badly; that was the same with most Jewish firms. '*Kaufft nich bein Juden*' (Don't purchase Jewish goods). But not from her ... not from her.

Mother told me that Lila Guggenheim's father had helped, as was only right. She told me that after the War, Father had, with a large loan, put Julius Guggenheim back on his feet. He had never looked back. He had repaid all, of course.

I hoped Father was not borrowing any money from Aunt Felicia. It must be that rash. He did not always prescribe medicine, especially in cases of nervous origin, and I (Dr Sylvia!) was sure it must be some kind of nettle rash; I'd seen it before.

If she would pay me *properly*, I could give him the money. She was saving two people's wages. I was sure old Emmy had not worked for anything less than a good wage; she was a *Herrschaftskoechin* (an experienced cook who would normally only work with adequate help in the kitchen). Jews had to be glad to get anyone, let alone a *Herrschaftskoechin*. The charwomen had been paid by the hour, but that too was expensive.

How could I ask Father if he was borrowing money? How could I ask him anything like that? It must have been the rash.

I was shocked when I looked at my watch. Good heavens! I'll never be finished in time. I was at least a quarter of an hour behind.

In the 1930s, it was fashionable to arrange everything according to a timetable. Even the 'baby nurses' were expected to feed the children by the clock. Some had alarms going at feeding time – it saved one the trouble of waking the infant – and the lucky child had his bottle on time, not five minutes before, not five minutes later.

Aunt Felicia was very quick, efficient and methodical in all work done. She seemed to have endless energy.

She had arranged my housework according to a timetable; she timed herself doing each job. If I had had to do only one room for every day I could easily have emulated her feat, but to clean the whole house at the prescribed speed was more like doing it in double time. The children would play with plasticine – this had to be scraped from table and floor; or they played trains with the chairs, leaving deep marks on the lino which had to be polished. Then the doorbell would ring. Often friends phoned and wanted to leave a message, and somehow there was never a pencil handy, the master having taken the lot. Each interruption, every extra job, meant precious time wasted and something had to be skimped so that I did not fall behind according to my time-table, which I carried in my apron pocket. I knew better than to forget to dust the skirting boards since this was a place my mother had always looked. Aunt Felicia tested them with her white handkerchief. However, I regularly got scolded for not wiping the window ledges of the dining room. These, for no reason except the architect's fancy, were high up. I could not reach that far, without a kitchen chair. Aunt Felicia, being much taller than I, could reach easily. In order to make me aware of my negligence, she would pull me along by the ear to show me, pretending it was a huge joke. 'Now if you were a servant,' she said, 'it would not matter very much, but your parents have sent you here so that I should teach you properly.'

This phrase was used regularly when I was scolded. The large coconut mat in the hall was another sore point. I lifted it a foot all the way round and polished that far. I was completely defeated by the obstinacy of this mat; it snapped back when I tried to roll one end up, while the other end stuck up straight and rigid in the air, and wouldn't budge. One morning when I felt it really could not wait any longer – the dirt was now visible – after unsuccessfully struggling, I asked the chauffeur to help me. He was standing about in the hall waiting for the master. A cloud of dust rose and settled on his navy blue uniform; he beat it off with his leather gloves. I apologised and started brushing him. He smiled and said it didn't matter. However, behind my back, he complained bitterly, standing on his dignity. He declared he was employed by the factory and was not a servant.

A job I loathed was to dust her dressing table with its thousand and one bottles and jars; this had to be done every day as the powder spilled was tell-tale. I once knocked a bottle of expensive French scent over. The stopper slipped out and almost half of it spilled on the glass top of the dressing table before I could catch it. I mopped it up and then washed the duster immediately in the house-maid's sink. The scent still hung about the room, though I had opened the windows and doors, so I fetched a vase filled with lilacs and put it on the dressing table.

It took more than week before it was discovered. I was sitting in the pantry polishing silver, my usual Thursday afternoon job, grumbling to myself because Aunt Felicia had ordered the egg-mayonnaise to be dished up on a silver platter and it took me quite a while to get rid of the resulting discolouration. I must hurry, I'll never get through this pile before the boy gets home from school.

She came in and asked me, 'Have you pinched some of my scent?'

I replied, 'I haven't pinched any,' and, before I could explain, the telephone rang and came to my rescue. She went to answer it, as my hands were black. To my surprise, she did not pursue it any further.

The same week, Aunt Felicia enquired if I had seen some of her stockings. I had a guilty conscience as it was one of my tasks to do all the mending and I had pushed several pairs with long runs to the bottom of the mending basket. The ladders had to be hooked up with an extra-fine crochet hook.

'I don't mean those,' she said. 'Silly girl! The new ones I bought last week; I bought twelve pairs of "Elbeo" stockings and now there are only nine left, and I have not worn any yet.'

214

'Perhaps they slipped down the back of the drawer,' I suggested helpfully.

'I have already looked there. Are you quite sure you don't know where they are?'

When I went to my room to wash and change, as I had to cycle to town to do the shopping, the villa being on the outskirts, I found her going through my drawers, systematically piling my undies on the floor. I was so furious I did not know what to say.

'I am looking for my stockings,' she explained.

'You'd better have a *good* look and then you'll be satisfied that they are not *here*.'

'You are the only one who has access to my things.'

'Nothing is locked. Anybody can get at it.' I thought, Why, only on Monday at the party everybody used her dressing room and the man who repaired the window frame was over two hours alone in the room, although it wasn't likely to have been him. Why should I care? She'll probably find them somewhere else.

I left her still rummaging through my underclothes.

They always took their coffee in the drawing room about half an hour after dinner. Just in time I noted that I had forgotten the sugar again, so I put the tray down on the hall table. I heard my name mentioned, the door was ajar, and I could not resist the temptation to listen – this has always been a weakness of mine.

'I would have smelled it,' I heard Aunt Felicia say. 'It's very powerful, and you know how long it lasts. I'm sure I would have smelled it had she spilled it.'

'Did you ask her?' he said.

'Yes, I asked her if she had taken any. Of course, she didn't admit it, and now with the stockings. I couldn't find them in her room but that does not prove anything; she could easily have taken them home.'

'I don't like it,' he said. 'I don't like it. She doesn't seem to me to be that kind of girl. I would look again; you can't be certain... Are you sure?'

'Of course I'm sure. She is the only one to go to my drawers.'

'What reason has she for going to your drawers anyway?'

'To put my clothes back after she's mended them.'

'Why don't you do your own mending? She has enough to do.'

I stamped a bit outside the door before I took the tray in.

Aunt Felicia's cousin, who was a close friend of my Mother,

visited her one afternoon. I was very apprehensive when I caught Aunt Felicia's last words as I entered the room with the coffee: '...surprised and stealing.' I listened again at the door. Unfortunately this door was a flush one and I could only catch odd words like 'terrible liar', 'weak character', 'would upset the parents'.

Why did she want to brand me a liar? I could not imagine why. Later on a possible explanation came to me.

Aunt Felicia went with male friends to the Beecherwoods. Father had often taken us there. These men never came to the house but waited in the car for her. Once, her husband came home, unexpectedly, early. When I told him she had gone to the woods he was most surprised. That evening there was a big row. He shouted that she had promised to be a good wife. She answered that she had gone shopping, shopping. One cannot believe what this 'idiot child' says, 'this liar'. True, she had not told me that very afternoon where she was going. She had said nothing, but I had seen her in the same car.

One thing I was certain of: she tried to undermine my reputation, my good name, so that if I blabbed, no-one would believe me. I would have been branded a liar and a thief. I did not know who had stolen her stockings, most probably one of her lady friends.

I was very unhappy that night; I wished my year to be over. Other girls did a Household Jahr – and they stuck it out. Why did my Father send me there? Did he not know what she was like? I supposed not. He meant well. Aunt Felicia was very efficient and I would get a reference at the end of the year. Since she had not really accused me openly to my face, I would have to confess that I had listened at the door if I brought the matter up. If I told my parents they would probably take me away and then Aunt Felicia would tell everybody in the town that I had left because things disappeared, and that I was such a liar. According to the law in Germany you are guilty until you are proven innocent. How could I prove anything? Aunt Felicia was always telling me to work well, '...because you will be a servant all your life'. The easiest way for a young girl to emigrate was to become a domestic servant and get a work permit. These were rarely given for other jobs.

I was supposed to get pocket money – ten marks a month – but Aunt Felicia bought canvas slippers and clothes of the cheapest quality for me instead. She used to spend more than ten marks – and let me know it. I didn't want them, but I was afraid to say

216

so. I was not used to the somewhat gaudy, though hard wearing, stuff she picked for me. She did not consider my clothes suitable for housework; they were too good and my leather shoes made too much noise on the parquet floor. But the flat canvas slippers made my legs ache.

I had to eat with the family even when they were entertaining business friends. Then, I was the daughter of the house. I would have preferred to eat in peace in the kitchen. The master had a genius for finding fault, whether it was that the mineral water was flat, or he wanted red pepper instead of black, or brown bread … whatever it was I had to get up to fetch it. The family was finished with lunch and my plate was still half-full. I gulped my food to catch up. Aunt Felicia said, 'She has not been fed for a year.' Small helpings were the obvious answer. 'Other girls would be grateful to get a decent helping of such wholesome food.' The food was elaborately arranged on silver dishes with covers (more cleaning), and to carry the large, heavy tray from the kitchen without mishap was always, and every day, a new strain. Sometimes I was so frightened when I clutched the outsize tray that the whole room seemed to recede, getting smaller and smaller, and the voices faded further and further away. Sometimes I rested on the stairs – I could hear if anyone approached.

My hands could not stand the excessive water or the cleaning materials and became swollen, red and cracked in the lines, until they bled almost every day. When Aunt Felicia discovered my sore hands, she arranged for me to see a skin specialist. On his door was a big brass plate: 'Specialist in skin and venereal diseases'. This combination seemed to be favoured in Germany. I hoped no-one had seen me go into the house and when I sat in the waiting room I hid behind a magazine, the largest I could find. The doctor suggested treatment with an infra-red lamp and said that I should wear rubber gloves for work. Perhaps I had some horrible disease and he was only pretending that it was 'sensitive skin' so that I should not feel embarrassed. Too ashamed to let anyone see my sore hands, I walked about with my thumbs tucked in my fists. Aunt Felicia said wearing gloves to work was 'sissy' and what next? She did not wear any. Perhaps, I thought, I was too good for the work? But that was exactly what I was there for. When my gloves had disappeared next morning, I did not dare to ask her about it. My Father made up an ointment for me and my hands healed quickly.

217

Aunt Felicia had decided that they would emigrate to America and slowly they prepared themselves. They took English lessons, read English books: Shakespeare, Uncle Tom's Cabin, and other classics, as well as some of the bestsellers in fiction, such as Steinbeck and du Maurier. These had been translated into German and so could be compared with the English. My Father spoke perfect English fluently. He had studied in London for a year. His French had an Alsatian accent, however, because Grandfather came from Muelbach.

Two young Americans arrived in town. They received many invitations to the Jewish houses; it was good for one to practise English. 'How do you do?' 'It's a fine day, isn't it?' 'The penwiper of my aunt!' The two young men, I was told, were Mormons from Salt Lake City. They came to supper. They fell very short of my expectations. Mormons marry many wives, but those well-scrubbed, pink young men with crew cuts, looked less than harmless. I was lost in my thoughts and when I handed the soup round, I poured it down the neck of one of them. He apologised for being in the way, blushed, and was very nice about it. Aunt Felicia called me a clumsy child. He sent me a small bunch of flowers the next day.

I never understood Aunt Felicia's children; I could not take to them. The boy, Gert, was eight years old. He rarely talked normally, instead he whined and whimpered. This irritated me, and I'm afraid I sometimes became impatient with him. But I was sorry for him; he wet his bed often. I tried to conceal this from his mother, lest she smack him. Little Gert was in his second year at school and had difficulties with his homework. He did not understand what was required. He would approach his mother, asking for help.

'No, not now, I am going out. Go and ask Sylvia.'

'But she is an "idiot". You said she was an "idiot", she can't help me.'

'She was clever at school *Ja, schulgescheit und lebensdumm.* [School clever, not street wise.]'

I could clearly see Gert had no confidence in my teaching ability; he did not trust me.

'You are an idiot.'

'Mind your tongue,' I replied. What could I do? I took him to his grandmother who lived next door. 'Mrs Rothenberg, please could you help Gert with his homework?'

'Where is my daughter?'

I answered, 'She is not at home.'

Gert whined, 'My mother has no time. She has gone out with Uncle Veit; she has gone to Beecher Wood. I don't want Sylvia, she is an idiot.'

'Who called her an idiot? She was top of her class in school.'

'My mother said she is an idiot.'

I was glad his granny agreed to help out. It was Thursday, my silver-cleaning day.

Ruth, a little girl of almost five years, was a strange child. Some mornings she woke up crying. I was at a loss and did not know what to do.

'Why does she always cry?'

Aunt Felicia said, 'Give her one, and then she will know why.'

I could not possibly hit a crying child. I picked her up and tried to comfort her, but she bit me hard.

As soon as Ruth was dressed she was quite cheerful and all was forgotten. She never cried during the day, not even when she fell and cut her knee.

One day I could hear her screaming right from the kitchen. Running out, I wondered what could have happened – I was sure to get blamed for it. I was supposed to keep an eye on the children and I was still doing the dishes.

I found her sitting huddled on the steps leading to the garden.

She looked up at me, stopped, and then screamed some more.

'Ruthy, what's the matter?' I noticed a bulge under apron.

'I am going to have a baby.' And she pulled out her doll. 'Boo-hoo, boo-hoo. I am playing with Charlie,' she explained. Her playmate, Charlie, was also five years old.

* * *

A communal holiday had been arranged for the older Jewish children, aged between ten and seventeen, to the Allgau, an area bordering Austria and Switzerland.

Aunt Felicia, as sports teacher of the girls, offered her services. Bruno Mainzer was to take charge of the boys.

A cabin in the mountains was to be rented for two weeks. Such cabins were unoccupied during the summer months, as the cattle were grazing higher up. It was all very exciting, if not primitive. It was to be low cost, self-catering – the dearest item was the train

219

fare to Oberstdorf and then by hire bus to the Lechtaler Alps, the whole journey about 150 kilometres.

Aunt Felicia said she would take me, treat me – it was to be my holiday. Gert and Ruth were to stay with Grandma.

I helped with the grocery list, which was quite extensive. 'This is called "mass catering", part of your training,' said Aunt Felicia. 'We must not forget anything; the nearest shops are a good distance away, down in the valley. Our chauffeur will bring the groceries and some of my kitchen equipment. We are bound to need it.' Bread, milk, butter and cheese would be supplied by a local farm. The Allgau was famous for dairy products.

Yes, the most expensive item was the fare – she told me several times.

I was looking forward to the trip. I remembered that Father had taken us to the Lechtaler Alps, with their beautiful scenery – picture postcard country.

I told Arnold about my forthcoming trip. 'There will be about thirty of us, or more. Aunt Felicia is paying for me – the fare is very dear.'

Arnold laughed. 'Bemmerle, she is not paying for you. The railway allows party rates: for every ten you get one free.'

I was stupid, or naïve, or both.

The train journey was uneventful. We ate our packed lunch. The bus was of the old, shaky, rattling kind with wooden slat seats. It started to rain. The mist came down, like cotton wool. The hut was damp. Bruno lit a fire in the enormous kitchen range, which acted as a stove, heating the whole cabin. We ate the rest of our packed lunch.

'Bed now!' It had been a long day.

We climbed the ladder to the upper storey. Hay had been laid on two rows of planks, with a gangway in the middle. On the side were neatly folded oversize sheets in gingham. These we tucked over the hay – what fun! No night attire was to be worn, only tracksuits. There were no blankets – after all, it was high summer. Aunt Felicia had marked the wooden walls with chalk, allocating each girl a space of about a metre on our hay bed – what fun!

Lights out. The oil lamp was removed. We settled down.

Ouch! Something was pecking me. I was not the only girl who complained. By the light of our torches we removed the sheets and went on the thistle hunt. We rummaged in the hay; it created a tremendous dust storm – sneeze, sneeze, cough, cough.

I was woken at 5.30 by my miniature alarm clock – it was already quite light. I was to help Aunt Felicia with the breakfast. This was simple enough, being continental style, with the addition of an apple.

An excursion had been planned, to familiarise us with the immediate neighbourhood. I had kitchen duty. I was to wash the breakfast dishes, but the water was not hot enough, so I started with the spuds, putting them in water, in a sort of wash tub, to stop the discolouration.

Bruno had lit the fire, which had gone out. 'Mind the fire, there is plenty of wood.'

'Yes, Bruno.'

'I've put the milk on; we have to boil it, it's safer,' said Aunt Felicia. 'Watch it.'

After the group had departed, I poured myself a mug of coffee from the large enamel can which had been left, forgotten, on the top of the range. I discovered the biscuits on the shelf.

The fire was now roaring. Occasionally I glanced at the milk, which was in a very large double-handled saucepan. Now it started to bubble in the centre. I stopped peeling my potatoes. Just another minute – it must boil properly.

The milk saucepan had been put on the very back of this large range. I cannot reach this blooming pot ... the milk is rising ... where is a stool? ... the chair? It's too high and it's wobbly ... I'll fall into the fire.

Then I remembered the rake, which was leaning on the wood stack next to the door.

Quick, quick, it's boiling over! I managed to hook the rake through the handle. That should do it, I thought. I pulled the massive pot forward. Whoosh! It slopped all over the kitchen range. Spilling, spilling ... it would not stop. By now the range was glowing red hot – Bruno had done a good job. It started to smell. Again I tried to lift the pot off, almost searing my arms. When half the milk had been spilled, I finally managed to get the still heavy pot onto the floor. I felt like crying from frustration, because I could not even clean up the stinking mess. I dared not touch the glowing range.

I opened the door. A grey, acrid cloud wafted out.

'We could smell it a mile off,' exclaimed the group on their return.

Luckily I had their lunch ready. It was simple: continental sausage, cheese, gherkins for those who liked them, and the excellent black bread, which had been delivered from the farm.

I refused the offers of kind souls to help me with the washing up; they were bound to wash up 'dirty' and then I would get the blame. This very clever kitchen range had a water container attached, complete with thermometer and gauge for contents. I read the gauge and found that the water was well down, almost empty. Perhaps I had used too much on the washing up. I must tell them to scrape their plates clean. Water was in short supply. It had to be collected from the trough with a pump, which was two hundred metres downhill – what a bore! I trundled down with my two pails and pumped and pumped; one pail was now full. When I tried to lift it off the board, a lot spilled on the ground, which was bare from frequent use. The soil, which must have been clay, slowly turned into a creamy mess. By the time my second pail was full, my shoes had become well and truly stuck.

One of the young cow hands who had been watching me came over. 'Do you want a hand?'

'Yes, please.'

He carried both buckets up to the hut.

'Do I get a kiss? I deserve a kiss.'

'No!'

'Well, I thought not. No harm in asking.' He laughed. '*Gruess Gott, Miss.*'

On my earlier exploration around the hut I had discovered in the outhouse, a number of large empty milk churns. I should have used these, they had lids. One is often clever after the event.

Dinner went without further mishap.

When I had washed up, I was tired, I did not join in the parlour games and the singing. I went up the ladder to my hay bed.

But it was too early, I could not sleep. Why? Why, do things always happen to me? I must be stupid, clumsy. Arnold calls me *Bemmerle*, Aunt Felicia said 'school-clever, life-stupid'. But she is a malicious cow. Are these my trials and tribulations? Overcoming difficulties builds character, so they always teach one. Blow character! I'd rather have my comfort. Odysseus, the hero from the antique world, fought ogres. Girl, you are no hero, no heroine – certainly not. Heroines weave nettle shirts for their swan brothers... You are no princess, you are a *Haushalts Lehrling* (household apprentice, a drudge). Aunt Felicia is almost twice my size. She is almost six feet tall; she should know I cannot reach that far. She has long arms. Moan, moan, moan. Never mind, protect yourself. How?

At breakfast everyone was asked, 'Would you like some burnt milk? It's not that bad.'

'No, thank you.'

They discussed the muddy area I had created, saying one was dirtier after one's ablutions than before.

The day passed uneventfully.

I peeled my potatoes, cleaned my carrots, dividing them into all the smallish saucepans I could find, particularly the milk, making sure I could lift them. It created a lot of extra washing up, but that could not be helped.

After dinner I joined the group. I did not mind having missed the excursions. I've never been one for 'shinning up' the mountains, not unless there was a special treat at the end of it, like a castle to view, a lake for swimming, or a good restaurant. I liked the sing-songs. Bruno Mainzer had a beautiful voice; people said he could have been a cantor in a synagogue. 'God forbid,' said Bruno. Aunt Felicia had rehearsed a new song with the children:

Was kann die Sylvia denn dafuer das sie so dumm ist
Und alles was sie macht ist ja verkehrt
Die Milch ist verbrannt
Es stinkt im ganzen Land
Gesundt ist das baden in dem Lehm
Das ist wohl sehr bequem.

It's not Sylvia's fault, she is so stupid
And everything she does is wrong
She burns the milk
Creates a mud flat
This is her story
In a song.

I got up and went out. How dare she! I really must do something now. And I did. The next evening I was ready. I joined the sing-song, but I continued with the 'Sylvia stupid' song. 'Now comes the second verse,' said I. All went quiet.

It's not Sylvia's fault she is so small
Not at all
Not everyone can be so tall
It's not her fault her arms are short
I report ... that.

She was afraid to fall into the fire
Burnt flesh stinks even more
Now sing the encore
It's not Sylvia's fault she is so small
Not at all.

I sang it loudly, pronouncing everything very distinctly. Then I went out. I am happy to say they never sang 'my song' again.

* * *

This was my holiday; this was what Aunt Felicia had promised. I did not mind my kitchen duty. I could see she had to accompany the girls on the excursions, as there were several quite young ones. But I felt the older ones should share some of the work. Aunt Felicia made the menu, giving me detailed instructions. I liked to work single-handed, preparing the lunch. It made me feel grown up.

I decided, however, that I no longer wished to be the water carrier. The young cow hand, who had helped so gallantly, was no longer around. There were other time-consuming jobs, too, which I wanted to get rid of.

On the general notice board were the instructions for the day, both from Bruno and Aunt Felicia.

Now was the opportunity. I would add my instructions. I owned the same notepaper; everyone had it. It came from a Jewish shop we all 'patronised'.

I printed, in capitals:

WATER DUTY:

OLDER BOYS TAKE TURNS BEFORE BREAKFAST
MILK CHURNS ARE IN SHED, PLEASE WASH OUT
CAREFULLY

GIRLS: LAYING TABLE   LUNCH AND DINNER

EVERYONE: CROCKERY MUST BE STACKED
CAREFULLY
CUTLERY TO BE PUT INTO SAUCEPANS CONTAINING
WATER

THANK YOU

My notes looked the same as their notes; even I was hard put to spot any difference. I hoped both our 'leaders' would think the other one had written it. Why should the children not contribute to the work? Fair is fair.

I had by now solved the problem with the kitchen range. In the shed I had found an old fashioned men's clothes hanger, with a crossbar at the bottom. By removing two thirds of the bar, I had turned it into an admirable hooking device. I had to take care not leave it lying around though, or Bruno might use it for firewood.

At lunchtime the children talked enthusiastically about their morning outings.

'You should see the mushrooms. There are ever so many. Not far from here.'

'Bilberries, too.'

'On the heath.'

They showed me their hands. 'It won't come off!'

'Take Vim. That usually does the trick, even if it's very blue – ink too.'

I also liked mushrooms. I offered to go on a hunting expedition on my free afternoon. Two boys asked if they could accompany me.

'If Bruno says yes.'

Growing under the trees, the mushrooms were prolific. I restricted the picking to the golden yellow ones, the *Pfifferlings*. I explained that the brown ones sometimes got mixed up with the poisonous ones, as they are so similar, and that recently, on market day, a country woman had had all her three baskets confiscated by the inspector who had found one single mushroom which was poisonous.

It did not take us long to fill our baskets with the golden treasure.

I promised to make 'Hunter's Stew'. Only this morning, a lad had brought in four rabbits. I was glad our mushrooms would 'stretch' the meal so everyone could have a decent sized portion. Hunter's Stew was a recipe of my mother's. It was a pity the red wine to be

225

used for the marinade would be missing. The dinner was a great success. Everyone praised me. Next day, I went bilberry picking. This time I took two girls. I made bilberry and apple pie. The children were surprised that I could cook so well. 'You are only fourteen!'

I explained that our Liesel had taught me; she had been a 'smashing' cook.

At Aunt Felicia's there was no time to help with the 'interesting' cooking. Preparing vegetables, yes, but I was too busy with cleaning chores to get to the kitchen in time to watch and learn.

My catering skills had helped to eliminate the 'stupid Sylvia' image – most of it anyway.

At least the stress and the tension had gone. I returned refreshed from the 'holiday'.

'Bemmerle, you are learning to protect yourself,' Arnold said.

* * *

Rarely did I see any of my former friends. I had no time. I was allowed to receive visitors, but it was all so embarrassing.

I felt I had to spend my Sundays – every other Sunday afternoon it was – at home. It usually happened that on my free evening Aunt Felicia had guests. Guests meant extra courses, stacks of washing up; by the time I had finished it was often past nine o'clock. It was not worth going out – I had to be in by ten.

Once I had asked if I might leave the dishes until morning. Aunt Felicia looked at me horror-struck, saying it was most unhygienic to leave remains of food in the kitchen. Please, not in her kitchen. At the dinner, the last course, she bade me, most pointedly, farewell. She explained to the guests that it was 'the child's' free evening. Would they excuse her? She would join them after she had done the dishes. I offered to stay, with a martyr's air, but she declined. She had been offended.

I never tried that again.

My former schoolmate, Helga, came to stay with us for a couple of days. The family was leaving for the States. Her parents had sold their house, and Aunt Felicia had offered to put Helga up.

Helga and I had never been very chummy at school. We went to parties and functions and were polite to each other for our parents' sake, who were friends, but she bored me.

I had made up a bed for her on the couch in Aunt Felicia's private sitting room.

226

This, a rather small room, had been 'designed' for her by an interior decorator. Under the windows were bookshelves – not much on them I approved of, mostly romances – which were made of black opaque glass. I had reason to dislike those glass shelves. The dust showed again, almost immediately after dusting. The long-haired fluffy rug did not help matters. I always dusted them before Aunt Felicia asked her lady friends in for coffee; the hausfraus would surely notice.

Whilst Helga was having breakfast I did her room and I made up her bed. I did not mind doing this, though it was complicated to get all the blankets back into the box. Whilst I was clearing her breakfast tray she called me. How tall she looked standing there in the morning sun. I felt like a dwarf next to her, especially as I wore my canvas slippers.

'I want to show you something,' she said.

'Yes?' I entered the room.

'It's dirty over there.' She pointed to the black glass shelves. I slapped my duster into her hand. 'Here you are.'

She slapped it back into mine. 'I am not a servant,' she said snootily. 'That may be so,' I answered. 'But it's your dirt. I've done it once, that's enough.'

Under the heading of apprenticeships in the 1920s and 1930s it was quite acceptable that young persons, even children, be exploited in employment situations. The grown ups declared that a little strict discipline can only do them good, adding that they had had to get through that stage as well. Teenagers were usually employed at a very small wage or for nothing. It was frequently pointed out that they were very lucky no money had been demanded from their parents for their apprenticeship, as had been customary before. Often they worked long hours, as additional duties, such as the keeping clean of the premises, were expected from them. There were also 'good employers', who had the interest of the youngsters at heart, but these were in the minority. In my own case, I realised that Aunt Felicia's offer had come after she had found out that during my mother's illness and stay in hospital, I had looked after the whole family, including doing the cooking. I would be useful, and very cheap.

Yes, I know people looked on me as a servant, a *Dienstmaedchen aus guten Hause* (a servant coming from a good family), a poor fish. The work was the same, but for the 'privilege' of eating with the family one received no wages.

They always talked about getting a maid or a cook-general but that was as far as it went.

Once, a cook called Anna came. I cannot remember very much about her, except the rows of bottles of patent medicine she had arranged on the kitchen dresser – for her nerves, she explained. I don't believe she stayed a fortnight.

However, they engaged a Nanny, one who had been with the family in the past.

Life was a little easier for me after Miss Katherina, the new nanny, arrived. She was a very tall woman with a saturnine face, her black hair parted in the middle. She had extraordinarily long, bony hands.

She was a good disciplinarian and the children did not dare tell fibs; when they first tried, she just raised her eyebrows and said, 'Is that so?' and took not the slightest notice. Even Aunt Felicia was reasonable in front of her. Miss Katherina helped me with many little jobs. I knew they were not expected of her, but it was such a help to me when she did the laundry or laid the table, that I just said, 'Thank you,' and didn't question it. Her influence in the house was soothing and I no longer felt so persecuted. When I was depressed after a 'telling off', Miss Katherina recounted to me stories about the Frau Generalin, her previous employer. They made me laugh. Aunt Felicia was an innocent baby by comparison. Every morning, the Frau Generalin had called, '*Antreten.*' The whole staff lined up in the hall, presenting their hands. Those with dirty finger nails got rapped over the knuckles with a little stick as she walked past them. Her children were not much better off.

All good and all bad things come to an end, and soon my year was over. Aunt Felicia asked me to stay on and offered me a substantial wage. It gave me a great pleasure to tell her politely, but firmly, that I could not manage another day. She asked me why. Caught unawares I had to think quickly and said that my grandparents needed my help.

I decided to pay them a long visit there and then.

228

Chapter 25

The Berlin Episode and my Grandparents Arrange for my Education

I stayed with my grandparents for several months. What a relief it was to be with normal kindly people. Everyone was so friendly. They spoiled me, and how I enjoyed that.

I slept in my Mother's former room. It was pretty with its mauve wallpaper, brass bedstead, hand-made lace coverlet and quaint white-painted furniture. On the what-not in the corner was my Mother's collection of shells, collected abroad on holidays. There was a beauty, a large one, all pearly-pink and smooth, from Blankenberghe. I sometimes took it to bed with me and listened to the sea. I had never been to the seaside. From my window there was a glorious view which reached over gardens to the far distant Taunus Mountains.

I was surprised that there was much more anti-semitism in Camberg than at home. But then in small places everything is more personal. Camberg had 2,519 inhabitants, of whom 72 were Jewish, according to census. Overnight, boys chalked swastikas or 'Jews' on the door and old Maria, the maid, would try to wash it off before my grandparents got up.

My grandfather used to supply the blacksmiths and farmers in the surrounding countryside. But his main trade, wholesale in ironmongery had almost come to a standstill and his warehouse, where the iron girders stood, was kept locked now. All the staff had been given notice; August, his chief clerk was the last to go. Occasionally a customer would enter the retail shop and perhaps ask for half a pound of nails or screws. I would then serve him. For the bigger items I called grandfather, or when a wholesale customer came in. The farmers took great pleasure in haggling over the prices and this they could only do with 'Moritz', my grandfather. Sometimes they suggested that they should pay a deposit – followed by monthly instalments and a dozen fresh eggs every market day. Their hens laid the biggest and the freshest. If they had spent a large amount, they expected grandfather to give them a present from the shop, such as a good saucepan for the wife, or a new household gadget – 'nothing too new-fangled, mind!'

But the bell of the shop rang less and less. During the summer holidays, when the town was packed with visitors 'taking the cure', one could have expected a certain amount of casual trade. But the Hitler Youth posted pickets in front of the door – holiday duty. I had just served a young lady with a frying pan and when she left the shop, our 'sentry' stopped her, calling her a Jew-lover. Through the window, I saw her brandishing her pan and calling out, 'Baby-face, would you like a taste of this?' and I quite believe she would have let him have it if had he not run away. He returned with a reinforcement.

I was never actually molested during my stay, apart from children running after me, chanting, 'Jew! Jew! Dirty Jew!' I would straighten my shoulders and walked on.

Most of the younger Jews of the town had emigrated by now. 'Emigration' cast a shadow over us all. The neighbours would drop in in the evenings after supper and read their children's letters. How hard it was to find a foothold in the 'foreign land'. It was rare indeed if they could keep their own profession; one was glad to get any kind of work. To relieve the situation they told little jokes of a new kind: 'emigration jokes'. The old Viennese gentleman says, 'I must emigrate, I cannot bear it any more; emigrate even if I eat only dry bread, but in a free country.' And he emigrates to England. 'What! No central heating?' Or the joke about the Jewish marriage broker, called a Shadchen. (He was more a figure of imagination and of the past than of reality; I had never heard of anyone actually practising.) The father comes to the Shadchen and says, 'I have a daughter, Elsie, she is young and pretty. My Elsie, who is a good girl. I would give her twenty thousand marks for her dowry.' So the Shadchen goes through his list. 'Well, here we have a lawyer, a former councillor, perhaps a doctor, or a business man?' says the old Jew. 'I had actually thought of an artisan,' replied the father. 'You know, somebody practically minded; it's so much better nowadays, so much easier to emigrate.' The Shadchen says despairingly, 'Everyone wants an artisan or a farmer or a labourer. I have dozens of lawyers and Doctors and philosophers on my books and you come with a measly 20,000 marks and ask for an Artisan!'

Cousin Erica was preparing to leave for Palestine with the Youth Alijah. I was invited to stay with her for a week. She spoke excitedly about the life of the Kibbutz, how she was prepared to live in a tent, and dig and drain the land. Her enthusiasm was catching – she seemed so idealistic, saying that the only hope for Jews to avoid persecution was to have a country of their own. Theodor Herzl had said so. She tried to persuade me to join her.

This was all very uplifting, but then I thought of the practical side. In the hot summer months, I would have to stay indoors, as the heat made me feel ill. When exposed to strong sunrays I got prickly heat, small blisters all over my arms and hands. As a small child I had had to wear a special straw hat with a large brim to shade my face. Erica said, 'Better not. You'd most probably be a nuisance.' And so the subject was dropped.

Cousin Erica's father had died of appendicitis. He had arrived home from a sales trip, complained to his wife that he felt ill and wanted to go straight to bed. In the morning he was found dead. So my parents arranged for little Erica to join us on all excursions and generally spend much time with us. She was my senior by two years. She had arrived late, having grown-up sisters and a brother, who was born in England, when her father worked for our branch factory in London.

Eugene Ries was an exceptionally tall man, six foot four inches. He was often teased about his height for 'Ries' in German means 'giant'. This blond, blue-eyed giant had great imagination and was popular in his new job, when he returned to our town to work for Gentner's. They produced Nigrin, the black boot polish which was made of the finest quality black soot. Eugene took over the publicity. He engaged a circus artist to walk on super-high stilts, dressed as a chimney sweep, with top hat, blackened face and chimney sweeping brushes to walk through towns and villages. Children of all ages accompanied him, yelling 'Nigrin, Nigrin', hoping to get a little tin man chimney sweep present. Newspapers published the times when the 'Nigrin' man would arrive in town.

One day, walking through his kitchen, Eugene smelled burning. What was burning? On the cooker was a large copper pan in which bubbled what was supposed to be plum jam. Where was the maid? She was in the garden, talking to her fiancé.

231

Eugene thought it looked like brown boot polish. Why did no-one manufacture brown boot polish? Many brown boots were sold.

The new, much advertised brown polish was called 'Eri', after his little daughter, Erica, who was proudly telling people, 'I am Eri, it is called after me.'

Aunt Paula kept a Jewish newspaper. I had never seen one before. At home we seemed to believe in the 'ostrich' policy: the Nazis were crazy or misguided people, it could not and would not last. This newspaper carried a large, diverse advertisement section: Jewish homes for elderly ladies and gentlemen; Jewish schools for children no longer allowed to attend municipal schools; long and short training courses for all sorts of jobs, to prepare people for emigration. A large section of 'Help Wanted' was the result of Christians who had left their Jewish employers. Domestic servants were also in strong demand because of the Nuremberg Laws.

My eyes were on the tastefully presented, large format of an advertisement for the Fashion School Bendit, Passauer Strasse, Berlin, offering courses in pattern cutting for people in the textile trade. The courses were held in their Salon, in the evenings, between 7.00 p.m. and 9.00 p.m. I remembered vaguely cousin Herta, who lived in Berlin, having spoken about this salon. It was *haute couture* and very expensive. Interesting this! I wrote for a prospectus. Well, they did not ask or stipulate age and my family were, or had been, in the textile trade. Could it be possible for me to attend?

What about finance? Berlin was a dear place.

The 1,000 marks per month the Nazis allowed Jews to withdraw from their frozen bank accounts were insufficient for our family needs. Father's income was nil; he considered it wrong to charge for his gifts, and he mostly supplied his 'patients' with the medicaments free. Susan was still attending the Ladies' Seminary for Young Ladies, Richard was still in the Jewish Orphanage in Esslingen. Even brother Arnold, who was apprenticed in Uncle David's paper factory in Eislingen, could only just make his small salary cover his fares and other expenses.

I was a fully qualified domestic servant. Had I not spent – suffered – a full year with Aunt Felicia, to get the 'certificate'?

I discussed this new idea with Aunt Paula, Erica's mother. She was my father's sister. She and my mother did not get on. She said to me, 'I cannot understand your Father letting you go to Aunt Felicia, a woman like that. She is *"boshaft"* [wicked, depraved, vicious].'

232

There was an advert from Doctor Hohn, who needed a young lady for reception work and to assist with laundry and other light duties. Pocket money was offered. Aunt Paula wrote that I was of a good family, intelligent, tri-lingual, and needed a part time situation, as I wanted to attend evening classes in Berlin. Almost by return I received the offer of the situation.

Mother had raised no objection to this project, although I had expected difficulties because of my age. She had only said, 'My daughter does not consult me any more; she does not need her parents.' Father was always easy with anything I really wanted to do.

There was an undercurrent of resentment between me and my Mother and I felt that the less said the better.

Somehow I wanted to be independent. I hated to ask Mother for favours or permission to do anything, let alone for large sums of money. Her attitude towards me – and I was then convinced it was only to me, and not my brothers and sister – was that I should be grateful that they had brought me up so well – be grateful, 'because other children have not got it', be grateful to one's parents, 'honour one's father and mother, it is written so in the Ten Commandments'. To be grateful, to be grateful ... I often wondered why I was brought into the world. I had not asked for it. The closeness and one-ness I felt with Father as a small child receded and became a dreamlike vision, and then only a memory. I had been his child; he had loved and wanted me. Now he appeared to be a different man, so tired, trying to make peace between my Mother and me, although there had been no argument, no open hostility. 'Don't upset your Mother, you know she is very excitable.' Mother was annoyed that I had discussed Berlin with Aunt Paula, so she said, 'My Fraulein daughter is too grown-up to ask me about anything.'

It was essential for young people to learn something practical, but this was easier said than done. Universities and technical colleges were closed to Jews and the Nazi Government made it difficult, almost impossible, to transfer money abroad, even for educational purposes.

The few existing factories still under Jewish ownership and control took as many trainees as possible. My Mother's dream of my becoming a dress designer gradually turned into one of my becoming a dressmaker; it was more practical. In spite of my fifteen years, I felt very grown up. I was determined not to lose any time in starting to train, otherwise Aunt Felicia would be right: I would be a servant all my life.

My grandparents offered to pay the large fee for the Fashion School Bendit.

Now I had arrived in Berlin. The doctor's practice was in a large, old apartment block, a seven and a half room flat, which included their living quarters. I was shown to my room, the half room, the former maid's chamber, with bed, small chest of drawers, a chair and a few nails behind a curtain, doing duty for hanging clothes. To my delight, I had a washbasin of my own. There was even a shelf above for toilet articles.

The work routine was as follows:

Private patients used the front staircase, the parquet floor one, and were shown into the waiting room with the little gold chairs, upholstered in red velvet. *Krankenkasse* (insurance) patients used the side stairs, the ones for servants and deliveries, and sat in a miserably depressing room with an assortment of chairs, and a large wooden bench.

I entered all the patients' names and other details into books.

The 'other help', was a charwoman, who came everyday. She soon gave notice to leave – she could not stay, her husband did not like her to work in a Jew house. She said she had stayed until the Frau Doctor could get someone else, but she would keep doing the two staircases. Nobody would know, as the other flats had Christian tenants. So, after a month, she had left. I now started work at 6.00 a.m.; the consulting rooms had to be done by 8.00 a.m. sharp. Everything had to be disinfected, as the doctor was a specialist in skin and venereal diseases. It was quite a rush, but by 8.00 a.m. I was in my white overalls, all smiles.

Frau Doctor cooked lunch. She was a jolly good cook. I laid three places in the dining room. For the privilege of eating with the family, I was addressed as Miss, and received pocket money, not wages. We shared the washing up. I swept the waiting rooms, emptied the ashtrays, did the dusting, tidied the magazines, not forgetting to look behind the sofa and other furniture for stray lunch papers or sweet wrappers discarded by patients.

Then came the laundry. All the linen from the practice was

234

washed at home. The former maids' bathroom was used as a laundry room. A strong solution of disinfectant was made in the bath, and in this the linen was immersed. After a while it was wrung out, then given three rinses, then taken to the loft to dry. I was given long rubber gloves, so as not to touch the linen. If I was lucky, I would be finished by four o'clock. I got myself ready to walk to the fashion school, if the weather was clement.

The Salon was very impressive, with thick carpets, chandeliers and fresh flowers, beautifully arranged. Some long, large tables had been put in the former workrooms, which were available because the Salon was not busy now, being Jewish owned.

Most of my fellow students were male, sales people who had been, or were, working in men's or women's clothing, mantles, tailoring or textiles. They were all around thirty or forty years old. When the Directrice found out that I was only fifteen, she said she would reserve the right to cancel my agreement; they had never had anyone so young. Admittedly, I acted older than my age.

I found the pattern cutting, drawn to a quarter scale in a graph book, very easy to follow, having been good at maths, geometry and drawing at school. I even helped some of the other students, when they asked me. The directrice of the course was delighted with my fashion drawings, so she said.

No longer did I walk to school; I was too tired. The day was too long, what with starting work at 6.00 a.m. At lunchtime I was too tired to eat, and the Frau Doctor complained that I was spoiled. The food was wholesome and tasty, but I was just too tired.

Instead of preparing my homework, I flopped on my bed when I had finished the laundry. This was the same situation as at Aunt Felicia's, who had also claimed that there was domestic help.

Meanwhile I had developed some spots and scabs above my wrist. Frau Doctor said that the Herr Doctor could not claim from the *Krankenkasse* if he treated me, so he sent me to a colleague. He diagnosed impetigo and said, with a puzzled expression, shaking his head, 'Mrs Hohn told me it was caused by being dirty. I certainly don't believe that.' On my return home, I demanded an explanation from Frau Doctor. She said it was because I did not clean my teeth in the morning. This was true. I did not at 5.45 a.m.! I did them later, but only sometimes.

'How did you know?' I asked her.

'Because your toothbrush is dry.'

My Father sent me medicine, the rash soon vanished.

Then a good idea came to me. That Jewish newspaper I had read at Aunt Paula's had had so many advertisements for Domestic Help. Perhaps I could find something easier. A small ad. costs practically nothing, so I took one: PART-TIME JOB, HALF-DAY, FOND OF CHILDREN, COOKING. I asked for replies to be sent *Poste Restante.*

Surprisingly, many replies awaited me at the Post Office. Most of them, however, were quite unsuitable. Did they not read that I wanted *part-time*?

There was one which sounded quite promising: 'One little girl, some cooking, 2 and a half room flat, part-time, until 2 p.m.' I looked up the address. Hooray, hooray! It was near the Fashion School. It had said Hinter house, which meant it was one of the cheaper flats at the back of the building – a small flat. Not much work there – that might be all right. I would save the fare money, too.

I went to the Hinter house. A timid little lady welcomed me. I was wearing my navy dress with the lace collar – which I did not like, because it looked too prissy (I had thought I would need it for reception duties at the doctor's) – my navy gabardine raincoat and beret. My hair was scraped back, so that my curls could not escape. This was my would-be Nanny outfit.

When I said I needed to live in, the lady said she could only offer me a share of the child's room.

'Does the little girl sleep well?'

'Oh, yes, Lori sleeps very well; she normally wakes up at eight o'clock in the mornings.'

The lady explained that she was helping her husband in his office in the mornings. I was to give Lori her lunch. So I agreed to start work as soon as I had given notice at the doctor's. The money offered to me was more than the pocket money I received now. The Hohns had never increased it in spite of the large savings made from the charwoman's wages.

I gave one week's notice to Frau Doctor. She replied that I must give her one month. I told her, 'I get weekly money, therefore I can give weekly notice' – although I was not certain about this. I said it cheekily and with conviction.

After the week was over, and having received my money the day before, I got up extra early, cleaned the surgery, left a note to

236

tell them I had done so, and slipped out at seven o'clock, before they were up, to avoid any argument or recriminations. She had called me an ungrateful girl. What had I to be grateful for?

The Lamm people were pleasant, the child Lori delightful. The work was very easy. No longer did I almost fall asleep in my lessons. I mentioned I had looked after two children for a year, before their family had emigrated to the USA. There was no need to show my Household Apprentice certificate.

Mrs Lamm had not asked my age at the interview, and she never asked for my insurance cards. I was glad about this as my birthday was on these cards.

After I had dressed the child, we breakfasted. I cleaned the small bedroom and the bathroom. Then we went for walks, to the playground or the park. I sat on the bench marked. 'No Jews', knowing that with my blonde hair no-one would suspect I was Jewish. We sang nursery rhymes, and I told her fairytales; if I could not remember the details, I made them up. (Please forgive me, Hans Andersen.)

A little shopping on the way home, then I cooked lunch for Lori and me. She liked my food and ate it up without any trouble. I offered to cook for Mrs Lamm as well, who returned home after working in the mornings in her husband's office – another extra portion to cook was no extra work. Mrs Lamm was very grateful and praised me. Lori was put to bed for her afternoon rest, then I cleaned the kitchen and did some washing and ironing for the child only. I noticed Mr Lamm's shirts rolled up, ready for ironing. However, I resisted the temptation to be helpful. I thought, if I do it once, it will be my job, I'll never get rid of it. I had learnt my lesson.

'It's going to be fine today. You'll like that,' said Mrs Lamm to her daughter.

'No, I like it better when it rains.'

'Explain, why?'

'Then Sylvia makes paper chains, boys and girls dancing, and I can say what they are wearing and help to colour them.' Paper, crayons and scissors, praise be! Lori scribbled, with the crayons, on the paper. I used this as 'material'. I drew the clothes, to Lori's instructions, cut them out and pasted them onto the children on the paper chain. They wore only vests and knickers. Then I scrubbed the kitchen table for unavoidable crayon marks and glue spots. We did quite well – what do you expect from a budding dress designer?

237

Sadly, there was a lack of toys in this family: just a doll, and not a very nice one – she had lost two fingers – and a ball. No books whatsoever. When I telephoned home to ask my Mother to send some of our old toys and books, she said she had given them away. I thought of our two crammed-full cupboards in the day nursery – one for toys, and one for books!

'You are spoiled,' she had said. 'Other children have not got it!' My Mother was right. There were no books of any kind to be found in the Lamms' flat, only the *Illustrated Racing Times*.

The street kiosk at the corner had some cheap cardboard children's books. I selected a farmyard one. It was not a success: Lori did not know the animals. She knew 'dog' and 'cat', and 'fly' and 'bird', no other. I woofed and meowed, and I mooed. 'Sylvia makes funny noises,' she told her mother. Once on the street we saw a horse and cart. This was fascinating. We trotted alongside for quite a while. I could only do 'giddy-up, giddy-up' – whinnying was beyond me.

Saturday had been baking day at home. I thought a *Hampelman* (a gingerbread man, without the ginger), would be nice but I could not find a weighing machine, so I guessed the ingredients. I must have used too much butter, for the leg broke off. I mended this with jam, red jam.

'Sorry, his leg is broken.'

'Hospital, hospital,' called Lori. The jam really did look like blood oozing from a wound.

I signed on for the second and more advanced part at Bendit's, and I thoroughly enjoyed it.

Unbeknown to me, the school had written to my grandparents, expressing their opinion that I was very talented and should do well in the fashion trade. There was a Jewish fashion school in Hamburg for full-time students. My grandparents decided they would support me.

I was sorry to leave the family. They had been kind, and I had grown fond of Lori. 'Your education is very important, we know,' they said. 'We'll miss you.'

238

Chapter 26

The Fashion College

Arrangements had to be made regarding fashion school in Hamburg, and my lodgings. A small family conference was held. 'Whom do we know in Hamburg?' It was established that we had no relatives there. 'Relatives' in our family were cousins of even the fourth degree, or good friends of a friend. Aunt Herta said that an old school friend of hers had recently been appointed matron of the Jewish Orphanage in Hamburg, and she was sure she could be helpful. A letter was drafted.

In due course the reply arrived. The matron regretted that there was no room at the orphanage or the attached School of Domestic Science, but she could arrange for me to stay temporarily at an Old Ladies' Home. The Home was in the same district as the fashion school. Furthermore it was promised that she would keep an eye on me and occasionally invite me on weekends.

How kind of her, I thought, how condescending! I suppose there are always conditions attached if one asks for something and I would willingly have put up with much more.

It was a Sunday evening in spring when I arrived in Hamburg. I hoped somebody would be waiting for me at the station; I had not been told of any arrangement, of the newspaper, carnation or handkerchief sort. Would they recognise me? I waited a little while on the platform; a stream of people hurried past, then only a trickle. I sat down on my suitcase for a few minutes. The train had been punctual; possibly they were late. After a short time I enquired how to get to the Home. The tram took me right through the centre of the town, over the Alster Bridge, past colonnades of shops to the residential quarter. The houses there had been built around the turn of the century, possibly for prosperous merchants. They were

239

large and had individually laid out and well cared for front gardens. 'Your stop, Miss.' I alighted with my heavy suitcase. 'The second turning on the left past the telephone kiosk.' This was the second turning but the street had a different name. Had I counted properly? I'll ask again. There were not many people about on a Sunday evening. I hoped I would get there before it got really dark. The suitcase was heavy, so I rested; I wound my handkerchief round the handle. No, I had been given the wrong direction; it was the second turning on the right. I wished I had taken a taxi; the case was getting heavier and heavier, and my shoulders ached. Taxis are expensive and I did not know how long my pocket money would have to last. Finally I found the 'Home for Old Ladies of Gentle Birth'.

The bell sounded very shrill in the silence. Nothing happened; then footsteps over a stone floor, and a bolt was pulled back. A maid with a starched white apron and cap, and very red hands, opened the outer door.

'Yes?'

'I am Sylvia. You are expecting me.'

'Please wait in the hall,' and she closed the bolt again. Why, it's just turned nine o'clock, I thought. What time do they go to bed here?

She returned with a tall lady whose erect posture and springy walk belied her age, her white hair, and wrinkled face. She said, 'Miss Schmidt, the matron, is out and I was not told she was expecting anyone.' I told her that arrangements had been made for me to stay at the home. 'Miss Schmidt will probably return shortly. Please wait in here.' She switched on the light and pointed to a chair near the door. 'Will you excuse me – I'm sure it won't be for very long. It's Matron's day off.'

It was the dining room and the tables had been laid for breakfast: long rows of cups turned upside down, individual napkin rings and different pots of jam to break the monotony. The china was plain white, hospital type, but the silver was burnished bright.

I looked round. The long narrow room was oak panelled. At intervals along the wall, a photograph of a man in an old-fashioned suit, high stiff collar and pointed beard, or a lady with her hair parted in the centre, sitting bolt upright next to an aspidistra, a group of serious looking men and women; the Committee of X on the occasion of X. A Persian rug, with a piece of fringe missing, lay on the parquet floor; the once olive-green velvet curtains had faded to yellow in the folds. Several glass cases were arranged along the wall; they held ornate, ugly silver, strangely proportioned. At the large window stood a table with half-withered plants. Why don't they nip off the dead leaves? On the sideboard lay some purple knitting with steel needles stuck through the fat ball of wool from every direction.

Matron's night out; I must have waited an hour. I looked out of the window. Night had fallen, and I could see very little. The view of the street was obscured by the bushes planted near the fence.

The erect lady returned. 'Miss Schmidt won't be long. Are you comfortable?'

'Yes, thank you.'

I was thirsty and took out of my case the last orange remaining from those packed for my journey, and started peeling it. No waste paper basket. I put the peelings back into the paper bag in my case. At this precise moment, Matron arrived. I stood there, oozing orange in my hand, not quite knowing what to do with it.

A white overall covered the ample contours of early middle age; she looked frighteningly efficient but the effect was slightly softened by her rosy apple cheeks. She said, in a brisk manner, (no nonsense there), that she had not expected me until the following day, but not to worry, would I please go with her, and that my room was upstairs – rather high up, but as I had young legs, this would not matter. The porter would bring my case.

I followed her up the highly polished stairs, still clutching my orange and wishing I could lose it somewhere.

My room was on the fourth floor, sparsely and shabbily furnished. The brass bedstead had a beautifully mended white coverlet. The light brown paint had chipped off the wardrobe revealing previous layers of cream and dark green paint. A worn piece of American cloth, scalloped at the edges, with a garland of faded and scratched-off roses, covered the washstand. The water jug said 'Good morning' to me, but the letters were too big and one had to turn it round to read what it said.

A wizened little man brought up my luggage. Should I tip him? He wished me good night and was off before I had time to decide. I pulled my pyjamas out of my case. A good wash would have been essential because I had travelled all day, but I was so tired that 'Good morning' would have to wait until next morning, and I scrambled into bed.

241

The gong woke me. What time had Matron said breakfast would be ready? This must be the first call. I found 'Good morning' very cold, after being accustomed to hot water. Another gong! I went downstairs. The doors were opening. Little old ladies, and fat old ladies, and scraggy old ladies, were going downstairs, some clutching the railings, others thumping their sticks.

'Good morning, Mrs Goldman.' 'Goodmorning, Mrs Myerhofer.' 'Have you had a good night?' 'Oh, my rheumatism...' 'Weather warmer now...'

A place had been allocated to me at the bottom of the table. Matron presided. Next to her stood the lady who had let me in. She handed the mail to the fortunate ones. 'A letter for you, Mrs Kahn.' 'Here you are, Mrs Levy.'

Matron said, 'Good morning, ladies. I must ask you ladies not to leave your personal belonging, books, knitting, and other things in the dining room; no responsibility can be accepted...' Aha, I thought, she must mean the purple knitting of last night. Who would want to pinch that anyway? Matron continued, 'There are still two places vacant in the coach for this afternoon's outing to the park. I shall be in my office after breakfast to accept applications.'

She gave a signal and the maid with the red hands started pouring the corn coffee. No, this would not affect the old ladies' hearts. Plum jam, rather watery, bread and butter – was it butter? Never mind, butter was rationed then in Germany. Goering had said, 'Cannons for butter' – but I'm sure this was only an excuse.

On my right sat a little thin lady. She wore a lace fichu around her neck, arranged like a clown's frill. On my left the place was empty. The door slowly opened. Everybody stopped eating and looked in that direction. The offender, a small plump woman of about thirty-five tried to creep in – have you ever tried to creep in over a parquet floor, with high heels? Matron pretended not to notice and said, just a shade too loudly, 'Would you please pass the sugar?'

The small plump one sank into the chair next to me. She did not seem to feel at all guilty and laughed. The many tight curls on her head jumped with each movement she made. I secretly christened her 'Bubble Curls'. 'You're here now ... why did you come here? ... where is your room? ... what is your name?...' Not waiting for an answer, she continued, between mouthfuls, 'Come and see me whenever you like, a bit of a dump here, don't

242

say I said so, my fiancé wants me to stay here.' So she had a fiancé! Well, I never. This fiancé was a very important man (although I never found out in which way he was important), and I was to hear more of him.

Matron stood up and, coughing in a genteel manner, said, 'Good morning, ladies', and left the room. The ladies rolled up their napkins. Bubble Curls said, 'You had better bring a napkin ring or a bag, or the maid will mix them up.'

I went upstairs to tidy my room and make my bed.

My appointment with the headmistress was at eleven o'clock. The Fashion College was in the same district as the Home, so I would walk. It was a nice morning and the sun was shining.

The college was housed in a Victorian red-brick building with little turrets. Brown lino was everywhere, with dark green and buff-coloured paintwork – serviceable. I called this combination of colours 'decorators' delight'.

The headmistress was a thin, pale woman, of about fifty-five, with freckles, and red hair arranged carefully over her ears, frizzed out to make it look thicker. She looked me up and down, made me sign a book, and then gave me a short lecture on the glories of good workmanship and how much better everything had been when she was young. 'The Good Old Days.' She showed me my classroom, reminded me that punctuality is the virtue of kings, and walked over to one of the girls. 'Hand me your garment, child – no, this will not do at all.' And with her pale anaemic hands, she picked up the scissors: snip, snip, snip.

One could breathe again after she had left. 'Old fusspot,' said the girl next to me, 'You have to make two inch seams so that she can cut them away. Really!'

The assistant teacher said that I must do the usual practice blanket; this was so called to show all kinds of stitches, seams and buttonholes. Miss Preisser (the 'old fusspot'), would then decide if I were fit to stay at the school. What happens if you are not good enough? Do you get thrown out? These questions remained unanswered.

The very sight of this practice blanket became hateful to me. I sat for weeks over it, unpicking it again and again, until the white material had turned pale grey. One weekend I washed the whole thing. Old Fusspot remarked that she had not given me permission to do so. The practical work became boring, even though it had been interesting in the beginning. No garment can still be exciting after four weeks' work on it, no matter whether the over-sewing looks like Chinese embroidery or not. The school supplied most of the materials and they remained the property of the school, to be sold in a bazaar or a raffle. We had an endless stock of woollen material which a philanthropically-inclined clothing manufacturer had given us, probably because he could not sell it. The material was scratchy and came in shades of rust, grass green, and light navy. You try and design model gowns in this! Day dresses, afternoon dresses, two pieces, skirts, pleats and drapes – all had to be designed in the same material! As a concession Old Fusspot would occasionally allow us to buy a ribbon for trimming or white pique for a collar, but this was a special privilege.

Butter muslin and unbleached calico were used for the evening gowns, and we dyed them in the scullery of the school in many startling shades. I disliked dying the blue ones most, because the blue stain remained on my hands for days – but blue was fashionable then.

Sometimes I longed for the stiff crêpe paper from Uncle Daniel's factory, from which I had made theatrical costumes when I was a child. We made countless sketches for our models and I found the cost of the paper high for the school did not supply the brown paper for the patterns, nor the drawing paper.

'Theory' was more interesting. We had lectures given by outside specialists on textile production, wool, fibre, etc. We paid visits to museums, conducted by 'Old Fusspot', and occasionally received invitations from Jewish stores to attend their fashion parades, with complimentary tea and cream cakes. There were life classes, although the model was fat and middle-aged. One of the students assured us – she had heard it from a reliable source – that the model had six children.

Twice a week we were given a lecture by Miss 'Quick-quick' on mass production, medium trade.

Languages, either French or English, were compulsory at the school; twice a week we had games. Why this was included in the curriculum I never found out.

My fellow students were mainly residents of Hamburg with a few provincials like myself. These lived as paying guests with families, sometimes in digs (they must have had very modern parents!), or in small residential hotels called 'pensions'.

244

I was chronically short of cash. Did I suffer from excessive pride about money? My grandparents sent the exact money for fees and lodging. Could I ask them for more? I calculated that I was costing them more per month than a labourer would earn. They were giving most generously. My parents never sent anything and I did not dare ask them. I suppose they did not think that I needed money for fares, shoe-soles, or toilet articles. Shoe-soles were a big problem, as I always walked to college to save the tram fare, but I don't suppose it was more economical. Apart from this, I had the cost of the paper for the school. We used so much – paper to make patterns, drawing paper, cardboard for mounting successful designs; I had never realised that paper could cost so much. But a dressmaker, even a student dressmaker, can always earn a little extra.

My first job in the Home turned up when the matron asked me to help a blind lady. Her dressmaker, who had called on her every fortnight, had emigrated. This work consisted mainly of exchanging the white collars on her dresses. She was most meticulous about her appearance and told me that white collars gave her confidence. Before leaving I always threaded a whole row of needles for her as she was quite capable of sewing on buttons and doing minor repairs herself. She insisted on paying for the little services I did for her, and when I protested that the job was really a very small one, she said that if I did not take the money she would not ask me again; it was difficult to find anyone who would be prepared to do one hour's work for her.

She had a sweet, patient expression and the corners of her mouth were always turned up. I have often noticed the same expression on the faces of other blind people.

My fame as a dressmaker spread and soon many of the ladies asked me to do minor repairs and alterations. Bubble Curls, the lady with the fiancé, asked me to design a trousseau for her, mainly underwear. I tried to persuade her to keep off chiffon and other transparent materials. Yes, I knew that Zarah Leander, the film star, looked divine in a negligée just like this one, but then Bubble Curls' waist was twice the size. She said, 'My fiancé does not want me to be slim. He likes me the way I am.' We compromised, and she got classic lines with chiffon frills – the fiancé sent me a box of chocolates.

I spent most of my evenings with my extra sewing jobs, sitting near the open window until the light failed. It was impossible to do any work later than this as the Home had to be very economical – at least that was what they said – and they had put a light bulb of the smallest possible power in my room. I had only seen this kind of bulb used in corridors, as an all-night lamp. If it was a fine day, I went for a walk. The maid with the red hands had given me a key for the side door, unofficially of course.

The Home was situated a short distance from the Alster, a lovely large lake in the centre of the town, which was surrounded by trees, almost a miniature woodland, and it was considered the best district of Hamburg. There were illuminations on the roads around the Alster during the summer months and paper lanterns swayed gently in the breeze on the small quay. Many boats were anchored there and young people would alight, amidst laughter, and walk towards the lakeside hotel for the dance held there in the open air. It all looked so festive, and I stood there on the bridge staring into the water, watching the lights dance on it, longing for a prince, but when the prince appeared in the shape of a fat old man who asked me to have dinner with him at the hotel, I ran away.

The fare at the Home was monotonous. It was one of the new regulations of the Third Reich that there should be no 'kosher' meat. The Nazis maintained that the animals would suffer by being slaughtered in the Jewish manner. Because many of the old ladies would eat no other, there was no meat at all on weekdays. For Jewish holidays, meat was imported from Denmark at great expense, and served in minute proportions with a good deal of gravy. There was a special soup kitchen attached to the Home, run by charitable ladies, where for ten pfennig you could get a plate of swedes and potatoes, or cabbage and potatoes, or turnips and potatoes, according to the day of the week, together with a slice of brown bread and margarine and a cup of corn coffee served in a tin mug. The corn coffee (foreign currency was not available for 'luxury' goods), was served in the smaller room adjoining the soup kitchen, where the Intelligensia held court. On the walls hung the newspapers, a reasonable selection of dailies, nationals and Jewish ones. These were clipped securely onto sticks – this is customary in continental coffee houses. Also on the wall was a notice board which not only displayed the weekly programme of the Grindel cinema (Jewish owned – Jews were no longer admitted to cinemas and theatres), as well as matters of general interest, such as rooms to let. Aryan landlords had been told by the Party to 'throw out' their Jewish tenants. On this board were also private notices: articles for sale, mostly at give-away prices, but there was no demand for these as people were emigrating.

I made acquaintance with the soup kitchen when Matron decided that it was a bother to keep the ordinary lunch for me; I could not get home from school in time for lunch and it was a nuisance if I went down to the kitchen to warm it up when the maids had already finished washing up. 'Why not have some nice, hot, steaming swedes and potatoes from the soup kitchen instead?' The vegetables, cooked in such very large quantities, were most unappetising, but the worst was the cabbage smell.

Most of the Hamburg coffee houses had by now *'Juden unerwuenscht'* (not wanted) signs, so the soup kitchen became a meeting place of many unemployed, former municipal servants, teachers etc. There was even a Herr Doctor, a *Kommerzian Rat*, (Commercial advisor in the former government). The gentlemen welcomed the opportunity to discuss the newspapers with their cronies. Besides, the room was well heated, even if the food was not exactly *'haute cuisine'*!

On weekends, when I had time, they often offered me a place at their table; they said they liked to have a pretty girl around. I found their discussions very interesting.

Dr Goebbels had prohibited art criticism. He claimed the Jewish critic-aristocracy had over-run German culture. Hitler had declared that it was not criticism that was wanted, but a 'unity of mind and will'. Dr Goebbels played on the fears of the people. The middle class was to be frightened by reports of the Communists' actions in foreign lands against the middle classes. Never fear, Adolf Hitler will look after you. The working classes could be stirred up by reminders of the not so distant past of unemployment, hunger, housing shortages and lack of social welfare. Farmers were shown what happened in Russia with their collective farms, and women generally were made to feel pity for the many abandoned children in the Soviet Union.

Everything was the fault of the Jews.

Dr Goebbels preached the need of *'Lebensraum'*. His propaganda was most active in Austria, for of the intended *'Anschluss'* (annexation to the German state). First Austria, then Czechoslovakia with the Sudetenland, then Poland and the Latvian States. He claimed all these *Auslandsdeutsche* wanted to be reunited with the *Vaterland*, by rights they belonged to Germany. The rest of the eastern people were *minderwertig* (worthless, slave labour).

Hermann Goering, the fat, be-medalled, important Nazi had been elevated to General Fieldmarshall (four-star General). He gave orders for an armed 'Action' against Austria on 13th March. He demanded that the Austrian chancellor Kurt von Schuschnigg must resign to be replaced by the Nazi Seyss-Inquart. Austria was now ready to be invaded. Church bells were to be rung and fires to be lit on mountain tops for the celebrations when the German army entered; this was shown on the news reels in all cinemas. There was a plebiscite, it was claimed that ninety-nine per cent of the Austrian population had voted for the *Anschluss*. The friends at the coffee table found this hilarious, they said it did not even allow for spoiled voting papers, unavoidable from the large illiterate population of the mountainous hinterland. Several years later I met an Austrian girl, whose father had been a judge. She told me that at the plebiscite the 'No' votes simply disappeared.

Adolf Hitler had been born in Austria, another good reason to declare Austria German. The news reels showed a jubilant reception when Adolf Hitler drove through Austria on his way to Vienna.

When my 'alteration business' at the Home was good, I would buy myself sandwiches and didn't trouble to go home. Occasionally my expenses were very heavy. When I had to buy paper or have my shoes soled, it was difficult to manage on the money. I studied the windows of the food shops with new interest and most carefully. Herrings were a good buy and very filling – ham sausage was already more extravagant. For the price of two rolls purchased in the delicatessen one could get three and a half in the baker's shop. On a notice board I saw the following announcement:

Gut Bürgerlicher Mittagstisch for Students
Three courses: eighty pfennig per day
Two courses: sixty-five pfennig per day

Underneath was a specimen menu. This was very cheap. I deliberated for a long time, longing for the hot, delicious food. I imagined *knoedels* (dumplings) filled with meat and sausage. Once when I received a larger sum than usual for my sewing, I plucked up courage and went there.

A very stout middle-aged woman in a floral overall with a white apron over it received me suspiciously. 'For how long did I wish to book?'

'Well, I don't know. One week, perhaps more.'

'It's only for regulars,' she said. 'My young men book for a term at least.'

'Did you enjoy your dinner?' she smarmily asked, a fair, pimply youth, who passed us. Then, turning back to me, she said aggressively, 'I've got a waiting list. Everybody wants to eat at Mother Koeller's.' I apologised for troubling her and left.

I didn't dare to write home and complain about the food because my mother might easily have written back saying that if I was not satisfied, if I was so spoiled, I might as well come home. I was afraid of my mother's irony.

After about six months in the Old Ladies' Home, the matron of the orphanage found a vacancy for me, saying I could share a room with another girl. The orphanage had been given additional beds by emigrants who could not take them abroad. She wrote to my grandparents that the fee for my board and lodgings was less than at the Home. As they deducted the difference, I didn't profit by this economy.

The food there was plain, but plentiful, and no longer did I have to spend my 'sewing money' to supplement my ration. The orphanage was a red-brick building, painted inside like all institutions, buff and green, with serviceable brown lino on the floors. The dining hall was enormous and there were several long tables with perhaps twenty children to a table, at the end of which sat an assistant house mother. Every available space at the orphanage was taken up, and many spare beds were now put in the dormitories. The Nazis had forbidden Jewish children to attend ordinary schools in many towns and villages; the orphanage, therefore, had many boarders, as the Jewish community in Hamburg ran its own schools.

There was a college of Domestic Science attached to the orphanage, which I thought was a very clever idea. The young girls learnt cooking, sewing, laundry work, and housework. No domestic staff was required as these students did all the housework. Apart from a porter and his wife, there was no other servant in the whole place. The girls paid rather a high fee to be taught, although admittedly they had French lessons, English lessons, hygiene, child psychology, and all sorts of other lessons which members of the

249

Hamburg Jewish community gave free. There was always a long waiting list for the Science College, as the orphanage had a very good reputation; the students received the much sought-after certificate at the end of the year to say that they were fully qualified domestic servants.

Musical evenings were arranged twice a week, and one of the house mothers, Miss Elsie, who was acting as assistant matron, played the piano for us: the lighter pieces of Beethoven, Mozart, Schubert. Miss Elsie used to be a piano teacher and I think she was my favourite among the teachers there. On sewing evenings Miss Elsie read to us (the domestic science students, and myself) books such as Axel Maunthe's *St Michele*, and with her soft and trained voice she made the story exciting and wonderful, and the characters seemed more alive than when I read the book myself. I read it again, many years later, and it was a disappointment; then I found it shallow and conceited.

The sewing room in the Orphanage was situated on the third floor overlooking the street and the parade ground of the Hamburg Police Training School. The sewing machine on which I did my homework for the Fashion College, and the work for the children, was facing the window. My eyes sometimes wandered from my work. The shrill commands given by the instructors echoed on the red brick walls and the sound of their goose-stepping on the gravel was multiplied a thousand-fold. They were always in a perfect line. Knees bend, up, down, up, down. They all looked alike in their white singlets and khaki shorts.

I wondered whether in their free time they would also be all alike, drinking in the Bierhallen, making slightly obscene jokes, or taking their girls to dance halls. As I was fair-haired, uniformed Nazis often tried to make passes at me. Fair hair was something special; fair hair was approved of. And now they were goose-stepping again. Crunch, crunch, crunch. I closed the window.

The dressmaker who had attended part-time to see to the alterations had emigrated. I inherited her job. Matron was satisfied with my work, saying I was better, in spite of my young age. She would pay me the same. No longer was I hard up; I could even buy the longed-for odd art book. Jewish people who were emigrating donated surplus clothing, and new fabrics were donated by shops which had closed down. Whilst many children were paying boarders, these gifts were intended for the real orphans or children with parents in reduced circumstances, of which there were now many. I moved my sewing machine away from the window, so as not to be distracted.

A girl at the orphanage had told me that they not only trained police there, they also trained the SS. I wondered if this was true. They all looked alike – which one was a police man, which one an SS man? When they had finished their training, would they be detailed for duty at the concentration camps? The brutalities committed there were only whispered about. Were they capable of those brutalities or was everything gross exaggeration?

In a big town at that time one was further removed from anti-semitism. There was the usual swastika daubing, but this was confined to the synagogue and the Jewish stores. Nobody called after one in the streets. Cinemas had 'Jews not wanted' signs, but there was one in the Grindel to which one could still go; it was Jewish owned. The cinema industry in Germany had been created by Jews – now it was Aryanised.

I found Hamburg a beautiful town, the mellow red brick buildings so tall and stately. I liked to go for walks in the twilight. Often there was a fine drizzle; it rained much more in Hamburg than in South Germany. I did not mind, for then the town looked even more romantic. The pavements shimmered and the oil spots in the road glistened like jewels. I would walk down to the old part of the town and watch the barges gliding past in the canals.

The local girls in the college had told me many wild and woolly tales about the Reeperbahn, the town's amusement centre, to which all the foreign sailors went for a good time. One could meet sailors from all over the world there – even Negroes and Chinese – and in those stories there was so much excitement and vice that I felt I would not have 'lived' until I had seen it. One afternoon, I arranged to go there with one of the girls. She would show me round. She would call for me at four. At the last minute she phoned and said she could not come. So I set off alone.

When I arrived there, everything was deserted.

I bought myself a slice of melon from a wagon and slowly walked down the street, waiting for something to happen.

Nothing did.

I drank a glass of lemonade in an open-air café, served to me by a sleepy waiter. It tasted exactly the same as anywhere else.

The decorations and illuminations looked rather sad and shabby in the daylight.

The merry-go-round was revolving, but no-one was riding the little horses.

The photographs of 'Les Girls' weren't a bit risqué; in fact, I thought some of them looked rather old and haggard.

I had permission to stay away for supper so there was plenty of time left, and nothing to do.

I passed a shop selling underwear. There were some very cheap stockings in the window; they didn't look bad at all, so I went inside.

'Anything else?' asked the blowsy saleslady, who was wearing a black satin dress. 'We have some special cami-knickers here, very special.' She showed me some pink ones with lots of black lace – I would never have dared to wear them, especially in the orphanage.

'No, thank you.'

'I'll reduce them. They'll really do something for you,' she said in a familiar way which embarrassed me.

I picked up my stocking and practically ran out of the shop, saying to myself, Well, if you *will* buy things on the Reeperbahn, what can you expect?

Consulting my watch, I realised that I had over three hours left, so I decided to go to the cinema.

The film was a love story, sexy and sentimental. Then came the news footage of the Munich agreement. Everybody laughed at Chamberlain's umbrella. 'Mr Umbrella!' called a youth who sat near me. Chamberlain – I disliked him because of his name. I did not trust him. I thought of Houston Stewart Chamberlain (was he a relative?), who had married one of Richard Wagner's daughters. He was an author who wrote fantastic tales, proving that Jesus Christ was not Jewish at all and that Christianity was essentially German. He was an Aryan supremacist who claimed that the rebirth of the West could be achieved only by the total removal of the Jews. He also preached Darwin's theory of natural selection and survival of the fittest. He had even become a naturalised German, perhaps to please his wife. He was a great believer in 'the master race'. Absurd! On screen there were flags everywhere; the Germans were jubilant.

The Fuehrer had done it again. Heil Hitler. To myself I said, 'Hell Hitler.'

Deutschland, Deutschland, ueber alles, ueber alles in der Welt. Die Fahne hoch...

I saw the big film half way round again getting up just before the sexy bit which had embarrassed me. The woman next to me was furious because I blocked her view at the crucial point.

Chapter 27

The Pogroms of November 1938

On 7 November 1938 a seventeen-year-old Jewish refugee boy shot and killed the third secretary, Ernst von Rath, of the German Embassy in Paris. The boy's father had been recently deported to Poland, herded together with thousands of other Jews in box cars, which the railway normally used for the transport of cattle.

The assassin, Herschel Grynspan, had intended to shoot the German ambassador, Count von Welszeck; Herschel had asked to see the ambassador and did not know it was Secretary von Rath who came out to see him. Ernst von Rath was no anti-semite; he was himself under 'supervision' by the Gestapo for his anti-Nazi attitude.

When we read about this in the papers, we knew it would be bad for us Jews.

'A German Jew? His name does not sound a bit German,' said one of the domestic science students at the orphanage.

'Perhaps they made him change it,' said another student. 'I have heard they've forced some people to take peculiar names on their passports. They were so glad to get a passport out of Germany they let the Nazis put those middle names on.'

One of the Nuremberg Laws had decreed that Jews must carry a Jewish middle name – most Jews took Israel or Sara. This was on the 'approved' list of names 'suitable for Jews', which had been concocted by the 'expert' Globke, from the Interior Ministry. The old testament names, like Jacob or Ruth, were not included because these had been 'Germanised' and were in general use in Germany. There was a whole list of names 'suitable for Jews'; mostly they were figments of the imagination of Herr Globke – names like Sharne (meaning all burnt up), Schlemche (meaning muddy), Feibisch and

Sprinzi. These names sounded awful; the latter was a name I found in records of the eighteenth century, so Globke was something of an expert after all. Herschel (young stag) was a Jewish name but not in general use. I don't know if this was on the list.

'Perhaps it is not true at all, just propaganda,' said a third girl.

But true or not, one thing was certain, we were afraid. And then came 9th November.

9th November had been Grandfather Samuel Fleischer's birthday. It was also the anniversary of the Weimar Republic.

9th November was the anniversary of the Beer Hall Putch. The Nazis always celebrated the Beer Hall Putch. The storm troopers who had died in the Munich street fight had been declared national heroes, heroes who had been martyred in the sacred cause of delivering Germany from the 'traitors' of the Weimar Republic.

9th November is now the anniversary of the Cristall Nacht (night of the broken glass), the night of the burning of the synagogues in Germany – at least 267 were destroyed – the night of the beginnings of the pogroms.

I was not aware of anything unusual, that fateful night. I was asleep.

When I got up in the morning, I found the house deathly quiet.

On my way to the washroom I passed one of the Kindergarten teachers.

'Good morning,' I said cheerfully. 'How silent the children are today ... perhaps my watch is fast. What time is it?'

'Sh ... Haven't you heard?'

'Heard what?'

Then she told me the dreadful news: the synagogues burned, the men arrested, the shops and stores burned, smashed and looted.

The children were told at breakfast that their school had been closed until further notice. 'We live in difficult times. We know you all will co-operate by being on your best behaviour.'

The silence in the house was broken only by the telephone, which rang very frequently.

The phone calls came from all over Germany. They brought bad news: somebody's father, or brother, or relative had been arrested by the Nazis.

The older children and the students hung around in groups in the corridor outside Matron's office, waiting, terrified, for those phone calls.

Whose turn was it next? Some girls cried openly and some prayed. Others just stole off to their rooms. We were too afraid even to discuss it.

They arrested approximately 20,000 Jewish males. Within the span of a few days the SS had called at most Jewish houses and rounded up the men. They had even called at the house of an aunt of mine whose husband had been dead for two years. This shows that their lists must have been prepared far in advance. There was no escape. If you did not open the door, they knocked it down with the butts of their rifles. If you went into hiding, someone had seen you and gave you away. If you were caught hiding, you were usually shot, 'trying to escape'. You could not flee to another country; the passports had been confiscated by the Reich.

I also had my phone call.

My Mother was in Frankfurt with the grandparents when the Nazis called to take my Father away. It was in the early hours of the morning; two SS men had come.

Later I was told what had happened.

Father had woken Arnold and Susan. Richard, of course, was away at the Jewish Orphanage in Esslingen. Father had gone over to the window and drawn back the curtains. 'Look, the sky is quite red – it's the synagogue. I saw it from the laboratory upstairs. I got up a little earlier than usual because I had a lot to do today.'

He pulled his watch out, Father wore an old-fashioned gold repeater watch, he could not bear anything constricting his wrist. 'Almost four thirty now. I think I'll go and have a look at how things are going. I've called the fire brigade. They knew already, they were all out. I supposed by now they have the fire under control. I wonder what could have started it?'

Arnold and Susan were looking out of the window, speculating as to the cause of the fire.

'Do you think it could have been arson?'

'I don't know,' answered Susan. 'I would not be surprised.' Only yesterday, coming home from school, some big boys had run after her shouting, 'Jew, Jew, Jew.'

'It looks worse,' said Arnold. 'I'll go upstairs. I can see more from there.'

'Call me if you can really see something,' said Susan. 'I'm going back to bed. Sh ... did you hear that? It sounded like an explosion.'

'I did not hear anything with you jabbering all the time. Perhaps it was the backfiring of a car.'

'Bit early for a car.'

'Lorry then.'

Susan closed the window and went back to bed.

After a while the bell rang.

Arnold called down, 'Open the door, Susan. Father must have forgotten his key.'

Susan slid downstairs on the banisters. In the vestibule, she quickly pressed the buzzer, then started to run upstairs. She did not want to be caught without her dressing gown. Mother always said, 'carelessness', 'catching cold', 'no slippers on', etc.

Bang, bang, bang. Someone was hammering on the glass door. Susan peered over the banisters. She saw two SS men. Bang, bang, bang.

'It's open,' she called.

They saw her. 'Come here!'

Susan became still, as if she had grown onto the stairs. She did not move. She stared.

'I said, come here, you brat!'

They were slowly coming upstairs. Susan could not take her eyes off the revolver which the SS man was pointing at her. The other one was holding a briefcase. He opened it.

'Julius Fleischer. Your father. Tell him we want him. Be quick.'

'He is not at home.'

'When is he coming home?'

'I don't know.'

'Where did he go?'

'I don't know.'

They obviously did not believe her; they brushed past her and started to search the rooms, slamming doors as they did so.

Arnold came out of the laboratory. 'What's going on?' He sized up the situation in a second and planted himself in front of Susan.

Susan was silent. She was shivering. She looked younger than her age – she was fourteen then – particularly so because she had grown out of the striped pyjamas she was wearing.

Both Arnold and Susan were small; they took after Mother.

The SS men consulted a list. 'No, I don't think so, he can't be the one. He's not eighteen. Not that one.'

They searched very thoroughly – the closets, the cellar, but clearly didn't think anyone there was over eighteen.

257

'Let the boy look after the child,' said the one with the revolver to his companion. Then he barked at Arnold, 'We'll be back.'

They tramped downstairs. It echoed.

'I wonder where Father is. Oh, dear,' said Susan, 'what are we going to do?'

She sat down on the stairs. Arnold fetched her dressing gown.

'Let's go and make some coffee.'

Father was hardly through the door when the SS men returned to take him away. They must have been waiting for him.

'I'm just going to the police station with these gentlemen,' Father said. 'For inquiries. I'll be back soon. You'd better go back to bed, both of you. If I am not home by breakfast, ring your Mother. Not to worry.'

It was Mother who rang first, at six in the morning. This was good thing because later on in the day the telephone did not work any more.

Arnold told her the bad news about the synagogue.

She said the synagogue in Frankfurt was also burning. The grandparents were as well as could be expected. She did not like to leave them, but she would catch the morning train. Mother cautioned Arnold and Susan that under no circumstances were they to leave the house. No, she did not think they were burning down private houses. She was wrong: they did, though not in our town. 'Promise me,' she had said, 'that you won't go outside the door. There are riots in the streets.' She warned them to be sure to lock all doors and windows, but not to stand near them, and to draw the curtains because they were throwing stones. She would be home in the afternoon. She would get a taxi.

Mother was glad that the driver accepted her as a fare. She vaguely knew him, though the rank at the station was not his usual one.

He drove slowly.

He pointed to Heiman's, the large Jewish clothing store on Market Place. All the plate glass windows were smashed – they had been exceptionally large ones. A dummy was lying half in and half out of the window, its uncovered legs with the painted-on shoes sticking up obscenely.

The taxi driver said, 'I was there, when it happened. No offence meant, Mrs Fleischer. We all had a call, we had to report right away. Everybody. I don't hold with things like that. My wife bought

258

a coat at Heiman's over three years ago. It's still good ... but he [Herschel Grynspan] shouldn't have shot him, no ... he should not have shot him. They told us all about it, about International Jews. What I don't understand, the Jews here, what did they have to do with it? I might be wrong ... I don't believe they had anything to do with it ... Yes, I was there when they smashed the windows. Kleinknecht, the one who has the little shop in the Graebergasse, he threw the first brick, or something like a brick, and he shouted ever so loud, "*Ich werd, dir den Laden schoe' renoviera*" [I am going to renovate your shop for you.] And when it crashed – what a noise it made! "*Jud, jetzt hast dei', shoe' Auslag' g'habt!*" [Jew you've had it, your nice display window.] No, I don't think that's the way to go about it.'

He shook his head. 'Kleinknecht should "renovate" his own shop. It's a miserable hole, that shop of his in the Graebergasse, and not much passing trade either. It's a one-way street now – one could never get through there – out of the way it is.'

When they drove past the synagogue, it was still smouldering. 'They had half the brigade out, spraying the boy's school next door, all night long. They were afraid it might catch fire with the wind last night... They even used detonators. Nope ... he shouldn't have shot him.'

The taxi drove on. Personally he had nothing against the Jews; they tipped well, and were courteous. Not like some people he could think of. Mother gave him a good tip. He put the luggage in the vestibule. 'Shall I take it up for you, Mrs Fleischer?'

'No, thank you, it's all right.'

Later the details of the arson became public.

Hitler and Goebbels had been attending the festivities celebrating the Munich Beer Hall Putch in the Alten Rathaus in Munich, when they were informed of the murder of von Rath.

Goebbels, as Minister of Propoganda, gave the signal for the onslaught against Jewry.

The full machinery of information was used all over the German Reich to inform the various leaders of the District-Groups of the SA and the SS. The Group South West, the SA, Brigade 56 Ulm received the order to burn all the synagogues, and to transmit this order forthwith to their branches. This was done. The local chief of the fire service was told to turn off the alarm calls which called the local firemen at their houses. Later an order was given to protect only the

Christian houses and premises adjacent to the synagogue. It seems that the local Nazis were asleep, as it was two SA men from nearby Geislingen who committed the arson. They climbed in through a window, and with the straw and petrol they had brought with them, 'made a wonderful fire'; they bragged about it later. The cupola fell in, the benches and the whole interior was burned out; only the outer walls remained. There was a small crowd watching, perhaps about fifty persons, mostly in uniforms, 'on duty'.

Opinions were mixed, about this outrage. One SA man said, 'Tonight we really did a thorough job.' Others said they were disgusted. When the Judge of the local Police Court (*Amstgerichtsrat*), Dr G. Mueller, was heard to say, 'That is no way to go about things', an SA man asked him, 'Is this not to your liking?' Dr Mueller replied, 'Do you know who I am?' The man screamed at him, 'It does not matter who you are, this is no concern of yours', and he threatened him with his loaded pistol, held at his chest. This Dr Mueller later became the Ministerial President of Baden-Wuerttemberg from 1953–1958. From 1958–1971 he was President of the Bundesverfassungs Gerichts. The Commandant of the Fire Service had also expressed his distaste for the 'action'.

*   *   *

The clean up of the place where the synagogue had stood, cost 3,858 Reichmarks – to be paid by the Jewish community. On the green, there is a memorial tablet, erected in 1971.

As mentioned before, Germany was very short of foreign currency. All kinds of measures were taken to help in the export drive. The November pogroms had set them back considerably. The foreign buyers, and by no means were they all Jewish, had cancelled contracts, withdrawn agencies, and boycotted German goods.

Countries were horrified at the behaviour of Nazi Germany. Germany had been known for a cultured country; it had produced many great men in the Arts, Sciences and Philosophy. People liked to think that perhaps the reports were exaggerated, mere newspaper propaganda.

German goods were reliable, German goods were cheap. One need not have 'Made in Germany' stamped on the goods, if it offended the customer; 'Foreign' was quite within the custom regulations. I don't think that people were aware the goods they bought so reasonably were subsidised by the Reich, sometimes by up to fifty per cent. In order to be competitive in the world market the Germans had to under-bid. The Reich made up the deficit and reimbursed the manufacturer.

Foreign currency earned with exports belonged to the Reich; the Reich had to be notified of every transaction. The penalties for crimes against currency regulations were heavy, especially in the case of a Jew, where everything he owned would be confiscated immediately and the whole family put in concentration camps.

By now most firms – those with overseas branches or overseas connections – said that they wanted to help the former owners, directors, salesmen and other staff. The Jews had given good service to the firm; therefore it was only right that a job should be found for them abroad.

This gave many Jews a chance to emigrate, quite legally. It gave them and their families safety and security.

The Jewish salesmen had always been considered good at their job. They sold German goods abroad for the much needed foreign currency. The kind-hearted foreigners gladly helped those poor refugees, and placed considerable orders with them.

The merchandise was good, the price was right, and Mr Bernstein, that nice Jewish traveller with the quaint sing-song accent – he was Viennese, not even German – could bring his family over. Yes, the Home Office had granted a visa.

Still the exports fell.

The German ambassadors complained that the pogroms had made their relations difficult, the goodwill was gone. The ones who complained too loudly were recalled.

Another measure to liquidate Jewish assets was taken in February 1939 when all Jews had to hand over, in the official state pawnshops, gold and silver, jewellery, silver plates and coffee sets, gold watches, etc.

Mother was very upset, especially that her beautiful pearl necklace, Father's engagement present, had fetched only 13 Reichmarks (less than a pound). The pearls were large and well matched; once, when Father was hard up at the factory, he had used the necklace as collateral for a bank loan. I can well remember the row it caused between my parents. This necklace had been the 'exchange present' (*Gegengeschenk*) for Mother's dowry, which had amounted to 150,000.00 Gold Marks. I had been told that Mother had been the richest girl in Hessen Nassau (a county in Germany) and that Great

Grandfather – I remember him vaguely; he let me comb his red beard – had been able to live on the interest of the interest (*zinses-zinsen*). He was said to have lived modestly, having only one carriage, unlike my father's family who were 'wasters' and had large stables. Father seemed upset only over the loss of the Grand Prix and other gold medals awarded to the corset factory. With Mother's jewellery went the few bits and pieces belonging to Susan and me – relatives believed in 'starting girls off' with something. The official 'receipt' showed only a few items. Father explained that the Nazi was obviously suffering from writer's cramp. He said, even if he had thought it wise to try to persuade the man to 'write some more'; it might only have resulted in another few marks.

We were allowed to keep one set of solid silver cutlery per person; I've still got mine. These were part of a set in a box for twenty-four people. It was far too dangerous not to obey these regulations. One was too afraid. One could not hide jewellery or get it easily out of the country. Most people had put things in the banks for safety when the Nazis came to power. These were now frozen assets, and the Nazis had lists of them.

Another way to control Jewish property was by way of the Reichs Flight Tax. This had been in operation since the beginning of the Hitler régime. All German Nationals had to pay one-fourth of their money if they wished to leave the Reich.

This was to stop people taking their capital out of Germany. By 1939/40, 900,000,000 Reichmarks (£56,000,000) had been collected in Reichs Flight Tax. Persons with small incomes and little capital did not have to pay anything. If the Christian Germans were doing well they had no reason to emigrate, unless it were for political or religious reasons.

Communist sympathisers were emigrating, catholic priests were emigrating, the theosphists and anthroposophists were emigrating.

The Rudolf Steiner School – The Waldorf School – in Stuttgart, the largest private school in Germany, was closed by Nazi order, even though it was not a Jewish school. (It re-opened after the war.) The anthroposophists had had bombs in their meetings as early as 1933. I think the Nazis were afraid of them, because they openly reported what the Nazi's 'were up to'.

*   *   *

Life was very different from the time – in 1777 – when His Grace the Baron, High-and-Mighty and well-born (the popular style of address at that time), had granted 'his Jews' free religious worship. The Jews had been truly grateful, the Baron had been a just and fair protector. Life was very different now – in 1938.

* * *

Back in Hamburg, a few days after the pogroms, the Matron of the Orphanage had arranged for a Jewish photographer to prepare passport photographs for all the children. I asked him to do some for me as well, just in case I might be lucky.

Matron put the children's names down on a list to be sent to England. She asked if she should add mine. 'You might be too old, but there is no harm in trying. Perhaps,' she said, 'a family might even prefer to have an older girl.'

Individual families offered to take children into their homes. The so-called 'Children's Transports' were arranged by the Society of Friends in conjunction with English Jewry. Over the next few months, almost every week a 'Children's Transport' left one or other of the larger German towns.

The English people were very generous. They took over 10,000 children into their homes. They were absolute strangers, but were made welcome. Not all these children were Jewish. Approximately 10–15 per cent were children of parents persecuted for political reasons: Communists, writers, etc. I shall always be grateful to Miss Edith Rosenthal, the matron, for adding my name to the list, and I shall always be grateful to the couple who signed the guarantee for me.

Aunt Frances Rossendale (Rosenthal), the widow of Adolphe Rosenthal, my grandmother's brother, refused to give a guaranty for my parents. The sum was £500 per person but she could have afforded it. She was a very rich person now, as the London factory had been 'written over' to her in 1914 as a temporary measure – free, no money paid. My Father never claimed the factory back. It closed in the 1950s.

Chapter 28

Braune Schwestern *(Nurses in Brown Uniform)*

On 10th November, the Jewish schools were closed by Nazi order; this included the Fashion College.

I don't know what reason, if any, they gave when they closed the school. That it was a Jewish school would have been sufficient, I suppose.

I was hoping that the college would re-open soon, so I stayed on at the orphanage for the time being.

The orphanage often received materials and good, cast-off clothing from people of the Jewish community. I made myself useful doing alterations and making simple clothes for the children. Matron allowed me to design them, and she mostly approved my handiwork.

I buried myself in the work to avoid thinking.

I was terribly upset about my Father – what would they do to him? All my shortcomings and childish misdemeanours came to mind. I prayed for a chance to make amends.

Father had been annoyed over the infrequency of my letters home. He wrote once asking me if all the ink was dried up in Hamburg. If only I had the chance to write to him now! But the inmates of Dachau, the camp to which he had been taken, were not allowed letters. I worried so much that I became quite numb and paralysed with fear. Then, after a little while, I wouldn't allow myself to think about it any more. Three months later, Father returned home. I received a cheerful letter from him, saying he was in good health. He wrote that his breathing exercises had kept him quite fit during his stay at the camp. He didn't wish me to come home and he hoped that the school would re-open soon. After reading the letter through again and again that night, I put it underneath my pillow. I was in a high state of tension and found it difficult to sleep; I woke up continuously. I walked over to the window and looked up at the inky sky with its thousands of stars. It was so clear that I tried to recognise the constellations. My heart was thumping, my throat was so dry that it hurt, and I felt hot all over. Digging my nails into the windowsill, I could not take my eyes off the stars, and suddenly I thought I was flying right into the sky.

I woke up in the children's sick bay. I had no idea how I got there. Miss Elsie, who looked after me, told me that I had fainted and they had found me on the floor. Falling, I had knocked over a chair, and one of the teachers had come to investigate the noise.

Miss Elsie said she hoped the doctor would come soon, but I must be patient. I knew how difficult it was. With most doctors in 'Camp', the remaining ones were overworked. An elderly, retired doctor came. He looked at my throat and hummed; he didn't like it. I'd better have some tests taken at the hospital. Miss Elsie told me to get dressed, but I just couldn't; I could hardly raise my arm for her to pull my clothes over me. At last they got me into a taxi.

After what seemed an interminable ride the taxi stopped at the hospital reception. I gratefully sank into a chair. But apparently it was the wrong place – they wanted me to go to another department. I remember the muddy pathway and the desire I had to sit down on the ground, puddles and all. When I arrived, I passed out again.

I woke up in bed wearing a stiffly starched night-gown – buttoned all wrong, not that I cared or could have altered it; it was also very scratchy. A nurse passed by and I asked her to give me some water, but she just walked on. After a while, I saw another one and called out to her. She said I had to wait until the trolley came round. The trolley did not come round, or perhaps I missed it. When the doctor examined me, I said, 'Can I have some water, please?' He waved dismissively, 'Later.' I replied that I had asked several times, but not got any. The nurse defended herself by saying, 'Those Jews are all the same – spoilt', and that she was not there to be at their beck and call.

The test came through – diphtheria. I was put in isolation. My temperature was high. I can remember very little of the next few days, except that I was woken up continuously and made to drink black coffee. I was now all on my own in a tiny room. I felt frightened and lonely when I was gasping for breath. There was no air, though the window which ran the whole length of one wall, was kept wide open. Outside was a strip of garden, fenced off. Visitors were allowed to go as far as this fence where notices were placed at intervals – 'Halt', 'Danger', 'Isolation'. I could hear the convalescent patients shouting out of their windows to the visitors. When I was better I was on the look-out during visiting hours. I had many letters from home and then one from Miss Elsie who wrote that Matron had decided it would be better if no-one came to see me because diphtheria is so dangerous.The disease had a high mortality rate in those days.

How glad I was when I could leave the hospital. The nurses had been so severe and strict, I was afraid of them. In our home town the municipal hospital was staffed by Sisters of Mercy who were sweet and gentle. These here were *Braune Schwestern* (Brown Nurses – affiliated to the Nazi Party). One red-haired one scolded me, saying I had been a lot of extra work; she had had to sit with me when she had so much else to do. I did not remember that at all, but I worried about it. Another one complained that I wouldn't eat the food, and she would get into trouble. I suppose she meant well. However, I was so scared that I couldn't distinguish between a kind reproof and a telling off. I was not hungry, swallowing hurt, and rather than leaving the food on my plate, I flushed it down the lavatory, which was in the room because of the danger of infection. The linen was changed every day, even the letters I wrote were fumigated before being sent out.

On the day of my discharge I sat on a little bench in the corridor for hours, waiting for the various articles of clothing to be brought out, one by one, from the fumigation chamber.

I made my goodbyes and thanked the Sister. She answered, 'Your parents have paid. You can go.' She did not even say goodbye.

When I arrived at the orphanage I found my things in great disorder, piled on my bed. The Health Authorities had come to seal off my room for three days, the sewing room as well. What a mess! I almost cried – I did not know where to start first. Mechanically, I picked up some clothes and started to fold them. I'll do it later, I must just have a little rest, I thought, pushing the things to the side of the bed. Hours later I woke up, crooked and stiff.

Mother had suggested I should spend my convalescence at home. I packed my suitcase as well as I could, having to sit down to rest every five minutes.

Next day I travelled home.

266

Chapter 29

The Young Man Does not Like Peroxide Hair

Having found an empty compartment, I settled myself in a window seat facing the engine. The train was due to leave in a few minutes and I hoped – I always do – to keep the compartment to myself. However, at the last minute, a young man pushed the door open and sat down opposite me. I tried to read my book, but somehow I was too tired to concentrate properly. I thumbed through the magazines I had bought at the kiosk at the station; feeling extravagant I had purchased several. Dutifully I looked at the fashions, criticising them; I was not impressed. They were cheap magazines, so I picked up my book again. The ticket collector came in. The young man engaged him in a long conversation, asking about branch line connections and so on. He spoke too loudly and glanced occasionally in my direction. I felt this was an act put on for my benefit – he was the type who would know the timetable by heart. He was a mousy-looking young man, his fair hair plastered down meticulously over his forehead and worn with a middle parting.

Feeling restless, I got up to look out of the window in the corridor. My book slipped onto the floor. Very quickly he picked it up for me – I had to thank him. I didn't want to give him a chance to speak to me, so I put on my 'don't speak to me face'. But, sure enough, he took this opportunity and said, 'Interesting book you're reading, Miss.'

'Yes, thank you,' I answered and went outside. Half way through the door he stopped me. 'Excuse me, would you mind if I looked at your magazine?'

'Oh, do, help yourself.'

I stood in the passage a while and looked out of the window. The country was bare and flat, devoid of trees. Out of boredom I went to the dining car for coffee. On my return he thanked me profusely – Oh, do be quiet, I thought – for the loan of the magazines. He made several clumsy attempts to open a conversation. He had even looked at the fashions! One magazine had a big advertisement for hair-bleach.

He pointed to it and sighed. 'So very few women have real blonde hair. I don't believe in all that dyeing and that bottle stuff, do you, Miss?'

I said, 'I don't think it matters what colour hair one's got, as long as it suits one.'

'But you're so wrong, Miss, you're so wrong.'

'Why?'

'We must have fair hair to keep the race pure.'

I got a bit aggressive. 'To keep the race pure is very important to you, I suppose.'

'Yes,' he said. 'Yes, Miss, very important. Now you, Miss – what should I say – you're ash-blonde...' He mused. 'I suppose when the sun falls on your hair you're golden blonde. It's beautiful. You must marry a blond man and have blond children.'

'I find dark men more attractive.'

'How could you?' he said, as though this were a personal insult. 'No,' he said emphatically, 'we mustn't be selfish in these matters. We must breed a pure blond race for our Fuehrer.'

I retorted, 'I'm afraid I'm not very interested in this.'

He looked at me in perfect horror. 'A young German girl like you – it's your duty.'

'Perhaps I'm not a young German girl, and I don't think it's my duty. I'm Jewish.'

With a slightly embarrassed laugh he said, 'You mustn't joke about these things, Miss. The Jews are rotten people; you don't know them. We must get rid of them. You know, it's like a tree which has a rotten fruit on it – it's diseased. We must cut the disease out; we must nip it in the bud.'

'No, really,' I said, 'I am Jewish.'

He stammered, 'Please, please, stop joking, Miss. It isn't right. I'm a very patient man, but that's not right. You with your fair hair and blue eyes and pink complexion – Jewish, hah!' He laughed.

'Would you like to me show you my Jewish *Kennkarte*?' (Identity card for Jews.) 'And I'd like you to know, that my Father was a frontline soldier for years; he received the Iron Cross and other medals.'

The train was now slowly approaching a station.

The young man hurriedly stood up, gathered his belonging and stumbled out of the compartment with a hasty goodbye. From his conversation with the conductor I knew this was not his stop.

I remember well when, last November (1938), I had collected my *Kennkarte* from the main police station in Hamburg, a young policeman rose from behind his desk to conduct me, solemnly, to an inside room, where with a messy black roller my fingerprints were taken, to be filed and stored away. I felt like a criminal and didn't dare look up.

All Jews in Germany were given a *Kennkarte*, on the cover of which was a big 'J' for Jew. The inside held a passport photo with the left ear exposed.

The additional middle name of Israel or Sara (or any other from the 'approved' list), made it possible to recognise a Jew or half-Jew by the name alone. It was illegal to 'forget' to write down this middle name.

Our Passports were also marked with a red 'J'.

The journey seemed endless. I was relieved when the familiar landmarks of our home town appeared. I couldn't see very much as it was dark and people were getting their suitcases down from the rack. I craned my neck to see whether they had yet taken down the names of the Jewish factories, most of which had large neon signs. They were built along the railway which ran parallel to the river. Mother had written to me that by now almost all the Jewish factories and shops had changed hands. The Jews who had emigrated had had to sell, usually at a ridiculously low figure. The others hardly dared go near their own businesses after the pogroms in November; usually a Works Management of Nazi Party members was running them.

My parents were waiting for me outside the barrier. I had a shock when I saw them. Father looked so thin and that crew cut was terrible, I remarked on it; Mother smiled. 'It's much better now; you should have seen him when he came out of the camp. He was shaven close then.' Mother looked fragile; I noticed a white streak in her hair.

The luggage hadn't arrived. Father suggested I collect it next morning as I looked so tired. Mother had cooked my favourite dish, but I was too exhausted to eat even that; after a few mouthfuls I put down my fork, and went to bed.

Next morning I rose early. My sleep had failed to refresh me, but I offered to help with the chores. Mother declined, saying I still looked pale; if I wanted to do something, I should go and collect my luggage.

Slowly I walked down to the railway station. In the market place the plate glass windows of the large Jewish clothing store had been smashed; they were boarded up. A little swastika flag on a wooden stick had been wedged between the wood and was waving in the wind. Pretending not to notice, I walked past it. Hilde Schmidt, one of my former schoolmates, turned round the corner when she saw me approaching; at least this was preferable to being cut in the street. A band was playing 'Hitler' music, and all the people stopped and raised their arms, saluting the flag. I went into a doorway.

At the Left Luggage Office, I had to wait until they found my two cases. Looking round, I saw one which looked like Uncle Georg's, high up on the rack. It was stuck full with gaily-coloured hotel labels; my Father had often teased him saying it was vulgar, but he cheerfully kept sticking them on till there was hardly any space left. When I got them they felt as if they weighed a ton. My bones were aching all over, and I treated myself to a taxi.

When I got home I went back to bed. I was to stay there for two months with acute rheumatic fever.

My father nursed me, listening patiently to my never-ending complaints about my aching limbs. The worst of it was that I was unable to read, let alone hold a book. Mother propped the daily paper up in front of me, a doubtful pleasure; it was most upsetting as it seemed that every page held something about Jews, even in the advertisements: 'We have pleasure in announcing that the former Kaufhaus Levi is now under pure Aryan management.' Or in the gossip column: 'With the departure of the occupants of Number Five Hofstrasse, we have pleasure in announcing that the street is now *Judenrein* [cleaned of Jews].'

Father used to sit with me some evenings. Once I plucked up enough courage to asked him what it had been like in Dachau. He replied that it had not been too bad for him. 'You know, I'm used to fasting; I think it is very good for the health. It did not make any difference to me that roll call was at five o'clock, that is my

270

normal hour; in summer I get up earlier. But poor Mr Oppenheimer – you now how fat he is, and how he loves his food – it was very hard on him. Do you remembr young Stolts? He got frostbite and couldn't get into his shoes any longer; that's why they wouldn't release him at the first parade, when we were let out. He is home now, though. Mr Baruch – he was also in my hut – he broke his arm jumping over a fence when they set some dogs on him. They didn't set his arm properly and the silly man wouldn't let me do it for him. Of course, it had to be broken again.'

'That must have been painful.'

'It was a clean break,' he continued. 'Do you remember old Pastor Mueller, who disappeared two years ago? There were then all sorts of rumours – people said he'd gone to Rome. Well, I saw him. I couldn't speak to him as he was in another section, behind a fence, with other priests. They all wore purples patches. I don't think he saw me. He looked quite well – a bit thinner perhaps.'

Father stopped himself; he seemed to have said more than he intended. He could see I was becoming distressed. Gently he stroked my hair.

He said, 'I should not tell you all this. When I was discharged from Dachau they warned me – Fleischer, if you tell your friends about your holiday in Dachau, we'll have you back for another one – so don't you talk about it, my dear.'

We sat silently. He seemed to be thinking, concentrating.

Very slowly he said, 'Have no fear. You'll be protected.'

Many a night I lay awake just thinking, wondering. What would happen to us? Could we ever emigrate? The chances weren't good now. Our waiting number, given by the American Consulate, would not come up for at least another eighteen months, the quota was so small. There were difficulties in entering most countries. They would take you if you had a large sum of 'gold marks', but the Nazis would not allow you to 'export' your money, and if you could finally get a passport ten marks was as much as you were permitted. Young people didn't mind if they had the prospect of a job, but the older generation couldn't face it if they had no relatives waiting for them. Girls over eighteen could go as domestic servants; several countries would take them for that type of work. Young men could fill different types of jobs according to the needs of the country. But an advertisement in a paper would mean thousands of applications. Or there was Palestine – if one had been a Zionist of long standing, or belonged to their youth groups. For other Jews, emigration was almost as difficult as elsewhere. One felt like a mouse caught in a trap.

In the stillness of the night every sound was magnified. The footsteps echoed and it was easy to differentiate between a man's and a woman's. The SA was always holding night manoeuvres, the Labour Corps was holding night manoeuvres, the Luftwaffe had exercises; then there was the *Wehrmacht* – tanks rumbled through the street, from far off sounding like thunder. The sound would grow nearer and nearer until the houses were vibrating, and then stillness again. On Sundays the airmen – strangers to the town – stood at the street corners, whistling at the girls, and trying to pick up anyone who would let them. Mother laughingly told me that even she was not safe, but little Susan was frightened – she ran home as fast as she could. 'Fraulein, Fraulein, wait for me! Not so quick,' they would call.

I was surprised how Susan had grown whilst I was away. She was a pretty teenager now. A velvet ribbon held back her hair, which she wore shoulder length in ringlets.

She told me, 'They don't care how young you are, you can always become a *Deutsche Mutter* [a German unmarried mother]. Do you remember Irmgard, who used to be in my class, the one with the freckles and the red plaits? She's a *Deutsche Mutter* now. She's had it, two months ago, a boy, in the Municipal Hospital in Stuttgart – she's been living there with an aunt. I saw her pushing a pram when I went shopping. They say it was one of the athletes at the Sports-Tagung last year, some boy called Kurt – she did not even know his surname. But if I had been her I would not have created such a rumpus.'

'What happened?'

'You know she was a Leader of a Group of *Jung Maedel* – they do things with men ... they don't care if they get a baby.'

'But she is only fifteen now!'

'That's just it. At her confinement the nurse said when she brought her the child, 'Here you are, baby, hold your baby!'' Irmgard said, 'I am a German mother and proud of it!' And the nurse said, 'You should be ashamed!''

'Believe it or not,' Susan continued, 'Irmgard reported that nurse to the Party, and she had to apologise to her – in public!'

I had very few visitors during my illness, but Lisa Lendt – my former schoolmate, called quite often. Most of the Jewish girls I had grown up with had emigrated. My cousin, Lila Guggenheim, came to say goodbye before she left for England to stay with friends. She had spent two years in Switzerland. The Guggenheims and the Littles had met in Nice several years ago on holiday and had kept up a correspondence. The Littles, who lived on the Isle of Wight, had offered to apply for a work permit for Lila as soon as she reached eighteen. Then she could join their household as a 'servant'. Lila's oldest brother had gone to South Africa, the other one to the USA. And now, all the children having emigrated, the parents prepared to go to America; their waiting number would soon be reached. The restriction on Jews for emigration, for property and passport, varied from time to time. By now most Jews had lost their German citizenship and to obtain passports was extremely difficult. Little objection seemed to be raised to their taking a certain amount of household goods, providing they submitted the appropriate list. Valuables such as cameras, works of art etc., mentioned on the list, were then collected by the SS, but permission was usually given to take furniture, linen and clothing.

273

PART FOUR

ESCAPE STORIES

Chapter 30

The German Blood and Honour Must be Protected

The Nuremberg Laws came out by order of the Reichstag on 29th July 1935.

Signed on 15th September by the: Fuehrer Adolf Hitler
Minister of the Interior
Reichsminister of Justice
Deputy of the Fuehrer

To take effect by 1st January 1936, which meant the Nazis would imprison anyone who contravened these new statutes.

The following extracts will give an idea of their highly restrictive nature.

Racial Disgrace

Paragraph 1 Marriages between Jews and German Nationals are forbidden, even if they have been sanctified in a foreign country.
Paragraph 2 Sexual intercourse between Jews and German Nationals is forbidden.
Paragraph 3 German Nationals below the age of 45 are forbidden to work in a Jewish household.
Paragraph 4 Jews are forbidden to insult the German National flag.
Paragraph 5 Should anyone oppose Para 1 of this decree, the punishment will be Zuchthaus
Against Para 2, for the man, prison or Zuchthaus
Against Para 3 or 4, prison up to one year or a monetary fine.

Already as early as 1933, the Nazis had ordered a boycott against the Jewish shops and businesses, to begin on 1st April.

Jewish shops were marked with a black square, with a yellow circle in the centre. There were stickers to be attached: 'The Jews are our Disaster'. People were advised to shun Jewish medical doctors as well as Jewish lawyers.

The criminal behaviour against Leo Neuburger, in July 1933, comes to mind. He had a relationship with a Christian girl who worked in his factory. There had been an article about him in the local press, and he had been called a '*Rassen schaender*'.

The screaming populace dragged him out of his house, led by their Nazi District *Leiter* (Leader). They put a strong rope around his neck, pulled him through the streets of the town. They attached a cardboard notice which read, 'Racial shame, seducer'. At every lamp post Neuberger was made to call out, 'I am a perpetuator of racial disgrace'. To encourage him, the District Leiter kicked him and pulled at the rope on his neck, so that the poor man fell down. Then he was dragged to the Police Station. However, the police protected him and cut the rope off.

For mixed marriages, divorce was advocated. Couples emigrated. To be married to a Jewish partner meant loss of your job. Jewish ladies often begged their husbands to divorce them, because of the loss of income and other economic disasters, even if they saw each other secretly. Pressure was put on Christian husbands to leave their Jewish wives and racially impure children. One Jewish grandparent was sufficient to make you racially impure, tainted by the blood of an inferior race.

An acquaintance of Father's, the glass artist, Wilhelm von Eiff, had spent his youth in the town and had served his apprenticeship at a firm making art glass. He had invented a new method of etching glass – suitable for large window-like panes – using an electric attachment like a dentist's drill.

He became famous throughout the world, and was made a professor in Stuttgart at the Art Academy, where he had many foreign students. He was married to a Jewess. The Nazis put pressure on him for a prolonged period of time; they did not wish to lose such an important artist. Finally he succumbed and divorced his wife. It was said that a large commission was put his way. Father was of the opinion that von Eiff could have found employment abroad. But if you are not so young one might not have the courage to start afresh. One can understand that...

Arnold was interested in statistics – he told me they were more interesting than the lies and the cover-up propaganda in the newspapers, particularly about the economic situation. He gave me an example of why the unemployment money had been cut. 'Do you know, about two million German soldiers were killed in the war, about 800,000 are still on pensions with war wounds or such like. There are 300,000 war widows on benefit, and an enormous lot of fatherless kids. Who is to pay for all this? Who can pay – State Welfare, Local Welfare? With our reparation payments the money is not there.'

Mother had told me that after the war young girls could not find a husband, so many men had been killed, not unless they had a very good dowry, or were prepared to marry a much older man, perhaps a widower with children – women still died in childbirth, though fewer than before. Arnold said the reason was that conditions in the home were cleaner and there were more hospital births.

So, 'Racial Hygiene' was advocated: 'eugenics' – sterilisation of the *minderwaertig* (the worthless people). This included not only the incurables, but cripples and the insane; such people were using up hospital beds. Persistent criminals, thieves, the work-shy, vagrants and prostitutes were also ripe for sterilisation. If nothing else, it would save a lot of money.

Count Gobineau from France and Lanz from Liebenfels were widely read. There were also 'programmes' in the United States and Sweden, declaring that bad genes were inherited. Doctors attending births should decide which babies were fit to live.

'This is monstrous, Arnold,' I said. 'I know, in Sparta, they put the weak babies out for dinner for the wild animals, and there was Romulus and Remus of Rome. Perhaps wolf's milk is better than human's. But our cousin Karl, born weighing just over one kilogram, is now six foot two inches tall. Of course Uncle Emil was a doctor and looked after the baby himself. The Nazis want to kill off all the malformed babies; they are not wanted by the Aryan race which is so superior to all other races. What about Dr Goebbels, this ugly monster? He has a club foot – oh, he is very clever. He is a devil. He married a beautiful woman, a Venus, just like the god Vulcan who lives in the Hell of Vesuvius. I wish Goebbels would burn in Hell. He deserves it for telling so many lies about Jews. I wonder if he'll get club-footed children?'

Later I was told that rumours had been flying around about a hospital situated in the nearby countryside.

279

It admitted no visitors. Was it an Isolation Hospital for infectious diseases? Staff working there were forbidden to discuss their employment. People said that once you went there you came out only in a box, or mostly not at all. Perhaps they transferred you to another hospital, perhaps it was for incurables, perhaps for crippled people – everybody seemed to know a different tale.

One thing was certain, it must be a specialist place; not many local people had been sent there.

Chapter 31

Eighteenth-century Books

Whilst I was at the station collecting my luggage, fumbling in my bag for the luggage ticket, I thought I had recognised one of the cases on the rack, its gaily coloured labels seeming familiar, but I paid no further attention when my suitcase was handed to me and hailed a taxi. I was glad to get back home because I felt so tired and ill.

In fact, two cases had been standing for months on the racks of the Left Luggage Office: one, a battered hide suitcase, grained to resemble crocodile skin, covered with fancy hotel labels, now partly torn, camouflaging its worn appearance, No. 348; the other, a slightly larger one, a grey and black Revelation suitcase, new and efficient looking, No. 349.

'Been here a long time, Fritz. Have a look at them labels,' called the elderly porter to his youthful assistant. 'At least four months ... well, it's not my money.'

Fritz slowly spelled out the name: 'Dr G-e-o-r-g A-d-e-l-s-h-e-i-m-e-r ... what a scrawl!'

The old porter scratched his head slowly. 'Sounds familiar. Wait, might be wrong, though ... Adelsheimer, Dr Adelsheimer...'

'Sounds Jewish,' said Fritz.

'That's exactly what I thought. Fritz, go and ring the police. Ask if they have any information. 348 ... get the date first from our book.'

Fritz grumbled. 'Go on,' said the porter. 'I'd do it myself but I can't leave here. Inspector hasn't been round yet.'

Fritz returned after a little while, a smirk on his face. 'You're quite right, ha! The *Judenschwein* is dead! My *Abteilungsleiter* [Group Leader in the Nazi Party], says every time another Jew kicks the bucket, "*Heil Hitler!*" So, *Heil Hitler.*'

281

The old porter shook his head sadly. 'So, so this was Dr Adelsheimer's luggage...' and looking at the case said, half to himself, 'Amen.'

In his Daily Report Book he wrote, laboriously, later,

10.34 a.m.   Handed to Police Officer on duty
             as per instructions
             Luggage no. 348 & 349
             Contents not examined
             Fee unpaid
             Reason: Owner deceased
             Dr G. Adelsheimer. Signed Alois Schufner.

Mother had written to me that Uncle Georg had died of heart failure. He was a friend of my Father's and not a relation. I was very upset by this news, because I had got on especially well with Uncle Georg; he and I had discussed beetles over coffee with *Schlagsahne* (whipped cream), and chocolate éclairs at the local patisserie, sitting on gilded chairs at marble-topped tables. He had been a Professor of Entomology.

'Uncle Georg was not very old, Daddy. Only forty-six. Was his heart so bad?'

'No, my dear, it might have lasted him another thirty years.'

I got alarmed. 'He didn't die in a concentration camp?'

'Oh, no, he died last October, before we were all sent there.'

'Daddy, what is it? You are hiding something from me!'

'It would have been better if you hadn't asked me. Well, I suppose you'll find out anyway. One night the hooligans got him – mad men, criminals!'

'Here, in our town?'

'Here in our town,' Father answered, and, shrugging his shoulders, he left the room.

I tried to get further information from my Mother, but she remarked, very bitterly, that Uncle Georg's friendship with Fraulein Heller had brought him no luck. I remembered her quite well and I recalled vaguely that she had at one time been engaged to Uncle Georg. She had served me often when she worked in her cousin's book shop, before she had the position in the library.

Mother maintained that Christians and Jews should not inter-marry and had said this often, even before the Nuremberg Laws came into force. She was far more orthodox than my Father's family. The majority of my Father's friends were Gentiles. He used to say, 'I am a German of Jewish faith, and he is a German of Protestant faith, and he is a German of Catholic faith, and there are Moslems and Buddhists – what matter, if we are decent people?' But now, in 1939, even the most courageous stayed away from their former Jewish friends. It was understandable. They would have risked too much: their jobs, their reputation as a true German, perhaps even concentration camp.

Gradually I pieced together the information. Our charlady told me of the funeral, that the grave was covered with flowers, the wreaths and bouquets spilling over to the footpath.

'Never seen anything like it! Most of them anonymous, too. Fancy that! Guilty conscience, I call it!'

Old Anna, who used 'to do' for Uncle Georg, now had to take in a little washing to supplement her small pension, and nobody could iron men's shirts as well as she.

Once, whilst collecting a small parcel from her, I asked about Uncle Georg. 'The Herr Doctor, the kindest gentleman there was...' and she shouted, 'God will punish them.'

I said, 'Sh.' I was afraid someone might report her.

'I am an old woman – they can do what they like to me – and I don't care who hears it. I've known him since he was so high, and I was very proud when he got the prize, and I was not a bit surprised when he became a professor.' She continued, 'I said to him, "It will come to no good, Herr Doctor, but I'll tell Fraulein Heller what you've said." That was in the morning on the day it happened. And I told her; now I wish I hadn't. Nobody but I knew that he had the post in South America; they had even sent a ticket for him to Switzerland.'

Anna was wrong, my father knew.

And then she cried a little, and I made her sit down. I poured us two large cups of corn coffee.

'She has disappeared. Nobody knows where she's gone. Not that I have anything against her, she is all right.'

*　*　*

This is what actually happened.

Dr Georg Adelsheimer paced through his flat, which was denuded of ornaments and personal objects. Two rooms were locked. He

283

turned the key of one of them, entered. Anna, the daily woman, had covered the furniture with dust sheets. He lifted the corner of the one covering the red velvet *fauteuil*, sat down on the edge. He looked at the large portrait of his father, hanging on the wall opposite. He could scarcely remember him, he had died when he was a small boy. The portrait, oils, was in a heavy wooden frame. A mild looking man, with thinning reddish hair. Mother had said the painting did not do him justice, it was not a good painting but the artist was fashionable at that time. He leaned against the high back of the chair, Mother's favourite chair. I must be crazy, what am I doing here? He left the room, muttering that he had so much to do and must not waste time. His luggage was already at the station. For the third time he checked the entire contents of his brief case and his pockets. Too late if I forget anything, and he packed it all back again. Ah, handkerchiefs. He smiled. 'Georg, have you got a clean handkerchief?' He could still hear his mother. He was almost glad she was dead; the old lady died three years last June. She would never have understood the crazy happenings, she could not have adjusted herself to 'The New Order'.

Two large packing cases stood in the hall; he had arranged to have them collected by a courier, after dark, saying there was no one at home to open the door if they came earlier. One has to be discreet; one must not arouse suspicion.

From time to time he looked out of the window, and then he sat down again. 'Everything is under control, everything is under control,' he told himself. 'All packed.' Anna had left a dish of lentils and Frankfurter sausages in the oven for him. 'Your favourite, Herr Doctor, the last time.' And she had wiped her eyes with the corner of her apron, but he was not hungry.

Early this afternoon he had sent word by friends in the library where she worked. He had to tell her, had to know how she felt. Now at last he had something to offer her.

It was unbearably hot; the central heating sputtered. He opened the window and took this for an excuse to scan the well lit street, the shopping centre of the town.

No, there was no sign of her. She would go home first, prepare supper for her brother and herself, as usual. Perhaps she would come then – if not, he couldn't blame her.

He smoothed his sandy hair, and started polishing his glasses, and then lit, automatically, a cigarette. He paced up and down.

284

Again, glancing in the mirror as he passed. He returned to the mirror, searching, taking stock of his physical self. Paler than usual, his freckles looked more pronounced, I'm putting on weight, he thought. No wonder with all this sitting about; I don't get enough exercise. Since his 'resignation' from the university (Jewish professors were not employed any more), he had spent his time writing, completing his book on scarabs. Yes, I have been putting on weight, I am not getting any younger. Well, not too bad for forty-six. He felt suddenly chilly, and closed the window.

Sitting on the old fashioned horse-hair settee, always an uncomfortable piece of furniture, reading a newspaper, he noticed that he had read down to the bottom of the page without having the slightest inkling of what he was reading. The bell rang three times. He jumped up – Frieda – ringing the same way she used to ring. Why shouldn't she?

Going down the two flights of steps, he rehearsed a little speech, but when he finally stood face to face with her, he could only bring out a rather hoarse, 'Hello, Frieda.'

'You know,' she said, 'I had invited a girl from the library for supper and I couldn't get rid of her. It would have to be tonight. Finally I had to plead a headache. This helpful creature insisted that I took two aspirins and, to play the part, I took them. Now I am supposedly having a breath of fresh air.' She laughed gaily, though it did not quite ring true.

'Let's go upstairs.'

When he helped her out of her coat, she leaned against him. 'Georg, how have you been? You're leaving,' she said, noticing the cases.

'Yes.'

'When?'

'Tomorrow. I'm not even offering you a chair, ha, no manners at all – forgive me – I have not seen you for such a long time.'

'Oh, Georg, please...'

'I was not sure you would come – it's a risk for you, your job. Anna thought you might come.'

'Old Anna has gone amongst the readers, God bless her. I talk to her if nobody watches. She chooses some peculiar books.'

Georg laughed. 'She doesn't read them, you know, she just picks one at whatever section she happens to be standing. She says she likes to know what is going on.'

There was a long silence. Georg lit another cigarette. Frieda twisted her lace edged handkerchief. Frieda looked very fragile, sitting in the big easy chair, small and lost. She was tall, but her bone structure was delicate; her eyes were large, wondering, sometimes hazel and sometimes green, and her arched black eyebrows complimented her prematurely grey hair. Frieda was thirty-eight.

Georg watched her playing with her handkerchief. He noticed she was not wearing the engagement ring. She became aware of his gaze and smiled. Opening the top button of her blouse, she fingered for a fine gold chain with the ring on it, worn like a pendant.

Georg fairly stuttered, 'I didn't know whether it was all off – and, do you know, I hadn't the courage to ask you.'

Frieda looked up at him and said miserably, 'Georg, I don't think I'll ever see you again.'

This remark shook Georg out of his almost trance-like state, and he sat on the arm of Frieda's easy chair. 'Wait till you hear my news – it's going to be all right, my darling, it's going to be all right. I've been offered a post in South America. Imagine! I heard of the job through Haeberlein, you know, my school friend. We studied together in Heidelberg, he runs an Art Gallery in Zurich. I applied. The Dean wrote me a letter, most flattering, saying he had read my book. He called it a classic, blah, blah, blah... I must confess, though, I felt I could have kissed him when I got it – the letter. So tomorrow I am going on a holiday in the Black Forest – that's what I am telling everybody. I've got my passport – they've slipped up this time, forgot to call it in. You know, they issued me a new one only last year for the Paris Conference. A stroke of luck, this is.'

'Darling, do be careful.' She looked at him with a worried expression. 'What are you going to do about money? You are only allowed to take ten marks with you.' (Ten marks was then about sixteen shillings.)

'I've drawn as much as I've dared "for my holiday", and to hoodwink the manager I've asked them to transfer some to a branch of the bank in Baden Baden, in case I "get short" later. I didn't know how much I could draw without them reporting it. They won't get suspicious this way.'

Georg got up and started to walk backwards and forwards. 'I am taking nothing with me, just some of my books, papers and specimen cases; I mean to say, Haeberlein, who is going to meet me in Baden Baden, is going to take them for me. He is Swiss, nobody will question him at the border. I'll also give him the money, little as it is. That leaves me with just two hand bags, a real tourist.'

'It's just like a detective novel! Oh, Georg, I didn't mean that. I meant you're awfully clever.'

'I had not thought of it that way, but now you remind me, in my student days I once wrote a thriller, did you know that? I never finished it, quite.' He smiled sheepishly.

'No, you never told me.'

'It was not very good. Now coming back to more important things. As soon as I get settled, you come. Take your holiday, sick leave or something, say you are going to the Riviera. I've got it all worked out. Providing they don't freeze my account, as soon as I'm safely out of the country, I'll arrange for a transfer of some money to you, or better still, to Anna. I was making arrangements for her anyway. One never knows – if they gossip, it would be unpleasant for you.'

'Georg, don't let's talk about that. It's not important. Anyway, I've got some savings.'

'Darling, you are forgetting that I can't contact you. Walter Haeberlein – by the way, he is not Jewish – will write to you from me, so do not be surprised if you are getting love letters from a Swiss gentleman. You had better take his address. Got some paper?'

While she was scribbling, he went to the cabinet for some brandy. 'I think we could both do with some.'

'What are you going to do with all this?' asked Frieda, pointing to the furniture.

'Oh, this? The orphanage can have it. Couldn't sell this stuff, probably, even if I wanted to, but mother was used to it. I told Anna she can have what she likes; I am afraid, my dear, you are marrying a poor man. We have to start from scratch.'

'I am not worried,' Frieda laughed. 'Besides I can work.'

'Not in South America. I have been told it is not customary for ladies, and you are a lady.' Georg bowed to her.

'What are you doing with your beautiful bookcases, and the Louis Seize vitrine?'

'Anna is keeping them for us, with the china, the pictures and a few odd things.'

'You know, Georg, you are awfully practical. I would never have thought it.'

'Necessity, just sheer necessity.'

The bell rang.

'I expect it is for the cases. I have told them to collect them in the evening. Excuse me, my dear.' And he went downstairs. When he returned, he said, 'It's your brother.'

'Did you tell him I was here?' Frieda arose, looking anxious.

'He knew.' After a pause, he repeated the conversation: 'I have come for Frieda,' her brother had said. 'What makes you think Fraulein Heller is here?' 'She was seen entering this house. I've had a phone call to tell me; so I would advise you not to make any further trouble.'

'He is waiting outside, in SS uniform. You'd better go, my darling. Now don't cry, there.'

Georg helped her into her coat. 'I'll write very soon … that is, Walter will write very soon,' he corrected.

Frieda tried to smile. 'First thing I'll do tomorrow is get my geography up to date.'

'Remember that I love you.' They descended the stairs slowly, hand in hand. Georg kissed Frieda on the forehead. 'Frieda, Frieda.' Then he opened the door. She quickly joined her brother and left without turning around.

Without looking at each other, silent, Frieda and her brother walked home. She did not notice it when he raised his hand, giving a sign to a group of SS men. She was deep in thought, holding an imaginary conversation with her brother. There would be a big row – he had a temper – but it would blow over. She would keep quiet and bide her time. The knowledge of her love made her strong, courageous, defiant. But for Georg's sake she would be submissive; he was not yet out of the country. Most probably her brother would lock her in her room tonight. She smiled inwardly. Tomorrow, she would go to work as usual, as if nothing had happened. They continued walking.

Georg opened the door, but instead of the carriers he expected, he found himself face to face with five SS men.

Collecting himself, he said, trying to appear calm, 'Can I help you, gentlemen?'

One laughed – a long coarse laugh, which sounded down the passage.

'Adelsheimer, we are here to take you to the station for questioning.'

'I'll get my coat.'

'Oh-no-you-don't,' said the leader of the party. 'There is a back exit.'

A blond SS man, very young, tapped meaningfully on his revolver.

Slowly, dignified, his bare head erect, Georg walked down the main street. Window curtains were pulled back, passers-by stopped, stared, making way for the small procession. The street was black, shiny from the autumn rain, reflecting the arclamps and the illuminated shop windows.

'This way,' commanded the leader. They entered a narrow ill-lit cobbled thoroughfare. Their steps echoed, swelling when they reaching a passageway. Georg stopped to wipe his glasses, misty from the rain.

'*Vorwaerts*,' shouted the one behind him.

'*Vorwaerts*,' repeated the one beside him, giving him a push. The glasses fell to the floor, breaking in pieces. Georg instinctively bent down to pick them up.

'Did you not hear me, *Saujude*? I said *vorwaerts*,' kicking him from behind with high boots. Georg stumbled, fell. Trying to get up, he groped, short-sightedly.

'And this will teach you, Jew... Racial Disgrace ... seducer ... serve you right ... and that. Damned Jew.'

Georg raised his arm, trying to shield his head, still crouching in the gutter, bleeding profusely, his suit spattered with mud.

When Georg fell face forward, the young blond one laughed shrilly, hysterically.

* * *

Frieda and her brother walked silently home. She intended to go straight upstairs, trying to avoid any discussion.

'I would like some coffee,' said her brother. She spread a cloth on the table and fetched the tin with the home-made biscuits which were his favourites.

'Frieda,' he said, not unkindly. 'Whatever came over you? A Jew. I had no idea this was going on. I thought you had got over this girlish crush years ago!'

Frieda did not reply, looking sullenly in front of her.

'Promise me you will never...'

'There is nothing to promise,' she interrupted him haughtily. I am going to bluff my way out, he can't prove anything, she thought to herself.

'You were up there a long time, Frieda. *My* sister, with a Jew!'

'*Your* sister talked about some rare eighteenth-century books, which Dr Adelsheimer wanted to dispose of. I can take care of myself, thank you.' If he suspects something he'll watch me day and night, she thought.

'No woman can take care of herself. Damn the books. I wish I could believe you, but I know you're lying.' However, he felt a little shaken. Had he been rash to report Adelsheimer? The idea of the Jew touching his Frieda had roused him to blind fury. The Fuehrer was quite right: they were rotten, one had to stamp them out. He felt uncomfortable under Frieda's searching gaze.

'Promise me you will never go to his house again and if you should see him on the street, you don't speak to him, understand!'

'I promise,' said Fried flippantly. (I won't have the opportunity anyway.) She said, 'Don't make such a fuss over nothing.' (Keep the pretence up, librarian, keep it up.) 'It was books we talked about, eighteenth-century books.'

The rest of the evening was spent in silence, Frieda knitting and her brother reading a detective novel. The phone rang.

'I've got to go out,' her brother said, putting the receiver down slowly. 'Something to do with the Party. I might be late, so don't wait up for me.'

Frieda slept badly that night. She dreamed of books, large, dusty old books, eighteenth-century books in leather bindings, books opening up with yellowing leaves, hundreds, thousands of them. The letters climbed down from the pages and advanced singly – sinister, menacing, crushing her, suffocating her. 'You will release us, you will release us,' they cried. Frieda awoke. She was perspiring. She dried her forehead with her sheet.

She slipped into the cosy, comforting warmth of her dressing gown. For early October it was unusually chilly. Closing her window she stared at the broad trunk of the horse-chestnut tree where the wind had blown together a heap of brown leaves, now sodden with rain.

There was the new catalogue of the library to be finished. 'I'll never manage it today. Saturday is always extra busy. Perhaps if I get there a little earlier, I might get it done before the rush.' Georg would be on his way by now. She selected a jersey dress with matching jacket. 'I must tell Kroeder, the porter, to put the central heating on. If it gets too hot I can take the jacket off.'

Knocking at her brother's door, she entered the room. She looked disapprovingly at the untouched bed and then went downstairs to boil the corn coffee. All the lights were on; she remembered switching them off – he was usually so careful. She entered the sitting room which was stale-smelling from old cigarette ash. Her brother was slouched forward on the dining table. Drawing himself upright he asked, 'What time is it, Frieda? I must have fallen asleep.'

Frieda pulled the curtains back and threw the windows open. 'A quarter to eight. Coffee is ready in the kitchen.'

'I would like it in here. Bring yours as well.'

Slowly, whilst he was stirring the sugar, he said, 'That telephone call I had last night – it was about Adelsheimer ... he's dead.'

She looked at him with terrified, widening eyes. 'No... He can't be. What happened? You didn't do anything to him?'

'Apparently he was already dead when they rang me. Heart failure.'

'He was all right when I saw him.' Oh, God, please don't let it be true... They must have caught him... Nobody knew he was leaving, only old Anna. Trembling she leaned back on her chair. The wooden crossbars dug into her.

'I had to report him, Frieda. It was my duty, I had to. The boys were a bit rough... On the way to the station...'

'A bit rough! You murdered him! You...'

'They found the books in the hall when they searched the flat. I told them about the books, I told them I was wrong. Frieda, we've killed the Jew because of his books ... I thought it would teach him a lesson, a night at the station would do him good. Believe me, I did not want this.'

'I was going to marry him,' she said, in a tiny voice. 'You murdered my Georg.'

'Are you mad? You can't do that, it's against the law. *Du bist ein deutsches Maedchen!*' He shouted, 'Crazy, you must be crazy.'

'Yes,' Frieda breathed, 'I'm crazy. Everybody is crazy, the whole world is crazy ... and my Georg is dead... And my brother killed him; me and my kind, we have killed him.'

'I am glad he is dead! I was sitting up all night. Ha, books!' He laughed wildly. After a pause, he said, 'There is no sense in

291

getting you involved now – and for that matter, it might cost me my promotion in the Party. I am going to stick to that story of yours, eighteenth-century books … I almost fell for that one. And if you know what's good for you, you keep on sticking to it.'

Frieda sat with hunched shoulders and folded arms on her chair. The morning air blew in through the wide open windows; she shivered. She said, 'Will you ring the library for me? Kroeder will be there by now. Tell them that I am ill.'

'I am not going to do that – advertising it. Are you out of your mind?'

'I don't care.'

'But I do. Have you not done enough? It could ruin me.'

'You're not responsible for me. I'm over age.'

'You are going to go, if I have to drag you there,' he said threateningly.

She looked at him coldly, contemptuously.

He pleaded, 'Frieda, you must … do it for me. We will both get into trouble – they'll say…'

'I don't care what they say … All right, I'll go, I'll go.'

Frieda was quite numb; her fingers, her arms, her legs, they did not belong to her. 'My legs are walking upstairs to fetch my coat, my coat slips around me and it is buttoned, buttoned, buttoned. I do as I am told … perhaps I am dead. Frieda, it's Georg who is dead, *you* are alive.' Without touching the banisters she descended. 'I can't feel my feet; I must be gliding.'

Frieda smiled. She catalogued and she gave mechanically, without being conscious of what she was saying – nearly always the correct answer.

Anna swore and muttered some terrible curses. After that she cried so much that she had to be given a sedative to calm her.

My father made the necessary arrangements for the funeral.

Nobody saw Georg Adelsheimer. The coffin was sealed.

The Nazis sealed the flat as well.

When Walter Haeberlein telephoned, the bell rang a long time, then the operator cut in and told him that the number was discontinued.

Only Mr Duisberg, the florist, had a good day. He was rumoured to have pro-Jewish sympathies. He had lived in England for a long period and was therefore expected to be different. He was extraordinarily busy with funeral orders, most of them placed anonymously.

Frieda and her brother politely avoided each other for the rest of the Saturday. On Sunday morning Frieda had stayed in bed. She did not prepare the lunch. Her brother, reluctant to ask her to do anything for him, went to the *Gasthof sum Baeren*, but he did not enjoy his meal. The buxom waitress scolded him for leaving most of it on his plate. Afterwards he lingered over his quarter of '*Heurigen*' (the local new wine). When it was time for his usual Sunday game of skittles he got up, relieved.

Frieda, glad to be alone in the house, listened into the still Sunday afternoon. She strained her ears to the clap-clapping of women's heels on the pavement and, not wanting to hear it, buried her face in the pillow, but the steps penetrated, and children's laughter, roller-skating, then the bickering of a couple which was drowned by a passing motorcar. Then the roller-skates screeched past again. They shouldn't allow them to make this row on a Sunday, she thought. Why not? The kids enjoy it.

She was woken out of a dreamless sleep by the doorbell.

'Go away,' she said aloud, and turned over. At the third ringing she got up and peeped through the curtains. It was a friend of her brother with his schoolgirl daughter. I suppose they are on their way to the wood and want him to come along with them, she thought. She opened the window and called down.

'He is out. Why don't you stop ringing? He is out!' She crept back into bed. 'Can't one have any peace? No peace, no rest.'

On Monday morning a letter arrived with a Zurich postmark. Walter, she thought, and she slid it quickly into her apron pocket. After her brother had left for work, she tore open the envelope. Instead of the expected letter were two small square pieces of cardboard, nothing else. She studied them with a puzzled expression.

'The honour of your company is requested at the private view of water colours by Schibli, at the New Era Galleries, on Thursday next. Refreshments will be provided.'

There was no sender on the back of the manila envelope. 'Water colours ... I don't particularly like water colours...' Suddenly Frieda understood. She could almost hear Georg telling her again, 'Walter Haeberlein, you know, my school friend, we studied together at Heidelberg, he runs an Art Gallery in Zurich!'

'But why doesn't he write? Of course, it is too risky. He obviously does not know what has happened. I must write to him. I'll do it tonight...'

She looked at her watch. 'I'm late.'

When she arrived at the library, her assistants were already dusting the shelves. She had almost finished the catalogue before the mid-morning break when the senior assistant approached her.

'Fraulein Heller, could you order some more copies of *Mein Kampf*. We've had several applications this morning, and they're all out.'

'I'll see to it,' Frieda replied. The girl was still standing in front of her and, so it seemed to Frieda, eyed her curiously. 'Anything else?' Frieda asked, businesslike.

'No ... except we are very busy this morning, quite unusual for a Monday.'

'In that case you'd better go back to your work.'

The girl obeyed, moving slowly away.

The catalogue finished, Frieda took up her position behind the main counter. The library, especially the fiction section, was crowded this morning, mostly *hausfraus* carrying bulging shopping nets and baskets. Filling out the cards, she noticed that many of the ladies had not borrowed a book for as long as six months. They tried to draw her into conversation, enquiring how she felt. They asked after her brother. In every question, every glance, Frieda felt a hidden meaning; every smile was a smirk. When she put on her coat at lunchtime, she was thankful the morning was over. Hurriedly she walked home.

Her brother was already sitting at the dining table reading the newspaper when she entered with the tray. They ate in silence, the brother looking at the newspaper between mouthfuls, Frieda staring out of the window.

'I'll be home late tonight, we have drill. Don't wait with supper.'

She nodded, cleared the table and proceeded to wash the dishes.

'What can I write to Walter?' Thoughtfully, she rubbed the same plate for a long time. 'It's so difficult to write. If only I could talk to him, if only I could talk to him!' Reaching for her handkerchief in her pocket she felt the stiffness of the cardboard of Walter's invitation cards. The honour of your company is requested...

She packed, slowly, methodically, filling first one case, then another. A large hold-all held her bags and shoes.

'For how long am I going?' she asked herself. She refused to think about the answer and went on packing.

She took down the diploma which hung over her bed, noticing

that the wallpaper had faded, and packed it together with some of her favourite books.

The housekeeping accounts did not balance; she went through them once more, then added the missing money from her purse to the one in the tin box kept in the kitchen drawer.

'I am going away for a holiday,' she wrote to her brother. 'You will understand. I'll contact you as soon as I have reached my destination. The bills are all paid up to the first, except the milk, which is weekly. Your sports jacket is at Schlemmer's [the cleaners]. Love, Frieda.'

She folded the note and stuck it on the mirror in the hall; then, changing her mind, went upstairs and pinned it on his pillow.

I might make the express at three-thirty, she thought. She telephoned for a taxi; it arrived almost immediately.

'Stop at the bank on the way to the station.'

'How much is in my account?' When the clerk reappeared and hand her a scrap of paper, she made out the cheque for the same amount as the figure on the paper, and looked away, pretending to study an announcement about the bank rate whilst he rapidly counted the notes and put the rubber bands around the bundles. Her handbag was too small to hold them all; it would not close. She pushed two bundles into her coat pocket.

'How do you do, Miss Heller,' said the booking clerk at the railway station. 'Where to?'

'Stuttgart, please.'

He gave her a return ticket.

She thought, 'Anyway, I have to change at Stuttgart and the difference between single and return isn't much.' She took the return ticket.

The cases were small enough to take into the compartment. A grey haired gentleman stood up to let her pass and helped her put the luggage on the rack.

'The sun has come out. Would it disturb you if I opened a window?' he asked. 'I take it your going on holiday.'

'No,' Frieda replied, quite pleasantly. 'I'm attending an art exhibition.'

'How interesting – paintings?' he inquired.

'Watercolours,' she said.

Chapter 32

The Nest Egg

Uncle Julius Seeheim and Aunt Pauline, Lila's parents, sat round their circular coffee table, the sole remaining piece of furniture in their lounge not yet packed up by the transport firm. They both supervised the packing, and Aunt Pauline was fussing like an old hen. Uncle Julius seemed to be interested only in his suite of club easy chairs, upholstered in pale green leather. He kept impressing on the men to be careful with it, until one of them offered to sew it into sacking as protection. The police had returned the packing list to them, and now it was duly stamped with the Nazi seal. This was the third time they had received the list back asking for further details and deleting permission to pack some of the more precious items. There was a set of Sèvres plates and dishes which Aunt Pauline had inherited from her grandmother in France. (She was born in Alsace-Lorraine and had lost her French nationality by marrying Uncle Julius.) These were still at the Polizei Amt for 'inspection'; she doubted if they would ever be returned to her.

When the packing men had departed with the furniture van, they both walked round the nearly empty house. He said, 'Well, we can say we once had a beautiful house.' And they looked out through the glass wall of the dining room.

'Do you remember how much trouble and argument we had over this glass wall?' Finally a compromise had been reached between him, his wife, the architect, and the planning authorities. Glass walls were revolutionary in the 1930s, but Aunt Pauline had set her heart on it. The view over Stuttgart was beautiful, reaching far over the valley, and at night a thousand lights twinkled. They had spent a lot of time in that room admiring 'their' view. To have a villa built near the Bobser meant something. They hadn't as yet sold the house; he couldn't bear anybody living in *his* house. After all, he would never see the purchase price. That would go into his frozen bank account, if the Nazis even bothered to make the gesture.

'Pauline, let's have a cup of coffee,' he said.

'We've packed the percolator, but I think I can manage with a saucepan.'

They went into the kitchen and he sat down on the folding chair and pulled the stool out for her. There were only old, or large, or cumbersome pieces of furniture left in the house now; the best had been packed for the 'lift'. Wardrobes would not be required in America with all the built-in furniture. He doubted whether he would be able to afford anything but a small flat.

Uncle Julius had been very impressed with the wonders of America and used to tell us children fantastic tales about his visit in 1930:

'My hostess had bid me goodnight and told me breakfast was at eight. I couldn't see a bed anywhere in the room! Maybe she didn't have one for me. Perhaps she had meant to put the two easy chairs together; they were quite large. I tried that, but they kept coming apart, so I spent the night on the carpet. I didn't like to worry her again. In the morning she came in with some orange juice and said, "My, my! You continental folk are rather tidy. You shouldn't have troubled to make the bed because I have to change the linen anyway." She pressed a button and the bed slowly descended from the wall. It was hardly noticeable as the frame had been so carefully papered.'

And he told us about the Chinese restaurants, open day and night. 'All you had to do was to go in, sit down and say, "Chop, chop," and they brought you half a dozen different little bowls. Couldn't tell for the life of me what was in it, but it tasted very good.' At that time he didn't speak a word of English, and this was much simpler than to go into an ordinary restaurant and laboriously work out a few sentences with the help of his dictionary.

Or the tram. He'd asked the Negro conductor to tell him where to get off and had paid his few cents. He hadn't realised what a long journey it was, but he thought for the little he had paid he couldn't travel very much longer. Surely, the man would come round and tell him. He travelled for two and a half hours to the terminal. The Negro turned round and grinned at him: 'Guv'nor, you're still here?' and he let him ride back for another two hours

297

without paying extra. When he arrived his friends told him that he had been invited for *lunch*, not dinner. This could never have happened in Germany where an inspector keeps checking tickets all the time.

That visit to America had altogether changed his outlook on life and business. When he returned to Germany, his mind was made up. He was going to copy one of those marvellous red and gold Woolworth stores and one of them was set up in our town. He made as faithful a copy of the original as he could, and almost everything was cheaper there than anywhere else. As a special attraction, at the very end of the store, he opened a soda fountain and a cooked meats counter. There he sold the best quality ham at two-thirds of the ordinary retail price. He laughingly explained to me that by the time the customers had reached that counter he hoped they would have bought half the shop on the way, so he would be well able to afford to sell the ham without profit. Naturally, this made him unpopular with the local butchers but the store was a great success. At weekends he would advertise in the local paper in verse, sometimes with funny drawings. These advertisements were witty in a childish sort of way, and very suitable for their purpose.

That, however, was the past. The future would be quite different. If he was lucky he would get a job in America, but when you've reached fifty-six, even if you are younger looking and in good health, nothing is easy. The idea of a chicken farm interested him – he'd once seen a film about one – and he imagined that the chickens would lay eggs like mad and all he would have to do would be to pick them up. Of course, one needed 'connections' for finance. But then America was a rich country and, God permitting, his 'lift' would arrive safely. He had a little nest-egg hidden in it and nobody knew about it.

For a long time he had deliberated over the money question. Very distant relatives in America had given him an affidavit, but it was an unspoken agreement between refugees that once one arrived in the new country, one would make one's own way. His son was there, yes, but he wasn't earning very much. He had to learn the language first. He was a good boy, though in no position to keep his parents. Had he been alone, it wouldn't have been such a problem. He always said, 'I don't mind washing bottles!' However, the idea of Uncle Julius Guggenheim washing bottles was like one of his own jokes. He'd always been a good provider and was prepared to do anything. Some of the younger ladies had taken on jobs as cooks or helps in cafeterias shortly after their arrival in America. Hannah Kraemer had even started a small confectionary business, baking Viennese and South German specialities in her oven at home. She got three dollars for a pound!

But his wife Pauline was far from robust – to work like that would be an imposition on her. In the early years of their marriage she had helped him in his business by sitting at the cash desk, but he was grateful when trade improved, so that she could stay at home – as was only right. He had to take the chance. Anyway, nobody knew about it and the money would help to put him on his feet.

For the next few days they lived 'primitive', making do with their one and only saucepan for everything, carrying the kitchen chairs around with them as required.

At last, their letter from the American Embassy arrived. It would take only a couple of days to get the visa and book the berth. However, they would have to wait until next month as their bank account was frozen, apart from their monthly allowance of one thousand marks. The tickets were expensive: Aunt Pauline had set her heart on First Class travel.

In the early hours of the following morning, the bell rang and two Gestapo officers collected both Julius Guggenheim and his wife for interrogation. Somehow, the Gestapo had been informed that money might be hidden in the 'lift'. The chairs packed in sacking seemed so obvious, and in the upholstery they found what they were looking for, carefully hoarded over the past year.

They were put in prison to await their trial for defrauding the German Government by illegally smuggling money out of the country – a serious offence for Jews. They would not let them communicate with any lawyer and wouldn't answer Aunt Pauline's questions: Was her husband in the same prison? Was he well? When was the trial coming up? Letters were not allowed.

One day the wardress brought in her clothes and said she could go. She tried to make enquiries about her husband at the police and the Jewish Welfare Office – with no result. So she went home to wait. Next day she again went to the police and she spoke to the young man on duty. He kept her sitting for a long time outside the room on a wooden bench. Plucking up her courage, she knocked at the door again and asked whether he could give her any details, please. This snivelling woman was a nuisance. There had been too many interruptions of a similar nature recently. Besides, he was busy. He thumbed through some papers. 'Oh, yes, yes. Guggenheim, shot trying to escape. Good day, Madam.' That got rid of her.

Aunt Pauline boarded the tram and rode back home, slowly ascending the Stuttgart hills to the Bobser. From there it was only a few minutes walk to her house, but it took her hours to get there.

She sat on the folding chair in the kitchen for a long time. Then she tore the curtain down to stuff into the gap underneath the door, a rather large gap as the carpets had gone. After she had opened all the gas taps, she sat down again on the folding chair and waited patiently. That's how she was found.

Julius Guggenheim was released from prison in time for his wife's funeral. Several days later he left for America, having traded the two first class tickets for one steerage in order to pay the fines imposed on him. The 'lift' was, of course, confiscated.

Chapter 33

Story of a Hat

I had been ill for several weeks and was becoming irritable, so Lisa Lendt was a welcome visitor during my illness. The days are so long when one cannot move at all. Lisa had just finished a course in Beauty Culture. She came to practice on me – that's what she called it when she arranged my hair and gave me special make-up. It was very soothing when she patted and creamed my face. I could hardly wash myself, let alone do my face, as my arms were still painful, and I had to rely more or less on my sister Susan for help.

She held the mirror in front of me.

'Now, how is that?'

A stranger, sophisticated me looked back from the mirror; Lisa's powder was so dark that I looked as if I had been to the Winter Sports. And that bright lipstick!

'You'd better take it off.'

'Why? Don't be silly, it suits you – good for your morale.'

'I am only allowed pale pink lipstick and if Mother sees that eye-shadow there'll be a row!'

'Oh, shucks!' she said, but she wiped the eye-shadow off. 'Mine won't allow it either. She called it "Ready for the Footlights", or worse!'

Lisa was a graceful attractive girl, looking older than her seventeen years. She had almond eyes and what I called a magnolia skin – that was before she covered it with make-up.

Her parents were hoping to emigrate to South America soon, where her father had connections. We discussed the clothes she was going to take. She complained bitterly about her mother. 'She's got no understanding, treats me like a schoolgirl, and she absolutely hates that hat.' She put it on, flicked at the brim, and then posed for me.

'What do you think of it, honestly?'

'Well, honestly – it suits you – but you look twenty-five!'

'Goody-goody.' She pirouetted round the room.

* * *

Lisa was in quite a different mood next time she called on me. I had already heard of the trouble.

'Tell me about it. Is your Grandfather back yet?'

'No, I have just called there. I rang the bell and knocked and knocked, but Granny did not open – she's afraid. I'd better ring her from here and tell her I'm coming. It's all boarded up, you know. Perhaps now my grandparents will come with us. Grandfather always said he was too old to learn new tricks, that at his age one does not think of emigration. My father is trying to arrange now for them to come with us.'

Two boys, about thirteen or fourteen years old, in their brown uniform, had thrown a brick and broken the large plate glass window of the Lendt's store. They stood in front, laughing, admiring their handiwork, when old Mr Lendt came out to see what had happened. One of the boys ran away; the other mocked him and chanted: 'Dirty Jew. I've got another brick for you!'

Mr Lendt became so enraged that he grabbed hold of the boy and gave him a good box on the ear. They were separated by the crowd which had gathered by them.

'I'll get my father after you, Jew. He's in the SS.'

'He ought to give you a good hiding.'

Mrs Lendt persuaded her husband to come in. 'Please, Joseph dear, it's not good for your blood pressure.'

Mr Lendt was interrogated at the police headquarters. It was an offence apparently for a Jew to lay hands on an Aryan youth; the boy had a fine record in the Hitler Youth. Besides, his father was an active member of the SS.

Three days of anxiety followed, watching and waiting. Mrs Lendt did not dare ring up the police station. She was frightened in her large flat above the shop, and kept all the curtains drawn.

During the night after the 'incident', the remaining glass of the shop-front had been smashed.

The trouble she had had to get a local firm to board it up during

302

the morning – one could hardly believe it. They were all busy, had commitments, no men available. Finally, she found someone, but he only nailed some planks across. It was not safe, not safe at all.

And so the old lady sat in the hall on a chair all day and the next day. If someone knocked she peered out behind the curtain; she would not open, not even for the rabbi when he called on her.

Lisa's father tried to persuade her to stay with them; she would not hear of it, but she consented to consult her lawyer. The lawyer in turn instructed an 'Aryan' colleague to make enquiries about her husband's whereabouts. The news was good. Grandfather Lendt was still in police custody, had not yet been sent away.

'What do they want? What are they waiting for? I'll do anything,' wailed Mrs Lendt.

'They might let him go with a fine and say the shop will have to go. You'd better sell the shop,' said the lawyer.

'He won't like that.'

'My dear lady, how can I advise you? Do as they say. It might be this or Dachau – I don't think you'll have any choice.'

This or Dachau.

Before Mr Lendt was released, his wife had signed a paper to say that she voluntarily vacated the shop. The figure for the purchase would be settled later. (This sort of thing was called *Zwangsverkauf* – Forced Sale by the Jews.)

Lisa's father had received no reply from the Embassy to the application to take her grandparents with them, only an acknowl-edgement of the letter. Their own visa had not come through yet either.

Once a week, Lisa's father called personally at the Embassy. Sometimes, waiting his turn, he was there for hours, before being told that 'his case was under consideration', 'the Minister was away', and so on.

Finally the whole family was asked to come for an interview. They had their medical check-up. Still, they received no visa. There was the question of the health of Lisa's brother, a boy of eleven who had always been sickly, and the grandparents' age. The consul was very kind; he promised he would do all he could and seemed hopeful. 'Call in a few days. I might have some news then – just one of you will do.'

303

'I've come to say good bye,' said Lisa. 'We're finally going. The boat leaves Hamburg next Monday.'

'Darling, I'm so glad. I'll miss you.'

Lisa did not say much – she looked sullen. I fetched my present for her, an art book – small, but with excellent reproductions. My legs were no longer painful and I was up again.

'Thanks,' she said, not even looking at it.

'What's wrong? Surely you're not sorry to leave? If I were you I would be jolly pleased, and all of you going together.'

'Oh – shut up.'

'Look here...' There was a silence. Then she blurted out: 'It's killing me, I must tell somebody. Promise me you won't tell a soul. Swear and hope to die.'

'I promise.'

'Well, Daddy was busy, so I went to the Embassy before him; he was following later. They told me the visas had come through. I felt so happy, so grown up. I was wearing my new hat. Then he asked me to have dinner with him.'

'Who?'

'He's the second-in-charge there. I think he is the First Secretary or Vice-Consul. He took me to The Excelsior.' This was the best hotel in Stuttgart.

'Oh, I've never been there. What did you wear?'

Lisa ignored my question.

'We had dinner in a private room. All the time, I was thinking, if I walk out now, we might not get those visas, or something will go wrong. So I was nice to him and drank his lousy champagne ... I never thought it would hurt as much as that...'

I did not know what to say to her. We were both silent.

'Do you know, he even swore at me – in Spanish – I understand that much Spanish: "The Devil! I don't like Virgins."'

Chapter 34

The View of the Limmat is Wonderful, if . . .

Father had arranged for a check-up on my heart at our Municipal Hospital. He said I was all right, but he wanted a second opinion. Diphtheria and rheumatic fever are not 'exactly beneficial' for the heart.

'Say "Hello" to Uncle David whilst you're there,' he suggested. 'If they keep him on a strict diet he ought to be home soon, and mention that card you received this morning from Lisa. It might interest him – he used to play cards with Jo Lendt.'

My footsteps echoed when I walked down these well-polished corridors. I passed a small table with a notice on it saying 'Silence Please', and guiltily crept along. Ah, there was the number. A 'Do not disturb' sign hung on the door. Should I knock and chance it? Perhaps he was asleep.

A nun dressed all in white came along and asked me if I was expected. The hospital was completely staffed by the Sisters of Mercy.

I replied, 'No.' I gave her my name, adding I was a relative.

She announced me and told me I could enter.

'Are you better, Uncle David? I was afraid they would not let me see you.' I drew up a chair.

'Oh, I am fine. That sign is to keep out certain people.' His eyes twinkled, 'I am here for a rest. The telephone is not connected either. My, you're quite a young lady now.'

That must be the hat, I thought. Lisa had given it to me before she left. She had exclaimed, dramatically, flinging it on the table, 'I'll never wear it again after what happened!'

'You can hardly blame the hat for that,' I observed.

'I am sick of the sight of it.'

I tried it on. 'It's rather chic. Thank you, Lisa.' So now I was wearing Lisa's hat.

I put a small bottle with tincture on his night table. 'Father sends his love. Ten drops three times a day after meals.'

'How is the old quack?' He always referred to my Father in this way.

'All right. He said if you wouldn't stuff yourself the way you do, you need never be ill and he hopes they put you on a strict diet.'

'Don't be cheeky, young lady.' He smiled. 'But seriously, what can I do? I have to eat what Minnie puts in front of me. When my wife was alive, she watched me. Now there you are.'

Opening the locker next to his bed he pulled out a box of liqueur chocolates and a terrine of pâté de foie gras. 'I suppose you'd better have it – from well-wishers – just what I needed.'

'Oh, thank you. I adore pâté! I had a card from Lisa Lendt from Hamburg this morning.' I showed it to him. 'Actually, you are looking very well. When are you coming home?' Uncle David was still a handsome man. His face was deeply bronzed and he had snow white hair.

'Oh, I like it here, best place to be.'

A Sister came in and made him swallow some pills.

'No, don't tell your father – and I won't tell her about this,' pointing to the tincture.

'It won't do you much good this way.'

'Well, it won't do any harm either.'

'Have you heard from Herman and Walter?'

'Rather.' He smiled. 'They write that the weather is bad. Very English. They write about the weather – everyone talks about the weather in England; that is considered good manners.'

'I know,' I said. 'We learnt it in school.'

'They all live in London. Rita too! I suppose you know that?'

'No, I didn't. Any other news?'

'No, no. Rita went with that friend of hers, Ellen. You remember her, the good-looking dark girl?'

'The one who was with Rita in Finishing School?'

'Yes, that's the one. Ah, something else. This might interest you – you're a dressmaker or something like that.'

'Trying to be.'

'You know Rita – she was never good at needlework. Remember my socks? Well, believe it or not, Rita has now found a position

306

in a school in the country, in one of those small private schools. She is teaching languages. Montreux was very useful, after all. And she is teaching "needlework"! She was so happy to get the job that she said "yes" to everything at the interview. She wrote, that she has bought a book on needlework and is glad she does not have to do it herself.'

'Rita's socks' were famous in the family, a standing joke. All girls have to knit a pair of socks in their primary school, men's socks. I had also knitted a pair of socks for my father. Rita knitted and knitted and dropped many stitches. The socks would not grow. Uncle David teased her saying that there was nothing else he would like better for his birthday than a pair of socks knitted by his own Rita – but they must be knitted by her and no-one else. So Rita, in order to please him, rushed and finished the socks for his birthday. One was almost perfect, but the other was three inches shorter.

I never got to know her well, nor Herman and Walter. They were half a generation older than we were and had no interest in children – they called all children brats and nuisances. Herman was supposed to be the intelligent one, the Herr Doctor of Chemistry. Walter's only claim to fame was that, once at Yom Kippur, he had entered the synagogue sucking a sweet.

'I'd better go now.'

'Just a minute. It's your birthday tomorrow – here you are.' He handed me some money. 'Buy something pretty.'

'You know perfectly well it isn't – it was last month. Thank you very much.'

Uncle David always said this when he gave us children money, explaining he could not be expected to remember dates. 'When my wife was alive she did the remembering for me. Come and see me again.'

'You'll be out before then.'

'Tell your brother Arnold to watch the factory for me.'

'He might just do that!'

'I was joking, of course. No, forget about it.'

Suddenly he looked serious. 'I don't want him to get involved, understand?'

'Yes, Uncle David. Bye, bye.'

'Look after yourself, my dear. My! what a big girl.'

* * *

307

The original factory started in 1837 in the village. There were a lot of local spinners and weavers of cotton and linen and in this type of work one gets a lot of waste. The large textile mill of Moritz Fleischer supplied waste to a local paper factory (in those days writing paper was made from linen). That factory got into financial difficulties and went bankrupt. No-one was willing to buy or take over the factory so, as the main creditor, Moritz Fleischer got it cheaply.

Now the family had a paper factory – what to do with it? They decided to have a go at paper-making, but the porridge-like mixture was not correct and the paper came out transparent and thin, not suitable for writing. That is how tissue paper was born.

In 1871 Moritz moved the factory to the nearby town. His son, my Uncle David, entered the firm in 1892. Again the premises were moved, to Eislingen, when Robert Kraft's factory there, next to the River Fils, was purchased. The making of paper was now mechanical. This time the temperature controls of the machinery were complicated and the new owners did not have the required technical knowledge. The paper came out all shrivelled. That's how crepe paper was invented, the first in Germany and possibly in the whole world. The Fleischer paper mills became one of the largest in Germany, exporting to forty-seven countries by the 1930s.*

* * *

Arnold told me about the latest development in the paper mill. During the last year there had been a lot of trouble in the factory. The *Ortsgruppenfuehrer* had approached Uncle David and his brother Kuno several times with propositions to take over the factory. He would like to buy it, so he had said. Where would this little man get the money from? He did not own a penny. But that would not matter as he would probably pay with a piece of paper, a promissory note. Since the Jewish bank accounts were frozen or supervised, one could not get hold of one's own money anyway.

When Herman and Walter did not return from a business trip abroad, that little Nazi was promoted first – he more or less promoted himself – to Departmental Chief, then Manager, not that

---

*It was customary for the Nazis to deny that Jews had invented anything, whether poetry, music or something technological. Even in school we were given stickers to place over authors' names.

the man was either qualified or capable of it; however, his rank in the Party made up for that. Herman and Walter were well out of it. They had been lucky: they were allowed to keep their passports. These had not been called in because, as the mill exported to many countries (the need for foreign currency being almost greater than the hatred for the Jews), Herman and Walter supervised the foreign sales as part of their job. So, after one of their 'selling' trips, they simply did not return. They even managed to get Rita and her friend Ellen out of Germany by bribing Nazi frontier guards on the Belgian border to escort them through the lines.

The pressure for a 'sale' of the mill was on just now, Arnold said.

Uncle Kuno stalled them, explaining he could do nothing until his brother, the senior partner, was back. Uncle David had had his phone disconnected in hospital, and showed no inclination to return to the factory. He studied Lisa's postcard which I had left on his locker. Yes, he knew that type of liner: a fine ship of the Hansa. He had travelled once on a sister ship.

'Sailing tonight. We are all very happy and send our love from Hamburg.'

It was only a few weeks ago when Jo Lendt had told him he was definitely not going to sell. 'They don't get rid of me as easily as that,' he had said. 'Anyway, my customers come specially up from the country to see me; they're used to me, I've served them in the shop for more than fifty years myself.' Jo Lendt was deluding himself; the shop was empty like every other Jewish shop. Uncle David did not have the heart to tell him so. Everywhere one heard of forced sales, prison, concentration camps or worse.

'Damn it! I'm not going to sit down and watch it,' Uncle David. 'I must prepare myself better next time. I slipped up because I have no head for geography, no sense of direction.'

A week ago the *Ortsgruppenfuehrer* had demanded an appointment from his private secretary. The girl did not dare refuse and had fixed one for the next morning.

He was in a bad temper that very morning. He knew it would be a hot day, an unpleasant day and he did not want to face the 'little runt'. He sat for a long time over his breakfast. When Minnie, the maid, asked if she could clear away, his mind was made up.

'Pack my briefcase, just pyjamas and a change of underwear, I am going to Stuttgart for the day. I'm meeting some friends. If the weather keeps fine we might go for an excursion, so I might be going overnight.'

Yes, he had decided to try out the Number One plan. Two years ago, on a holiday in Switzerland, he had stayed in the same hotel as a Swiss lawyer. They got on well together; the man was a good chap and very discreet. Uncle Daniel's interests abroad were considerable and he instructed this lawyer to act for him. At that time he still had his passport. I was a fool not to quit Germany there and then, but of course at that time I was not prepared to leave all my money behind, he thought.

Things had got rather out of hand lately with the foreign sales – one could not write for fear of censorship. The Swiss lawyer had visited him a couple of months ago. He had said, 'If you have to leave illegally, I have a plan.' In fact, he had two plans.

Uncle David put on a tweed jacket, stout boots and a Loden hat. He selected a knobbly stick from his collection.

He took the express for Stuttgart but alighted at Plochingen. From a public 'phone box he telephoned the lawyer and told him that he was trying Number One plan, tomorrow or the day after. Then he bought a ticket to Constance at Lake Constance. There he boarded a cross-country bus and got off in one of those small, picturesque Black Forest villages. He had no difficulty in booking a room in a simple country inn, *en pension* for a week. People who went for early out-of-season holidays were usually careful with money and *en pension* was much cheaper. He explained that his luggage would come later.

Next morning he bought a couple of good detailed maps of the locality.

Whilst he was sitting in the Gaststube planning his 'excursion' the landlord joined him, making helpful suggestions, telling him about local beauty spots. Uncle David made a note of them and put it in his pocket.

'Will you be in for lunch today?' asked the waitress.

'No, I don't think so.'

They supplied him with a packed lunch in a small paper carrier.

He walked a few kilometres, consulted his map and turned off the main road, heading in the direction of the Swiss Frontier.

'All you have to do is get across in the woods. Approach the Swiss guards. Tell them you have no papers, your Swiss lawyer is holding them for you.'

It had sounded so simple when the lawyer had explained – it *was* simple.

Nature's borderline between Germany and Switzerland is the River Rhine, but at Singen – Kanton Schaffhausen – there is a small patch of Switzerland wedged in, so to speak, between German soil. It is an area of thickly wooded country.

Uncle David was heading for this place. The sun was right up now, and it was getting hot. He took his jacket off and tied it to his stick carried over the shoulder, tourist fashion.

From far off he could see the frontier marked in red and white stripes, so he left his path and started climbing the hill where he hoped to slip, unseen, through the undergrowth on to Swiss soil. It was a steep climb and he was not getting any younger – the stick came in very useful. The paper carrier was a nuisance but he did not dare abandon his food as he did not know long it would have to last.

He had almost reached the top of the hill when, to his dismay, he saw another frontier post with two German guards, one strutting up and down, the other eyeing him through binoculars. They were shouting something to him, so he waved to them. Now he had to think fast. No bright idea came up. He sat down on a tree trunk and started eating his lunch in full view of the guards, hoping they would get tired of watching him. After a little while, he got up, waved to them, and proceeded with his climb. They shouted, and as he did not stop, blew their whistles. In no time at all he was arrested and taken for interrogation.

They could not get anything out of him. He was an old man. He was on holiday. He was just eating his lunch. 'Look, you can see, this is my lunch, or what's left of it.' And he showed them the bag. 'Of course I wasn't leaving the country. You can see for yourself, I have no luggage or papers.' He had no papers, no passport – why should he? He was on holiday. He had a Kennkarte, stamped with 'J' for Jew. Long he had deliberated whether he should he take the Kennkarte or not. In the end he had decided for it. It was the law, and without it, he could hardly have insisted that he was having a holiday. He also had on him a list of beauty spots he was going to visit. This finally convinced the Nazis. They asked him why he did not stop when they called him. He answered apologetically that at his age his hearing was not all that it should be.

They put him on a train home with the warning that next time he showed his face around these parts, they would shoot him on sight.

When Uncle David arrived home he did not feel so good and called the doctor. He ordered a rest. Uncle David decided to rest in hospital.

He did not risk putting a call through to Switzerland when he returned home. There was a rumour that calls from Jewish homes, especially long distance ones, or those going abroad, were tapped. One had to be careful and he himself had been 'tipped off', so to speak, by Minnie, that he was being watched. Minnie's brother-in-law was in the party, in the SA, and he continuously tried to get information out of her, so the good Minnie told him things which did not matter, and in exchange received confidences which she passed straight on to Uncle David. Minnie had been serving the family for the last thirty years, initially for Uncle David's mother. When her fiancé did not return from the 1914–18 war, and she found herself with child, the family had kept her, instead of putting her on the street, as her own father had threatened to do. Minnie always said they'd been better to her than her own. Anyway, she had been engaged, 'all proper', with a ring – that made a great difference in her eyes. Franz, her boy, called after him, had had a good start in life in spite of being illegitimate. Uncle David had paid the fees to put Franz through High School. He was a bright, industrious boy. Later he was apprenticed in one of the new garages, where they did repairs; he learned a lot. Now he was settled, and married to a good girl. Minnie was part of the family, and since the death of Uncle David's wife she had been his housekeeper.

Every time Minnie went home her brother-in-law nagged her: 'Why don't you leave the *Juden-haus*?'

'Frankly,' Minnie replied, 'it's the money. You find me a job as easy as that for the same money, I'll take it. And, all those presents! He gave me all her clothes, too, when she died, a pity the shoes did not fit – she had such small feet.'

Minnie looked at her sister who was wearing some of these very same clothes. Every month Minnie gave a part of her wages to her sister. They were buying their house and it was difficult. They were short since there was no longer any overtime money in his wage packet – with all those duties in the SA he could not spare the time.

'We're watching your old Jew,' he informed her after Uncle

312

Daniel returned from hospital. 'We've got it all laid on. Let me know if there is any news.'

'Sure I will,' said Minnie. 'I'll keep in touch. He has not gone back to work.'

'That I know, too. That's no news.'

'Mr David,' said Minnie, 'do be careful. They're watching out for you. My brother-in-law told me that they report all the railway tickets bought by Jewish people straight to Headquarters. Not, of course, the local ones. And they're after you. Oh, my God.'

The Jews of the town had been aware of this for some time, and if movements had to be concealed they bought dummy tickets or changed trains. This was the reason Uncle David had purchased a return ticket to Stuttgart instead of Constance. Most people shopped for important items in Stuttgart, which was only twenty-five kilometres away; this did not arouse suspicion.

Jews carrying suitcases did not get far, usually no further than the barrier, before being questioned as to where they were going. As it was a small town everybody knew everybody. However, when people emigrated – that is when they finally received their passports and papers – they were never stopped, not even questioned; so the railway employees must have been well informed – clearly they were hand in glove with the Gestapo.

'Mr David.' Minnie came in, looking worried. 'That's the third time they have phoned from the factory. I wish you'd talk to them – they won't believe me when I tell them you're not in.'

'Minnie, I know it's not fair to you, but you know how things are at the factory – I think I'd better make a move. Sooner or later they'll come to the house. I know I can trust you, Minnie, but please, please, don't breathe a word to anyone – not even my brother or Mr Julius. I'll be leaving tomorrow.'

'As soon as I am finished in the kitchen I'll be packing for you then. Which case did you want to take?'

'No cases, my dear. I'll go as I stand.'

'Mr David, you can't. It's wicked they should do this to you.'

'The risk is too great. It's not worth it.'

'If I might make a suggestion, Mr David. My niece just had a baby. I could go and see her – sort of – and take your cases to Stuttgart for you.'

'I would not like you to take any chances.'

'But it's quite safe, I'm sure; I'll tell my sister I'm going to

313

visit Dora ... oh dear, oh dear, what am I going to do, after all the *Herrschaft* has gone?' (*Herrschaft* was the respectable way of referring to the family.)

Minnie cried and sat down and Uncle David, always embarrassed by female tears, in trying to comfort her said all the wrong things.

'Don't cry, Minnie. I'll arrange for the bank to send you some money every month.' She interrupted him. 'I don't want any money!'

'Minnie, I hope they will pay it,' he continued. 'At present my account is not completely frozen... You'll soon find another position, you know that. Now, here, have a drink.'

'Oh – Mr David, you know perfectly well I am teetotal. Drink is rotten stuff – bad enough when I have to wash the glasses.'

Minnie was annoyed, and her old self again. She stamped across the room, collected some glasses and put them with a bang on the tray.

'Once I am abroad I'll arrange for a transport firm to pack up the furniture and things, providing they can get permission. In any case, Minnie, it's a good idea if you help Dora with her new baby. Here, buy some nappies, a rattle or something for her.'

Minnie packed two cases with his best clothes, carefully wrapping some family photographs in the underwear. With a sigh she slipped in 'Rita's socks'. Yes, he'll want these.

In the morning, she took the early train to Stuttgart. She deposited the cases in the Left Luggage Office and met Uncle David in the Second Class waiting room in the afternoon, as arranged. 'I could not wait in the First Class with all those fine people,' she had said. There had been no hitch. Minnie, dressed in black, handed the Left Luggage tickets over.

'You look as if you're going to a funeral, not a christening,' he joked. 'What are they going to call the baby?'

'Adolf,' Minnie said shamefacedly. 'You know, Sir...'

'I had an Uncle called Adolphe myself,' he said, 'in England.'

Adolf was the most popular name that year.

'Remember me to Dr Herman and Mr Walter, and the ladies.'

'I can never thank you enough, Minnie – the way you looked after me. I wish it could be more.' Uncle David handed her an envelope. 'All the best.'

'You shouldn't really... Thank you so much... God bless you!'

He had phoned the lawyer and told him which train he was taking. Plan Number Two was working so far. A steward brought

314

coffee to the compartment which he had to himself. The First Class was never very full in the ordinary express trains. It was unwise to wait about on the railway station – one never knew if one would meet someone familiar – so he had taken the first train out to Basle although it was only semi-fast. He did not dare to drink his coffee in the dining car for the same reason. The train rattled on. At Karlsruhe an elderly lady entered the compartment. Politely, quite from habit, he helped her with her luggage, though he knew his doctor had warned him not to exert himself in any way. She tried to involve him in conversation, but soon gave up as there was no response. She started to knit.

The train neared the border. When it stopped at Basel Stadt, which is still German, the Passport Control and Customs, German and Swiss, entered the train. They always check between Basel Stadt (German) and Basle (Swiss).

Uncle David asked the German officials if he could buy a drink at the refreshment room. 'Yes,' they said, 'but hurry up. You have only three minutes.'

He walked to the refreshment room, went in, and walked out at the other side.

Two policemen, in Swiss uniform, stopped him.

'Your papers, please.'

'I have no papers.'

'What is your name?' He told them. 'We arrest you for being on Swiss soil without papers, please follow us to the police station.'

He was safe. The plan had worked. The lawyer's chief clerk was waiting for him at the police station with some makeshift papers and asked what he could do for him.

'I was sitting in Compartment M4. Would you please arrange to have my luggage taken off in Zurich.'

'The "old man" [that was how Uncle David was generally referred to in the factory], has hopped it and they took Uncle Kuno to Headquarters for interrogation,' Arnold told me a couple of days later.

Uncle Kuno had received a card, postmarked Zurich, saying, 'The view of the Limmat is wonderful, especially when you look down from the bridge.' Unfortunately, he had the card on him when they searched him at Headquarters.

'Good Lord! He's not still there?'

'No, they did not keep him. He told me about the card himself

315

when he came back, called me into his private offices in fact, and asked me to take a message to Aunt Clare, saying he did not want to phone. "You know who is on our switchboard – this bitch listens in to everything! It's now only a matter of days before we get Aryan management." '

'Will you get the sack?'

'Eventually, but who cares? I'll go to Munich just a little earlier.'

* * *

Arnold had always been interested in cooking, in good food, and now he decided to take a concentrated, three months chef's course in Munich.

This particular school had not asked on their application form for either religion or Party Number and some other Jewish men or boys had attended it without incident.

The next day, Uncle Kuno was arrested and taken to Stuttgart gaol. They claimed there had been irregularities with foreign currency at the factory and they had to make a thorough investigation. Uncle Kuno was kept three months in 'protective custody'. His wife, Aunt Clare, moved heaven and earth for his release. She 'sold' the factory to the Nazis, at their valuation. Needless to say, no money changed hands.

However, this was not enough to secure Uncle Kuno's release.

The Nazis had found out that Aunt Clare had wealthy relatives in the USA. One morning she received a 'confidential' visit from a high-ranking officer in the SS who made her the following proposition: For $20,000 they would release Uncle Kuno. The SS officer said he would personally guarantee their safety – in fact, he would go further than that, he would arrange to get permission for them to take some of their personal belonging with them.

Aunt Clare immediately phoned her mother who lived in New York. The old lady promised to arrange to send the money as soon as she could.

Father had been allowed to visit Uncle Kuno in prison, a most unusual concession. He told me that Uncle Kuno's health had very much deteriorated. He was suffering from kidney trouble and his ankles were swollen, so much so that he had been unable to lace up his shoes. 'If he stays there much longer, with that diet and without medical attention and all that strain of continuous interrogation, it won't be "very good" for him.'

316

One day a letter arrived from Alsace, France. The authorities asked what should be done with the French factory, our corset factory, which was now closed.

Mother exclaimed emphatically, 'Ignore it, Julius. Do not answer it; it is much too dangerous.'

If the Nazis found out one had property abroad they put one in the concentration camp until the property was signed over. A token price would be paid, or more often only a promissory note.

*   *   *

In a locked first class compartment of the Stuttgart-Zurich express sat a silent Jewish couple. The two SS men guarding them had, after locking the door, taken the safety catch off their revolvers. After a while they decided to play cards and laid the revolvers next to them on the red plush seat.

'You'd better not try any tricks,' they barked.

Playing cards was a thirsty business. The SS men ordered beer.

'The gentleman will pay you.' Uncle Kuno paid the waiter out of the small sum of money allowed to any Jew – ten marks for himself, ten marks for Aunt Clare. The SS men were thirsty and had several refills.

At Basle they alighted and were met by a representative of the American Banking House who handed the SS men the banker's draft made out in favour of Heinrich Himmler for $20,000 according to instructions.

'Have a pleasant journey, Sir, Madam.' The SS men bowed ironically and clicked their heels. *'Heil Hitler!'*

The money had been sent by Aunt Clare's brother-in-law. He was a wealthy man, as he and his family owned some of the largest stores in New York, among them Gimbels. Luckily the Nazis did not know this, otherwise they would hardly have been content with $20,000. His lawyers had arranged for the pay-off to take place on Swiss soil, in order to guarantee the safety of the prisoners. Too many had been shot 'trying to escape'.

Chapter 35

'You Don't Need a Winter Coat on an Excursion'

Arnold sent enthusiastic letters from Munich. He seemed to be enjoying the course tremendously and sometimes he enclosed a specimen menu. With the diploma he hoped to get a job abroad; he was even considering a domestic job if he could not get into the hotel business.

Our immediate chances of emigration, however, were very small. The matron of the orphanage in Hamburg had put my name down on the list, along with all the children and household students under seventeen years of age, for a Children's Transport. These were leaving quite often from large cities – destination England. Susan and Richard's names were down in Stuttgart. Arnold, then over eighteen, was too old. The only chance for my parents was America, but their waiting numbers would not come up for at least another eighteen months. Arnold had booked them himself after a discussion with my father, which had ended in an argument.

Occasionally people left Germany illegally, without papers. Unless they had friends or relatives abroad who had arranged for visas or permits, it was a very risky business. I had heard of people being sent back, under police escort and being sent straight to Concentration Camps. One thing was certain: one either needed to have money abroad or good friends or relatives willing to give a guarantee for one, the amount of which usually varying with the age of the person. For instance, England would accept £500 for a young person, but for a middle-aged person required the assurance that they would be kept for the rest of their days as, over a certain age, labour permits were not usually granted. There was no-one who would offer to do this for my parents. Father had written to England to our relatives, but they had refused. Aunt Frances had replied that she had already given full guarantees for several of her brothers and sisters, and this was as much as she could do. Father replied, sending her details of his waiting number for the USA, writing that it would be only for two years at the outside before we would re-emigrate to the States. He also suggested he could help in her factory; he had done so as a young man and his English was almost perfect.

'To have helped us would not have hurt her. She was well off – in fact rich,' Father explained. As a young girl she had been a governess in England. She came of good family but there had been sixteen of them. All her brothers had studied medicine, law or some other profession. As her father was unable to supply his daughters with a dowry, as was customary then, he let them have an education. Frances had a situation at the turn of the century and had married well. Her husband, my grandmother's brother, who ran the English branch of the corset factory, had died more than twenty years ago. After his death she ran the factory, and very ably, so I was told. She had no children of her own.

It was natural that people would look after their closest relatives first, but Father felt that financially she had some obligations to our family, as our share of the English branch of the business had been given to her husband, a naturalised Englishman, at the outbreak of the 1914–1918 War to avoid being seized by the English Government as enemy property. (I don't know how much our share in the factory had been worth, but when Aunt Frances died in the 1950s, her estate ran into six figures, which went to her side of the family, with the exception of approximately £1,500 'in mementoes' – as published in *The Times*).

Walter and Herman obtained permits from the Home Office for Rita and her friend Ellen to join them in London. A good lawyer had helped them over the quite considerable difficulties caused by Rita and Ellen not possessing their German passports, which had been confiscated, like those of most Jews, by the Nazis. The two girls were inseparable and had refused to be parted. Also there was their own paper factory in Swanley, Kent (Swanley Mills).

Walter and Hermann had arranged to meet them at the Belgian Frontier. Their 'travel instructions' had been pieced together from letter and telephone calls, double-checked and re-checked; one had to be so careful as calls from abroad were often monitored. Walter had insisted they should bring some of his things as well, although he had stipulated one suitcase only for each of them. They were to visit a Herr Klausner in Aachen, who was to introduce them to his friends.

Whilst Rita and Ellen were taking coffee with Herr Klausner, two young men in Nazi uniforms came in. They were Frontier Guards. They clicked their heels and gave the Nazi salute. Herr Klausner addressed them as Herr Korporal and Herr Soldat (a private) respectively.

Staring at Rita and Ellen, one said, 'This is a pleasure, I think I am going to like this consignment, Herr Klausner, different from what we had last week, eh?'

Rita and Ellen were both in their early twenties and looked elegant in their tailor-made suits and silk shirts.

'Why complain about last week?' said Herr Klausner. 'You received double for the old lady.'

'It was not worth it. I had to practically carry her the last bit of the way. I wouldn't take it on again and *"Grossmutter"* [grandmother] was "jammering" all the way.'

'Don't talk about money in front of my wife. It's the only chance I get for some pocket money. Quiet – she's coming in.'

'Ja so,' said Frau Klausner, who brought fresh coffee. 'It's your day off, you're going for another excursion.' She turned to Ellen. 'That's a nice coat, warm too – the one you were wearing when you came in. Don't you think it's too hot for it today?'

Ellen agreed with her. She had worn it only to save carrying it. It was an off-white winter coat with a lynx collar. Frau Klausner asked if she could try it on. Rather surprised, Ellen consented. It was much too long for Frau Klausner and also a little tight. She stroked the fur with her rough, red hands, preening herself and admiring her dumpy figure in the glass.

'You won't be needing it, going on an excursion, young lady.'

Ellen wanted to protest, but Rita nudged her. The coat had been a favourite, the light colour complimenting her dark hair and exotic looks.

A ramshackle old car stood outside the house. The Herr Soldat apologised, saying he was saving up for a Volkswagen (The People's Car. People paid monthly instalments and were put on a waiting list but the cars were never produced in Hitler's Germany.) Herr Klausner put the luggage into the boot. Rita sat down next to the driver, Ellen in the back with the Korporal. Nobody could have guessed that this little party was anything else but a couple of young Nazis with girl friends on an outing.

After driving half an hour down a country road they all get out at an inn.

The Nazis refreshed themselves with beer; they insisted that the girls had some too. Rita opened her purse.

'Put it away, girlie,' said the corporal, smacking her bottom. 'We can afford it.' He grinned. 'It comes out of the advance we've had.'

They spent almost two hours at the inn, till nightfall.

'Surely this is asking for trouble,' said Ellen to the men, 'sitting here in public.'

'Don't you worry. We don't bring our other customers here – it's better if we wait until after dark.'

They were getting merry. The corporal crooned, *'Du schoene Spanierin mit schwarzen Haaren, ich liebe dich.'* ('You beautiful Spanish maiden, raven-haired, I love you'.)

He leaned forward and whispered confidentially into Ellen's ear, 'Spanish – that's what you are for me.'

The strong smell of beer nauseated Ellen; she drew back. Rita, who was a shy girl, smiled nervously and looked at her watch from time to time.

Once a friend of the Nazis approached them. 'Introduce me to your girl friends,' he had demanded.

'You'd like that, wouldn't you – nothing doing,' they replied.

'I can't blame you, they've got class,' he remarked as he went back to his table.

Finally they went off in the car, driving through a beechwood.

Rita's companion edged closer to her. She gently took his hand off her thigh and said, 'Mind the road.'

In the back, Ellen sat huddled in the corner. She felt chilly in the night air; she missed her coat.

'That's as far as we go.' They stopped the car in a lane.

'We are near the frontier now – it's not patrolled here. The rest we make by foot.'

'What about the luggage?' asked Rita.

'That we bring over later in the car. It's much too conspicuous to carry it. We declare it in the normal way in Customs as our luggage: they never check ours. You've got some men's clothes in it?'

'Yes, of course.'

'Now I understand why Walter insisted I should bring some of his things,' Ellen said to Rita.

She opened the door to get out.

'What's the hurry?' asked the corporal. He grabbed hold of her and tried to kiss her. She struggled to get out. 'Come here, girlie, it's much more comfortable in here.'

Ellen jumped out of the car. Rita, who was watching anxiously, quickly went out to her and put her arms around her, as if to protect her.

The corporal stared at them furiously. He slowly took his revolver out of the holster and seized Ellen's arm with his free hand. Automatically she slapped his face. A second later she was terrified at what she had done, thinking, that way they'll never take us across, I've ruined everything now.

He slowly rubbed his chin. His revolver was pointing towards them.

The private was leaning against the car, undecided what to do.

'I'll have this dark piece,' the corporal said to him. 'I've wanted her all night. If you like, you can take the other – what's her name? Rita. Meet you at the usual place.'

Chapter 36

Perhaps it's Hidden Under the Floorboards

Mother had gone to Frankfurt to stay with her parents. They had moved there from Camberg on that fateful night of the pogroms in November 1938.

Uncle Albert, Grandfather's youngest brother – he was more than twenty years younger and he had red hair and a lovely red beard – had tried to sell Grandfather's business. He put an advertisement in a newspaper and was successful. That means that an Aryan had offered to buy the business and at a give-away price. This was usual for Jews at that time but better than nothing!

When the deal was made and sent up to the Town Hall for sanction, the Nazis said that they could not pass it. It was too much! The price was further reduced. Then the deal was completed. The purchase price, which consisted mainly of stocks and shares, went into Grandfather's frozen bank account.

By a miracle, Grandfather was spared – or perhaps it was his age, although men older than he were in Dachau with Father.

My Grandparents had found a flat in Frankfurt, in the Guillettstrasse, right next to the English Consulate.

They kept open house for their friends and acquaintances who went there seeking visas or information. Many stayed overnight, as the majority of hotels would no longer take Jews.

At first Grandmother managed the flat with the help of a daily cleaner. Later, when she stayed away in spite of the high hourly rate my Grandmother paid the woman, she had to do all the work herself.

Mother used to visit them about every six weeks for a few days, especially since Grandfather's heart had been troubling him.

Grandfather was pacing up and down. 'Husband,' [my Grandmother

323

always addressed him in this way], 'Husband, please sit down, here – have a pipe.' And she brought him a selection from the pipe rack. 'You know you must not get excited. You shouldn't read the paper either.' She took it from him. 'I am going to stop the paper.'

Grandfather could not get used to the idle life. Right up to their departure for Frankfurt he had been pottering about in his shop and warehouses; in fact, as all the staff had left, he opened the store himself every morning at 7.30 and closed it at night. Sometimes there was not a single customer during the whole day. Only strangers passing through the town would come in for a small purchase, if this was not prevented by Hitler Youth pickets, 'Doing Duty'.

He did not like going for walks; he had never been the outdoor type. Besides he now tired easily and the public benches were prohibited for Jews.

When Uncle Albert 'sold' his share of the Karlsruhe store to an Aryan he stayed with them for a few days. Of course it had been a bad deal, a real swindle, but he had been lucky enough to receive part in cash payment. He intended to use this cash to help him escape. One of his sayings was, 'Cash goes a long way; underneath that brown uniform ticks a greedy little heart as often as not.'

The SS must have been informed about the cash transaction almost immediately. They maintained it was illegal to pay cash to a Jew. They even brought a search warrant with them, a matter of form not usually adhered to.

They questioned Uncle Albert for hours. He said he had left the cash in his office safe. They told him it was not there, they had searched it already.

'Who gave you the keys?'

'We don't need keys, we have experts. Where did you hide the money?'

Uncle Albert insisted he had put it in the office safe; if it was not there, it must have been stolen.

'Your secretary says you have not been to the place during the last week.'

'She wouldn't know – I put it there in the evening – she leaves at five-thirty. It must have been almost seven o'clock when I went to the office.'

They searched the flat most thoroughly, turned everything upside down, with no result. One SS man noticed that a floorboard had been prised up – the edges were slightly damaged. They lifted a good part of the floor, although my Grandmother assured them, several times, that she had had the boards up because they creaked and she offered to give them the name of the carpenter who had done the job. It was late at night when they finally left. They had not found anything.

'Albert, dear, tell me, I would like to know, where did you put the money?' asked Grandmother. They were having a little brandy with their coffee, relaxing in the drawing room after the ordeal.

Uncle Albert grinned and pointed to his brief case which had been lying on a chair in full view of everyone.

'All in there.'

Chapter 37

Arnold 'Loses' his Camera

Arnold returned from Munich with a chef's hat, a long white apron, and a glittering array of carving knives. Nobody was allowed to touch these without his permission. Mother's absences gave him plenty of opportunity to practice his new art. He prepared elaborate dishes, more suitable for banquets than a family in reduced circumstances. Father complained, after the novelty had worn off, saying this rich food was hard to digest. Everything was served most artistically, covered with pastry shapes or done up in gelatine with fancy vegetable cut-outs – in fact, *pomme nature* was a thing of the past.

I was most impressed by his Beef Wellington, but shocked at the cost of the fillet of beef. Arnold assured me this dish was popular in an up-market restaurant. 'They'll pay,' he said.

It was the season for soft fruit and berries. I asked if he could make *clafouti*? This was a favourite of mine, a dish from the Alsace made with black cherries. Our cuisine contained many Alsace dishes, not least the *choucroute garnie*, made with white wine, apples and onion, cumin and juniper berries (the German Sauerkraut is a poor relation).

I said, 'I'll go, and get some from the orchard, the cherries should be ripe by now.'

'You must be very careful, and stay on the footpath,' said Father. 'I've let a farmer have the grass. The grass is high now. You must not trample it, so stay on the footpath.' Father had never let the grazing rights before, or the grass for hay.

I knew the layout of the orchard, where every tree was, where the best fruit was. A tree with black cherries was right next to the path, so that was all right. The red and black currants were also

326

in season, blackberries too and the berry bushes bordered the path. I picked a whole basket of fruits. I also picked some quinces, although I could not tell if they were ripe; one never can. They are stone hard, even when ripe, and quite inedible raw.

This orchard was the one adjoining the north side of the factory. Our factory had been sold several years ago, the production, such as it was, having been removed to smaller premises. The building had been bought by the town, to be converted into the College of Trade for the whole district. Built in 1890, it was situated in the 'best part' of the town. The Town Council had always maintained the area was not really suitable for a factory, even one producing 'clean' goods.

The *clafouti* was a great success; also the summer pudding.

We made red currant jelly, which I found insipid, and tangy blackcurrant jam, as well as quince jelly squares. These are really a sweet for Christmas, but we could not think of anything else to make with this strange fruit.

I really enjoyed being his kitchen maid and happily washed stacks of china and saucepans. I learnt more in a couple of weeks by assisting Arnold than during my whole year as Aunt Felicia's unpaid drudge.

If we did the washing up together, Arnold was certain to make his little speech that 'it was not customary for the chef ... etc., etc.'

The responsibility of keeping the household account book was mine. Mother had insisted I kept it up to date whilst she was away. We seemed to spend a good deal more than she did. Arnold therefore decided to cook some economy dishes. Unfortunately these were not cheap either, as they required so many exotic spices and things which Mother did not normally use, all of which had to be purchased.

Susan did the greater part of the cleaning. She enjoyed polishing and dusting, I preferred to think – I hated it. Every afternoon she went to a Jewish lady who gave private lessons on how to make artificial flowers from felt, silk and other materials.

Since 1936, Richard had been attending school in Esslingen, fifteen miles away. Richard was a big boy and very strong for his age; he had been the tallest in his class. When some of his former classmates had called him a 'dirty Jew' he had given them a good hiding, to make sure they would not do it again. He had called out: 'Anybody else want to call me a dirty Jew – come on then!'

327

After this incident, Father thought it advisable to send him to a Jewish school. Most of the weekends Richard spent at home. He told me he enjoyed the life at the boarding school very much: lots of games and no girls – wonderful that, no interfering females at all!

Susan had taken it upon herself, in Mother's absence, to supervise his toilet, which he bitterly resented. *'Willst du Kartoffein wachsen lassen unter deinen Fingernägeln?'* she had asked him. (Do you want to grow potatoes under your fingernails?)

I had helped Arnold with his packing; he was leaving for England. Aunt Frances had decided, after all, to send a guarantee for him. Arnold was to escort Aunt Frances' widowed sister, Anna, as she had refused to make the journey to London by herself. She said she would not go by boat as she was a bad sailor; she would rather fly. Those new fangled devil's machines were supposed to be quite comfortable. Yes, she'd fly – but not alone – impossible – she could not risk it. She had never travelled alone, she sighed to Arnold. After her dear husband died, bless him, she had not moved out of the house. Arnold said to me that in his opinion she had not opened the windows either – ugh! – all red plush and lace mats. Mind you, she must have been quite good-looking in her time – about a hundred years ago!

Aunt Anna liked Arnold. Most elderly ladies did and were charmed by his good manners.

I knew I was going to miss him very much. When would I see him again? Perhaps in America in two years' time, all being well.

'It's a pity about your camera.'

'Yes,' he replied. 'Several times I've called at the police station for it, but they always say it has not been passed yet.'

'Did you have to tell them about it?'

'Of course, it was on my list. I need the permission to take it with me, otherwise they will confiscate all my luggage on the border.'

Arnold had saved up for more than a year to buy this camera, a Retina. It meant a lot to him. His watch, an inexpensive sports model, had been returned to him after 'inspection' – not so his camera.

'I think I've had it,' he said. 'Blast them! They're so expensive in England, duty and so on.'

'Those thieves.'

328

All evening I had been knitting. 'Sorry I can't finish your pullover. I'll have to send it. It will be ready in a couple of days. If I mark the parcel "Free Gift", it will go through Customs. I'm sure you won't have to pay anything.'

Any minute now I was going to cry, I could feel it. I got up quickly and went to the kitchen to make coffee. My tears annoyed me. 'You should be pleased he is going away,' I told myself over and over again.

Arnold insisted that no-one should see him off. Joking about his departure, he had said, 'Railway stations are miserable; railway stations plus relatives are downright depressing.'

If Arnold had had any visions of working in the London factory, he was soon relieved of them. He thought, I have passed my Merchandising Exam with honours, my knowledge of English is quite good, especially where commercial business is concerned since I've done the sales correspondence in English in Uncle David's factory. However, Aunt Frances had found him a job in a slipper factory in Hinkley near Leicester as a machine operator. She obviously did not want him near the London factory; Adolphe Rosenthal in Margaret Street, London, W1.

In all fairness, I must state that Father had never bothered about the English factory. I suspect he was quite glad to be rid of it. Aunt Frances had been running it for twenty years and since her retirement her nephew Jeffrey Frank, son of her sister, had taken over.

Chapter 38

The Red Sports Car

In our factory, which had previously employed several hundred workers, the machinery stood idle. Only the office was kept open with the help of one clerk. Whatever business was still left – people did not buy Jewish goods – was given out to homeworkers, checked once a week by a forewoman who had formerly worked full time at the factory. Occasionally Father managed to sell some of the special machinery to help our financial situation. Exactly how bad it was I could never make out, as my parents would not discuss money matters in front of us children. However, when we needed something special the money always seemed to be available. Once Father sold part of his collection of antique corsets to a museum. This unique collection had been started by my great-grandfather.

'A pity they found out it was a "Jewish" collection,' Father remarked. 'They paid me well below the value.'

He worried over commitments. Karl, the gardener and Wanda, my Grandmother's house-keeper, received a small pension and there were others from the factory receiving assistance. Grandmother had died whilst I was in Hamburg, aged eighty-two. She was quite blind, very weak and spent the greater part of the day in bed. Up to the very end everyone pretended, when visiting her, that all was exactly the same as in the good old days and, as much as possible, stories about emigration and Nazis were kept from her.

Twice weekly Father held 'surgery' in the surrounding villages. This was conducted in great secrecy, sometimes in the private room of an inn, in the vicarage, or in an outlying farm, always at a different place. Father's whereabouts would be quickly spread by word of mouth. It was forbidden for Jews to practise medicine except on other Jews. Even so, his former patients kept on sending messages. As it would have been too dangerous for them to consult him at our house, Father cycled to the villages and hamlets wearing sports clothes, knickerbockers trousers, and with a rucksack.

I worried and dreaded the day when someone would report him. But Father seemed to be quite unconcerned. 'I have to do my job,' he said. 'I will be all right, dear. Please – you must believe me.'

People referred to him as 'The Healer'. The predominantly Catholic country population treated him with great respect, almost amounting to reverence. I believe all the secrecy added to his prestige.

Once one old lady said to me, 'Of course, we must not forget, already in the Bible, all the healers were Jews, and it had to be all secret then.' I felt embarrassed by this over-simplification.

Often in the morning we would find at the front door a basket of new-laid eggs, fruit, vegetables or flowers, always the choicest, which had been left by grateful patients. Father was most pleased when he received the special herbs which he needed to make tinctures. He rarely took payment, saying his gift (that of medical clairvoyance), surely would go if he abused it by commercialising it.

Deda (Sister Paula) had kept up some correspondence with my Father, mostly on medical subjects, apart from sending birthday and Christmas cards. She was now Chief District Supervisor of Midwives in the Black Forest, an important position. Hospital confinements there were generally advised only if complications were anticipated.

One weekend she paid us a surprise visit. I told her she looked exactly the same as the day she left us. She did not look older: the same ageless, parchment coloured face, mousy hair and no make-up. She wore a belted gabardine raincoat, an unbecoming felt hat and lace-up shoes, sensible ones, like men's.

She hugged and kissed us. I remembered how she used to say, 'Kissing is unhygienic.'

She had brought flowers for Mother.

'Oh! I forgot your present in the car,' she said. 'Just a little something. Ricky' (she had always called Richard Ricky), 'go and get it – on the front seat.'

Richard returned quite excited. 'Deda, your car is super-duper. Sylvia, you must go and have a look at it.'

Richard was most impressed and kept on talking about the car.

331

'I want to see the present first.'

We carefully unwrapped it. There it was. A large, rosy marzipan pig, just like the ones we used to 'slaughter' after many a Sunday dinner when Deda was still with us. Father had ceremoniously carved them, after pretending to sharpen the knife. We had not had one for years, not after the patisserie Bliederhauser closed down. It was a wonderful present.

Deda accompanied Father to his laboratory; he was going to show her something to do with his research on the predetermination of sex. I had asked him several times to tell me about it, but he had always said, 'Later.'

Meanwhile we went outside to have a look at the car. I was most surprised – it was not at all what I had visualised. It was a bright red streamlined sports model, long and low-slung. Richard pointed out the finer details and kept guessing about the speed it could do. Deda had put the car straight in front of the house.

How careless of her, I thought. If it was reported that she had been visiting Jews, it could be dangerous for her, as she was a Civil Servant. I suggested she should move it, but Deda laughed, and when I pressed her, pointing out that the Nazis might make difficulties for her, she swore a popular, but very rude, Swabish curse. Richard squealed with delight, saying he never would have believed it, had he not heard it, and she having been a children's nurse.

I kept watching through the window to see if anybody was noting down her licence number. Sometimes people glanced with admiration at the car before passing on. It made me nervous and I was almost glad when she left. It had spoiled her visit for me.

Chapter 39

Growing up

Grandfather was very ill. Mother had gone to Frankfurt to help Grandmother; I looked after the household as well as I could.

With the morning mail, Father received a letter from the Welfare Department for Jewish Youth in Stuttgart, telling him that the West London Synagogue Committee had sent a guarantee for Susan. Could she be ready in two days? If so, she would be able to join a Children's Transport which was leaving then.

By showing the letter at the police station, Father obtained her passport quickly. There were no difficulties as she was a child of fifteen years of age.

I stayed up half the night, washing and ironing. It was a warm summer night and the excitement and a sense of duty kept me awake. Mother had decided not to return home – Grandfather was worse – so she asked me to pack for Susan. Next day I laid out all her clothes, underwear and shoes, so that she might choose the wardrobe she was going to take. It was a difficult choice as only one suitcase was allowed. Summer clothes, winter clothes – I must not forget anything; the responsibility weighed heavily on me. The case would not shut; there was far too much. By applying the training I had had at the fashion school, seeing that the clothes matched and interchanged, I managed finally to cut it down. There was even room to slip in extras, such as a bottle of hair shampoo.

Susan had gone to say 'goodbye' to our few remaining friends and relatives. She told me that Karl had cried. 'I shouldn't laugh, I know, but he looked so funny with the tears on his handlebar moustache, like dew-drops' – because it was waxed, I suppose. Wanda had spoken to her in English, showing off the few words she knew.

During the afternoon, I received a phone call from Hamburg, from the matron of the orphanage, Miss Rosenthal. They had been able to include me in the next transport to England. 'Could I come right away?'

I thanked her and replied I would leave at once.

Hurriedly I packed. Susan helped me by polishing shoes and fetching and carrying. I almost threw the clothes in the case. 'I am bound to forget half of my things, to be sure. My books – I wish I could take them – they weigh a ton – perhaps one can send them. I selected three small art books of the Insel Verlag, my favourites and my treasures, two small oil paintings: *The Weather Prophet* and *The Card Sharp*. I hoped these would not be confiscated at the border. Also my little silver fish, a needle cushion mother had given to me.

Father went to the station to enquire about trains and try to reserve a sleeper to Hamburg. Of course, it was too late – nothing was available.

As I was leaving with a Hamburg Transport, I had to be officially domiciled there. My passport would be issued there. Matron was going to put the application in meanwhile to save time.

Susan and I had to sit on my suitcase to close it. With the careful re-packing which I hoped to do the next day, it would be all right. My cosmetics and toilet articles I put in a brief case, taking a chance that I would be permitted to take it on the Transport.

'We might even get to the same place,' said Susan. 'We'll have a reunion – with Arnold too.'

'I doubt that. We'll meet as soon as we can.'

Arnold had been staying with Aunt Frances whilst looking for a job.

Father accompanied me to Stuttgart where I changed for the night express. He bought me some magazines and a hot dog on a cardboard plate from the vendors on the platform.

'I'll phone your Mother to tell her you'll be in the middle of the train. The train stops for only a couple of minutes in Frankfurt – I hope you'll see her. When you get to England, you'd better see the dentist right away – it's only a temporary filling.'

'Don't worry, Daddy. You'd better leave the train now.' I kissed him. He embraced me.

'Have no fear. You'll be protected.'

334

'I know, Daddy.'

Once before he had said that to me … when, I could not remember.

'Try and sleep in the train.'

'If I can.'

He was getting off.

'Write soon.'

'Yes.'

A trolley with flowers passed us and he purchased a small bunch of violets. The train started to move.

'Catch.'

I waved for a long time.

What luxury to travel First Class; normally I travelled Third. 'Most probably it will be empty,' Father had said. 'You'll have a chance to stretch out.'

I had had only a few hours sleep the previous night.

Two elderly gentlemen sitting opposite me discussed sales promotion. I tried to doze. Snatches of their conversation drifted past me: '…sent my men out in full strength … very disappointing … poor result, poor result, poorresult, poorresult, poorresult.'

When I woke up the compartment was empty.

The train arrived in Frankfurt. I got out and walked up and down the platform but I could not see Mother. It was a very long train. I craned my neck – 'Where can she be?' The porters started to bang the doors shut – the whistle blew. Quickly I jumped back on. I do hope everything is all right, I thought.

One feels a sort of resentment, if only for a few seconds, when one has to give up the privacy of one's compartment and share with a stranger.

A tall youngish man was putting his luggage in the rack. Turning round he asked: 'This is not your seat?'

'No, I am on the other side.'

He smiled at me. 'Good evening.'

What a handsome man, I thought. I was intrigued. Almost automatically I started our childhood guessing game: How old? Thirty-two to thirty-five. Tall, over six feet. Profession? Don't know yet – later – good face, strong but sensitive – looks tired – permanently tired. Perhaps over worked, or too many parties? No, not the type. Oh! Lovely long hands, nails immaculate, manicured, done in a shop – I don't like that, none of my business anyway.

335

I continued with my assessment. Well cut clothes, expensive. That olive green gabardine suit is handmade, very suitable in this hot weather. I don't know – everything is too perfect, matches too well. He must be a self-made man – none of that easy carelessness. My girl, you are a snob! His luggage – pigskin – much travelled – no, not a commercial traveller, definitely not – looks too artistic for that. He's no artist though – much too tidy, his shoes are well polished, they're polished every day.

I had liked his voice; it was pleasant, quiet, but had authority.

Good posture, but not muscular – probably he's not played any sports since his college days. Profession?... '

Then, almost as if to help me with my guessing game, he opened his brief case to take out some technical drawings and blue prints. He started to study them, making notes in a little book.

Without appearing too obvious, I peered at them: No, it was not a building or a machine – you're nosy, my girl – that's what you are. Leave the man alone.

He had put down his plans and was looking at me. To avoid his eyes I picked up my newspaper. After a little while I glanced over the top of it and saw he was still looking at me.

'Can I offer you one?' he asked, holding out his cigarette case. I noticed it was brown leather, gold-tooled. Probably Florence, I thought.

'No, thank you.'

'Do you mind if I smoke?'

'Of course not.'

'I am going to Hamburg. How far are you travelling?'

'Hamburg.'

'Oh!' He seemed pleased. 'Do you live there?'

'No, not now. I used to live there. I'll be going to England.'

'For a visit?'

'I suppose one could call it that,' I said pensively. I picked up my newspaper again as I did not wish to talk about it.

After a while he said, 'Do look at this sunset. It's really quite something – you'd get a better view from here.'

I got up and we looked together out of the window.

The sky was striped pink and orange, framed pale grey, the trees sharply silhouetted, deep black. Up and down, up and down the telegraph wires danced.

He said, 'One should paint it.'

'If you would paint it, you wouldn't like it. You know those calendars with sunsets – ghastly – much too sentimental. They are really bad taste – well, all the ones I've seen.'

'There is only one painter who could do it – the Englishman, Turner.'

I was surprised he knew Turner who is hardly known in Germany.

'I like Turner very much. He knows about light. Do you know Breughel? The black trees remind me of the winter scenes; his light is even more exciting. Exciting – that's not the right word for it.'

'I know exactly what you mean – you can feel everything about the light, the heat and the chemical quality as well.'

He understands. It's wonderful if somebody understands, I thought. 'Have you been to the Hamburg Museum?' I asked him. 'There is a Rembrandt there, a Nativity. All the light seems to radiate from the Christ Child. One can feel the warmth of it, it's almost a physical experience. It's a dark picture, the whole world being shadows.'

'I've not seen that. I'll make a point to have a look at it as soon as I can, though I doubt whether I'll have the time. I'll only be in Hamburg two days. How long will you stay there?'

'Just a few days, I am not certain how long. It depends.'

'On what?'

'I've got to get my passport – things like that.'

'There might be a war. What do you think?'

'I really don't know – it looks bad.'

'Why are you going to England at a time like this?'

What should I say? Because the time is like that? I did not answer.

A steward walked past in the corridor. He called him in, ordering two coffees and two brandies.

'Thank you for the coffee, but I don't like brandy.'

'You're not supposed to like it at your age, but it's good for you. Tell me, how old are you?'

'Seventeen.'

'Even younger than I thought. You did not answer me before. Why are you going to England?'

'I want to finish my studies.' This was a half-truth anyway, because I hoped I could go to school, or perhaps to evening classes.

'What are you studying?'

'Fashion, textiles. I want to be a dress designer.'

'England!' He looked puzzled. 'If you had said Paris, I could understand that.' After a pause, he said, 'I do like your clothes, your suit especially – the simplicity. Did you design that?'

'Yes, and I made it. The coat too.'

'It looks most professional. Do you know, you're good!'

I could feel myself blush at his praise. 'One must be better than average, otherwise one should forget about it. What do you do?'

'I am an architect.'

'Tell me, those plans, what are they?'

'A bridge.'

'Do you specialise in bridges?'

'I build all sorts of things. At present I'm doing a warehouse and a block of flats as well.'

'That's a big job.'

He smiled. 'I'm lucky. I've graduated to the "big jobs" now, as you call it.'

'Luck alone won't do it.'

'No. Talking of luck, I was cross when I could not get a sleeper – don't get enough sleep as it is – but if it had not been for that I might never have met you.'

'My father tried for me, too. They had all been booked.'

The coffee arrived. I sipped the brandy reluctantly – it tasted like medicine.

'Surely it is not as bad as all that – your face – you ought to see it!' He laughed. Then he became very serious. We just sat looking at each other. It seemed as if the atmosphere became filled with us and nothing else existed.

I got up and reached for my brief case. He quickly rose to help me. He held me a long time in his arms before he kissed me. I felt I had never been kissed before. Never had I felt like this.

We were sitting close together, holding hands, my head resting against his shoulder. 'It is as if I had always known you ... your hair smells delicious. Darling, darling ... don't go to England, I am certain you can learn, whatever it is, just as well in Germany.'

'I really must go.'

He pulled me, almost roughly towards him and kissed me hard. 'You belong to me, you can't go away now.'

I wanted his kisses. I wanted him to hold me forever and ever.

My God, this is crazy – remember who you are! I thought.

'We'll spend a lot of time together,' he said. 'I have an assistant, permanently on the job there. I'll just see how things are going, then I'll be free. Let's look at that Rembrandt,' he continued. 'We'll have lunch at the Alster, if the weather holds.'

'It's so close, I think we'll have a thunderstorm.'

He was thoughtful. 'Berlin is quite good for fashions I believe. I am often in Berlin. I want to see a lot of you. At present I am building a warehouse in Siemenstadt – that's near Berlin... Please, darling, talk to your parents.'

'Really ... I can't.'

'Why, but why?'

Slowly I reached for my bag and took out my birth certificate. Only this afternoon Father had obtained a copy for me; I needed it for the passport.

In the margin was typed: 'And the said Sylvia Fleischer will take on the additional Christian name "Sara" and that no document will be legal without this name on the signature.'

Sitting opposite I watched him reading it. He seemed shocked and went quite pale. Carefully he folded the document and returned it to me. I waited for him to speak but he kept silent. After what seemed to me a long time, he got up, sat next to me, and stroked me very gently. Then he kissed my eyes.

'Of course you must go to England. I'll have to go there, to London, in two months' time, for an International Conference ... if the war does not start before ... if you'll see me ... you might not even want to talk to me then.'

I said nothing.

'I don't understand. You're so fair. I thought all Jews were dark and semitic ... I look more Jewish than you – I never thought Jews were like you. Of course I don't know any – personally I mean. You have a lovely face, an interesting face.'

'We are not exactly like those portrayed in the *Sturmer* – we're just like anybody else, good, bad, indifferent.' Hearing myself utter this cliché, I inwardly winced.

'You must hate me.'

I smiled at him. I was sad, and shook my head. Hate? I did not hate him or anybody else. I hated the madness. And then I thought, I did not even hate that, I could not understand it – it was like an infectious terrible disease, like an epidemic.

Black is white and
Wrong is right and
I am getting out of it and
I can't sort it out.

I felt helpless. 'No, I don't hate you.'

He said, with embarrassment, 'Of course, I am a member of the Party – everyone is. I've no "duties" as I am in the Reserve Police. They've put me there because I travel about such a lot and I can't attend the meetings. I care little for politics.'

We sat in silence for some time.

I was wondering why Mother had not met the train in Frankfurt, and I decided I must telephone her as soon as I got to Hamburg. All kinds of unpleasant thoughts flashed through my mind. No, they don't arrest women … not usually, not for nothing.

I dearly would have loved to say goodbye to Mother. I knew she was glad that I could go away. She had been just about my age when she had gone away to Finishing School. It was not going to be Finishing School for me. I did not know what it would be, but the main thing was, I was on my way.

I re-lived the last few hours Mother and I had spent together. It had been late at night when Grandmother phoned to say that Grandfather had suddenly got worse. I offered to help Mother with her packing. She said she was not taking much, it was a pity that she had worn her white blouse only today, the blue ensemble would have been just right. This ensemble, to which the white blouse belonged, had been the last thing her Grandparents had ordered for her at the Salon Wintermeyer.

Mother had been surprised when the familiar striped box arrived on her birthday. No longer could she afford to patronise the Salon Wintermeyer. The Prussian blue ensemble was loosely cut, the edge-to-edge style was the latest fashion, and it was very elegant. I was impressed with the workmanship and had turned it inside out. Mother had been amused. We got on much better now. Perhaps the bad times had brought us together. To quarrel – about nothing – one just did not do that anymore. Mother had taken a great interest in the Fashion College and what I had learned there. She kept on saying that she wished her father had allowed her to learn dressmaking. The clothes her daughter Sylvia made did not look 'home-made' at all.

Quickly, to surprise Mother, I washed the blouse and rolled it in towels. If I got up very early in the morning, I could press it. I was sure it would get dry enough over night. However, when I ironed it in the morning, a big yellow streak appeared in front – I had not rinsed it properly in all the hurry. Mother was most particular about her clothes. When I went to her to confess she was not a bit annoyed; she said it did not matter at all, and she had given me a kiss. Her eyes looked suspiciously as if there were tears in them.

Good God, why did she not come to the station?

I was tired.

'You should try to sleep. Here, rest against me.'

A wave of feeling surged over us and we kissed as if this would save us from drowning.

In the early hours he rolled up his coat to make a pillow for me, then, carefully, covered me with mine.

Very gently he woke me up. 'We shall be in Hamburg in ten minutes.'

I went to have a wash. The train was entering the station when I returned to the compartment. Hastily I packed my things together.

Through the window he waved to two men standing on the platform, a big one with a red face and a thin young one with glasses. I suppose that's his assistant, I thought. They both wore rain coats; I noticed that they were wet on the shoulders.

I hailed a porter. Without saying 'Goodbye' I slipped out of the train and followed my bags down the platform. I could not resist turning round. He was talking to his friends. I saw him handing them his suitcase. They bowed respectfully. Then he walked quickly after me. I hoped he would catch up with me but I did not slacken my pace. When he reached me, I was getting into a taxi.

'I haven't got your address.'

I shook my head.

'Your address, please.'

'Don't be hard on him, Miss,' chipped in the cabby.

Turning to the driver, I said, quite loudly and distinctly, 'Thirty-seven Laufgraben.'

'I'll wait for you at twelve o'clock outside, darling. Goodbye.'

Matron welcomed me. 'After breakfast, I'd like you to go straightaway to collect your passport. You've got the photos?'

'Yes, I had those done ages ago.'

Everything went smoothly. I was less than a quarter of an hour at the police station Passport photographs are horrible – I looked much older, not that I minded that.

When I returned to the orphanage, Matron had very kindly given me my old room which one of the Domestic Science students had specially vacated for me. I decided to repack my case. To my surprise, I could even get my briefcase inside. A clock struck – I looked at my watch – only ten o'clock. I phoned home. Mother answered. She was sorry she had missed me at Frankfurt, but she had been in a train going in the opposite direction, hoping to reach home before I left.

I had time for a bath. Afterwards I rested on my bed.

Although I did not expect him, I dressed slowly and carefully. It started to rain again – that very fine rain which always lasts for hours.

I'll endanger his position. I must not see him – anyway he won't come! He shouldn't come. 'You must be shameless,' I said to myself, 'carrying on with a Nazi.'

And another voice in me whispered, 'He is no Nazi.'

The first said, 'Don't be absurd, they're all Nazis.'

And the little voice said again, 'He's taking chances, too.'

I walked over to the window and scanned the street just to see if he would turn up. At a few minutes to twelve I saw him coming along, slowly, looking for the number.

Quickly I put on my raincoat and beret. I ran downstairs. When I saw him I asked, 'Did you ring?'

'No.' Then he said, 'I am so glad you've come.' He took both my hands. 'I don't know whether I would have had the courage to fetch you from "inside".' And his eyes travelled to the inscription over the door: 'Jewish Orphanage'.

We held hands and walked around many streets, not knowing where we were going – somewhere in the old part of the town.

On a bridge we stopped and watched the barges go by. One motor boat pulled six tied together, all filled with glistening black coal. Men with bright yellow oilskins guided them with poles through the narrow canal. It was still raining. He wiped my face dry with his large handkerchief. The initial on it scratched my cheek.

'Ouch!' He kissed it better.

'You do look a mess – I love you.'

The rain was gradually penetrating our clothes and shoes. I hardly noticed it.

'Let's go and eat.'

'I'm not hungry.'

We turned down a side street.

'Looks all right in here.' He held the swing doors open for me. It was one of those slightly old-fashioned comfortable restaurants where elderly businessmen go, the food and service usually being very good.

'Perhaps there is a "Jews not wanted" sign,' I whispered to him.

'I doubt it – who cares? Don't worry, darling, nobody knows us.'

The place was almost empty as it was late.

We sat down in one of the oak-panelled cubicles.

'Really, I can't eat. My tummy is all funny.'

He beckoned the waiter. 'Chicken soup – that's all right for you?' I nodded. 'Some plain boiled rice and a small omelette – the lady is on a diet.' Then, turning to me, 'You don't mind if I have something different?'

'Of course not.'

We sat for a long time after lunch, sipping china tea. I held the little bowl to the light. One could see through it.

Leaning back against the upholstery I relaxed. We listened to the music which was very quietly relayed.

'I know this piece. It's "Song without words".' He winked at me. 'Mendelssohn – he was a Jew.' In Germany, music by Jewish composers had been banned since 1933. 'They must have slipped up,' he laughed. 'I've fixed a meeting for four o'clock, we'll have to go.'

We sat in silence in the taxi. He stopped it at the corner when it turned into the Laufgraben.

'How pale you are – all black shadows.' He traced around my eyes with his finger. 'Perhaps you'll write to me.'

I had no words. 'Come on, smile,' I said to myself.

Straightening my shoulders, I walked away. I did not want him to see me cry.

*   *   *

Matron entered my room.

'That's clever of you, you're in bed already. I've only come to tell you that the Transport leaves tomorrow at ten-thirty.'

343

Next morning I got up extra early to repack my suitcase. I realised the crocodile case had been a bad choice: it was too heavy and had too many extra compartments, bag-like fabric sections which took up space. Yes, they were detachable, held by clip-on studs. I stuffed the sections in the waste bin. After everything was carefully folded, I could once again get my briefcase inside.

The dining room was very quiet. We assembled in the hall. The whole orphanage was there, including the Domestic Science students. The children were giving us a special send-off – go-away songs – Miss Elsie, as usual, accompanying at the piano.

A small bus was waiting outside. The driver was loading the suitcases standing in the hall. The younger children were wearing rucksacks; I had never seen such tiny rucksacks before.

The instructions had been:

Take only what can be carried comfortably.
Small children: washbag with small hand towel, change of underwear, socks, warm pullover or cardigan, one favourite toy.
Older children: one medium-sized suitcase, same as above, additional clothing, rainwear, scarf.

By my guess there were about fifteen children, between the ages of four and twelve.

Goodbyes were said.

I thanked the matron, Miss Edith Rosenthal, to whom I was deeply grateful. Then I said, 'I must go to the Post Office, to send a registered letter.'

'If it is important, yes. Your case is on the bus. Yes, there is plenty of time.'

'I'll take the tram straight to the station.' I thanked her again.

I wanted to return my surplus money. Father had given to me extra, for the passport, and other essentials. At home money was short, otherwise I would have put it in the orphanage kitty.

One of the Domestic Science students stood at the door. 'Here, from all of us. I'm glad I caught you. Good luck.' She gave me some sweets in a paper bag for the journey.

'Oh, thank you.'

I caught up with our group outside the station. 'We are early,' said Miss Rosenthal. 'I'm afraid I have to leave you now. Here is

344

your Helper.' She handed to the lady a list of our names. 'Have a good journey. Do write. Bless you all.'

It was a bright summer day, this 25th of July 1939.

Epilogue

My sister Susan arrived in London two days after me. She was 15 years old and had been placed with a doctor's family. Many people offered to take children after an appeal in the newspapers and on the radio.

The doctor's wife had decided to help her husband in his surgery, as his receptionist had talked of doing some war work, should there be a war.

So Susan had charge of two small girls, escorting them to school and kindergarten. Then she cleaned the house, which, according to her employers, she did rather 'sloppily'. No pocket money was given, after all one had to be grateful to receive board and lodging.

This 'job' lasted until the doctor was called up, when there was no further need for Susan.

The Refugee Children's Movement, also called the Board of Guardians, situated in Bloomsbury House, took a close interest in us. They had found that people taking in older children did not always do this for altruistic reasons. My East End family told me that they had chosen me because I came from an orphanage, it had stated I was good at sewing, therefore they thought I would not be spoiled. 'You work well, we must say that, even being a college student!'

There were families who took the children, because of love and pity. I knew of a small girl taken by a family in Gloucester. The lady had lost her own little daughter. She said God had heard her prayers and sent to her this lovely child for adoption. The girl became a lawyer and later on a judge.

No news from our parents, not even through the Red Cross, via Switzerland. Only at a later date did we find out that they had

346

been deported, with Richard, to the East, possibly Poland, or Riga. I tried to block this from my mind – somehow I was still in shock, so I became rather silent and did not talk very much.

I was looking forward to meeting my brother Arnold, who had been placed by Aunt Frances in a job in Hinckley near Leicester. It was in a factory making slippers, as a trainee machinist. He wrote that his digs were excellent, his landlady urging him to eat more, so that he should grow – he was only four feet eleven inches tall!

He wrote that when he had saved enough for the fare he would visit me. I was surprised that no job had been found for him in the London factory, Adolphe Rosenthal. He was well qualified for office work. Then it occurred to me that our side of the family was not to go near that place!

Soon Arnold's Waiting Number from the American Consulate 'came up'. The US was neutral, had not entered the War – therefore there were no boats leaving for that destination, the only way was via Canada.

The British Government was interning foreign nationals on the Isle of Man, prior to shipment to Canada. Arnold volunteered, but had to wait his turn to get a passage. To his surprise, he was shipped to the centre of Canada, where he became a lumberjack.

Far removed from any settlement, there was absolutely nothing to do in the evenings, besides there were guards. So he and several of the other internees, boys of the same age, decided to take the Canadian Matriculation, a correspondence course, which they thought might come in useful. He passed with flying colours.

Now in Toronto, the Jewish community had heard of these clever young boys. They came to visit them, surely these lads were University material. Most of them were sponsored by them – Arnold missed out. They thought he was too young, his height was against him.

After he was released from the lumber camp he decided he would like to become an accountant, surely a well paid job. A small firm having diverse accounts would be more useful than one of the larger firms who specialised in just a few lines. At that time the customary fee for apprenticeships had been lifted. As now, there was a shortage of young recruits to the profession.

To support himself, he took on a part-time job as a machinist in a slipper factory from 6–11 p.m. After all, he was experienced in this kind of work.

Luckily his employer had many restaurant accounts. Arnold,

having previously had training in cooking, understood their problems and was very popular. He tried to arrange his visits near lunchtime, it helped his rather tight budget.

His fellow internees kept up their friendships, they called themselves the Refugee Mayflower Club. Most of them became lawyers or doctors and they remained lifelong friends.

Arnold graduated after two years. He became a most successful accountant and business adviser, and had many important clients, including one of the royal houses of Europe who had large properties in Canada. He was still interested in the arts, and would travel to New York for the theatre or opera.

He married late in life, a divorcee with a teenage son. Unfortunately he died of the Asian Influenza in 1968. This was a great loss to me, it took me a long time to get over it.

Arnold was a very creative business advisor. To give one example – one day a would-be client arrived, saying he was in trouble and going bankrupt. Arnold found out the only asset the man still owned was a paper cutting machine, but he could not afford to pay for the raw materials.

Arnold's advice was this: every week the newspapers pay good money to have taken away, by lorries, the left over paper rolls. They have to stop their machines early, which run at high speed otherwise they get clogged up, which could be a big and costly job. Shall we offer to collect these rolls for free? This was done and it became the start of the Phoenix Paper Co., a concern dealing in note blocks from the cheapest to the finest handmade paper. Turnover soon reached a million. Needless to say, Arnold had training in Uncle David's paper mill. 'Mr Fleischer, will you consider being my partner?'

Arnold – the little man with the big brain.

* * *

Continuing about myself. I had been working for two weeks in their hat factory, the family were satisfied, even praised me sometimes. They had booked a holiday in Margate, the children were looking forward to the seaside. The car was small and there was no room for me. What should I do? The factory was closed for the week. I suggested I could give it a good cleaning, it was really needed. Perhaps I could pay a visit to Aunt Frances in Gerrards Cross, Father had said previously I should make myself known.

348

From the 10 Marks (16 shillings) we had been allowed by the Nazis to take out of the country, I had sufficient for the fare, having only spent on postage stamps. Needless to say I had not received any pocket money. My good lady had left me some tinned food and milk was delivered.

I arrived at my aunt's house in the afternoon, without a previous telephone call because I had been unable to follow the complicated instructions on the apparatus at the railway station.

It certainly was at the wrong time. There was a tea party in progress for auntie's lady friends. I was directed to a small chair at the back of the room, whilst the plight of the refugee children was discussed. Surprise, surprise, the girl lives in London's East End! Whitechapel! Surely not?

I was wearing ankle socks and one of the ladies noticed that I had red spots on my legs. Auntie took her walking stick, lifting my skirt for inspection. A lively discussion took place about the prevalence of bugs in the East End.

Auntie was shamed into offering me a home, she had several guest rooms. I moved there just before the beginning of the war, in time to hear the Prime Minister's announcement. War. War, this had been generally expected, talked about, but not believed.

I was busy doing the flowers, writing pretty labels for the jam the housekeeper had made, grooming and walking the dogs, running errands to the village, which was a good two miles away, laying the table, cleaning the silver, mending the linen, including some lace, and picking up windfalls and berries in the garden, these were ripening just now. Just the things for a young lady.

The aunts were forever criticising my appearance. I wore my blonde hair shoulder length. It was fine, blow away hair. 'Not neat, tie it back, you're not an actress!'

'Have you not got a better brassiere? Your bosom is sticking out.'

'It's young,' said Aunt Anna, 'it's the fashion.'

'You are wearing ankle socks, hardly suitable for your age.' I had been saving my precious pure silk stocking for important occasions.

'Here, have some lisle ones.'

These were heavy weight and wrinkled at the ankles, even if I tried to pull them up quite hard. Oh, well, good enough for taking the dogs for walkies.

Shortly after I had arrived, the house parlour maid gave notice, she was joining the Forces. I inherited her job. Au pair. My weekly pocket money which had been one shilling was increased to half-a-crown. What a good saving for the aunt.

Some time later we had to attend a Tribunal for Aliens. As our family was well known, Susan and I were Class C Friendly Enemy Aliens, so the same call up as for British born persons applied to us. My call-up papers had arrived on my 18th birthday. I never saw them, my aunt must have opened them. She took me to the local Labour Exchange, where they decided I should work for the evacuees housed in a former Rothschild Mansion in Buckinghamshire.

The housekeeper there said she did not like Germans – that made two of us. She gave me mostly scrubbing to do, on my hands and knees, with disinfectant, as the poor children had brought with them nasty infections. They mostly came from poor districts and were in a sorry state.

I did not last long at this job. The scrubbing gave me a severe case of housemaid's knee. The doctor I consulted was quite firm. 'This work must stop.' I bought a long-handled scrubbing brush, but the housekeeper would not allow me to use it. When I showed her the Doctor's Certificate, and asked for alternate work, she regretted she had none.

On my next day off I went to London, taking my sketch books. I found a job as an Assistant Designer, after I called at about twenty different clothing firms. I left my long-handled scrubbing brush for the housekeeper as a little going away present. I tied a nice ribbon bow on it, with best wishes.

Alas, this job also did not last very long. The firm closed down from lack of materials. They had decided not to manufacture uniforms. Both of the partners joined the forces.

All 'Refugee Children' had to keep in touch with Bloomsbury House whenever we had a change of job or accommodation. They decided at Bloomsbury House that I would be useful to teach girls how to use a sewing machine, so that they could be employed by the factories making uniforms or parachutes. My teaching hours were easy, two hours in, the morning, two in the afternoon. I took my lunch in the Lyons Corner House at Tottenham Court Road.

There I met the professor, who also took his lunch there. He discovered that he knew my family, he and his wife were bridge partners with Aunt Herta, who had lived in Charlottenburg, Berlin.

Aunt Herta's husband was a Regierungs Rat (a high-up animal in the German administration).

'You and your sister must come for tea and meet my wife, not in the evening, my wife retires early, she suffers from migraine.' I was working in the afternoons.

The professor was fully occupied with his work for the Beveridge Report, he did statistics. I listened spellbound – what a wonderful thing, free healthcare for all, it led to the founding of the National Health Plan.

Again my job as a sewing instructor did not last very long.

The educational and social background of the refugee children was well documented at Bloomsbury House. They worked together with the Labour Exchange (now called Job Centre), to find suitable employment for their charges.

Susan and myself received a notice to present ourselves at the Denmark Street Labour Exchange, which is the specialist Labour Exchange for the catering trade. We were handed a menu in French, and asked to read it. 'Do you understand this? Can you explain? What food is this?' We had often had French food at home, our cook Liesel had been a *Herrschafts Koechin* (a sort of Mrs Bridges from *Upstairs, Downstairs*). Certainly our mother gave out the menu sometimes in French, including the Alsace cuisine. We both passed with flying colours.

Now we were pronounced qualified to become waitresses in the Grill Room of a large hotel. The French and Swiss kitchen staff refused to speak English, they were professionals. They turned a deaf ear to anything other than the orders given in French. We were able to advise our customers, who could not read the French menu.

We joined a nice set of young refugee waitresses, all from good middle-class families; the daughter of a judge, one of a professor, and one whose family had Kempinksi's, which was a famous hotel in Berlin. If only the working hours would not have been so long, all one could do on one's day off was sleep.

This was considered Essential Work for the time being.

Again the job did not last very long, we got a further call to do war work. I was sent to an Engineering Training Centre to learn benchfitting, which is another term for tool making, correct to the thousandths of an inch.

Susan was sent to do engine cleaning at the railway. Susan claimed this very, very dirty job was given to her because the

Labour Exchange clerk seemed to take exception to her well manicured nails (colourless polish only) and her immaculate appearance. Susan was always neat and tidy, her hair was coiffed in the latest fashion in contrast to mine which could be quite wild when the wind was blowing. She was small boned with a pretty pert face, in contrast to my Neanderthal bones.

Work at my Engineering Training Centre was hard. One had to start at 7 o'clock. This meant getting up at 5.15; the underground ran infrequently at this hour and then I had a long walk over common land. One must clock on in time.

I wondered why we were made to practise on odd shapes, cutting them out of the metal, which were then always thrown away. It would have been more encouraging to have made something for the war effort.

The dust from the filing! No masks were given. I suffered from severe hay fever and could not stop sneezing. My swollen face looked pitiful. They released me from this work, without me even asking for it.

What to do now?

The professor came to the rescue, he was a man of influence. He asked me what I would like to do.

'The American Red Cross,' I answered. I had admired the smart uniforms.

The professor answered, 'Perhaps I can help, the wife of my colleague is the personal secretary to the American Ambassador.' I got my interview, was engaged, and was fortunate and happy to work for them until May 1946. My salary was small, however I was allowed money for the uniform and received free meals whilst on duty. We worked three shifts of eight hours in the Red Cross resident clubs for the troops.

Susan and I had shared a small flat, and my new job affected our living arrangements. Because of my irregular hours, I could no longer cook for her, and I slept at different times, etc. So Susan moved to a hostel run by the Refugee Children's Committee. I was glad because my irregular hours had disturbed her. She also had a better social life, with the company of other nice girls.

There were dances, arranged for the Jewish American troops, where she met a charming sergeant, a medical student, Phillip Nassau. They soon got engaged. She was the prettiest, cutest girl. How fortunate he found her! They married, it was a very small wedding. When she became pregnant he managed to get her a passage on a military plane, so that their baby should be born in the States. His family lived in Philadelphia, they looked after her.

Dr Phillip Nassau was a popular GP in his home town. He and Susan had two children and their daughter Irene, not only married a doctor, but one of her sons also became a doctor. The other works for Walt Disney. Susan died in a car crash, on a rainy night, two years after her husband, who had died from overwork, always looking after his patients, even at night, so Susan told me.

* * *

Because we worked three shifts at the Red Cross I could attend lectures, missing only one in three. I could further my education in Art, History and especially Comparative Religion. For the latter I had the great fortune to have as my professor Dr Walter Johannes Stein. He transcribed from the originals, being versed in Greek, Latin, Aramaic and other ancient languages.

To amuse myself I designed clothes and theatrical costumes in my spare time for my actress and model friends. I was a good cutter and fitter, and one starlet recommended another. Soon I designed for principals, being employed by the directors of plays, and later by television.

After my release from war work I needed help with the sewing and also suitable premises, which were difficult to obtain in war-ravaged London. The premises I had found had no telephone – there were waiting lists for up to two years for these, even for shared lines. Fittings for clients were difficult to arrange, but this turned out to be a blessing in disguise. I offered my goods to the shops, which were delighted, not having seen this quality since before the war. So I became a manufacturer of high class clothing, with the Harrods group of stores (then the best) taking 60 per cent of my output. We mostly produced fancy blouses and evening separates. I designed my own lace and embroideries, which were made for me especially in St Gallen, Switzerland. This was to stop my designs being copied too quickly by factories in England.

I had married in November 1949 a writer and critic, and in 1962 my daughter was five years old. I felt guilty for not spending more time with her. I employed a lovely lady, called 'Auntie', as housekeeper and an au pair. My marriage had broken up and, after

353

sixteen years, I decided to give up the business, to spend more time with my child. Education seemed to offer a solution. On my first try I was awarded a senior position by Hollings College, now part of Manchester University, as Lecturer in charge of Design. *Vogue* magazine, Harrods and Hupperts, the fine shop in Regent Street, London, as well as the TV company, had given me the testimonals.

After two years I obtained a more responsible position, in charge of a large department in Tameside College.

When I was 55 years old, there was an opportunity of early retirement. I applied but it came to nothing, as it was difficult to find someone with the industrial experience to run the department. So I had to stay on for another five years.

When I did retire from college work I bought a country inn in County Durham. I always liked cooking, and this gave me the opportunity to practice the French and Alsace cuisine I had been brought up with. My daughter was the waitress and sommelier. We were awarded three Crowns by the Tourist Board. I retired when I was 75 years old.

Now, finally, I had time to follow my own artistic inclination. Previously I had always executed whatever was needed, nothing for self expression.

The Millennium of Jesus Christ was coming up, for which I had designed twelve glass panels, 'The Story of Christ'.

When finances to make the glass panels fell through, I learned to do the glasswork myself. I had always been a do-it-your-selfer. The panels measured 7 feet by 3 feet including wooden bases, and the work was exhibited for three and half months. It gave me much insight into religion, and I prayed for guidance every night. In my research I studied alternative Gospels in the Nag Hammadi Library rolls, which brought to mind the lectures of Dr Walter Johannes Stein, and what had been suppressed by the Church. What was the truth? I realised that most portrayals of Jesus Christ in the past had been incorrect. The nails must have gone through the wrists, the position of the feet was wrong as well.

I was grateful that our family was non-denominational. Father had said that religion is like different languages, to teach you to become a better person.

I have to bring my house in order, and close this book. A brief outline to describe what happened to the people in my story will

354

follow. Brief, yes. My book is getting too long; I am now 84 years old.

Cousin Erica Ries had left Germany with the Youth Aliyah in 1938. They were enthusiastic about their life in Palestine, sleeping in tents in the newly formed Kibbuz Ein Dor, sharing everything, including the clothes they wore, selected from the laundered stack – small, medium, large. Agriculture was difficult in these early days, with sand, waterlogging and drainage presenting many problems. The members of the Kibbuz experimented, growing improved strains which could tolerate the extreme conditions. These seeds became a profitable sideline to sell to other countries with inferior soils. When they discovered that Israel had to import all their wire, they set up a wire factory to produce this needed article. Cousin Erica was working in this factory for years, well past her retiring age.

Gradually their sacrifices paid off, the Kibbuz became well established, and people started to build their own houses. There was a swimming pool, sports facilities, good accommodation to invite your families for extended stays for free, of course, and an allowance for holidays to Europe or wherever they chose. She married Reuban, who had come from Holland. None of her four children remained at the Kibbuz.

Her mother, Aunt Paula, had joined her son Herbert, who had been born in England. He was called up in the army, as an interpreter. Inge, his wife, ran a boarding house near Kensington Gardens, looking after their small son. After the war, Herbert became an insurance broker. They moved to a most luxurious flat overlooking Holland Park. Old Mrs Ries had a small bed-sitting room in Earls Court, which sported a gas cooker in the corner. Perhaps it was a blessing in disguise that her eyesight was failing, so she did not notice her sordid surroundings. Her suitcases were stacked on every piece of furniture. Her daughter Elisabeth had always been a children's nurse, her main complaint in life was that her employers were more loving to a puppy dog, ignoring their darling children. Elisabeth was a most cultured lady, though untidy, who could converse on anything. Unfortunately very few people were interested in serious discussions. When my daughter was a toddler, we were lucky enough to have her help. When she was at retiring age, she spent most of her time sitting on the bench in the park giving advice to the mothers, mostly unwanted, supplemented by pamphlets from her capacious handbags. Her bags grew bigger and bigger, unkind people called her the 'bag lady'.

Herbert's son, Peter, did not appreciate the very materialistic attitudes of his parents. He lived alone in a flat, was said to be a recluse, his only company a parrot. His father once told me he had not seen him for two years.

My cousin Lilo Guggenheim had been invited to join a family on the Isle of Wight. Her parents had met them on a holiday in the Riviera, in former times. She was also declared a 'Friendly Enemy Alien'. She trained in St Alphege's Hospital, Greenwich, as a nurse. Her high theory marks at the exams earned her the Gold Medal* to the annoyance of the matron, who failed her at the practical work. She had to repeat a year.

She joined her family in the US after the war. Working in a TB ward, she caught it. She was sent to Saranac Lake to convalescence, where she met her future husband, Mel, a scientist, also a patient. They married, had three children, and lived on Long Island where Lilo had a studio teaching aerobics. They retired to Saranac Lake.

She wrote her story, which is included in *Portrait of Healing – Caring in the Woods* (2002), by Victoria E Rinehart. She also edited her parents' letters in German and hopes to translate them into English.

Ette Duisberg, our neighbour and former playmate, inherited her family's large nursery. She continued to grow exotic plants, particularly orchids, which were then rare. Her florist shop in the town was well known for artistic work. She taught for years in the local college, with her students winning many national prizes.

Her flower paintings are sold all over the world; I have seen a large one in the Reception Hall of the municipal hospital in Malta. Even now, in her mid-80s, she has regular exhibitions of her paintings. When I awake in the mornings, my eyes see her lovely watercolour of the silver thistles, which grow on the Schwaebische Alb (they are a protected species), hanging on the opposite wall.

Her ability to express herself in rhyme has stayed with her, 'poetry for the occasion', she calls it. It's so nice to receive her greetings in this unusual way, about twice a year.

* * *

---

*Received in the County Hall, Westminster, London W1.

356

The story of Christof'Spa must be told. The doctor-in-charge, Dr Fritz Glatzel, resisted the Nazi order to hand over his patients for the official euthanasia programme. The Nazis had forcibly acquired Schloss Grafeneck, a home for the disabled run by the Samaritans, to turn in into a killing station. It was the first one in Germany. This was part of their plan to create a more perfect German nation, by killing the handicapped and eliminating the 'useless eaters'.

Dr Glatzel was in charge of the Christof'sbad Asylum and private nursing home, which at the time had over 500 patients. He had received the standard questionnaire to assess his patients, according to how much they were able to work, how long they had lived in the institution, whether they were local and whether they paid their own fees or these were paid by the state. Dr Glatzel asked why this assessment was required and refused to fill out the forms. A Nazi assessor from the ministry in Stuttgart, a Dr Mauthe, came to carry out the assessment himself. Half the patients ended up in Grafeneck.

It is estimated that more than 60,000 of the inmates of institutions for those with mental or physical handicaps across Germany were killed off in one of the six killing stations at Grafeneck, Sonnenstein, Bernburg, Brandenburg, Hadamar and Hartheim. There were so many rumours about Grafeneck that the place was closed on Hitler's personal orders. The staff were transferred to Auschwitz-Birkenau and other places in the east, where they could practise their acquired knowledge.

* * *

I met Frieda Heller again, years later. She was a staff nurse in a Manchester hospital. Coming to England via Switzerland, she had entered the nursing service. She said her knowledge of English literature was not sufficient for a librarian's job. When I asked about her brother she said she had little contact with him. She smiled a sad smile. 'Even now, he insists there was nothing wrong with Hitler except he lost the war.'

* * *

I could not bring myself to visit Germany for a long time. About five years ago I plucked up the courage to look up our beloved governess, Hede. She lived in a beautiful village in the Schwaebische Alb. She was still hale and hearty in spite of her ninety years of age.

357

We talked of 'old times', and how she missed us children, wondering what had happened to us.

Twice the Nazis had arrested her, when she told people that the tales about the Jews were not true at all, that she knew better. When the Nazis threatened her with a concentration camp, which they could promise she would not come out of, she had to keep quiet. She had married, but her soldier husband, who had been a textile engineer in Basle, Switzerland, fell in the war, leaving her with two small boys. She supported herself as a talented village dressmaker, helped out by her parents, who were wholesale wine merchants.

I am still friendly with her sons, visiting them sometimes. They are good, deeply religious people.

* * *

After the war I renewed my acquaintance with cousin Eva, the girl who had called me a young, green vegetable (*légume vert*) – this is not an affectionate endearment like *mon petit choux*. Paris was very war torn and shabby, there were shortages of everything. Eva was married, with two little boys. They were lucky to get a flat in their family house in the suburbs. This mansion had been the residence of Jacques Gril's great grandfather, a former Postmaster General of France, and was now divided into eight three-room flats. The housing shortage was so acute that they had to go to court to get living accommodation in their own property, as Eva was expecting a baby.

The Gril family was easy to find in Paris, after the war. Ettienne Gril was a well known writer. Eva's father had been his best friend and they worked together till the collapse of France, when Arthur was arrested by the Gestapo and never seen again.

Eva had worked within the Maquis. '*Fait la Route*', where her knowledge of languages came in useful. Many Alsace people are tri-lingual, this was a secret kept well away from the Germans. Eva's name had become Jaqueline Brusset. She told me about her adventures in the strictest secrecy; it was still dangerous, as there were assassinations by the Right Wing and the former adherents of the Vichy Government, whom the Maquis informed on. 'I must not get my family involved, promise you never talk about it,' she said. The Vichy traitors had collaborated with the Nazis to send people to concentration camps, not only Jews, but also Communists, writers, artists, the clergy and gypsies. 'For God's sake, don't tell my family, they don't know.' I promised.

During the war ration books were used as Identity Cards. You could be challenged in the street to produce it, and could face arrest if you did not.

Eva, an extremely attractive girl, decided to brave the German Command Post where these ration books were kept. She showed the German sergeant where her book was de-faced, a big ink-spot where the J for Jew was now invisible. Could she please have another book? When the soldier was out of the room she stole a whole bunch of these ration books. She made a date with the sergeant, which she kept, twice.

In the night the Maquis broke the window, to show forced entry, and made a nice mess, to cover up. Her haul had been very useful. Eva only ever admitted the ink spot to her family, never the theft of the books.

Jacques and Eva had three sons: Jean Joel, who works in Lyon in water preservation; Dr Denis, who is Professor in Ancient Arabic languages in Aix-en-Provence University; and Dr Joseph, who is Senior Lecturer in Wood Science in Montpellier University. Between them they have fourteen children.

We are very close, they are now our family.

Eva's mother had contracted TB and died in a home in Pau, in the south of France. That's where her young brother Erwin, then sixteen years old, started his journey, he was aiming to get to Israel. A group of youngsters and children set out for the long, long walk, over 100 miles from the border. During daytime they played ball games in the meadows, so as not to arouse the suspicion of the military, and in the twilight and early evening they walked till they arrived in Andorra, where they climbed the Pyrenees. From there they entered Spain. The British Authorities gave these brave children permission to enter Palestine.

Erwin became a lecturer in engineering, married a very '*fromm*' (orthodox Jewish) girl. They have three daughters.

* * *

Now we come to the saddest part.

Victims of the Holocaust.

On the 26th of November my parents and Richard were arrested with another thirty-eight Jewish persons. After an overnight stay in a school hall on the bare boards without blankets they were loaded into cattle trucks. The journey to Poland took three days. Many people died on the way. These horrific journeys have been well documented.

My mother was gassed.

My father died of blood poisoning and gangrene from wounds received.

Brother Richard, twelve years old and tall for his age, was put to work and survived with the grace of God

The Russians rescued him, he weighed 32 kg. They nursed him back to health in one of their hospitals. He worked for the Russians for a while, then decided he would like to go HOME. Home? He jumped trains, it was a long journey, but finally he arrived in Wuerttemberg. This was now the American Zone. He worked for the American authorities before departing to Philadelphia, USA, to live with Susan.

He had found our family via contacts in Paris. Cousin Eva had our addresses.

Susan's brother-in-law had a large builder's firm and offered to train him in any department of his choosing. Richard thought tiling was the cleanest work, so he became a tiler. He was good at the work and decided to become independent after only a short time, working mostly in marble. He met his wife, a charming, dainty Canadian girl, on a holiday. He was drafted into the Army, so they married just before he was shipped out to Korea.

He had a very successful tiling business, specialising in very high class work. Three years ago they celebrated their 50th wedding anniversary. They have no children. They retired to Canada, where they live near the lakes, because Richard is a great fisherman.

The younger members of the family survived the Holocaust; the older ones were the victims, four persons from Germany and twenty-three from France.

Light P. 337